LANGUAGE TESTING AND ASSESSMENT

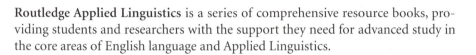

Routledge Applied Linguistics is a series of comprehensive resource books, providing students and researchers with the support they need for advanced study in the core areas of English language and Applied Linguistics.

Each book in the series guides readers through three main sections, enabling them to explore and develop major themes within the discipline.

- Section A, Introduction, establishes the key terms and concepts and extends readers' techniques of analysis through practical application.
- Section B, Extension, brings together influential articles, sets them in context and discusses their contribution to the field.
- Section C, Exploration, builds on knowledge gained in the first two sections, setting thoughtful tasks around further illustrative material. This enables readers to engage more actively with the subject matter and encourages them to develop their own research responses.

Throughout the book, topics are revisited, extended, interwoven and deconstructed, with the reader's understanding strengthened by tasks and follow-up questions.

Language Testing and Assessment:

- provides an innovative and thorough review of a wide variety of issues from practical details of test development to matters of controversy and ethical practice
- investigates the importance of the philosophy of pragmatism in assessment, and coins the term 'effect-driven testing'
- explores test development, data analysis, validity and their relation to test effects
- illustrates its thematic breadth in a series of exercises and tasks, such as analysis of test results, study of test revision and change, design of arguments for test validation and exploration of influences on test creation
- presents influential and seminal readings in testing and assessment by names such as Michael Canale and Merrill Swain, Michael Kane, Alan Davies, Lee Cronbach and Paul Meehl and Pamela Moss.

Written by experienced teachers and researchers in the field, *Language Testing and Assessment* is an essential resource for students and researchers of Applied Linguistics.

Glenn Fulcher is Senior Lecturer in the School of Education at the University of Leicester, UK.

Fred Davidson is Associate Professor in the Division of English as an International Language at the University of Illinois at Urbana-Champaign, USA.

ROUTLEDGE APPLIED LINGUISTICS

SERIES EDITORS

Christopher N. Candlin is Senior Research Professor in the Department of Linguistics at Macquarie University, Australia, and Professor of Applied Linguistics at the Open University, UK. At Macquarie, he has been Chair of the Department of Linguistics; he established and was Executive Director of the National Centre for English Language Teaching and Research (NCELTR) and foundational Director of the Centre for Language in Social Life (CLSL). He has written or edited over 150 publications and co-edits the *Journal of Applied Linguistics*. From 1996 to 2002 he was President of the International Association of Applied Linguistics (AILA). He has acted as a consultant in more than thirty-five countries and as external faculty assessor in thirty-six universities worldwide.

Ronald Carter is Professor of Modern English Language in the School of English Studies at the University of Nottingham. He has published extensively in applied linguistics, literary studies and language in education, and has written or edited over forty books and a hundred articles in these fields. He has given consultancies in the field of English language education, mainly in conjunction with the British Council, in over thirty countries worldwide, and is editor of the Routledge Interface series and advisory editor to the Routledge English Language Introduction series. He was recently elected a fellow of the British Academy of Social Sciences and is currently UK Government Advisor for ESOL and Chair of the British Association of Applied Linguistics (BAAL).

TITLES IN THE SERIES

Intercultural Communication: An advanced resource book
Adrian Holliday, Martin Hyde and John Kullman

Translation: An advanced resource book
Basil Hatim and Jeremy Munday

Grammar and Context: An advanced resource book
Ann Hewings and Martin Hewings

Second Language Acquisition: An advanced resource book
Kees de Bot, Wander Lowie and Marjolijn Verspoor

Corpus-based Language Studies: An advanced resource book
Anthony McEnery, Richard Xiao and Yukio Tono

Language and Gender: An advanced resource book
Jane Sunderland

English for Academic Purposes: An advanced resource book
Ken Hyland

Language Testing and Assessment: An advanced resource book
Glenn Fulcher and Fred Davidson

Language Testing and Assessment

An advanced resource book

Glenn Fulcher and Fred Davidson

Routledge
Taylor & Francis Group

LONDON AND NEW YORK

First published 2007
by Routledge
2 Park Square, Milton Park, Abingdon, Oxon OX14 4RN

Simultaneously published in the USA and Canada
by Routledge
270 Madison Ave, New York, NY 10016

Routledge is an imprint of the Taylor & Francis Group, an informa business

© 2007 Glenn Fulcher & Fred Davidson

Typeset in Akzidenz Grotesk, Minion and Novarese
by Keystroke, 28 High Street, Tettenhall, Wolverhampton
Printed and bound in Great Britain
by MPG Books Ltd, Bodmin

British Library Cataloguing in Publication Data
A catalogue record for this book is available from the British Library

Library of Congress Cataloging in Publication Data
Fulcher, Glenn.
    Language testing and assessment / Glenn Fulcher & Fred Davidson.
       p. cm.
    Includes bibliographical references and index.
    1. Language and languages—Ability testing. I. Davidson, Fred. II. Title.
    P53.4.F85 2007
    418.0076—dc22   2006022928

ISBN10: 0–415–33946–4 (hbk)
ISBN10: 0–415–33947–2 (pbk)
ISBN10: 0–203–44906–1 (ebk)

ISBN13: 978–0–415–33946–9 (hbk)
ISBN13: 978–0–415–33947–6 (pbk)
ISBN13: 978–0–203–44906–6 (ebk)

For Jenny and Robin

Contents

Contents cross-referenced

Figures and tables

FIGURES

TABLES

Series editors' preface

This series provides a comprehensive guide to a number of key areas in the field of applied linguistics. Applied linguistics is a rich, vibrant, diverse and essentially interdisciplinary field. It is now more important than ever that books in the field provide up-to-date maps of ever-changing territory.

The books in this series are designed to give key insights into core areas. The design of the books ensures, through key readings, that the history and development of a subject is recognized while, through key questions and tasks, integrating understandings of the topics, concepts and practices that make up its essentially interdisciplinary fabric. The pedagogic structure of each book ensures that readers are given opportunities to think, discuss, engage in tasks, draw on their own experience, reflect, research and to read and critically re-read key documents.

Each book has three main sections, each made up of approximately ten units:

A: An **Introduction** section: in which the key terms and concepts are introduced, including introductory activities and reflective tasks, designed to establish key understandings, terminology, techniques of analysis and the skills appropriate to the theme and the discipline.

B: An **Extension** section: in which selected core readings are introduced (usually edited from the original) from existing books and articles, together with annotations and commentary, where appropriate. Each reading is introduced, annotated and commented on in the context of the whole book, and research/follow-up questions and tasks are added to enable fuller understanding of both theory and practice. In some cases, readings are short and synoptic and incorporated within a more general exposition.

C: An **Exploration** section: in which further samples and illustrative materials are provided with an emphasis, where appropriate, on more open-ended, student-centred activities and tasks, designed to support readers and users in undertaking their own locally relevant research projects. Tasks are designed for work in groups or for individuals working on their own.

The books also contain a glossary or glossarial index and a detailed, thematically organized A–Z guide to the main terms used in the book, which lays the ground for further work in the discipline. There are also annotated guides to further reading and extensive bibliographies.

The target audience for the series is upper undergraduates and postgraduates on language, applied linguistics and communication studies programmes as well as teachers and researchers in professional development and distance learning programmes. High-quality applied research resources are also much needed for teachers of EFL/ESL and foreign language students at higher education colleges and universities worldwide. The books in the Routledge Applied Linguistics series are aimed at the individual reader, the student in a group and at teachers building courses and seminar programmes.

We hope that the books in this series meet these needs and continue to provide support over many years.

The Editors

Professor Christopher N. Candlin and Professor Ronald Carter are the series editors. Both have extensive experience of publishing titles in the fields relevant to this series. Between them they have written and edited over one hundred books and two hundred academic papers in the broad field of applied linguistics. Chris Candlin was president of AILA (International Association for Applied Linguistics) from 1997 to 2003 and Ron Carter is Chair of BAAL (British Association for Applied Linguistics) from 2003 to 2006.

Professor Christopher N. Candlin
Senior Research Professor
Department of Linguistics
Division of Linguistics and Psychology
Macquarie University
Sydney NSW 2109
Australia

and

Professor of Applied Linguistics
Faculty of Education and Language Studies
The Open University
Walton Hall
Milton Keynes MK7 6AA
UK

Professor Ronald Carter
School of English Studies
University of Nottingham
Nottingham NG7 2RD
UK

Acknowledgments

We would like to thank the series editors, Chris Candlin and Ron Carter, for their timely feedback on drafts of this manuscript, and their constant encouragement and help. At every stage in the writing process their wisdom and insight have been an inspiration, and we could not have asked for better editors with whom to work. At Routledge we would also like to thank Louisa Semlyen and Nadia Seemungal for their help, advice and efficiency.

The picture of the Golden Gate Bridge in Unit A4 is taken from http://www.sonic.net/~playland/ggsag.html. This picture is by an unknown photographer and is copyright-free, but we wish to acknowledge the source.

The examples of rapid prototyping in manufacturing in Unit A6 are reproduced by kind permission of Laser Prototypes Europe Ltd. The authors wish to thank Mr Tom Walls for his cooperation and advice while writing this part of Unit A6 (Tom@laserproto.com).

We would like to thank Mr R. J. Hann, erstwhile Staff Sergeant of Delta Company Fourth Battalion (4 RAR/NZ (ANZAC)), for permission to publish the picture in Unit C3, taken circa 1970 and published at http://www.diggerhistory.info/pages-uniforms/slouch_hat-b.htm.

The PERT and Gantt Charts used in Unit C6 are reproduced with permission of Alan Levine of Maricopa Community College.

The extracts in Section B are reproduced by kind permission of the publishers, as follows.

Unit B2
Moss, P. A. (2003) 'Reconceptualizing validity for classroom assessment.' *Educational Measurement: Issues and Practice* 22, 4, 13–25. Reproduced by permission of Blackwell Publishing.

Unit B3
Canale, M. and Swain, M. (1980) 'Theoretical bases of communicative approaches to second language teaching and testing.' *Applied Linguistics* 1, 1, 1–47 by permission of Oxford University Press.

Unit B4
Davidson, F. and Lynch, B. K. (2002) Chapter 3: 'Problems and issues in specification writing.' In *Testcraft: A Teacher's Guide to Writing and Using Language Test Specifications*. Copyright © 2002 by Yale University. Reproduced by permission of Yale University Press.

Unit B5
Alderson, J. C. and Wall, D. (1993) 'Does washback exist?' *Applied Linguistics* 14, 2, 115–129 by permission of Oxford University Press.

Unit B6
TOEFL materials selected from TOEFL Monograph Series MS-26 – *A Teacher-Verification Study of Speaking and Writing Prototype Tasks for a New TOEFL*, Educational Testing Service 2005. Reprinted by permission of Educational Testing Service, the copyright owner. However, the test questions and any other testing information are provided in their entirety by Routledge. No endorsement of this publication by Educational Testing Service should be inferred.

Unit B7
Hamp-Lyons, L. (1993) 'Scoring procedures for ESL contexts.' In Hamp-Lyons, L. (ed.) *Assessing Second Language writing in Academic Contexts*. Norwood, NJ: Ablex, 241–276. Copyright © 1991 by Ablex Publishing Corporation. Reproduced with permission of Greenwood Publishing Group, Inc., Westport, CT.

Unit B8
Reproduced with permission from Brown, A. (2003) 'Interviewer variation and the co-construction of speaking proficiency.' *Language Testing* 20, 1, 1–25. Copyright © Sage Publications 2003, by permission of Sage Publications Ltd and the author.

Unit B9
Reproduced with permission from Davies, A. (1997) 'Demands of being professional in language testing.' *Language Testing* 14, 3, 328–339. Copyright © Sage Publications Ltd 1997, by permission of Sage Publications Ltd.

Unit B10
Kane, M. T. (1992) 'An argument-based approach to validity.' *Psychological Bulletin* 112, 527–535. Copyright © 1992 by the American Psychological Association. Reprinted with permission.

How to use this book

Testing and assessment are part of modern life. Schoolchildren around the world are constantly assessed, whether to monitor their educational progress, or for governments to evaluate the quality of school systems. Adults are tested to see if they are suitable for a job they have applied for, or if they have the skills necessary for promotion. Entrance to educational establishments, to professions and even to entire countries is sometimes controlled by tests. Tests play a fundamental and controversial role in allowing access to the limited resources and opportunities that our world provides. The importance of understanding *what* we test, *how* we test and the *impact* that the use of tests has on individuals and societies cannot be overstated. Testing is more than a technical activity; it is also an ethical enterprise.

The practice of language testing draws upon, and also contributes to, all disciplines within applied linguistics. However, there is something fundamentally different about language testing. Language testing is all about building better tests, researching how to build better tests and, in so doing, understanding better the things that we test.

Sociolinguists do not create 'sociolinguistic things'. Discourse analysts do not create discourses. Phonologists do not create spoken utterances. Language testing, in contrast, is about *doing*. It is about *creating tests*.

In a sense, therefore, each section of this book is about the practical aspects of *doing* and of *creating*. And so each section has a research implication; no section is concerned purely with exposition. Research ideas may be made explicit in the third section, *Exploration*, but they are implicit throughout the book; put another way, the creative drive of language testing makes it a research enterprise, we think, at all times.

In the text we do not merely reflect the state of the art in language testing and assessment; nor do we simply introduce existing research. Our discussion is set within a new approach that we believe brings together testing practice, theory, ethics and philosophy. At the heart of our new approach is the concept of *effect-driven testing*. This is a view of test validity that is highly pragmatic. Our emphasis is on the outcome of testing activities. Our concern with test effect informs the order and structure of chapters, and it defines our approach to test design and development.

As test design and development is about *doing, creating* and *researching*, we have taken special care over the activities. With Dewey, we believe that through *doing* we grow as language testers, as applied linguists and as language teachers.

The book is divided into three sections. *A: Introduction* consists of ten units dealing with the central concepts of language testing and assessment. It contains activities for you to carry out alone, or with others if you are studying this book as part of a course. *B: Extension* provides extracts from articles or books relating to language testing and assessment which give you further insights into the concepts introduced in Section A. Each extract in *B: Extension* is accompanied by activities to focus your reading and help you to evaluate critically what you have read and understand how it links to a wider discussion of language testing and assessment. *C: Exploration* builds on the material you will already have found in the book. In this section we provide extended activities that help you to work through practical and theoretical problems that have been posed in the other sections. We also present ideas for individual and group project work, as well as suggestions for research projects.

The organization of this book allows you to concentrate on particular themes, such as *classroom assessment* or *writing items and tasks,* by reading the relevant units from *A: Introduction, B: Extension* and *C: Exploration* consecutively. Alternatively, you may wish to read the whole of *A: Introduction* before embarking on Sections B and C. In fact, you may decide to read the Sections in any sequence, just as you would read Julio Cortázar's novel *Hopscotch*: there is no one right place to start, and each path through the text provides a different experience. Whichever choice you make, the book is extensively cross-referenced and carefully indexed so that you can easily find your way around the material.

At the end of the book we provide a glossary of key terms that are not explained within the text itself. If you come across a term about which you feel uncertain, simply turn to the glossary for an explanation. We also provide an extensive list of references for additional reading.

In addition to the book itself, there is also a website http://www.routledge.com/textbooks/9780415339476 in which we provide very extensive additional reading, activities, links to relevant websites and further ideas for projects that you might like to undertake on your own or with colleagues.

SECTION A
Introduction

Unit A1
Introducing validity

A1.1 INTRODUCTION

Every book and article on language testing deals to some extent with validity. It is the central concept in testing and assessment, and so comes at the very beginning of this book. In other texts, it normally appears anywhere from chapter 4 to chapter 8. But this positioning implies that validity enquiry is something that is 'done' after a test or assessment has been written and is in use. This is to misunderstand the importance of validity. In this first chapter we are going to investigate the concept of validity. We are not going to shy away from asking serious questions about what it means, and why it is important. Only through tackling the most difficult topic first does everything else fall into place so much more easily.

Questions of validity impact on our daily lives and how we interact with people and the world around us; it is just that we don't reflect very frequently on the kinds of validity decisions that we make. We observe all kinds of behaviour, hear what people say to us and make inferences that lead to action or beliefs. One of the most pressing validity issues for humans is 'Does s/he love me?' The concept of 'love' is one that is virtually impossible to define, which is why it generates so much poetry and nearly every song ever written. The validity question a person faces when asking this question is: on the basis of what this person says and does, can I infer a set of feelings and attitudes that will justify me in taking decisions which, if I get it wrong, could lead to unwanted (and potentially disastrous) consequences?

But in our everyday lives we don't put validity questions formally, or try to list the kinds of evidence that we would need to collect before falling in love! In language testing this is precisely what we have to do, so that we can produce a chain of reasoning and evidence from what we think a test score means, and the actions we intend to take on the basis of that inference, back to the skills, abilities or knowledge that any given test taker may have. The closest we have to this for love is possibly the work of Stendhal (1975), who notes that in the infancy of love

> The lover's mind vacillates between three ideas:
>
> 1 She is perfect.
> 2 She loves me.
> 3 How can I get the strongest possible proofs of her love?

He goes on to explore the ways in which humans gather the evidence they need to 'dispel doubt'. In language testing this dispelling of doubt is removing as much uncertainty as possible that the scores mean what we think they mean, so that we can take actions without the fear of making serious mistakes. It is deliberate and planned, while in love, as other areas of life, it is intuitive and most often unconscious.

'Validity' in testing and assessment has traditionally been understood to mean discovering whether a test 'measures accurately what it is intended to measure' (Hughes, 1989: 22), or uncovering the 'appropriateness of a given test or any of its component parts as a measure of what it is purposed to measure' (Henning, 1987: 170). This view of validity presupposes that when we write a test we have an *intention* to measure something, that the 'something' is 'real', and that validity enquiry concerns finding out whether a test 'actually does measure' what is intended. These are assumptions that were built into the language of validity studies from the early days, but ones that we are going to question.

In this Unit we will take a historical approach, starting with early validity theory that was emerging after the Second World War, and trace the changes that have occurred since then. We will attempt to explain the terminology, and provide examples that will help to make the subject look a little less daunting than is usually the case.

A1.2 THREE 'TYPES' OF VALIDITY IN EARLY THEORY

In the early days of validity investigation, validity was broken down into three 'types' that were typically seen as distinct. Each type of validity was related to the kind of evidence that would count towards demonstrating that a test was valid. Cronbach and Meehl (1955) described these as:

- Criterion-oriented validity
    Predictive validity
    Concurrent validity
- Content validity
- Construct validity

We will introduce each of these in turn, and then show how this early approach has changed.

A1.2.1 Criterion-oriented validity

When considering criterion-oriented validity, the tester is interested in the relationship between a particular test and a criterion to which we wish to make predictions. For example, I may wish to predict from scores on a test of second-language academic reading ability whether individuals can cope with first-semester undergraduate business studies texts in an English-medium university. What we are really interested in here is the criterion, whatever it is that we wish to know about, but for which we don't have any direct evidence. In the example above we cannot see whether future students can do the reading that will be expected of them before they actually arrive at the university and start their course.

In this case the validity evidence is the strength of the predictive relationship between the test score and that performance on the criterion. Of course, it is necessary to decide what would count as 'ability to cope with' – as it is something that must be measurable. Defining precisely what we mean by such words and phrases is a central part of investigating validity.

Task A1.1

Consider the following situations where you may wish to use a test to discover something about your students:

How many students in my class are likely to pass the Certificate of Proficiency at the end of the semester?

If Mr Hassan starts work as an air traffic controller now, will he be able to successfully guide aircraft out of danger in near-miss situations?

My students of legal English are going to go on work experience later in the year. How do I know whether they will be able to help prepare the paperwork for court cases?

I need to plan next semester's syllabus for my class. I need to discover which elements of this semester's syllabus I need to recycle.

➤ In each case what would you use as a criterion (or criteria), and why?

➤ Try to think of other examples from your own teaching situation.

Predictive validity is the term used when the test scores are used to predict some future criterion, such as academic success. If the scores are used to predict a criterion at the same time the test is given, we are studying *concurrent validity*.

Returning to the example given above, let us assume that in this case 'ability to cope' is defined as a subject tutor's judgment of whether students can adequately read set texts to understand lectures and write assignments. We might be interested in discovering the relationship between students' scores on our test prior to starting academic studies and the judgments of the tutors once the students have started their programme. This would be a *predictive validity study*. We would hope that we could identify a score on the reading test above which tutors would judge readers to be competent, and below which they would judge some readers to lack the necessary reading skills for academic study. This would be the 'cut score' for making a predictive decision about the likelihood of future success on the criterion.

Suppose that my reading test is too long, and for practical purposes it needs to be made much shorter. As we know that shorter tests mean that we collect less evidence about reading ability, one of the questions we would wish to ask is to what extent the shorter test is capable of predicting the scores on the longer test. In other words, could the shorter test replace the larger test and still be useful? This would be an example of a *concurrent validity study* that uses the longer test as the criterion.

A1.2.2 Content validity

Content validity is defined as any attempt to show that the content of the test is a representative sample from the domain that is to be tested. In our example of the academic reading test it would be necessary to show that the texts selected for the test are typical of the types of texts that would be used in first-year undergraduate business courses. This is usually done using expert judges. These may be subject teachers, or language teachers who have many years' experience in teaching business English. The judges are asked to look at texts that have been selected for inclusion on the test and evaluate them for their representativeness within the content area. Secondly, the items used on the test should result in responses to the text from which we can make inferences about the test takers' ability to process the texts in ways expected of students on their academic courses. For example, we may discover that business students are primarily required to read texts to extract key factual information, take notes and use the notes in writing assignments. In our reading test we would then try to develop items that tap the ability to identify key facts.

Carroll (1980: 67) argued that achieving content validity in testing English for Academic Purposes (EAP) consisted of describing the test takers, analysing their 'communicative needs' and specifying test content on the basis of their needs. In early approaches to communicative language testing the central issue in establishing content validity was how best to 'sample' from needs and the target domain (Fulcher, 1999a: 222–223).

Task A1.2

➤ Consider these target domains. For each, try to list what a test may need to contain to be relevant to that domain.

1   Nursing in a hospital
2   Staffing the reception in a hotel
3   Check-in desk at an international airport
4   Taxi driver in a capital city
5   Tour guide in a tourist resort.

➤ Do you have students for whom the content domain can easily be defined?

➤ What makes it very difficult to define a content domain?

A1.2.3 Construct validity

The first problem with construct validity is defining what a 'construct' is. Perhaps the easiest way to understand the term 'construct' is to think of the many abstract nouns that we use on a daily basis, but for which it would be extremely hard to point to an example. Consider these, the first of which we have already touched on.

1 Love
2 Intelligence
3 Anxiety
4 Thoughtfulness
5 Fluency
6 Aptitude
7 Extroversion
8 Timidity
9 Persuasiveness
10 Empathy.

As we use these terms in everyday life we have no need to define them. We all assume that we know what they mean, and that the meaning is shared. So we can talk with our friends about how much empathy someone we know may have, or how fluent a speaker someone is. But this is to talk at the level of everyday concepts. For a general term to become a construct, it must have two further properties. Firstly, it must be defined in such a way that it becomes measurable. In order to measure 'fluency' we have to state what we could possibly observe in speech to make a decision about whether a speaker is fluent. It turns out that many people have different definitions of fluency, ranging from simple speed of speech, to lack of hesitation (or strictly 'pauses', because 'hesitation' is a construct itself), to specific observable features of speech (see Fulcher, 1996). Secondly, any construct should be defined in such a way that it can have relationships with other constructs that are different. For example, if I generate descriptions of 'fluency' and 'anxiety' I may hypothesize that, as anxiety increases, fluency will decrease, and vice versa. If this hypothesis is tested and can be supported, we have the very primitive beginnings of a theory of speaking that relates how we perform to emotional states.

To put this another way, concepts become constructs when they are so defined that they can become 'operational' – we can measure them in a test of some kind by linking the term to something observable (whether this is ticking a box or performing some communicative action), and we can establish the place of a construct in a theory that relates one construct to another (Kerlinger and Lee, 2000: 40), as in the case of fluency and anxiety above.

A1.2.4 Construct validity and truth

In the early history of validity theory there was an assumption that there is such a thing as a 'psychologically real construct' that has an independent existence in the test taker, and that the test scores represent the degree of presence or absence of this very real property. As Cronbach and Meehl (1955: 284) put it:

> Construct validation takes place when an investigator believes that his instrument reflects a particular construct, to which are attached certain meanings. The proposed interpretation generates specific testable hypotheses, which are a means of confirming or disconfirming the claim.

This brings us to our first philosophical observation. It has frequently been argued that early validity theorists were positivistic in their outlook. That is, they assumed that their constructs actually existed in the heads of the test takers. Again, Cronbach and Meehl (1955: 284) state: 'Scientifically speaking, to "make clear what something is" means to set forth the laws in which it occurs. We shall refer to the interlocking system of laws which constitute a theory as a nomological network.'

The idea of a nomological network is not difficult to grasp. Firstly, it contains a number of constructs, and their names are abstract, like those in the list above. In language teaching and testing, 'fluency' and 'accuracy' are two well-known constructs. Secondly, the nomological network contains the observable variables – those things that we can see and measure directly, whereas we cannot see 'fluency' and 'accuracy' directly.

What might these observable variables be? Whatever we choose makes up the definition of the constructs. For fluency we may wish to observe speed of delivery or the number of unfilled pauses, for example. For accuracy, we could look at the ratio of correct to incorrect tense use or word order. From what we can observe, we then make an inference about how 'fluent' or how 'accurate' a student's use of the second language is.

The network is created by asking what we expect the relationship between 'fluency' and 'accuracy' to be. One hypothesis could be that in speech, as fluency increases, accuracy decreases, because learners cannot pay attention to form when the demands of processing take up all the capacity of short-term memory. Another hypothesis could be that, as accuracy increases, the learner becomes more fluent, because language form has become automatic. Stating this kind of relationship between constructs therefore constitutes a theory, and theory is very powerful. Even in this simple example we could now set out a testable research hypothesis: fluency and accuracy are inversely related in students below X level of proficiency, and above it they are positively related.

Let us see if we can relate this back to our example from everyday life.

Task A1.3

Here we will set out Stendhal's theory of love as if it were a nomological network. Constructs:

1   Passionate Love, 'like that of Heloïse for Abelard'
2   Mannered Love, 'where there is no place for anything at all unpleasant – for that would be a breach of etiquette, of good taste, of delicacy, and so forth'
3   Physical Love, 'where your love life begins at sixteen'
4   Vanity Love, in which 'men . . . both desire and possess a fashionable woman, much in the way one might own a fine horse'.

➤   What do you think are the possible relationships between these four constructs?

For example, assuming that I could measure these types of love, I might hypothesize that as the strength of mannered love increases, passionate love might decrease. I may further hypothesize that there is a strong positive relationship between physical love and passionate love, and only a weak relationship between mannered love and physical love.

➤   Write down a number of hypotheses.

Stendhal went on to attach certain observable behaviours to each 'type' of love. Here are some of them. Which of these observable behaviours do you think Stendhal thought characterized each type of love?

- Behaviour always predictable
- Lack of concentration
- Always trying to be witty in public
- Staring at girls
- Following habits and routines carefully
- Always very money-conscious
- Engaging in acts of cruelty
- Touching.

➤   Try to list other behaviours that may be typical of a type of love as described by Stendhal.

Is your nomological net a satisfying theory of love? Probably not. Stendhal himself wrote: 'Instead of defining four kinds of love, one might well admit eight or ten distinctions. There are perhaps as many different ways of feeling as there are of seeing.'

➤   What are the implications of this for construct definition in language testing?

In philosophy, the logical positivists (some of whom Cronbach and Meehl reference) argued that only propositions that could be verified relative to empirical evidence were meaningful, and that all other propositions were not just false but actually meaningless (Ayer, 1936). In our examples of nomological networks above, meaning is created by measuring the variables (unfilled pauses, or predictability of actions, for example) and testing how these relate to the constructs that they define in terms of a theory that establishes relationships among constructs.

In testing and assessment this meant that if there is no possible way to test the hypotheses created by the relationship between observable variables, observable variables and constructs, and between constructs, the theory is meaningless, or not 'scientifically admissible'.

The underlying philosophical assumptions have been heavily criticized, and in 1989 Cronbach himself said that the position of 1955 was 'pretentious'. However, there were elements in the 1955 work that have continued to influence validity research – particularly the argument that construct definition lies at the centre of testing and assessment, and that at the heart of any validity study is the investigation of the intended meaning and interpretation of test scores. And central to understanding score meaning lies the question of what evidence can be presented to support a particular score interpretation. There is also one other aspect of the 1955 work that is still important. Cronbach and Meehl argue that it is necessary to institute a programme of research to collect the evidence that will be used to support specific interpretations, and 'make the evidence for the claim public' so that it can be evaluated by the community of researchers. They argue that 'confidence in a theory is increased as more relevant evidence confirms it, but it is always possible that tomorrow's investigation will render the theory obsolete'.

This is not positivistic in tone. It recognizes that our present knowledge and theories are tenuous and temporal, even incorrect. But they represent our 'best shot' at understanding what we wish to test, given our imperfect theories. The notion of the nomological network and the testability of hypotheses between variables and constructs to form theories was an early attempt to ensure that theory building was driven by data and the 'scientific method'.

This takes us to the heart of epistemology and what it means to say that something is 'true' or 'real'. In 1877 C. S. Peirce had put forward a pragmatic notion of meaning: 'Consider what effects, that might conceivably have practical bearings, we conceive the object of our conception to have. Then, our conception of these effects is the whole of our conception of the object' (Peirce, 1877: 146). To translate this into modern English: if we believe something to be true, will the effect be that we are better able to understand the world around us and use the idea to do something practical in a way that results in progress? Or as Messick (1989: 26) puts it (using the term 'instrumentalist' for 'pragmatist'): 'According to the instrumentalist theory of truth, a statement is true if it is useful in directing inquiry or guiding action.' Cronbach and Meehl could easily have argued that if a nomological network allows us to make better decisions in testing and assessment, then it is 'contingently true' (because it is practically useful) until it is shown to be a partial or inadequate explanation. The alternatives, Peirce argues, are believing something to be true on other spurious grounds, such as 'that's the way it's always been', or because the person who puts forward the theory is the most authoritative in the field at the moment. Messick (1989: 23) also added from a post-positivistic era that:

> Nomological networks are viewed as an illuminating way of speaking systematically about the role of constructs in psychological theory and measurement, but not as the only way. The nomological framework offers a useful guide for disciplined thinking about the process of validation but cannot serve as the prescriptive validation model to the exclusion of other approaches.

This quotation shows another shift in thinking about validation. The nomological network is just one approach to addressing validity questions. It is just one of the tools at our disposal, but there are many others that would yield validity evidence.

Secondly, Peirce held that theories may evolve or be overthrown by a community of researchers, and that with passing time, theories will evolve and become more adequate in their usability:

> This great law is embodied in the conception of truth and reality. The opinion that is fated to be ultimately agreed to by all who investigate, is what we mean by the truth, and the object represented in this opinion is the real. That is the way I would explain reality.
>
> (Peirce, 1877: 155)

Peirce believed that one day, at some point so far into the future that no one can see it, all researchers would come to a 'final conclusion' that is *the* truth, and to which our present truths approximate. Dewey (1938) was more concerned with the immediate future, and coined the term 'warranted assertion', which he trades in for the notion of truth (and prefigures more recent approaches to validity as argument that we discuss in Unit A10). A warranted assertion is a claim that appears reasonable because it is usually confirmed by further practice and inquiry. Such 'convergence of enquiry' is necessary in the short term for practical purposes, but even for Dewey it is always possible that we will discover new methods or new practices that produce results which give us a better handle on the world.

Validity theory occupies an uncomfortable philosophical space in which the relationship between theory and evidence is sometimes unclear and messy, because theory is always evolving, and new evidence is continually collected. The fact that so many articles and books on testing and assessment use statistics cannot have escaped your notice, but the service to which this evidence is put is not always clear in a larger picture of developing theories of language acquisition and testing.

Positivistic validity theory (emphasizing as it did the verifiability of nomological networks) and later the falsifiability of nomological networks passed away because it was increasingly realized that theory and observation cannot be kept apart. We see through our beliefs, and our beliefs change because of observation. They are not watertight categories.

★ Task A1.4

➤ What is truth? From your experience as a teacher and/or tester is there anything that you consider an unquestionable truth? If you answer yes, what are your reasons? If you answer no, what are the consequences for how you teach and test?

A1.3 CUTTING THE VALIDITY CAKE

Since Cronbach and Meehl, the study of validity has become one of the central enterprises in psychological, educational and language testing. Perhaps the most significant figure in this work since the 1970s is Samuel Messick. In perhaps the most important article on validity, Messick (1989: 20) wrote:

> Traditional ways of cutting and combining evidence of validity, as we have seen, have led to three major categories of evidence: content-related, criterion-related, and construct-related. However, because content- and criterion-related evidence contribute to score meaning, they have come to be recognized as aspects of construct validity. In a sense, then, this leaves only one category, namely, construct-related evidence.

Messick set out to produce a 'unified validity framework', in which different types of evidence contribute in their own way to our understanding of construct validity. Messick fundamentally changed the way in which we understand validity. He described validity as:

> an integrated evaluative judgment of the degree to which empirical evidence and theoretical rationales support the adequacy and appropriateness of inferences and actions based on test scores or other modes of assessment.
> (Messick, 1989: 13)

In this view, 'validity' is not a property of a test or assessment but the degree to which we are justified in making an inference to a construct from a test score (for example, whether '20' on a reading test indicates 'ability to read first-year business studies texts), and whether any decisions we might make on the basis of the score are justifiable (if a student scores below 20, we deny admission to the programme).

Table A1.1 presents this major step in our understanding of validity. In the left column is the 'justification' for testing, which can take the form of evidence or

Table A1.1 Facets of validity (Messick, 1989: 20)

	Test interpretation	Test use
Evidential basis	Construct validity	Construct validity + Relevance/utility
Consequential basis	Value implications	Social consequences

consequences of testing. In the first row is the 'function or outcome' of testing, composed of interpretation or use. These two 'facets' give Messick's four-way progressive validity matrix.

The evidential basis for test interpretation is construct validity, and the evidence to support score meaning may be sought from any source. In this view, all evidence supports or weakens the intended score meaning, or the inferences that the test designers intended to make from the scores. The evidential basis of test use is also construct validity, but with specific reference to the context for which the test is designed or used. For example, we might wish to ask whether a test is appropriate for a particular group of learners in a specific context. The consequential basis of test interpretation is concerned with the theory and philosophy underlying the test, and what labels the test designer gives to the constructs. Labels send out messages about what is important or 'valued' in performance on the test, and this is part of the intended meaning of the score. The consequential basis of test use is the social consequences of actually using the test. When the test takers get their scores, how are the scores used by those who receive them? What kinds of decisions are made? And what impact do these decisions have on the lives of those who take the test?

Messick did not intend the categories of Table A1.1 to be watertight. Indeed, he explicitly stated that the boundaries were 'fuzzy', and suggested that it might be read as a 'progressive matrix' from top left to bottom right, with each category including everything that had gone before but with additions: from construct validity, looking at construct validity in specific contexts, then theory, and then the social consequences of the testing enterprise.

Task A1.5

Think of a test that you are familiar with, perhaps one that you prepare students for.

➤ What construct(s) is the test designed to measure? Whom is the test designed for? Is it really relevant and useful for them? What are the parts of the test called? Are certain parts of language ability given preference or more highly valued, and does this impact on how you teach?

➤ What are the consequences for learners who fail, or get a low grade, on this test?

There are other ways of cutting the validity cake. For example, Cronbach (1988) includes categories such as the 'political perspective', which looks at the role played by stakeholders in the activity of testing. Stakeholders would include the test designers, teachers, students, score users, governments or any other individual or group that has an interest in how the scores are used and whether they are useful for a given context. Moss (1992) thinks that this is very similar to Messick's consequential basis for test use.

Messick's way of looking at validity has become the accepted paradigm in psychological, educational and language testing. This can be seen in the evolution of the *Standards for Educational and Psychological Testing*. In the Technical Recommendations (APA, 1954) the 'four types' of validity were described, and by 1966 these had become the 'three types' of content, criterion and construct validity. The 1974 edition kept the same categorization, but claimed that they were closely related. In 1985 the categories were abandoned and the unitary interpretation became explicit:

> Validity is the most important consideration in test evaluation. The concept refers to the appropriateness, meaningfulness, and usefulness of the specific inferences made from test scores. Test validation is the process of accumulating evidence to support such inferences. A variety of inferences may be made from scores produced by a given test, and there are many ways of accumulating evidence to support any particular inference. Validity, however, is a unitary concept. Although evidence may be accumulated in many ways, validity always refers to the degree to which that evidence supports the inferences that are made from the score. The inferences regarding specific uses of a test are validated, not the test itself.
>
> (AERA et al., 1985: 9)

The 1999 Guidelines go even further:

> The following sections outline various sources of evidence that might be used in evaluating a proposed interpretation of test scores for a particular purpose. These sources of evidence may illuminate different aspects of validity, but they do not represent distinct types of validity. Validity is a unitary concept. It is the degree to which all the accumulated evidence supports the intended interpretation of test scores for the proposed purpose. Like the 1985 Standards, this edition refers to types of validity evidence, rather than distinct types of validity.
>
> (AERA et al., 1999: 11)

Task A1.6

Imagine that you work in a large language school and one of your tasks is to place one hundred new students into appropriate classes on their day of arrival.

A test exists for this purpose, but there is no evidence to support the validity of the scores for its purpose. From the list below, which pieces of information would be most useful for your evaluation of this test? Rank-order their importance and try to write down how the information would help you to evaluate validity:

■   analysis of test content
■   teacher assessments of students after placement
■   relationship to end-of-course test
■   analysis of task types
■   spread of scores
■   students' affective reactions to the test
■   analysis of the syllabus at different class levels
■   test scores for different students already at the school.

➤   Can you think of any other pieces of information that would be useful for your evaluation?

While Messick's approach is now dominant in validity theory, there have been further developments within the field of language testing that we need to consider.

A1.3.1   Test usefulness

Bachman and Palmer (1996: 18) have used the term 'usefulness' as a superordinate in place of construct validity, to include reliability, construct validity, authenticity, interactiveness and practicality. They have argued that overall usefulness should be maximized in terms of the combined contribution of the 'test qualities' that contribute to usefulness, and that the importance of each test quality changes according to context.

Reliability is the *consistency* of test scores across *facets of the test*. Authenticity is defined as the relationship between test task characteristics, and the characteristics of tasks in the real world. Interactiveness is the degree to which the individual test taker's characteristics (language ability, background knowledge and motivations) are engaged when taking a test. Practicality is concerned with test implementation rather than the meaning of test scores (see Unit 8A for a detailed discussion).

The notion of test 'usefulness' provides an alternative way of looking at validity, but it has not been extensively used in the language testing literature. This may be because downgrading construct validity to a component of 'usefulness' has not challenged mainstream thinking since Messick.

A1.3.2 The validity cline

In a series of important papers, Chapelle (1998, 1999a, 1999b) has considered how validity theory has changed in language testing since it was conceived as a property of a test (Lado, 1961: 321). In her work, Chapelle has characterized three current approaches to validity.

The first is traditional 'trait theory'. For our purposes, a 'trait' is no different from the notion of a 'construct', as used by Cronbach and Meehl. It is assumed that the construct to be tested is an attribute of the test taker. The test taker's knowledge and processes are assumed to be stable and real, and the test is designed to measure these. Score meaning is therefore established on the basis of correspondence between the score and the actuality of the construct in the test taker.

At the other end of the cline is what Chapelle terms the 'new behaviourism'. In a behaviourist approach the test score is mostly affected by context, such as physical setting, topic and participants. These are typically called 'facets' in the language testing literature. In 'real world' communication there is always a context – a place where the communication typically takes place, a subject, and people who talk. For example, these could be a restaurant, ordering food and the customer and waiter. According to this view, if we wish to make an inference about a learner's ability to order food, the 'real world' facets should be replicated in the test as closely as possible, or we are not able to infer meaning from the test score to the real world criterion.

This approach is typified in the work of Tarone (1998), in which it is argued that performance on test tasks varies (within individuals) by task and features or facets of the task. She argues that the idea of a 'stable competence' is untenable, and that 'variable capability' is the only defensible position. In other words, there are no constructs that really exist within individuals. Rather, our abilities are variable, and change from one situation to another.

Fulcher (1995) and Fulcher and Márquez Reiter (2003) have shown that in a behaviourist approach, each test would be a test of performance in the specific situation defined in the facets of the test situation. 'Validity' would be the degree to which it could be shown that there is a correspondence between the real-world facets and the test facets, and score meaning could only be generalized to corresponding real world tasks.

Trait theory and behaviourism are therefore very different in how they understand score meaning, and we can understand this in terms of the concept of 'generalizability'. Let us look at two extreme examples that will help make this clear.

Example 1: We design a test in which learners are presented with written text that contains a number of errors judged to be typical of learners of English as a second language. The test takers are asked to underline the errors, and write a correction. The score reflects the number of identified and corrected errors. From the score we make an inference about a learner's ability to write in English.

Example 2: We design a reading test in which learners are asked to read a car maintenance manual and complete process flow charts that show how to replace a clutch. The score reflects the level of success in completing the flow chart accurately. From the score we make an inference about a learner's ability to read a car maintenance manual to successfully replace a clutch.

In the first example we generalize the meaning of the score from a very specific error correction task to an ability to write – perhaps in any context and for any purpose! The claim being made is that error correction is a key part of the construct 'writing ability' and can predict success in the real world. Whether this could be supported with empirical evidence is a validity question. However, the underlying issue is important: in any test we can use only a small number of tasks or items, but we want to draw conclusions from the test scores that can generalize well beyond the sample of tasks or items in the test. Compare this with the second example. Here the score meaning is very limited. It has minimum generalizability, only to doing a very similar task in a non-test situation.

In practice we wish to be able to generalize score meaning from a limited number of tasks, but we acknowledge that the score from any particular test cannot be used for any purpose in the real world.

Task A1.7

Consider a test that you are familiar with, particularly one that many learners take, such as one of those produced by Educational Testing Service (ETS) (www.ets.org), Cambridge ESOL (http://www.cambridgeesol.org/index.htm), or some other testing agency.

➤ Who is the target population for the test?
What does the testing agency suggest the scores can be used for?
What task or item types are contained in the test?

➤ Do you think it reasonable to generalize from the scores to the suggested uses?

A more pragmatic stance is possible, however. Chapelle (1998: 34, 44) describes an *interactionist* understanding of score meaning as 'the result of traits, contextual features, and their interaction' and says that 'performance is viewed as a sign of underlying traits, and is influenced by the context in which it occurs, and is therefore a sample of performance in similar contexts'. In this approach we acknowledge that the test contains only a sample of the situation or situations to which we wish to generalize. Part of investigating the validity of score meaning is therefore collecting evidence to show that the sample is domain-relevant, and predictive of the wider range of abilities or performances that we wish to say something about.

A1.3.3 Pragmatic validity

What we learn from the different approaches and definitions of validity is that validity theory itself is changing and evolving. We also learn that the things we look at to investigate validity may change over time. Similarly, our understanding of the validity of test use for a particular purpose is dependent upon evidence that supports that use, but the evidence and arguments surrounding them may be challenged, undermined or developed, over time.

What we call pragmatic validity is therefore dependent upon a view that in language testing there is no such thing as an 'absolute' answer to the validity question. The role of the language tester is to collect evidence to support test use and interpretation that a larger community – the stakeholders (students, testers, teachers and society) – accept. But this truth may change as new evidence comes to light. As James (1907: 88) put it, 'truth *happens* to an idea' through a process, and 'its validity is the process of its valid-*ation*' (Italics in the original).

The language tester cannot point to facts and claim a test valid. There are many possible interpretations of facts. What he or she has to do is create an argument that best explains the facts available. It is interesting to note that we talk of validity 'arguments' – a topic that we return to in Unit 10. The word 'argument' implies that there will be disagreement, and that there will be other interpretations of the facts that challenge the validity argument. 'Disagreements are not settled by the facts, but are the means by which the facts are settled' (Fish, 1995: 253). This is entirely in keeping with, but an expansion of, Messick's (1989) view that at the heart of validity was investigating alternative hypotheses to explain evidence collected as part of the validation process.

In a pragmatic theory of validity, how would we decide whether an argument was *adequate* to support an intended use of a test? Peirce (undated: 4–5) has suggested that the kinds of arguments we construct in language testing may be evaluated through *abduction*, or what he later called *retroduction*. He explains that retroduction is:

> the process in which the mind goes over all the facts of the case, absorbs them, digests them, sleeps over them, assimilates them, dreams of them, and finally is prompted to deliver them in a form, which, if it adds something to them, does so not only because the addition serves to render intelligible what without it, is unintelligible. I have hitherto called this kind of reasoning which issues in explanatory hypotheses and the like, *abduction*, because I see reason to think that this is what Aristotle intended to denote by the corresponding Greek term 'apagoge' in the 25th chapter of the 2nd Book of his Analytics. But since this, after all, is only conjectural, I have on reflexion decided to give this kind of reasoning the name of *retroduction* to imply that it turns back and leads from the consequent of an admitted consequence, to its antecedent. Observe, if you please, the difference of

meaning between a *consequent*, the thing led to, and a *consequence*, the general fact by virtue of which a given antecedent leads to a certain *consequent*.

In short, we interpret facts to make them meaningful, working from the end to the explanation. In order to understand this more clearly, we will relate it to the stories of Sir Arthur Conan Doyle, for it is 'abduction' or 'retroduction' that is at the heart of every single Sherlock Holmes story ever written.

Task A1.8

★

Read this extract from *Silver Blaze* (Roden, 2000):

> 'We have here the explanation of why John Straker wished to take the horse out on to the moor. So spirited a creature would have certainly roused the soundest of sleepers when it felt the prick of the knife. It was absolutely necessary to do it in the open air.'
>
> 'I have been blind!' cried the colonel. 'Of course that was why he needed the candle and struck the match.'
>
> 'Undoubtedly. But in examining his belongings I was fortunate enough to discover not only the method of the crime but even its motives. As a man of the world, Colonel, you know that men do not carry other people's bills about in their pockets. We have most of us quite enough to do to settle our own. I at once concluded that Straker was leading a double life and keeping a second establishment. The nature of the bill showed that there was a lady in the case, and one who had expensive tastes. Liberal as you are with your servants, one can hardly expect that they can buy twenty-guinea walking dresses for their ladies. I questioned Mrs. Straker as to the dress without her knowing it, and, having satisfied myself that it had never reached her, I made a note of the milliner's address and felt that by calling there with Straker's photograph I could easily dispose of the mythical Derbyshire.
>
> 'From that time on all was plain. Straker had led out the horse to a hollow where his light would be invisible. Simpson in his flight had dropped his cravat, and Straker had picked it up – with some idea, perhaps, that he might use it in securing the horse's leg. Once in the hollow, he had got behind the horse and had struck a light; but the creature, frightened at the sudden glare, and with the strange instinct of animals feeling that some mischief was intended, had lashed out, and the steel shoe had struck Straker full on the forehead. He had already, in spite of the rain, taken off his overcoat in order to do his delicate task, and so, as he fell, his knife gashed his thigh. Do I make it clear?'
>
> 'Wonderful!' cried the colonel. 'Wonderful! You might have been there!'

'My final shot was, I confess, a very long one. It struck me that so astute a man as Straker would not undertake this delicate tendon-nicking without a little practice. What could he practise on? My eyes fell upon the sheep, and I asked a question which, rather to my surprise, showed that my surmise was correct.'

➤ What do you think are the key elements of Holmes's method? See if you can write down one or two principles that he uses to make facts meaningful.

The stories of Sherlock Holmes are gripping because the detective holds to a key principle: one eliminates alternative explanations, and the one that is left, however unlikely, is the most adequate. In language testing, the most adequate explanation is that which is most satisfying to the community of stakeholders, not because of taste or proclivity, but because the argument put forward has the same characteristics as a successful Sherlock Holmes case. And in language testing, the validity method is the same: it involves the successful elimination of alternative explanations of the facts.

In order to conduct this kind of validity investigation a number of criteria have been established by which we might decide which is the most satisfying explanation of the facts:

Simplicity, otherwise known as Ockham's Razor, which states: 'Pluralitas non est ponenda sine necessitate', translated as: 'Do not multiply entities unnecessarily.' In practice this means: the least complicated explanation of the facts is to be preferred, which means the argument that needs the fewest causal links, the fewest claims about things existing that we cannot investigate directly, and that does not require us to speculate well beyond the evidence available.

Coherence, or the principle that we prefer an argument that is more in keeping with what we already know.

Testability, so that the preferred argument would allow us to make predictions about future actions, behaviour, or relationships between variables, that we could investigate.

Comprehensiveness, which urges us to prefer the argument that takes account of the most facts and leaves as little unexplained as possible.

★ **Task A1.9**

Read more of the Sherlock Holmes story in the previous text box, available online at http://www.related-pages.com/sherlockholmes/showbook.asp?bookid =4&part=1&chapter=1.

Imagine that Holmes had concluded that the facts could only be interpreted through a theory that aliens had taken over Straker's body – in fact two aliens, who were fighting for control of his mind, which would account for the double life. And that his death had been caused by a third alien who had inhabited a horse in order to kill the other two aliens as a punishment for crimes on another world. In order to do this, the host body needed to be destroyed. The last alien, having accomplished his plan, left the horse and headed back into space.

➤ How would this theory violate the principles of simplicity, coherence, testability and comprehensiveness?

When you have completed this task, you will have discovered why the argument is not adequate, whereas in the story the argument is adequate, because it meets accepted *criteria for the evaluation of arguments*.

We conclude this section by reviewing the key elements of a pragmatic theory of validity:

1   An adequate argument to support the use of a test for a given purpose, and the interpretation of scores, is 'true' if it is acceptable to the community of language testers and stakeholders in open discussion, through a process of dialogue and disagreement.
2   Disagreement is an essential part of the process in investigating alternative hypotheses and arguments that would count against an adequate argument.
3   There are criteria for deciding which of many alternative arguments is likely to be the most adequate.
4   The most convincing arguments should start at the end point of considering the consequences of testing, and working backwards to test design.

Since the 1980s, validity inquiry has moved away from positivistic trait theory to include not only context but the utility of tests for the particular purpose for which they are designed. Nevertheless, there has been growing concern with the context of testing, and how test method is related to the target domain to which we wish to generalize. This is linked to the interest in the consequences of test use and the extent to which we should say what test scores should not be used for. Hence validity has been forced to consider the social and political reasons for test design and score use (Davidson and Lynch, 2002; Shohamy, 2001).

Summary

In this Unit we have looked at the development of validity theory from the early tripartite definition of content, criterion and construct validities to the present unitary interpretation of validity. We have defined key terms related to validity, and considered what we mean by constructs and construct validity. In this discussion we have seen that it is necessary to look at epistemological questions about the nature of truth, and ask the difficult question about whether our constructs are human creations, or 'true' in the sense that they have a separate existence in the real world.

Finally, we have outlined a pragmatic theory of validity that provides a backdrop to the treatment of other themes in this book.

Unit A2
Classroom assessment

A2.1 INTRODUCTION

In Unit A1 we took a very broad look at validity theory, which is central to all educational assessment as well as language testing. Validity theory has grown out of the practice of large-scale testing and assessment. These are situations in which a test provider develops a test that is used on a national or even international scale. The test provider is required to ensure that the use of the test is appropriate for its stated purpose and target population. This includes investigating the extent to which score meaning can be generalized beyond the conditions of the test, to ability to communicate in non-test situations.

It is not surprising that some texts for teachers therefore draw heavily on the literature and approaches from large-scale testing. For example, Hughes (2003) couches much of his discussion in terms of 'types of validity', and the reliability of test scores. The latter he interprets as *consistency* in scoring. The teacher is introduced to some of the basic ways of looking at consistency in rating and criterion-related validity, such as the correlation coefficient. Even in texts that have a much more pedagogic purpose, the tendency is to look at classroom assessment in terms of traditional categories such as 'placement' (relating to establishing needs), achievement of proficiency as part of programme evaluation, and progress tests to inform lesson development (Bailey, 1998: 39). This leads once again into a presentation of *norm-referenced* statistics. Thus, despite the usefulness of much of the practical guidance in texts for teachers, the difference between the classroom and large-scale testing is not taken into account, leading to considerable confusion. This confusion can grow when technical large-scale definitions are mixed with everyday usages of common testing terms. For example, the word 'reliability' can also mean 'trustworthiness': if an employee shows up every day at work, then attendance is reliable because the employer can trust that the worker will do so. Ennis (1999) provides an excellent discussion of the tension between everyday and technical meanings of reliability.

We need to question whether what we have learned from large-scale testing, important as this is, can be directly applied to the classroom.

⭐ **Task A2.1**

Think about how you 'test' or 'assess' your own students in the classroom. Sometimes you may give a quiz that you have written, but there may be other times when you are assessing as well as teaching.

➤ Make a list of what you assess, and how you do it. Mark each item in your list as 'formal' or 'informal'.

➤ Do you normally see assessment in your classroom as a discrete activity separate from teaching and learning?

➤ Consult Ennis (1999). How do you use the term 'reliability' in your teaching and in your everyday life?

The main difference between classroom assessment and large-scale educational assessment is the context of the classroom. The learners are there as *learners*, and the teacher is there to engage with the learners in the learning process. This is true irrespective of whether the teacher is viewed as a facilitator, an imparter of knowledge, an expert interlocutor, or whatever other model one may choose to use. Moss (2003: 13) reflects upon her own approach to classroom assessment, and says:

> While from time to time I bring 'assessment' to the foreground as a discrete issue, I find it is artificial for me to separate out particular activities as 'assessment' when I design a learning environment and put it into motion.

⭐ **Task A2.2**

➤ How often do you or your colleagues design and administer 'classroom quizzes'?

➤ Why do teachers do this? What information do you get from these that would otherwise be unavailable to you?

Let us consider some of the key aspects of assessment in the classroom and relate these to validity theory. We will see that it is not always easy to take the principles from large-scale assessment and apply these directly to what is done in the classroom. This is often why teachers are 'wary' of the language of language testing, and wonder why it is relevant to their day-to-day work. Moss (2003) and others argue cogently that for the classroom we need other ways of looking at the world, or, as Taylor and Nolen (1996) put it, to challenge the 'misfit of the measurement paradigm' in a learning environment.

A2.2 PEDAGOGY AND THE MEASUREMENT PARADIGM

A2.2.1 Context

Teachers usually understand a great deal about the knowledge, abilities and skills of the learners in their classroom without the need to resort to formal tests. Over periods of time they have the opportunity to observe learners participate in a wide range of activities and tasks, working on their own and in groups, developing their ability to communicate with others. At the same time, learners grow as individuals as their horizons are widened through participation and the acquisition of new cultural knowledge. This is because of the context of the classroom, the tasks and activities, the learners and teacher, the interactions and relationships. As Moss puts it, the classroom is a social situation, in which our understanding of the learner is partly based on how they interact with their environment and the others in it.

In validity theory that has come from large-scale testing this context is not available. Rather, the 'context' of a language test is the environment in which the test takes place. This is the room where the learners will sit, the proctor or invigilator who shows them to their seats and supervises the test, the decoration, temperature, and all the other factors that might impact on the test performance of a person taking the test. All of these factors are assumed to be irrelevant to the test itself, and if any one of these factors became salient in the testing context we would suspect that there was something wrong. For example, if the test is being held in Egypt during the summer and the air conditioning breaks down, the temperature factor becomes salient and we may assume that the learners' performance on the test will suffer as a result. If a test taker is expected to write for an hour while seated on an uncomfortable wooden chair we may also suspect that the score may not represent the learner's optimal ability to write.

Context in validity theory is therefore usually referred to as one part of *construct-irrelevant variance*. All this means is that it should be the test taker's ability on the construct that causes the test score to be high or low. A learner with 'more' of the construct would be expected to have a higher score, and a learner with 'less' of the construct would be expected to have a lower score. If these scores vary – go up or down – because of a contextual factor, like hard seats or faulty air conditioning, the variability in the scores is construct-irrelevant.

In the classroom the context is the learning environment, constructed of sets of learning experiences that are designed to lead to the acquisition of language and communication. This context is not construct-irrelevant, but directly relevant to the assessment of the learners. How well they are progressing can be assessed only in relation to their involvement with the context and the others with whom they interact in the process of learning. The context is part of the construct.

⭐ **Task A2.3**

> Think of any classroom task that you have used in the last few months, which you have judged to be particularly successful.

➤ Describe the task and say why you thought it was successful.

A2.2.2 Tasks and items

In a traditional large-scale language test, learners may spend anything between one hour and five hours responding to a large number of tasks and test items, sometimes broken down into different 'papers', labelled by a 'skill' such as reading, or listening. It has become accepted that the more tasks or items a test contains, the more reliable and valid it is likely to be. The temptation for classroom teachers is to try to copy these task and item types, especially when there is an institutional requirement for a record of progress.

This needs to be considered very carefully. In large-scale language tests the assumption is that a fairly good picture of a learner's ability can be achieved only if that learner responds to many different items. Further, the response to each item or task must be independent of the responses to other items or tasks. This is because if the response a learner makes to one item is influenced, or even dictated, by a response to another item, that item carries less unique information. In the measurement literature surrounding multiple-choice items (the kind of item about which we know the most), this is referred to as the principle of stochastic independence. Each item must contribute as much unique information as possible to the meaning of the total test score.

The last sentence is very telling. In a test we collect pieces of information from many independent responses, we add them together in some way, and report a number or letter that we claim means something about the ability of the learner on the intended construct. But classrooms and learning aren't like this at all. In fact, what happens in the classroom differs in two very important ways. The first is that teachers almost never design tasks that are totally independent from everything else that is in the learning environment. In fact, a mark of good task design is for the range of tasks to be interlinked – so that each successive task builds upon what has gone before in a way that constantly takes the learner one step beyond what they can currently do. The second is that these activities are undertaken over a period of time. Sometimes learning is intensive, perhaps over a month in a short course. But for many, learning takes place over a year or many years, often with the same teacher. The formal test needs to be as long as possible in order to collect lots of pieces of evidence about a learner in a short period of time, whereas a teacher can take months or years to do this.

Task A2.4

What other types of evidence do you use to make judgments about the learning success of your students? Moss (2003) in B2 suggests these among others:

■ how students engage in tasks
■ ongoing conversations
■ interactions with others
■ knowledge of the resources available to the learners.

➤ Add at least four more of your own.

A2.2.3 The role of the assessor

In many large-scale tests the test designers try to design tasks that can be scored by machines. This accounts to some degree for the on-going popularity of the multiple-choice item, along with the fact that it is the most efficient item type in maximizing test information. Where human assessors or raters are used, usually to evaluate performances in writing and speaking, it is usually expected that they do not know the person whose performance they are rating. In the case of writing it is normally expected that the scripts are graded anonymously. In direct tests of speaking a great deal of research has been conducted into how the interlocutor(s) and raters are influenced by personal and contextual factors, and how these can be controlled so that the humans do not become part of the score meaning (see Unit A8 and Fulcher, 2003a: 142–152 for a discussion).

In large-scale testing it is important to try to control these factors, partly as a matter of fairness. If my speaking ability in a second language is just as good as my friend's, I would not want to get a lower grade just because I spoke to a different person, or had my writing marked by a different person.

In the classroom, however, the same arguments do not hold true. The teacher is familiar with each and every learner, and as we have seen above, can draw on a much wider range of evidence that informs judgments about ability. The teacher interacts with each learner, and the purpose of the interaction is not to assess in the most neutral, non-invasive way possible. Rather, it is to assess the current abilities of the learner in order to decide what to do next, so that further learning can take place.

In traditional terminology, this makes classroom assessment *formative*, rather than *summative*. As Brookhart (2003: 7) argues, assessment and learning are integrated within the classroom. She sees this in terms of Vygotsky's (1978) notion of the zone of proximal development, or 'that space between what the individual can accomplish independently and what he or she can do with assistance'. Teachers are constantly assessing, but the primary purpose of the assessment is to inform better teaching and more efficient learning. In the classroom the assessor is therefore deeply involved in the assessment, and cares about the outcomes of the assessment. There is nothing distant or neutral about intervening in the lives of learners.

★ Task A2.5

Most teachers instinctively – even unconsciously – evaluate the progress of a learner, alter input or processes, monitor progress, and then reassess. This is cyclical.

➤ Think of a particular student and describe this cyclical process. Try to be as explicit as possible when writing down how you assess, what you notice, and how this results in changes to the learning and teaching process. Share your description with another teacher. What do your descriptions have in common? How do they differ?

A2.2.4 Designing and evaluating

Language tests are designed by teachers with a particular skill and training in test design, or by people who specialize in test design. This is not because a test task always looks different from a classroom task but because a test task is usually designed with certain properties in mind (see Units A4 and A5). These are not necessary in the class, where any task is an opportunity for assessment that leads to an adjustment of the learning process.

Indeed, many classroom activities are not imposed by the teacher. The tasks grow out of perceptions of learning need that are negotiated by participants. Similarly, outcomes are not scored in traditional ways, but evaluated in terms of how successfully the tasks were undertaken. The evaluation need not be done by the teacher alone, but by the learners themselves, for themselves, in peer evaluation.

This approach to classroom assessment implies that learners are not 'ranked' in any way. The teacher and learners together negotiate what constitutes successful task completion and successful learning. The assessment that takes place is therefore 'criterion-referenced' – linked to the agreed criteria that if met show that a learner is ready to proceed to the next learning activity. This is something that learners and institutions may not always want. They prefer to get a 'grade' that shows where they are with regard to their peers and learners in other places. There is certainly a pressure to conform to the demands of external large-scale testing, but this is not necessarily the most appropriate model for the classroom learning environment, where progress in learning is more important than receiving grades from one-shot tests.

In the classroom learning environment it is feedback to the learner, from any source, that helps him or her to identify what needs to be learnt next to become an independent user of language in a new context. This means that the feedback must contain diagnostic information, and this is not usually found in formal tests.

Task A2.6

Who might be involved in:

- creating learning/assessment activities?
- evaluating outcomes and providing feedback to the learner?

➤ Make a list for each, and suggest what benefit the learner may get from their involvement.

A2.2.5 Assessment is performance-based

Performance-based elements in large-scale testing are usually restricted to a small number of controlled task types, usually involving writing and speaking. The reason for this is simply that they demand significant resources to implement, and are expensive. This is particularly the case for assessing speaking. But in the classroom the activities and assessment are almost entirely performance-based, and completely integrated. This is not surprising, because it is a social learning environment that encourages interaction, communication, achieving shared goals and providing feedback from learner to learner as well as teacher to learner. A particular feature of the classroom context is *collaboration* between learners.

We have seen above that one of the principles underlying task and item design in large-scale testing is that they should be independent. The same is true of the individuals taking the test. The responses of any one individual to a task or an item should be independent of the responses of any other individual. Collaboration in a test is usually described more pejoratively as *cheating*. The one exception to this is the group speaking test which, while still controversial, is becoming more common (see Fulcher, 2003a: 186–190). However, in a classroom context collaboration is encouraged, particularly in developing writing skills and the presentation of portfolios of work (Chapelle and Brindley, 2002: 281–282). Drafts will almost certainly have been reviewed by peers and others, and some pieces of work may be group constructions.

Anyone who thinks within the bounds of traditional validity theory will begin to worry whether it is possible to make inferences from anything (usually a 'score' or 'grade') to the abilities of an individual. Becoming trapped in this mind-set can sometimes be very damaging to institutions and teachers, and particularly so in contexts where external quality systems impact upon practice from only one epistemological perspective.

⭐ **Task A2.7**

> Imagine that you teach academic writing for ESL students in a university. You use a genre-based approach (see Gee, 1997) in which learners study the structure of texts from their discipline and construct texts of their own in group writing activities. You are present as a facilitator.

> ➤ How would you evaluate outcomes?

> ➤ If an external examiner asked for evidence to support a decision regarding an individual student's progression at the end of the class, what would you send and why?

A2.2.6 Generalizability of meaning

Validity theory in large-scale testing is extremely concerned with the generalizabilty of score meaning. That is, to what extent is a particular test score meaningful beyond the specific context of the test that generated the score? Part of this is the notion of reliability, or consistency. In a speaking test, for example, would the test taker get the same score if they took the same test with interlocutor B rather than interlocutor A? Here, the generalizability is across people.

The same notion can easily be extended to other facets. The most usual are time and task types. In the first instance, we wish to ask whether the same score would be given if the test had been given at another time. In the second, we need to know whether a learner would get the same score if he or she had taken other tasks drawn from the same domain as those tasks which they actually took.

When reliability is interpreted as consistency, it is very rare for it to be calculated in ways that actually involve giving multiple tests over time, or many similar tasks. Short-cuts are used, primarily those that estimate internal consistency. This is the extent to which independent items or tasks in the test correlate with each other and the test-total score. That is, there is an assumption that items are testing the same thing, and adequately discriminating between the better and weaker students. There are various ways of calculating internal consistency, such as the Kuder–Richardson formulae, and most usually coefficient alpha (α) (see a discussion in Unit 7A). Indeed, it is these kinds of formulae that books on testing for language teachers most frequently explain. But:

> Teachers simply do not calculate coefficient alphas, test-retest, or parallel form reliabilities for their classroom tests. They do not have the time or the inclination. Furthermore, I would argue that they might be misled by the results if they did.
>
> (Smith, 2003: 27)

Smith's position is entirely understandable, despite what teachers are frequently told about 'best practice' in the literature. Estimates of reliability in large-scale testing are based upon four assumptions:

- *Stability*: the abilities of the test takers will not change dramatically over short periods of time. It is interesting to note that the scores from many large-scale educational tests are given a shelf life of two years. But in the classroom the assumption is that the abilities of learners will change, as new teaching and learning grows out of on-going assessment. In other words, the very aim of assessment in the classroom is to make score meaning obsolete as quickly as possible.

- *Discrimination*: tests are constructed in such a way that they discriminate as well as possible between the better and poorer test takers, and the quality of the individual test items or tasks is dependent upon its discriminatory properties. However, in the classroom the teacher does not often wish to separate out all individuals and rank-order them, as it serves no pedagogic purpose. Rather, the teacher wishes to know if any individual has achieved the goals of the syllabus and can move on to learn new material, or whether it is necessary to recycle previous material. This is very much a 'yes/no' decision for an individual, irrespective of whatever position the individual may hold in class.

- *Test length*: traditional measures of reliability are also closely tied to the length of the test. Very simply, the more items or tasks are included in the test, the higher the reliability coefficient will be. Conversely, the shorter the test, the lower it will be. In the classroom there is very little reason to wish to spend many hours having learners take long tests, because teachers are constantly collecting evidence about their progress. Some task types, usually involving performance, take extended periods of time, and yet these still only count as one task – one 'piece' of evidence – when calculating reliability. Once again, we can see the definitions and practices related to large-scale assessment work on the presumption that the test takers are an unknown quantity and lots of pieces of evidence need to be collected in order to ensure that a 'score' adequately shows what a test taker knows or can do.

- *Homogeneity*: there is also an assumption in large-scale testing that all the tasks or items measure the same construct, and so the items are related or correlated to each other. So each 'piece' of information is independently contributing to the test score, and the test score is the best possible representation of the knowledge, ability or skills of the test taker. In the classroom it is much more likely that the teacher will use a whole range of tasks and activities that are not related to each other, and the teacher will see this as providing diversity of learning, variety of method, and encouraging the integrated learning of many different skills. The picture that the teacher creates of the learner is therefore very different and multifaceted.

In another very important article, Moss (1994) raised the question of whether it is possible to have validity without reliability, because it has always been stated in the language testing literature that without reliability there could be no validity. That is, if the scores were not stable and dependable, they could not be meaningful. In large-scale testing this is a reasonable assumption. But Moss considers situations in which validity can emerge where consistency is not present. One very obvious case is in the assessment of work submitted for a higher degree. Usually a very substantial piece of written work is submitted for assessment by a range of expert judges who are asked to decide whether the work is original, and contributes to the field of study. Each of the expert judges brings a different view of the work to the table, and they will frequently disagree. Through dialogue and debate a consensus will emerge, and a decision be made regarding the quality of the work. Moss argues that this process embeds validity in the decision, even though there is no assumption of consistency (in this case, across judges). Similarly in the classroom, the teacher, colleagues, parents and students may all bring something to the assessment process and outcome, in which the process is frequently more important than any outcome. The differences of opinion and perspective provide validity through dialogue, unlike the consistency of large-scale testing in which all judges must see with the same eyes.

From this perspective, how would we define 'reliability' in a classroom context? Probably as nothing more complex than whether a decision about what should be taught or learnt next, or whether it is necessary to recycle material, is the most appropriate decision for a learner at a particular point in time. Whether these kinds of decisions tend to be right for a range of individuals in a class over time would be the equivalent of generalizability in large-scale testing.

★ Task A2.8

Choose any text on language testing that you may have on your bookshelves or in your institution's library. Find the definition of 'reliability' that you find in the text.

➤ Is this a definition that you would be comfortable working with

- in large-scale testing?
- in the language classroom?

➤ How does this definition of 'reliability' reflect the points made by Ennis (1999)?

A2.2.7 Consequences

This takes us very smoothly to what Moss (2003) says about the centrality of consequences for classroom assessment. It is worth quoting the relevant section here.

Whatever one's definition of validity, with classroom assessment, understanding these effects is crucial to sound practice. I might go so far as to argue that validity in classroom assessment – where the focus is on enhancing students' learning – is primarily about consequences. Assuming interpretations are intended to inform instructional decisions and that instructional decisions entail interpretations about students' learning, it is on evidence of their (immediate, long-range, and cumulative) effects on which their validity primarily rests.

In short, does any assessment undertaken lead to better learning? Unlike the language tester who works for a large test-producing organization, the teacher is not a *dispassionate* collector of evidence. Rather, the teacher collects a range of evidence to make a 'holistic, integrative interpretation of collected performances' (Moss, 1994: 7).

A2.2.8 Validity evidence

We can see that the concept of validity is every bit as important within the classroom as it is in the context of large-scale language testing and assessment. It is just that the two contexts are very different. What is desirable within one context does not easily translate to another. For example, there are many aspects of what happens in the classroom that we would not wish to transfer to large-scale language testing practice.

Task A2.9 ⭐

Harris and Bell (1986) and Genesee and Upshur (1996) list some techniques for assessment. Which of these would be appropriate only in a classroom context? Why?

Structured interviews   Observing and recording
Unstructured interviews   Creating porfolios
Open group discussions   Completing self-reflection forms
Brainstorming groups   Writing essays to single prompts
Keeping a journal   Recording peer evaluation
Open questions   Multiple-choice questions

➤ Think of other activities that you use in the classroom. Suggest why they may or may not be appropriate for use in a large-scale language test.

But in both contexts it is important to collect evidence that contributes to the validity of decisions being made. It is just that the kind of evidence that we would collect in the two contexts may be very different.

Task A2.10

Consider the following set of questions from the Personal Reading Process Interview (Fradd and McGee, 1994: 263). This is a structured interview which may be used as one strand of evidence in the evaluation of English as a Second Language reading development in children.

1   What is reading?
2   Why do you read?
3   Do you know how to read in more than one language? Do you read more in one language than another? Which one? How did you learn to read in that language?
4   What did the teachers do to help you learn to read?
5   Do you know how to read well? How do you know, or what makes you think so?
6   What do you think makes the difference between reading well and reading poorly?
7   Is there something that you would like to improve about the way you read?
8   When you are reading and there is a word, a phrase or a sentence you do not know or understand, what do you do? Is there anything else you can do?
9   Do you know someone who reads well? How do you know this person is a good reader?
10 What do people do when they come to something they don't know?
11 Do you think your teacher is a good reader? What makes him or her a good reader?
12 What do you think teachers do when they come to something they do not know?
13 Pretend that someone you know is having a hard time reading a school assignment. What would you do to help the person? How would your teacher help this person?

The authors suggest that the responses to these questions would show a more or less 'effective understanding of the reading process'.

➤   How might you use information from this (or a similar) interview to inform decisions in your reading classroom?

A2.2.9 Empowerment and advocacy

It is not surprising that many language teachers see their role as assessor as contributing to *consequential validity*. It is suggested that the integration of evidence, including demographic information, student background, parental information and educational resources, as well as classroom performance, can be used to empower teachers as advocates for learners. One clear example of this is in the provision of resources for English language learners in the mainstream US educational system (Fradd and McGee, chapter 7). The process of integrated assessment could be used to improve educational systems beyond the school by showing what sociocultural and resourcing issues impact upon language learning and general educational development.

Summary

In the classroom the context of learning is important, and that context requires that the learning experience is integrated and relevant to the needs of the learners. For external language tests the context is potentially a source of invalidity, and the requirement to maximize information usually means that tasks and items should be independent. In the classroom, personal knowledge of the learner and the process of learning is taken into account in assessment that informs future learning, while in large-scale testing the learner is a distant, anonymous entity, about whom we need to collect as much evidence as possible in a very short period of time.

It is not surprising that sometimes teachers feel that language testing, and the *language* of language testing, is alien to their classroom practice (Fulcher, 1991). We have also seen that in some cases the mismatch between external large-scale testing and classroom assessment has taken on a political dimension as well. This shows that consequential validity as developed by Messick (1989) is applicable in a wide range of situations and contexts.

But classroom assessment may be seen as fundamentally different to large-scale assessment primarily in the focus on learning, where learners, teachers and other stakeholders are concerned with intervention and change. Wilson (1998) describes this as 'responsive feedback', and argues that:

> Responsive feedback . . . is part of a communication process which involves observation or other sensory input, interpretation, and response. It may in addition involve ongoing dialogue. Inaccuracy, in the sense of misinterpretations or misunderstandings may occur at any of these stages, as may obfuscations, denials, irrelevances, or contradictions. Empirically, this reduces to differences in interpretations, and there is no necessity in most cases to assume that there is some 'true' interpretation or description. The aim is not to accept or reject the other's meaning, but to understand it.

The usefulness of assessment, the validity of interpretation of evidence, is meaningful only if it results in improved learning.

Unit A3
Constructs and models

A3.1 INTRODUCTION

In language testing and assessment we have come to rely on models of what is variously called language proficiency, communicative competence or communicative language ability (CLA). The terminology that is used has become confusing, as pointed out by many recent commentators (see McNamara, 1996: 57–59; Celce-Murcia et al., 1995: 5–7). The confusion is further compounded because the terms 'model' and 'framework' are used with a range of different meanings in a testing context.

We take 'models' to be over-arching and relatively abstract theoretical descriptions of what it means to be able to communicate in a second language, and we reserve 'frameworks' to be a selection of skills and abilities from a model that are relevant to a specific assessment context (see Chalhoub-Deville, 1997). We will reserve the word 'construct' as describing the components of a model.

The real dilemma is navigation of these terms with respect to test development. We can distinguish three levels of increasing detail:

- theoretical models
- assessment frameworks
- test specifications (tests are actually built from these).

A framework is very different from a model. A framework document mediates between a model, which is a high-level abstract document, and test specifications, which are generative blueprints or plans for a specific test; it is not possible to write test items and tasks directly from a framework or model (see Davidson and Lynch, 2002, and Unit A4). If a model attempts to describe all that we know about language knowledge and language use, a framework might sample from the model to be relevant to a specific context. Furthermore, there can be several frameworks, which may or may not overlap (see Figure A3.1). Some aspects of the model will not be relevant to specific domains or contexts of language use, or may be untestable owing to constraints.

This understanding of the difference between models, frameworks and test specifications has provided the basis for critiques of the Common European Framework

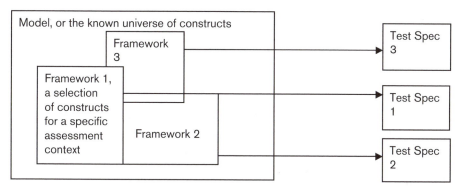

Figure A3.1 Models, frameworks and specifications

of Reference as a model, rather than a framework (Fulcher, 2004). Theoretical models and assessment frameworks are the subject of this Unit, while test specifications are the subject of the next Unit.

Task A3.1

Briefly look at the structure of the Common European Framework of Reference (Council of Europe, 2001), freely available on the Internet at http://www.coe.int/t/dg4/linguistic/Source/Framework_EN.pdf.

➤ Do you think this is a model or a framework?

A3.2 THE NATURE OF MODELS

McNamara (1996: 48) argues that all models of language ability have three dimensions, constituted by statements about:

- what it means to know a language (a model of knowledge)
- underlying factors relating to the ability to use language (a model of performance)
- how we understand specific instances of language use (actual language use).

The first is what Hymes (1972) called 'knowledge', and the second 'ability for use'. This second category contains all the factors that influence our ability to communicate. These may include individual factors such as how we feel, our general health or personality factors. As such they are not always related to language, but impact upon our ability to use language generally or in certain contexts. It is these first two dimensions that are often referred to as 'communicative competence' or 'communicative language ability', while the third dimension is actual language use, rather than the knowledge or ability for use that makes language use possible.

McNamara notes that models 'help us to articulate the "theoretical rationale" for such inferences' as we may draw from test scores to the abilities of an individual test taker. From specific instances of language use we trace the meaning of the score back to its meaning in a framework (which includes contextual features), and then to a model of communicative competence. This is a key part of what it means to consider the validity of the score meaning.

A3.3 CANALE AND SWAIN'S MODEL OF COMMUNICATIVE COMPETENCE

Canale and Swain (1980) produced the first and most influential model of what they called 'communicative competence', which is reproduced in Section B. They see the enterprise of defining communicative competence as leading to 'more useful and effective second language teaching, and allow[ing] more valid and reliable measurement of second language communication skills' (ibid.: 1). They attempt to do this firstly by reviewing how a variety of authors had so far defined communicative competence, and argue that for them it refers 'to the interaction between grammatical competence, or knowledge of the rules of grammar, and sociolinguistic competence, or knowledge of the rules of language use' (ibid.: 6). They firmly distinguish between communicative competence and communicative performance, the latter term referring only to the actual use of language in real communicative situations. For assessment, Canale and Swain argue that tests need to tap both aspects of communicative competence through tasks that require communicative performance.

Canale and Swain therefore present a model of knowledge, into which sociolinguistic competence is added. Note, however, that they do not have a model of performance, for as they say on page 7 'we doubt that there is any theory of human action that can adequately explicate "ability for use"'. For these authors, we therefore have a model that includes two components:

1   *Communicative competence* (a model of knowledge), which is made up of:

   ■ grammatical competence: the knowledge of grammar, lexis, morphology, syntax, semantics and phonology
   ■ sociolinguistic knowledge: the knowledge of the sociocultural rules of language use and rules of discourse (p. 30), and
   ■ strategic competence: the knowledge of how to overcome problems when faced with difficulties in communication.

2   *Actual communication*

   ■ the demonstration of knowledge in actual language performance.

Task A3.2

Canale and Swain outline Hymes's notion of a *speech event* in terms of participants, settings, form, topic, purpose, key, channel, code, norms of interaction, norms of interpretation and genre. The speech event is said to be the basis for understanding the rules of language use.

➤ Consider a speech event in a culture with which you are familiar, in which a novice may commit a serious communication blunder if unfamiliar with the rules of language use. Write down the rule of use that you may need to teach or test.

➤ Can you think of a test item or task for a test of this rule?

This seminal model of communication is relevant to language testing for several reasons.

Firstly, the distinction between communicative competence and actual performance means that tests should contain tasks that require actual performance as well as tasks or item types that measure knowledge. These task types would allow test takers to demonstrate their knowledge in action. This is a theoretical rationale for the view that pencil and paper tests of knowledge alone cannot directly indicate whether a language learner can actually speak or write in a communicative situation.

Secondly, as communicative competence was viewed as knowledge, discrete point tests were seen as useful for some purposes. Discrete point tests – using items that tested just one isolated item of grammar, for example – had been heavily criticized in the communicative revolution of the 1970s (see Fulcher, 2000a), but Canale and Swain argued that this criticism was not theoretically sound.

Thirdly, the model, especially if it were more 'fine grained', could be used to develop criteria for the evaluation of language performance, at different levels of proficiency. It is clear that the implications of a model of language competence and use have much to say about how we evaluate language performance, award a score to that performance and therefore interpret the score in terms of what we hypothesize the test taker is able to do in non-test situations. We will discuss this further in Unit A7.

A3.4 CANALE'S ADAPTATIONS

A3.4.1 Expanding the model

Canale and Swain explicitly claimed that explicating a theory of performance was impossible, as it would have to contain all the variables unrelated to linguistic knowledge that may impact on communication. However, by 1983 Canale (1983a; 1983b) began to introduce such a model, thus changing the definition of communicative competence to resemble more closely the original arguments put forward by Hymes. Further, Canale (1983a: 5) ceased to use the term 'performance' and began to use 'actual communication' to mean:

> the realization of such knowledge and skill under limiting psychological and environmental conditions such as memory and perceptual constraints, fatigue, nervousness, distractions and interfering background noises.

As Canale explicitly states that 'communicative competence refers to both knowledge and skill in using this knowledge when interacting in actual communication' (ibid.: 5), the introduction of factors such as those mentioned above certainly opens what McNamara has termed 'Pandora's Box' (McNamara, 1996). When modelling communicative competence and performance, we now have to account for both psychological and contextual variables.

Task A3.3 Performance conditions

It has only been relatively recently that models have included what we term 'performance conditions' – or descriptions of the context in which language is actually used. These tend to be attached to models that use the task facets to structure a difficulty continuum from the least to most demanding. One such model is the Canadian Language Benchmarks (CLB) (see http://www.language. ca/). Look at the following description of social interaction at the basic proficiency level:

What the person can do	Examples of tasks and texts	Performance indicators
■ Use and respond to basic courtesy formulas. ■ Indicate problems in communication.	*Hello, how are you?* *My name is Li.* *Thank you. Bye. Sorry.* *Pardon?* *Repeat please.* (negative + understand), (negative + speak English). Use the above phrases and others in short informal conversations, as needed.	■ Responds to greetings, courtesy, leave-taking. ■ May initiate the above. ■ Apologizes. ■ Indicates problems in communicating verbally or non-verbally.

We are told that the associated performance conditions are:

■ Interactions are short, face to face, informal, and with one person at a time.
■ Learner's speech is guided by questions from the interlocutor.
■ Learner's speech is encouraged by feedback from the interlocutor (e.g. *um, aha, I see, nod*).
■ Instruction is a short two- to three-word utterance.

➤ What do you think the performance conditions would be for an intermediate or advanced social interaction task?

➤ Is the CLB more like a 'model' or a 'framework'?

Communicative competence for Canale was now seen as distinct from actual communication, made up of knowledge (whether conscious or unconscious) and the skill needed to use this knowledge in actual communication. Knowledge and skill were seen as 'underlying capacities' while their 'manifestation in concrete situations' was actual communication. We illustrate this in Figure A3.2.

The notion of grammatical competence remains unchanged from the definition provided by Canale and Swain, but there are significant changes to the definition of other competences. Firstly, sociolinguistic competence now refers only to socio-cultural rules, and the rules of discourse have been taken into the new category of discourse competence. Sociolinguistic competence is the appropriateness of meaning (whether functions, attitudes and ideas are appropriate to context) and of form (how appropriate the realizations of functions, attitudes and ideas are in specific contexts), thus incorporating pragmatics. However, Canale clearly indicates that this notion has also been expanded to include the appropriateness of non-verbal behaviour and awareness of physical spaces and distances in communication (proxemics), as these are also involved in the creation of 'social meaning'.

In the 1980 model, strategic competence was defined as a set of compensatory strategies that could be used to overcome breakdowns or problems in communication. Canale here expands the definition to include strategies that 'enhance the effectiveness of communication' (ibid.: 11), such as changing the speed or pitch of delivery for rhetorical effect (see Kasper and Kellerman, 1997).

The new category of discourse competence is defined as the ability to produce 'a unified spoken or written text in different genres' (ibid.: 9) using cohesion in form and coherence in meaning. Although this does not differ in definition from the 1980 model, its appearance as a separate category indicates its perceived importance as both knowledge and enabling skill.

The Canale and Swain model, as adapted by Canale (1983a, 1983b), has provided the basis for all further work in this field.

Communicative competence				Actual communication
Knowledge and skill				
Grammatical competence	Sociolinguistic competence	Strategic competence	Discourse competence	Instances of language use

Figure A3.2 Canale's adaptation of the Canale and Swain model

A3.5 BACHMAN'S MODEL OF COMMUNICATIVE LANGUAGE ABILITY (CLA)

Bachman's model of CLA is an expansion of what went before, and does two things which make it different from earlier models. Firstly, it clearly distinguishes between what constitutes 'knowledge' and what constitutes a 'skill', which was left unclear in the model of Canale; secondly, it explicitly 'attempts to characterize the processes by which the various components interact with each other and with the context in which language use occurs' (Bachman, 1990: 81). The three components of CLA for Bachman are language competence (knowledge); strategic competence (the 'capacity for implementing the components of language competence in contextualized communicative language use', ibid.: 84); and psychophysiological mechanisms, which enable 'the actual execution of language as a physical phenomenon'. Strategic competence is also said to be affected by the knowledge structures (world knowledge) of the language user. This model is reproduced in Figure A3.3. Bachman's components of language competence are further developed and redistributed from earlier models, and presented in Figure A3.4.

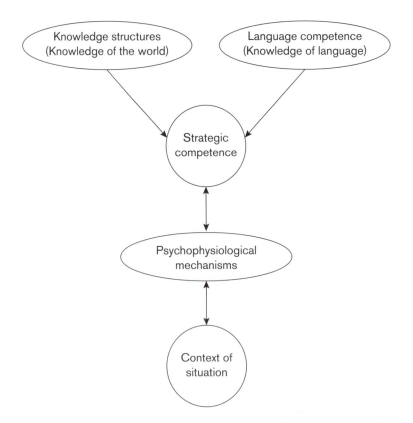

Figure A3.3 Components of communicative language ability in language use (Bachman, 1990: 85)

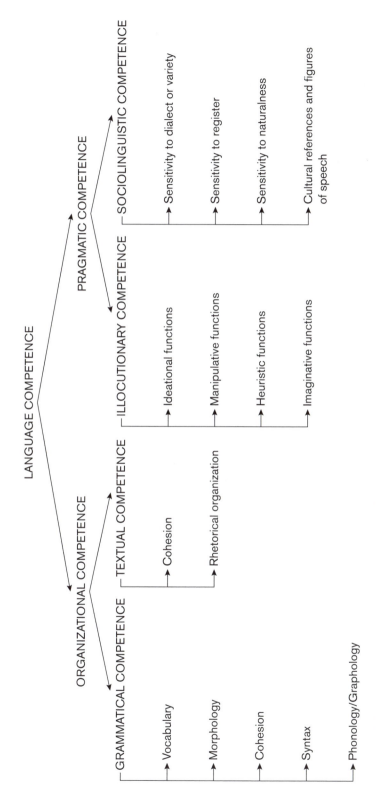

Figure A3.4 Components of language competence (Bachman, 1990: 87)

The two elements of discourse competence, cohesion and coherence, are split up. Cohesion occurs explicitly under textual competence, while coherence as a title disappears and is subsumed under illocutionary competence. This is because the left-hand branch of the tree concerns the formal aspects of language usage, comprising grammatical competence and textual competence. The latter concerns knowledge of how texts (spoken or written) are structured so that they are recognized as conventional by hearers or readers.

The right-hand side of the tree is now described by the superordinate term pragmatic competence, which is defined as the acceptability of utterances within specific contexts of language use, and rules determining the successful use of language within specified contexts. Pragmatic competence is therefore broken into two further components. Illocutionary competence concerns the performance of language functions, as described by Halliday (1973), and speech acts (following Austin, 1962). The functions listed in Figure A3.4 are:

- *Ideational*: expressing propositions, information or feelings
- *Manipulative*: affecting the world around us, including

    - *Instrumental*: getting things done through the use of speech acts
    - *Regulatory*: controlling the behaviour of others
    - *Interactional*: managing interpersonal relationships

- *Heuristic*: extending our knowledge of the world
- *Imaginative*: the humorous or aesthetic use of language.

Sociolinguistic competence is defined as 'the sensitivity to, or control of the conventions of language use that are determined by the features of the specific language use context; it enables us to perform language functions in ways that are appropriate to that context' (Bachman, 1990: 94). The components that are identified as being relevant are:

- dialect or variety
- differences in register

    field of discourse (context)
    mode of discourse (discourse domain)
    style of discourse (frozen, formal, consultative, casual, intimate)

- sensitivity to naturalness (what we would expect a native to say in the context)
- cultural references and figures of speech.

Everything that occurs under the hierarchy in Figure A3.4 is part of a model of language knowledge. It is strategic competence that now drives the model of the ability for language use. Bachman argues that strategic competence is best seen in terms of a psycholinguistic model of speech production, made up of three components:

Assessment component

- Identify information needed for realizing a communicative goal in a particular context.
- Decide which language competences we have to achieve the goal.
- Decide which abilities and knowledge we share with our interlocutor.
- Evaluate the extent to which communication is successful.

Planning component

- Retrieve information from language competence.
- Select modality or channel.
- Assemble an utterance.

Execution component

- Use psychophysical mechanisms to realize the utterance.

The 1990 model was amended and restructured in Bachman and Palmer (1996), a text which took forward and made more explicit some of the changes that Bachman had made to the Canale and Swain formulations, and which sought to articulate the model for the teaching of language testing. The changes that are most significant, as discussed by McNamara (1996: 72) and Celce-Murcia et al. (1995), are:

- the introduction of affective (non-cognitive) factors in language use
- re-labelling 'knowledge structures' as 'topical knowledge', and
- reconceptualizing strategic competence as a set of metacognitive strategies.

The 1996 model is presented in Figure A3.5, which again reinforces the central role given to strategic competence in the model. Affective schemata for Bachman and Palmer (1996: 65) are the 'affective or emotional correlates of topical knowledge', or the memories or past experiences that determine whether an individual will engage with a particular task and, if they do, the level of linguistic flexibility they will bring to it. This is discussed within two scenarios. Firstly, there may be highly charged topics with which speakers from some cultures or backgrounds may not interact. On the other hand, if a test taker feels strongly about a topic they may be motivated to engage more energetically with it. Hence, affective schemata interact with topical knowledge (previously referred to as knowledge structures, or background knowledge) to produce reactions to which the test developer should be sensitive. While the change in terminology is not significant, the introduction of affective factors is recognized as a major step forward in making the model much more complex.

Finally, strategic competence is defined as a set of metacognitive strategies or 'higher-order processes' that explain the interaction of the knowledge and affective components of language use. These are explained in terms of goal setting, assessment and planning.

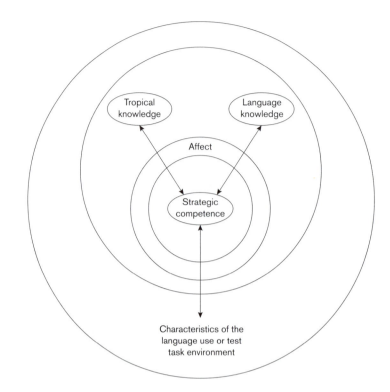

Figure A3.5 Some components of language use and language test performance (Bachman and Palmer, 1996: 63)

 Task A3.4

Bachman and Palmer (1996: 76–77) suggest that their model can be used directly as a checklist to aid in the design and development of language tests.

➤ Select a test you are familiar with and place a tick in the following list if you think the test measures this part of the model. What evidence leads you to each decision? Do you find this easy or difficult to do for each component?

Grammar: Vocabulary	Sociolinguistic: Dialect
Grammar: Syntax	Sociolinguistic: Register
Grammar: Phonology/graphology	Sociolinguistic: Naturalness
Text: Cohesion	Sociolinguistic: Cultural references/
Text: Rhetorical organization	figurative language
Function: Ideational	Metacognitive: Goal setting
Function: Manipulative	Metacognitive: Assessment
Function: Heuristic	Metacognitive: Planning
Function: Imaginative	

➤ Do you like a 'checklist' approach to evaluating a test or teaching activity?

A3.6 CELCE-MURCIA, DÖRNYEI AND THURRELL'S MODEL OF COMMUNICATIVE COMPETENCE

Celce-Murcia et al. (1995: 5) argue that since the Canale and Swain (1980) model 'there has been no serious endeavour to generate detailed content specifications for CLT that relate directly to an articulated model of communicative competence'. Although they refer to Bachman (1990) and Bachman and Palmer (1996), these models are criticized as relating only to the context of language testing. That is, they are seen as being conceptualized as tools for language testing, rather than as more general models of communicative competence. Secondly, Celce-Murcia et al. are critical of the types of content specifications that have been developed on an ad hoc basis for syllabus design, because they were not built on a model of communicative competence. What they attempt to do, therefore, is produce 'a detailed description of what communicative competence entails in order to use the sub-components as a content base in syllabus design' (1995: 6).

This model is made up of five components. Discourse competence remains a separate component as defined by Canale (1983a, 1983b), while actional competence appears as the knowledge required to understand 'communicative intent by performing and interpreting speech acts and speech act sets' (1995: 9). Indeed, it is the appearance of actional competence that makes this different from the Canale model, as it separates the ability to understand speech acts from sociolinguistic competence. However, sociolinguistic competence is re-labelled as sociocultural competence 'to better distinguish it from actional competence'. Grammatical competence is also re-labelled as linguistic competence as it includes lexis and phonology as well as syntax and morphology. The definition of strategic competence is essentially unchanged from Canale and Swain (1980) as a set of skills for overcoming communication problems or deficiencies in other competences, rather than the more general set of cognitive strategies envisaged by Bachman and Palmer (Celce-Murcia et al., 1995: 27). This model is presented in Figure A3.6.

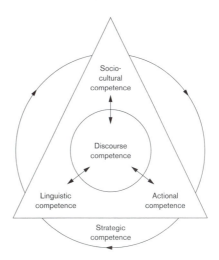

Figure A3.6 The Celce-Murcia et al. model of communicative competence

For Celce-Murcia et al., discourse competence, which appears at the centre of the model, reunites cohesion and coherence, which were separated by Bachman and Palmer. We should also note that unlike Bachman and Palmer (1996) there is no treatment of topical knowledge (or knowledge of the world), or affective factors.

Actional competence is said to relate to the knowledge of speech acts needed to engage in interpersonal exchanges (e.g. greeting and leave-taking, making introductions, and so on), impart information, and express information and feelings. It also includes suasion, dealing with problems (e.g. complaining or criticizing, apologizing and forgiving), and dealing with the future (expressing wishes, desires, plans or goals).

Sociocultural competence includes the knowledge related to context that impacts upon what is said, and how it is said. Contextual factors include participant and situational variables, while stylistic appropriateness relates to politeness conventions and stylistic variation by register and formality. While cultural factors include the usual dialect and cross-cultural communication, some background knowledge may be implied in this component, as it is said to include social conventions and awareness of values, beliefs and living conditions. Finally, the component includes non-verbal communication including body language, proxemics and the use of silence. However, this section is confounded with discourse competence as it is said to include backchannelling behaviour in addition to non-verbal discourse managing tactics.

Strategic competence is said to consist of avoidance strategies, such as avoiding a topic of conversation, and achievement strategies, such as circumlocution or the use of delexicalized nouns (such as 'thing'). Also included are stalling strategies, and self-monitoring strategies such as repair or rephrasing. Finally, but crucially, interactional strategies are listed, such as asking for help, seeking clarification or checking that a listener has comprehended what has been said.

Although the model presented is not unduly different from Canale (1983a, 1983b), and steps back from the non-linguistic elements of Bachman and Palmer (1996), it is nevertheless more specific about what each competence contains, and argues that the interaction of competences is the realm of strategic competence. It therefore contains a knowledge component and an ability for use component, following Hymes. This model appears to have brought us full circle. The authors are also explicit in stating that the model is not directly relevant as a whole to all teaching contexts. Celce-Murcia et al. (1995: 30) state that:

> as McGroarty points out, 'communicative competence' can have different meanings depending on the learners and learning objectives inherent in a given context. Some components (or sub-components) may be more heavily weighted in some teaching-learning situations than in others. Therefore, during the course of a thorough needs analysis, a model such as

ours may be adapted and/or reinterpreted according to the communicative needs of the specific learner group to which it is being applied.

We agree with this perspective. Ours is a book on language testing, and so the particular relevance of Celce-Murcia et al.'s work is to the design and validation of language tests, which would immediately limit its interpretation to other contexts of application.

A3.7 INTERACTIONAL COMPETENCE

Writers with a particular interest in the social context of speech and how communication is understood and constructed in a specific context have concentrated on developing the concept of *interactional competence*. With reference to the Celce-Murcia et al. model, Markee (2000: 64) argues that:

> the notion of interactional competence minimally subsumes the following parts of the model: the conversational structure component of discourse competence, the non-verbal communicative factors component of socio-cultural competence, and all of the components of strategic competence (avoidance and reduction strategies, achievement and compensatory strategies, stalling and time-gaining strategies, self-monitoring strategies and interactional strategies).

The conversational structure component, as we have seen, would include sequential organization, turn-taking organization and the ability to repair speech. This approach draws together aspects of models that we have already considered into a new competence that focuses on how individuals interact as speakers and listeners to construct meaning in what has been called 'talk-in-interaction'.

The origin of interactional competence can be traced to Kramsch (1986), who argued that talk is co-constructed by the participants in communication, so responsibility for talk cannot be assigned to a single individual. It is this that makes testing interactional competence challenging for language testing, for as He and Young (1998: 7) argue, interactional competence is not a trait that resides in an individual, nor a competence that 'is independent of the interactive practice in which it is (or is not) constituted'.

The chief insight is that in communication, most clearly in speaking, meaning is created by individuals in joint constructions (McNamara, 1997). This is part of the theoretical rationale for the use of pair or group modes in the testing of speaking (Fulcher, 2003a: 186–190), as these modes have the potential to enrich our construct definition of the test.

Opening up performance in this way has interesting consequences for how we understand the design of tasks and how we treat the assessment of test takers in situations where they interact with an interlocutor (either a partner or a tester or rater). In terms of tasks we need to ask what kinds of activities are likely to generate the type of evidence we need to make inferences to the new constructs. In inter-action, we need to investigate what constitutes construct-irrelevant variance in the score, or meaning that cannot be attributed to the individual receiving the score, and what part of the score represents an individual's interactional competence. These are challenging areas for test design and interpretation, and we shall return to them in A5 and A8.

We therefore need to ask what aspects of performance might constitute realizations of interactional competence that can be attributed not directly to an individual but only to the context-bound joint construction that occurs in interactions – including an oral test. Such aspects of performance would be those that arise directly out of the *adaptivity* of one speaker to another.

This definition of adaptivity is not to be confused with an oral 'adaptive test', which is a test where the rater adjusts and refines scores for a test-taker, live and in real time, by selecting tasks that optimize themselves to the test-taker's actual ability range. Here, we are speaking of the natural adaptivity that happens in all oral discourse, as human beings engage in complex conversational mechanisms to make themselves understood to one another.

The simplest example of the principle of adaptivity in second-language com-munication is that of accommodation (see Berwick and Ross, 1996), in which a more proficient speaker adapts their speech to the perceived proficiency level of the interlocutor, thus making communication easier for the other. One such example is lexical simplification, perhaps associated with slower delivery. The speaker makes an assessment of the abilities of the interlocutor, brings competences to bear in the adjustment of contributions to speech in real-time processing, and uses contributions that enable the interlocutor to make further contributions by drawing on their own current competences more effectively.

A3.8 FROM MODELS TO FRAMEWORKS: VALIDITY MODELS AND PERFORMANCE CONDITIONS

Models of communicative competence and performance form an important basis for what our test scores may mean, and they help us decide the extent to which the score can be generalized to other performances. The more we wish a test score to mean, the larger the claim we have to make for it, and the more evidence we need to supply to support that claim. There is rich territory in these models to build such evidentiary claims.

Still, we can never claim that a test score can predict all future performances in all conditions. This is why test providers need to specify the audience for their tests and the uses to which scores may be put. Tests have outcomes and impacts on the world, and, ultimately, it should be these test effects that drive the final design decisions about crafting particular items and tasks. We believe in 'effect-driven testing': test creation in which the ultimate test design decisions are driven by the impacts that the test will have on stakeholders.

The process of doing this involves careful consideration of the performance conditions under which the test takers are capable of operating, and these in turn provide the framework from which test specifications are generated (see Weir, 2004). Ultimately, the engineering of test creation is driven not by models such as those outlined in this Unit but by the nuts-and-bolts effect-driven work done in crafting test specifications – a topic covered next – which can (and should) be fruitfully informed by the rich history of models of human communication briefly outlined here.

Summary

In this Unit we have distinguished between three levels of description. At the most abstract level is a theoretical model that provides a description of the universe of constructs as we currently understand it. This may be expressed in terms of skills, knowledge and abilities, but may be extended to include a range of contextual and processing factors. All of these are relevant to language learning in general, but for testing we would need to select from these and demonstrate relevance to the specific purpose of our test. Such a statement would be found in a framework document that relates aspects of a model to a particular domain. The most specific document is the test specification that operationalizes the framework into an actual test. Tests can be built from specifications, but not from frameworks or models.

A model helps us to articulate the theoretical rationale for our test, and relate the meaning of specific test performance to language competence and ability for language use. Such models are constantly evolving and changing as our understanding of language acquisition and language use changes over time.

We have looked at a number of important models in the history of language teaching and testing, and argued that for the purposes of language testing these models may be treated as sources of potential constructs for specific testing purposes that are articulated in frameworks.

Unit A4
Test specifications and designs

A4.1 INTRODUCTION

Test specifications – usually called 'specs' – are generative explanatory documents for the creation of test tasks. Specs tell us the nuts and bolts of how to phrase the test items, how to structure the test layout, how to locate the passages, and how to make a host of difficult choices as we prepare test materials. More importantly, they tell us the rationale behind the various choices that we make. The idea of specs is rather old – Ruch (1924) may be the earliest proponent of something like test specs. We believe that specs are actually a common-sense notion in test development. Planning seems wise in test authorship.

Specs are often called blueprints, and this is an apt analogy. Blueprints are used to build structures, and from blueprints many equivalent structures can be erected. For example, we may find ourselves looking at a row of new homes, and, while each has unique design elements, we realize that all of the homes share many common features. Without going inside, we guess that the rooms are probably about the same size, with the kitchen and bath in the same location, with the bedrooms all probably in the same spot, and so forth. We surmise that all homes on this row were built from a common blueprint. Alternatively, perhaps we are in a housing development and we note that there are about five or six common models of homes. We see that one particular home resembles another some three doors down, and in turn, that another seems like one we saw on an adjacent street. In this second housing development, we surmise that the homes were built from a small set of some five or six blueprints. This second analogy is very like a test: there are a number of items or tasks drawn from a smaller number of specs, because we wish to re-sample various testing targets in order to improve our reliability and validity.

The classic utility of specs lies in test equivalence. Suppose we had a particular test task and we wanted an equivalent task – same difficulty level, same testing objective, but different content. We want this to vary our test without varying its results. Perhaps we are concerned about test security, and we simply want a new version of the same test with the same assurance of reliability and validity. This was the original purpose of specs. Following Davidson and Lynch (2002, especially chapter 7), we believe that test specs have a broader and more profound impact on test development. They serve as a focus of critical review by test developers and users. Equivalence, reliability, validity are all assured because, in addition to the mechanical blueprint-like function of specs, they also serve as a formal record of critical dialogue. In this chapter we will present the general concept of test specs, some examples and, most importantly, this critical review function.

A4.2 PLANNING IN TEST AUTHORING

A first and logical question might be: just how much can we actually plan in any test?

> Detailed rules of procedure in the construction of an objective examination which would possess general utility can hardly be formulated. The type of questions must be decided on the basis of such facts as the school subject concerned, the purposes of the examination, the length and reliability of the proposed examination, preferences of teachers and pupils, the time available for the examination, whether factual knowledge or thinking is to be tested, etc.
>
> (Ruch, 1924: 95–96)

Task A4.1

➤ Why is it difficult to have single set of 'rules of procedure' for test creation? Why must tests reflect the needs of a local setting? Conversely, what would be the advantages of a single set of procedures, for example in writing a multiple-choice item – procedures that would apply from one setting to the other?

Kehoe (1995) presents a series of guidelines for creating multiple-choice test items. These guidelines are spec-like in their advice. Here are the first two, which concern the stem of a multiple-choice item (a stem is the top part of a multiple-choice item, usually a statement or question).

1. Before writing the stem, identify the one point to be tested by that item. In general, the stem should not pose more than one problem, although the solution to that problem may require more than one step.
2. Construct the stem to be either an incomplete statement or a direct question, avoiding stereotyped phraseology, as rote responses are usually based on verbal stereotypes.

Here is a sample multiple-choice item. Let us assume the test takers are school-aged children in an English-medium school setting. Our item is part of a larger test that determines whether the student needs additional English language training – for example, supplemental English courses at the end of the school day.

> In a recent survey, eighty per cent of drivers were found to wear seat belts. Which of the following *could* be true?

(a) Eighty of one hundred drivers surveyed were wearing seat belts.
(b) Twenty of one hundred drivers surveyed were wearing seat belts.
(c) One hundred drivers were surveyed, and all were wearing seat belts.
(d) One hundred drivers were surveyed, and none were wearing seat belts.

 Task A4.2

➤ What does this item test? Does the stem test only one thing, as Kehoe advises in his first guideline? If the item tests more than one thing, is that a function of the stem, of the four choices, or of both parts of the item working in tandem? Clearly, the stem is a stated question – and so it fulfils Kehoe's second guideline. Is it a clear question or is it misleading?

There are two elements to this – or any – multiple-choice item, each functioning somewhat differently. We first see a statement and question, known as the 'stem'. We then see four 'choices'. Most likely, the test taker was told that each item has one correct choice (something that testers call the 'key') and three incorrect choices (known as 'distracters'). To answer the item correctly, the student must read carefully each word of the stem and each word of each choice; furthermore, the student probably knows well that three of the four choices are intended to be incorrect, and so this close reading becomes a process of elimination. Suppose that a particular testing or teaching situation routinely uses such close-reading items, and in that setting an item like this is actually very familiar to the students. In such a case, perhaps the students don't (really) read the item closely or analyse its component parts. They see it, recognize it as a familiar type of task, and engage the relevant cognitive and language processing skills – from their training – to attempt the item.

Ruch is making this point: we cannot really issue general guidelines (as Kehoe did) without knowing first the particular setting in which the test question will operate.

A4.3 GUIDING LANGUAGE VERSUS SAMPLES

There are many styles and layouts for test specs. All test specifications have two components: sample(s) of the items or tasks we intend to produce and 'guiding language' about the sample(s). Guiding language comprises all parts of the test spec other than the sample itself. For the above seat-belt sample, guiding language might include some of these key points:

- [1] This is a four-option multiple-choice test question.
- [2] The stem shall be a statement followed by a question about the statement.
- [3] Each choice shall be plausible against real-world knowledge, and each choice shall be internally grammatical.
- [4] The key shall be the only inference that is feasible from the statement in the stem.

■ [5] Each distracter shall be a slight variation from the feasible inference from the stem; that is to say, close reading of all four choices is necessary in order to get the correct answer.

Taking a cue from Ruch, we can assume one more important bit of highly contextualized guiding language:

■ [6a] It is assumed that test takers are intimately familiar with this item type, so that they see instantly what kind of task they are being asked to perform; that is to say, the method of the item is transparent to the skill(s) it seeks to measure.

An alternative would be to assume that our test takers are not familiar with this item type:

■ [6b] Test takers may or may not be familiar with this item type. The level of familiarity is not of any importance. The focus of this item is close reading, because the item must function as an assessment of proficiency, preferably of high-level proficiency.

Task A4.3

➤ Consider the sample item about seat belts and its guiding language: [1] to [6b], above. What other guiding language is needed to produce an equivalent item? Which presumption do you prefer, [6a] or [6b], and why?

A4.4 CONGRUENCE (OR FIT-TO-SPEC)

The seat-belt item was first presented, above, without any guiding language. We then encouraged a critical reflection about the item. This is rather typical in test settings. We have test tasks in front of us, and somehow we are not happy with what we see.

Our next step above was to induce some guiding language such that items equivalent to the seat-belt question could be written. For example, something like this should be equivalent – it appears to follow our evolving spec here:

The vast majority of parents (in a recent survey) favour stricter attendance regulations at their children's schools. Which of the following *could* be true?

(a) Most parents want stricter attendance rules.
(b) Many parents want stricter attendance rules.
(c) Only a few parents think current attendance rules are acceptable.
(d) Some parents think current attendance rules are acceptable.

⭐ **Task A4.4**

➤ Congruence (also called fit-to-spec) is the degree to which a new item fits an existing spec. Our existing item is the seat-belt question. It has guiding language above, points [1] to either [6a] or [6b]. Does this new item about school attendance fit our spec? If not, can you think of some new guiding language that clarifies what additional item characteristics are feasible.

A4.5 HOW DO TEST QUESTIONS ORIGINATE? REVERSE ENGINEERING AND ARCHETYPES

We have seen a test question (the seat-belt item), and from it we induced some guiding language (points [1] to either [6a] or [6b]). We stressed our evolving guiding language by trying out a new item – on school attendance. Certain problems began to emerge. Firstly, it is clear that our item requires very close reading – perhaps we want that; perhaps we do not. Perhaps we presume our students are accustomed to it from prior instruction; perhaps we can make no such presumption. When the attendance item is compared to the seat-belt item, there are some new discoveries emerging. It seems that the four choices have a kind of parallel structure. Both items have two choices ((a) and (b)) that follow similarly structured assertions, and then two subsequent choices ((c) and (d)) that follow a different assertion structure. We don't mention that fact in any of our guiding language, although we could. The precise grammar of each choice is different in the two items, but this choice pairing remains the same. Furthermore, if we do decide that the attendance item is congruent with our evolving spec, then it is acceptable for our spec to generate stems and choices either with precise numerical survey language ('eighty per cent of drivers') as well as items that do not ('the vast majority of parents'). Guiding language like this might be relevant, and note that this guiding language refers directly to the two sample items – a good idea in test specs:

■ [7] The purpose of this item is to test close inferential reading of assertions about scientific surveys. Items can contain precise counts and percentages (e.g. 'eighty per cent' in the first sample item) or generalities of a survey nature (e.g. 'the vast majority of parents' in the second).

Furthermore, we see in the second sample item that inference is broadly defined. Test takers may be asked to perform a mathematical calculation ('eighty of one hundred' is eighty per cent) or a double inference ('only a few' is the opposite of 'the vast majority'). This suggests:

■ [8] Inference is broadly defined. It can be relatively direct, oblique and indirect, or even inverted.

Spec writing is an organic process. Time, debate, consensus, pilot testing and iterative re-writes cause the spec to grow and to evolve and to better represent what its development team wishes to accomplish. We can follow this organic process by use of an audit trail (Li, 2006), which is a narrative of how we feel the test has improved; we shall return to audit trails in Unit C4. The beginning of this creative organic process is an interesting problem. We believe that most tests are created from tests we have already seen or have already experienced (perhaps as test takers). Often, test creation starts by looking at existing tests – a process known as reverse engineering.

A4.6 REVERSE ENGINEERING

Reverse engineering (RE) is an idea of ancient origin; the name was coined by Davidson and Lynch (2002), but they are the first to admit that all they created was the name. RE is an analytical process of test creation that begins with an actual test question and infers the guiding language that drives it, such that equivalent items can be generated. As we did the process here, it is a very good idea to stress an evolving spec by trying to write a new item during our reverse engineering. This helps us understand better what we are after. There are five types of RE, and the types overlap:

- *Straight RE*: this is when you infer guiding language about existing items without changing the existing items at all. The purpose is solely to produce equivalent test questions.
- *Historical RE*: this is straight RE across several existing versions of a test. If the archives at your teaching institution contain tests that have changed and evolved, you can do RE on each version to try to understand how and why the tests changed.
- *Critical RE*: perhaps the most common form of RE, this is precisely what is under way here in this chapter – as we analyse an item, we think critically: are we testing what we want? Do we wish to make changes in our test design?
- *Test deconstruction RE*: – whether critical or straight, whether historical or not, provides insight beyond the test setting. We may discover larger realities – why, for instance, would our particular test setting so value close reading for students in the seat-belt and attendance items? What role does close inferential reading have to the school setting? Are these educators using it simply to produce difficult items and thus help spread out student ability – perhaps in a bell-shaped curve? The term 'test deconstruction' was coined by Elatia (2003) in her analysis of the history of a major national language test.
- *Parallel RE*: In some cases, teachers are asked to produce tests according to external influences, what Davidson and Lynch (2002, chapter 5) call the 'mandate'. There may be a set of external standards outside the classroom – as, for example, the Common European Framework. Teachers may feel compelled to design tests that adhere to these external standards, and, at the same time, the teachers may not consult fully with one another. If we obtain sample test questions from several teachers which (the teachers tell us) measure the same thing, and then perform straight RE on the samples, and then compare the

resulting specs, we are using RE as a tool to determine parallelism (Nawal Ali, personal communication).

⭐ **Task A4.5**

➤ Have you ever done reverse engineering? Of what type? Why?

A4.7 WHERE DO TEST ITEMS COME FROM? WHAT IS THE TRUE GENESIS OF A TEST QUESTION?

Perhaps reverse engineering is at the basis of everything. It is extremely difficult to be truly original in a test question.

The evolving spec in this chapter uses multiple-choice testing – a known and comfortable path with ample general guidelines in the literature (e.g. Kehoe, 1995). And close inferential reading is a familiar high-level language task. If you are asked to produce a difficult item involving close inferential reading of scientific or survey data, might not something like this evolve anyway?

An 'archetype' is a canonical item or task; it is the typical way to measure a particular target skill. Specification-driven testing often falls prey to archetypes. If we then step back and look at that item, we will often see echoes of an item or task that we have authored in the past, that we have suffered (as test takers) or that we have studied in a testing textbook or testing lecture. Perhaps all supposed spec-driven testing is actually a form of reverse engineering: we try to write a blueprint to fit item or task types – archetypes – that are already in our experience.

It is often asserted that theory comes first and testing follows. External beliefs drive test creation. We decide – or we are advised to decide – our beliefs about the target language skills and then, and only then, build tests. Some authors (e.g. Bachman and Palmer, 1996) advocate particular theoretical models of language ability as guides for test creation. Theory before practice may work, and it may work well. And the converse may also be true in some settings: test developers may not have a clear idea of the traits they wish to measure. The beliefs we hold about language are not at issue. What is at issue is whether or not we carry in our professional baggage a certain – perhaps restricted – repertoire of archetypes by which we typically measure language.

Perhaps archetypes help validity and reliability in an entire teaching system. The common test forms we carry in our professional pockets, like so many worn and familiar coins, may help us survive and thrive as teachers.

Task A4.6

⭐

➤ Review a number of language tests at your setting. Review some that you have written: how much in these tests is really new? How much is familiar, worn territory?

➤ Are archetypes at play at your setting, and if so, are you comfortable with your archetypes?

A4.8 SPEC-DRIVEN TEST ASSEMBLY, OPERATION AND MAINTENANCE

Spec-driven testing lends itself very well to higher-order organizational tools. Specs are, by their very nature, a form of database. We might develop a test of one hundred items, which in turn is being driven by some ten to twelve specs. Each spec yields several equivalent items in the test booklet. When the time comes to produce a new version of the test, the specs serve their classic generative role to help item writers write new questions. Over time, each spec may generate many tens of items, and from that generative capacity an item bank can be built. The items are the records of the bank, and in turn, each item record can be linked to its spec. Over time, also, shared characteristics from one spec to another can be identified and cross-linked; for example, the spec under production in this chapter uses inferential reading.

Over time, the assembly and operation of a test represents an investment by its organization. Effort is expended, and there is a risk: that the value of the effort will outweigh the need to change the test. A kind of stasis becomes established – the stable, productive harmony of an in-place test (Davidson, 2004). Stasis yields archetypes, and that is not necessarily a bad thing. Well-established specifications which produce archetypes seem to produce trust in the entire testing system, and from such trust many difficult decisions can be made. In placement testing (for example), stasis helps to predict how many teachers to hire, how many classrooms will be needed, how many photocopies to budget and a host of other logistical details – because the educators who run the test are so familiar with its typical results.

There may come a time at which members of the organization find themselves frustrated. 'This test has been in place for years! Why do we have this test? Why can't we change it?' Grumbling and hallway complaint may reach a crescendo, and if funding is available (often it is not) then 'finally, we are changing this test!'.

There is an alternative view, best explained by an analogy from civil engineering.

A4.8.1 The Golden Gate Bridge metaphor

The Golden Gate Bridge in San Francisco was completed in 1937. Fifty years later – in 1987 – a big celebration was held to celebrate a half-century of service. Traffic was stopped, and people were allowed to walk out on to the bridge. This proved to be the greatest weight the bridge had ever carried, and it sagged at the centre of its span. The bridge did not fall, because it was very well built from the beginning. It was soundly constructed, to the best of the engineering knowledge of the 1930s.

In the intervening fifty years, and continuing after the 1987 celebration, engineering knowledge about earthquakes grew. San Francisco is prone to quakes, having had a terrible one in 1906. The Golden Gate Bridge is now being refitted for seismic safety.

The bridge was sound when it was built, and in fact it was very sound. It withstood all that weight in the 1987 celebration. Simply because it is being refitted for earthquake safety today, that does not mean that it was incomplete or weak in 1937.

This is how language test assembly and operation should happen. Tests should be built to the best of an organization's ability at the time that we first create them, and then, as and when matters change and the test needs refitting, the organization should refit it. A test should not remain in place simply because it is in place. Stasis is both a blessing and a curse, but its mixed nature can be moderated if all parties are willing to talk about the test – and such dialogue should happen at a higher, more productive level of conversation: it should be discussion about the specs and not only about the test.

★ Task A4.7

➤ Do you think that test development is like engineering? What other occupations seem similar to test development? What occupations seem different? Why?

A4.9 TOWARDS SPEC-DRIVEN THEORY

Test specifications suggest a theoretical model of test creation. A model of spec-driven test development, or 'spec-driven theory', seems to have several precepts when it works at its optimal state:

■ *Specs exist.* Somehow, somewhere, the system is able to articulate the generative guiding language behind any sample test items or tasks. At a minimum, this articulation should be oral, but it is far better if it is written down. Written specs have two great advantages: firstly, they spark creative critical dialogue about the testing; and secondly, they are wonderful training tools when newcomers join the organization. However, they are not written in granite. Rather,

- *Specs evolve.* They grow and change, in creative engineering-like response to changes in theory, in curriculum, in funding, and so on. Audit trails help to track this evolution, and evidence-centred design – as treated next in Unit A5 – contributes to the auditing. All along the way, there is transparency. If something changes, the test can change, and everybody knows that the test is subject to change, and, if the change does happen, everybody knows it happened, and everybody knows why. Change is acceptable, but it must be motivated by solid evidence of need for it, as well as (once the change gets under way) solid evidence that the changes are supportable. Much as the Golden Gate Bridge is amenable to earthquake refitting, now that knowledge of earthquakes has grown so dramatically, so too must tests be. At the same time,

- *The specs (and the test they generate) are not launched until ready.* Like the Golden Gate Bridge in 1937, the organization works hard to discuss and to try out test specs and their items and tasks, withholding a rush to production, examining all evidence available; the initial operational test roll-out represents the very best efforts of all involved. And this decision is feasible only because

- *Discussion happens and that leads to transparency.* Spec-driven testing can lead to 'shared authority, collaboration, [and] involvement of different stake-holders . . . there is a need for continuous examination of the quality of tests, for in-depth insight into how they are used, for the public exposure of misuses and for the awareness of the public as to the motivations for, harm and consequences of tests' (Shohamy, 2001: 161).

- *And this is discussion to which all are welcome.* Unit A2 explored notions of empowerment and advocacy. And the sample tasks coming in A5, next, should be seen not as final but as points of generative dialogue — as all test items should be seen: as targets always for evidence-driven critical reverse engineering.

Summary

Generative test specifications are blueprints for test creation – a common-sense and productive tool at least as old as Ruch's (1924) guidelines. Specs have two key elements: sample(s) of the items or task they intend to create, and guiding language – everything else. Beyond that, the form of the spec is up to its users, and both form and content evolve in a creative, organic, consensus-driven, iterative process. Reverse engineering of known tests is a likely starting point, and familiar archetypes most likely abound, but human creativity will also be given a voice if the debate and dialogue about the spec is one to which all are welcome. If we do our best, and produce the best spec we can, and if we then write the items and launch the test, and if we then find out that something else needs to be changed – the specs give us the tools to make those later operational changes. The bridge will not fall, but it can be made stronger, all because we have on hand and fully understand its blueprint.

Unit A5
Writing items and tasks

A5.1 INTRODUCTION

In Unit A3 we saw that in defining the construct we wish to test there were implications for the kinds of items or tasks that we choose to put in our tests. One of the most common mistakes made in language testing is for the test writer to begin the process by writing a set of items or tasks that are intuitively felt to be relevant to the test takers. And as we have seen in Unit A4, the process of defining test purpose and the items is one that needs careful thought and lengthy collaborative processes. In this Unit, which is complementary to Unit A4, we will investigate the process of item and task writing as part of the iterative process of writing test specifications. In order to do this we will draw on another paradigm in language testing, that of evidence-centred design (ECD).

An iterative process is one in which all tasks are undertaken in a cyclical fashion. Much of language test development has been presented as if there were clear steps to be followed, with the implication that if the reader works through the linear steps the end result will be a test that is more likely to be reliable and valid. But this is not the case. The process is much messier, because all the activities feed into each other. This is why test specifications are not set until the final test is ready to be rolled out in actual use. When specs function well, they are not set in stone, but rather they represent the best abilities of the test developers to build a strong product at a given moment in time, taking into consideration all feedback and try-outs available at that moment. Like the Golden Gate Bridge, which we discuss in Unit A4, a well-built test can be adapted and changed even after it is operational and as things change, provided that we have a clear record (specifications) of how it was built in the first place. Test specifications should be continually evolving documents, as construct definition becomes more precise and evidence is collected to support the link between the task and the construct.

This may need a little more explanation at this stage. A test task is essentially a device that allows the language tester to collect evidence. This evidence is a response from the test taker, whether this is a tick in a box or an extended contribution to a dialogue. The 'response as evidence' indicates that we are using the responses in order to make inferences about the ability of the test taker to use language in the domains and range of situations defined in the test specifications.

It has sometimes been said that tests are in some way *better* or *more valid* just because they are *direct*. But this is not the case, for, as Bachman (1990: 287) has pointed out, directness is problematic in language testing, as 'language is both the object and the instrument of our measurement'. The only value of any response to any item or task is given to it by the strength of the inference we can make from the 'response as evidence' to the construct as *language knowledge*, or as *ability for use* within specified parameters laid out in a framework and test specification.

This means that the arguments over task *authenticity* that dominated the late 1970s and 1980s are no longer meaningful for us. Proponents of the communicative approach to language testing argued that only tasks that mirrored language use in the 'real world' should be used in communicative language tests, reflecting the actual purposes of real-world communication, in clearly defined contexts, using input and prompts that had not been adapted for use with second-language speakers (see Morrow, 1979, and the discussion in Fulcher, 2000a). At the time, Alderson (1981) argued that this was a 'sterile argument', and we have since realized that authenticity, even conceived of as matching test method facets to facets of similar tasks in the real world (Bachman and Palmer, 1996), does not make test tasks automatically valid through directness; it means only that we may be able to model test-taker behaviour in ways that allow us to observe the use of *processes* that would be used in real-world language use. This distinction was made by Widdowson (1983) and is as relevant today as it was in the last century (also see Lewkowicz, 2000).

The old criticism of the multiple-choice item as being something that we don't do 'in the real world' (Underhill, 1982) is therefore one that we can no longer recognize as meaningful. Rather, we need to look at how sets of multiple-choice items are used within specific tests in order to judge whether responses to those items (and the resulting score) would support the inference from the evidence to the claims we wish to make about the underlying knowledge or ability of the test taker. It is the job of the test specifications to make our claim (about such responses) clear.

In order to investigate the place of the test item or task in more detail, we will look at a particular methodology in test design and see what the place of the item or task is within this paradigm.

A5.2 EVIDENCE-CENTRED DESIGN (ECD)

A5.2.1 What is ECD?

It is important that we see the tasks or items that we design for tests as part of a larger picture, and one approach to doing this in a systematic way is ECD, a methodology for test design and construction developed at Educational Testing Service (ETS) (Mislevy, 2003a). ECD is defined in the following way:

ECD is a methodology for designing assessments that underscores the central role of evidentiary reasoning in assessment design. ECD is based on three premises: (1) An assessment must build around the important knowledge in the domain of interest and an understanding of how that knowledge is acquired and put to use; (2) The chain of reasoning from what participants say and do in assessments to inferences about what they know, can do, or should do next, must be based on the principles of evidentiary reasoning; (3) Purpose must be the driving force behind design decisions, which reflect constraints, resources and conditions of use.

(Mislevy et al., 2003: 20)

The term *evidentiary reasoning* is what we have referred to in this book as a validity argument. The argument shows the reasoning that supports the inferences we make from test scores to what we claim those scores mean. Evidentiary reasoning is the reasoning that leads from evidence to the evaluation of the strength of the validity claim. As the second point in our quotation makes clear, the reasoning or validity argument should connect what a test taker is asked to do in a test, through the score, to its meaning in terms of the knowledge of abilities about which we wish to make a claim (see Unit A3). Finally, all decisions in test design should reflect the purpose of the assessment – why we are testing – in terms of these claims. But, as the third point makes clear, all design decisions will be subject to a range of constraints that should also be explained. For example, we may wish to test speaking ability for medical staff using extended role-play, but time constraints and the lack of human (supervisory personnel and assessors) and physical (room) resources may require us to design a very different kind of test from which we would still wish to make the same kinds of inference. Whether this is possible using alternative test methods would be a subject for research.

As we have argued, all tests are indirect. From test performance we obtain a score, and from the score we draw inferences about the constructs the test is designed to measure. It is therefore a 'construct-centered approach', as described by Messick (1994: 17):

A construct-centered approach would begin by asking what complex of knowledge, skills, or other attributes should be assessed, presumably because they are tied to explicit or implicit objectives of instruction or are otherwise valued by society. Next, what behaviors or performances should reveal those constructs, and what tasks or situations should elicit those behaviors? Thus, the nature of the construct guides the selection or construction of relevant tasks as well as the rational development of construct-based scoring criteria and rubrics.

This quotation makes it very clear that the role of task design in language testing is closely linked to what we argue will constitute evidence for the degree of presence or absence of the kinds of knowledge or abilities (constructs) to which we wish to make inferences.

Task A5.1

The way in which we do things reflects how we think we know things. Peirce (1878) argued that there were four ways of knowing:

- *Tenacity*: we believe what we do because we have always believed this and not questioned it. What we do is therefore based on what we have always done.
- *Authority*: we believe what we do because these beliefs come from an authoritative source. What we do is therefore follow the practice dictated by this source.
- *A-priori*: what we believe appears reasonable to us when we think about it, because it feels intuitively right. What we do is therefore what we think is reasonable and right.
- *Scientific*: what we believe is established by investigating what happens in the world. What we do is therefore based on methods that lead to an increase in knowledge.

ECD treats knowledge as scientific because it is primarily a method that leads to the test designer understanding more about relations between variables for a particular assessment context.

➤ Underhill (1982: 18) wrote: 'As ye teach, so shall ye test' and Underhill (1987: 105) argued that in language testing 'common sense' was far more important than what language testing experts did. What way of knowing do you think this position represents? How might we design a new test according to this philosophical position?

A5.2.2 The structure of ECD

ECD as originally proposed in the literature claims to provide a very systematic way of thinking about the process of assessment and the place of the task within that process. And it is here that we must revisit the confusing terminology discussed in Unit 3A, for the terms 'framework' and 'model' are given very different meanings within ECD. Firstly, ECD is considered to be a 'framework' in the sense that it is structured and formal and thus enables 'the actual work of designing and implementing assessments' (Mislevy et al., 2003: 4) in a way that makes a validity argument more explicit. It is sometimes referred to as a *conceptual assessment framework* (CAF). Within this framework are a number of models, and these are defined as *design objects*. These design objects help us to think about how to go about the practical work of designing a test.

Within ECD-style test specification there are six models or design objects, each of which must be articulated.

1. Student model. This comprises a statement of the particular mix of knowledge, skills or abilities about which we wish to make claims as a result of the test. In other words, it is the list of constructs that are relevant to a particular testing situation, extracted from a model of communicative competence or performance (see Unit A3). This is the highest-level model, and needs to be designed before any other models can be addressed, because it defines what we wish to claim about an individual test taker. The student model answers the question: what are we testing? It can be as simple as a single construct (however complex it might be) such as 'reading', or include multiple constructs such as identifying main argument, identifying examples, understanding discourse markers for problem–solution patterns, and so on. Whatever our constructs, we have to relate them directly to the target language-use situation by establishing their relevance to performance in that domain.

2. Evidence models. Once we have selected constructs for the student model, we need to ask what evidence we need to collect in order to make inferences from performance to underlying knowledge or ability. Therefore the evidence model answers the question: what evidence do we need to test the construct(s)? In ECD the evidence is frequently referred to as a *work product*, which means nothing more than whatever comes from what the test takers do. From the work product there are one or more observable variables. In a multiple-choice test the work product is a set of responses to the items, and the observable variables are the number of correct and incorrect responses. In performance tests the issues are more complex. The work products may be contributions to an oral proficiency interview, and the observable variables would be the realizations in speech of the constructs in the student model. Thus, if one of the constructs were 'fluency', the observable variables may include speed of delivery, circumlocution, or filling pauses. In both cases we state what we observe and why it is relevant to the construct from the performance, and these statements are referred to as *evidence rules*. This is the evaluation component of the evidence model. Mislevy (2003a: 6) says that:

> The focus at this stage of design is the evidentiary interrelationships that are being drawn among characteristics of students, of what they say and do, and of task and real-world situations in which they act. Here one begins to rough out the structures of an assessment that will be needed to embody a substantive argument, before narrowing attention to the details of implementation for particular purposes or to meet particular operational constraints.

As such, it is at this stage that we also begin to think about what research is needed to support the evidentiary reasoning.

The second part of an evidence model is the measurement component that links the observable variables to the student model by specifying how we score the evidence. This turns what we observe into the score from which we make inferences.

3. Task models. We can now see where test tasks and items fit into the picture. When we know what we wish to test, and what evidence we need to collect in order to get a score from which we can make inferences to what we want to test, we next ask: how do we collect the evidence? Task models therefore describe the situations in which test takers respond to items or tasks that generate the evidence we need.

Task models minimally comprise three elements. These are the *presentation material*, or input; *the work products*, or what the test takers actually do; and finally, the *task model variables* that describe task features. Task features are those elements that tell us what the task looks like, and which parts of the task are likely to make it more or less difficult (see below).

Classifications of task features are especially useful in language testing. Firstly, they provide the blueprint that is used by task or item writers to produce similar items for item banks or new forms of a test; secondly, if a test requires coverage of a certain domain or range of abilities, items can be selected according to pre-defined criteria from their table of classifications (see below and Unit A4).

4. Presentation model. Items and tasks can be presented in many different formats. A text and set of reading items may be presented in paper and pencil format, or on a computer. The presentation model describes how these will be laid out and presented to the test takers. In computer-based testing this would be the interface design for each item type and the test overall (see Fulcher, 2003b). Templates are frequently produced to help item writers to produce new items to the same specifications.

5. Assembly model. An assembly model accounts for how the student model, evidence models and task models work together. It does this by specifying two elements: *targets* and *constraints*. A target is the reliability with which each construct in a student model should be measured. A constraint relates to the mix of items or tasks on the test that must be included in order to represent the domain adequately. This model could be taken as answering the question: how much do we need to test?

6. Delivery model. This final model is not independent of the others, but explains how they will work together to deliver the actual test – for example, how the modules will operate if they are delivered in computer-adaptive mode, or as set paper and pencil forms. Of course, changes at this level will also impact on other models and how they are designed. This model would also deal with issues that are relevant at the level of the entire test, such as test security and the timing of sections of the test (Mislevy et al., 2003: 13). However, it also contains four processes, referred to as the delivery architecture (see further discussion in Unit A8). These are the presentation process, response processing, summary scoring and activity selection.

ECD can be summarized in Figure A5.1, in which we see the relationships between the different models. The role of the item or task designer is clear within ECD. Each item or task must elicit evidence that will be useful in drawing inferences to

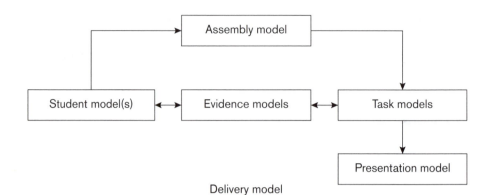

Figure A5.1 Models in the conceptual assessment framework of ECD (adapted from Mislevy et al., 2003: 5)

constructs. In order to do this, the designer must be clear about the kind of responses that are to be expected from tasks, and be able to define those features of tasks that are critical in eliciting relevant evidence. This requires us to be explicit with regard to the task form, and the expected response.

★ Task A5.2

Enright et al. (2000) describe a new construct for a reading test, which the authors entitled *reading to learn*. This is summarized in ETS (2005: 7) in this way:

Reading to learn depends on the ability to:

■ recognize the organization and purpose of a passage
■ understand relationships between ideas (for example, compare-and-contrast, cause-and-effect, agree–disagree, or steps in a process)
■ organize information in order to recall major points and important details
■ infer how ideas throughout the passage connect.

Notice the word 'ability' in the definition. This shows us that there is an explicit claim that *reading to learn* is part of a model of communicative competence that is directly relevant to academic reading, and that it is constructed of (at least) four sub-abilities.

➤ Take just one of the bullet points above. What evidence might you need to decide if a student could 'recognize', 'understand', 'organize' or 'infer'? Can you think of task types that you might use to collect this evidence?

A5.3 DESCRIBING ITEMS AND TASKS

It is perhaps items or tasks that first come to mind when we think of tests. This is because they are the most obvious, visible, part of a test. And for the most part it is considered 'easy' to write them, or copy them for use in test preparation classes. But we hope that the descriptions of test development and design from construct definition, specification writing and task design have shown that in fact this is not so. Mislevy et al. (1999: 6) argue that there are at least three steps in task design:

■ Identify the knowledge, skills or abilities (constructs) that we wish to test.
■ Identify the relationship between the constructs and the behaviours in situations that call for their use.
■ Describe the features of situations that provide the evidence to draw inferences from behaviour to constructs.

When it comes to describing tasks we need frameworks or typologies that will allow us to describe their key features. Pica et al. (1993), for example, argue that tasks should be goal-oriented, and should encourage learners to work towards achieving the goal. Their task typology also incorporates processes, which is especially useful in language testing as we frequently need to specify what types of strategies learners will use to complete the tasks set. Task activities and goals are broken down as follows:

■ *Interactional activity*

  With relation to information

  1 Each participant holds different information and needs both to give and to receive information in order to complete the task.
  2 One participant holds all the information and supplies it.
  3 Each participant holds all the information.

■ *Interaction requirement for activity*

  1 Each participant is expected both to request and to supply information.
  2 One participant supplies all the information.
  3 Each participant is expected to request and supply information but is not obliged to do so.

■ *Communication goal*

  With respect to goal orientation

  1 Participants have convergent goals.
  2 Participants have divergent goals.

With respect to outcome options

1   Only one acceptable outcome is possible.
2   More than one outcome is possible.

 Task A5.3

➤ Pica et al. argue that jigsaw-type tasks elicit the kind of language that is most likely to lead to learning. With reference to the Pica et al. typology, why do you think this is so?

Test task characteristics can be specified in many ways, and at levels of detail that suit particular situations. Bachman and Palmer (1996), for example, list characteristics of expected input, and characteristics of expected response in terms of format, language of input and topical characteristics. The language of input or expected response can be broken down in the following way:

Language characteristics:

■ Organizational characteristics

  ■ Grammatical (vocabulary, syntax, phonology, graphology)
  ■ Textual (cohesion, rhetorical or conversational organization)

■ Pragmatic characteristics

  ■ Functional (ideational, manipulative, heuristic, imaginative)
  ■ Sociolinguistic (dialect or variety, register, naturalness, cultural references and figurative language)

It is possible to assign labels to items (and the specs that produce them) such that test questions can be coded against schemes like that above. Coding tasks for specific features becomes important if we can demonstrate that those features are drivers of task difficulty; we shall return to the matter of coding in our exercises in Unit C5. In this case, if we knew that the use of a formal register by a speaker of higher social status in academic listening tasks always increased item difficulty, we would wish to ensure that we coded the item for these features in order to ensure that the test did not contain too many or too few such items to best represent the domain of academic listening. This is a special instance of evidentiary reasoning: we are arguing that particular features of the item do (or perhaps do not) trigger difficulty.

In ECD theory as outlined by Mislevy and his colleagues, with a clear understanding of what we wish to test and how we can describe tasks, it is possible to create highly formalized test specifications in which the production of the item is tightly controlled – the spec functions much as an intellectual template, guiding the item writer, shaping the test and ensuring evidentiary clarity all along the way. In order to under-stand precisely how this works, we will use an example from the well-understood domain of reading. Grabe (1999 and elsewhere) has summarized what we know about the reading process and the competences that are required for effective reading. Here are three of the fourteen identifiable 'abilities of the good reader':

1　fluent and automatic word recognition skills
2　a large recognition vocabulary
3　ability to recognize common word combinations (collocations).

(Grabe, 1999: 34)

As these concern vocabulary, they would be part of textual or discourse competence, depending upon the model of competence that we decide to use (see Unit A3), and which elements of the model we extract to place in a framework for a particular testing context. We would therefore wish our spec to generate a number of items that test the lexical component of textual competence, and specify key features of the items that may drive difficulty.

Task A5.4

★

Consider these sample items:

Identify the odd word out by drawing a circle around it.

1	dog	walk	lead	fish
2	take	elephant	horns	bull
3	chair	stool	furniture	sofa
4	bath	pot	pan	wok
5	impudent	insolent	audacious	pompous

➤ What is each item testing? Which items do you think are easy, and which more difficult? Do you think it is possible to make a claim from responses to these items to the textual competence of the test taker?

The kinds of features that may make our textual competence items easier or more difficult may include the following:

■ collocations or sets: does the item test collocation (words that tend to occur together in language use) or word sets that are usually considered to be alter-natives?
■ use of superordinates: is the correct answer in a set a superordinate rather than a co-hyponym (i.e. the relationship between 'animal' and 'dog' as opposed to the relationship between 'dog' and 'cat')?
■ cultural references: do the words in a collocation item collocate because they are part of a culture-bound idiomatic expression?

■ word frequency: are the words more or less frequent in language use? This may be difficult to define and could have many levels. For this purpose we will assume that any words that would not be in the top five thousand in a word frequency list would be less frequent.

■ abstractness: are the words more or less abstract in meaning? Again, this is difficult to define. Here we will assume that 'abstract' words are those that do not refer to objects in the physical world.

 Task A5.5

➤ Which of these features would you expect to make the items more difficult? Can you think of any other features that you may wish to include?

We will now produce an ECD-style basic task specification to match our samples.

A5.3.1 Claims to be made in relation to constructs

We can estimate the level of textual competence in test takers. We can generalize to the ability of an individual to read a variety of texts in the real world.

A5.3.2 Assumption

Items that test collocation test that part of lexical competence that requires a knowledge of how words are placed in chains that tend to co-occur in natural spoken or written discourse; items that test sets test that part of lexical competence that requires a knowledge of how words are selected from alternative words with similar meaning (hyponyms), or are related to more general words that name sets (superordinates). This ability is critical to decoding texts and efficient reading.

A5.3.3 Presentation material

Students are given sets of four words selected according to criteria set out in the task features. The instruction to the test taker for these items is always presented as: 'Identify the odd word out by drawing a circle around it.' The font is Arial 12, and at least three character spaces are left between each word.

A5.3.4 Work products

Test takers are required to identify the word that does not most naturally fit with the other three in the selection, either because it does not collocate or because it does not fit the lexical set. A circle is drawn around the word that does not collocate or is not part of the lexical set.

Task features

(1) Collocation item		(2) Set item	
(a) + cultural	(b) − culture	(a) + superordinate	(b) − superordinate
(c) + frequent	(d) − frequent	(c) + frequent	(d) − frequent
(e) + abstract	(f) − abstract	(e) + abstract	(f) − abstract

From this template we can see that the format of the item is completely set. There must always be four words, and these are drawn from collocations or lexical sets. However, they may vary along a number of vectors set out in the task features that our theory predicts will influence the difficulty of the items. Hence, if a student can answer the more difficult items correctly we will draw the inference that he or she has *more textual competence* than someone who cannot answer those items correctly.

If we now take one item:

impudent   insolent   audacious   pompous

we may now code this as: (2 b d e), and note that this coding could be used to select the correct number of items with this configuration for use in a test. This information would form part of the assembly model.

Note that in this example spec we have not provided a particular domain of inference, such as 'academic reading' or 'comprehending aircraft repair manuals'. We therefore have no task variables or features that relate to how words are drawn from a particular domain. Nor do we have any performance criteria that state under what conditions the test takers are to select the words. These could be added in order to make the inferences that we make from the scores to ability within specific domains more meaningful and hence more valid.

A5.4 TASKS AND TEACHING

In many parts of the world, language teachers are required to prepare their students to take language tests. As we have said, the most obvious part of a test is what it looks like in terms of tasks, and so it is likely that test tasks are going to influence what is done in test preparation classrooms.

Task A5.6

➤ Do you prepare students to take tests? Which tests?

➤ Does the test influence how you teach? How do you use the task types on the test in preparing your classes?

The term *washback* is used to talk about the effect that tests have on what goes on in the classroom. For many years it was just assumed that 'good tests' would produce 'good washback' and inversely that 'bad tests' would produce 'bad washback'. We now know that it is much more complex than this, as Alderson and Wall (1993) have shown (see Unit B5). And, of course, the whole notion of washback extends beyond the immediate impact on the classroom to how tests affect schools, educational systems and even countries, although this is sometimes referred to as the study of *impact*, rather than washback (see Wall, 2000; Cheng and Watanabe, 2004). The study of washback is also concerned with the political use of tests to implement changes in classrooms that are seen as improvements by governments.

However, here we are concerned only with the impact that the test has on the classroom as task types are frequently copied, either for practice or because there is an assumption that using the same tasks that appear on the test in teaching will result in higher scores for students.[1] But this is not necessarily so. Once students are familiar with a task type, that is all that is necessary to avoid the *test method* affecting the *test score*. What the teacher needs to ask is whether the test producers make it clear what each task type is supposed to test by setting out clearly the evidential link that they expect to hold between the task, the evidence that it is supposed to generate and the claim they wish to make about the test takers. If this information is available the teacher is given a very powerful set of conceptual tools that can lead to the generation of many different types of classroom activities that develop the communicative competences the test claims to measure. The formal test may have to use task types that can be delivered in a short space of time, maximizing the information that can be gained in that time. This was the subject of Unit A2. But teachers are not limited to the task types on the test to develop the abilities of learners in the classroom.

It is essential that we are critical of tests and the claims that surround them. Without the detailed information about constructs, all teachers can do is copy the test tasks for use in the classroom and hope for the best. With the constructs and evidentiary reasoning upon which a test is based, they are empowered to be creative in the development of communicative competence in the classroom. This is how testing can best help the teacher, in the classroom.

★ Task A5.7

➤ Select any test that you are familiar with, or for which you prepare students. Look at the test handbook and its specs (if written), or go to the website for the test. What evidence is provided about the task types on the test? Is there any evidence of evidentiary reasoning? Are you told which constructs the tasks are intended to measure?

In this Unit we have seen that designing and writing test tasks and items cannot be separated from the other processes of test design, and we have stressed that sitting down and writing content is never the first thing that we do when we need a new test. In addition, writing tasks and items is always a collaborative and iterative process that takes more time than is usually allocated for the task.

What we have tried to show is that the real question facing us when the time comes to think about test content is whether the tasks we intend to use are likely to generate evidence that can be scored, and whether we can convince others that the score will be related to the kinds of claims that we wish to make about learner ability. In order to illustrate this perspective on task and item design we have reviewed the approach known as evidence-centred design, which attempts to force test designers into considering questions of validity at the very earliest stages of the process. We looked at the kinds of questions that would be generated using a specific example from the field of testing reading.

Finally we considered washback in language testing, or how the test and its content may impact upon language teaching. We have argued that the dangers of 'teaching to the test' through the simple use of test-type materials in the classroom can be avoided if the teacher has access to the claims that underlie test design. When this information is available, the teacher is empowered to design his or her own approaches and materials that aim to develop the abilities that the test is designed to measure.

If all this seems complicated, it is. However, we believe that ECD is quite valuable in certain test settings. We find ourselves curious whether ECD must be defined as Mislevy and others have formalized it. In Unit C5 we provide some thought experiments on these points.

Unit A6
Prototypes, prototyping and field tests

A6.1 INTRODUCTION

The literature on evaluating test tasks and items does not clearly distinguish between writing prototype tasks and writing tasks from existing test specifications. The assumption in most cases is that test specs do exist, and that the problems surround how item writers can produce new items with item to spec fit.

For many test providers this involves a process of task *review*. Even with some high-stakes tests, the review of tasks may be conducted only by one or two 'senior examiners' or a 'chief examiner' whose expertise is thought to give 'validity' to the test. This kind of approach, sometimes conducted with a very light touch, is referred to as *moderation*. While we do think that this kind of moderation is very important, it cannot deal with the very serious questions of score meaning and validity that we have raised. Alderson and Buck (1993) and Alderson et al. (1995) deal extensively with how items are written and moderated, but the distinction between *prototypes* and *operational test forms* is not made.

The question that we wish to address in this Unit is: how do we know that the tasks we have selected for a test can be justified? To make this more specific, we wish to discover whether the responses to the tasks result in scores from which we may make valid inferences to constructs. In other words, we are still concerned with the process of how we construct a test, rather than how new forms are generated. It's about getting from nothing to something, rather than having something there that merely needs to be recreated in an alternative form.

A6.2 PROTOTYPES

Prototype comes from the Greek word *prototypo* (πρωτότυπο), which is sometimes translated as *archetype*, made up as it is of the two elements *proto* (πρώτο) or *first*, and *typos* (τύπος) or *type*. The meaning of *type* in this sense is of a mould or stamp, from which other examples could be created.

Task A6.1

➤ Look at the following definitions of *prototype*. To which range of industries and activities can the word be applied?

A model suitable for use in complete evaluation of form, design, performance, and material processing.
www.fibreglast.com/contentpages-glossary+of+terms+in+composites-163.html

The first working version of any device, software, product or service.
www.promitheas.com/glossary.php

A working model that is not yet finished but that represents the major technical, design and content features of the site. Prototypes are used for testing.
www.alco.org/help/help090.html

The original form which serves as a model on which successors are based.
www.worldimages.com/art_glossary.php

A facsimile of an end product used to demonstrate a concept rapidly, check feasibility and/or gain acceptance.
www.georgetown.edu/uis/ia/dw/GLOSSARY0816.html

The *Oxford Dictionary of Business* (1996: 407) defines prototype in the following way:

> **Prototype** A preproduction model developed to evaluate the feasibility of new ideas, materials, technology, and design techniques as part of new product development. In addition to the technological evaluation, consumer clinics may be used to establish the opinion of the potential customers on the acceptability of the product.

The purpose of a prototype in language testing is not dissimilar to its purpose in engineering. What we wish to do is produce an item or task that fulfils a particular function within a larger test. The function of the item or task is to generate a response from which we can make inferences. If we see the language test as a machine that needs designing and building, the first part of the design process is to ensure that the parts fulfil their intended function and contribute towards the working of the whole machine.

The first part of the design phase is referred to as *prototyping* – that is, the design and testing of prototypes. Before we look at this in relation to language testing, let us consider an example from industrial design.

A6.2.1 Laser Prototypes Europe Ltd

When manufacturing new products, companies need to build prototypes of these products to ensure that they work, and that the parts do what they are intended to do. If a company actually manufactured the parts in the way that the consumer would eventually see them, the costs would be extremely high. It is much cheaper to conduct tests for suitability and durability on prototypes that are quick and easy to produce so that as features are changed it is not necessary to retool machines completely or change the manufacturing process. This is why prototype parts are used for testing. Laser Prototypes Europe Ltd (http://www.laserproto.com/servicesmain.htm) is a company that specializes in prototyping. This is what it says are the benefits of prototyping:

Benefits of Rapid Prototyping:

■ Physical models in a few days.
■ Communicate your design intentions to your clients, toolmakers and to other departments easily and highly effectively.
■ Reduced time to market.
■ Fully functional testing before any commitment to tooling.
■ Ensures the right product to the market.
■ Shorter development cycles.
■ Lower development costs.
■ Accurate marketplace feedback.
■ Shorter lead times in comparison to using conventional methods.
■ Allows simple and effective design changes before expense of tooling

In language testing we need to ensure that the task we design engages the test takers in processes and produces a response which can be summarized in numerical or alphanumeric form, and from which we can make an inference to an unobservable variable – our construct definition. From that inference we then make a judgment about the likely ability of a test taker to perform in some future non-test situation. The task or item is the basic building unit for collecting evidence, summarizing it and making inferences. By building prototype items and tasks and engaging in prototyping, we can ensure that the task type is right for the market in that it does generate the evidence that we need.

Notice that this company uses the term *rapid prototyping*. In the early stages of testing a new product or a new task type, we need to find out very quickly whether it is going to work as an idea. Poor ideas are discarded; better ones are improved through iterations in the design process. The quicker this is done, the sooner we can arrive at decisions about which items may survive into an operational test. This is why specialists in prototyping talk about reducing design costs and speeding up the time to market, or, in language testing terms, the *roll-out* of the finished test.

In order to understand this analogy from manufacturing more easily, consider the following extract from the website of Laser Prototypes Europe Ltd.

Stereolithography is the longest established Rapid Prototyping process and is an excellent process for producing fast, accurate parts.

As the longest established RP bureau in the UK and Ireland, Laser Prototypes can offer an invaluable breadth of experience in providing many different industries with a very wide and varied range of models.

Prototype models can be built up to 500mm × 500mm × 600mm, while larger parts can be built in sections and bonded. These Stereolithography models can be used to check fit, form, function, and can be used as patterns in secondary tooling processes for short production runs of plastic or metal parts.

At LPE, we offer models in a range of resins, depending on the customer requirement, from snap fit requirements to high temperature resistance.

Task A6.2

➤ When brainstorming task types for a new test, why do you think it is important to generate more ideas for task types than will be needed on the final test?

A6.3 PROTOTYPING

At the end of Unit A5 we provided an example of a task template with specific claims about what the items were intended to measure. The item started from a requirement to test textual competence as a critical element of reading, and in order to test this it was decided that evidence was required from students which indicated that they were able to recognize lexical sets arranged in chains (collocation) and groups with similar meaning (sets containing superordinates and hyponyms). The task type is one of many we could design for which we could make this claim. In rapid prototyping we would subject this and other items to tests that would let us see whether the parts would work well.

Rapid prototyping of item and task types is made up of two parts, *alpha testing* and *beta testing*. Continuing our analogy from manufacturing, alpha testing is the

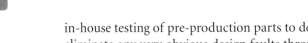

in-house testing of pre-production parts to decide if the design is adequate and to eliminate any very obvious design faults through expert judgment. In order to do this we only need a small number of sample items. Let us look at our items again:

Identify the odd word out by drawing a circle around it.

1	dog	walk	lead	fish
2	take	elephant	horns	bull
3	chair	stool	furniture	sofa
4	bath	pot	pan	wok
5	impudent	insolent	audacious	pompous

Identifying experts to comment on this item type as a means of measuring textual competence may not be unduly difficult. We would probably select two applied linguists working in lexis or corpus linguistics, two teachers who have extensive experience of teaching vocabulary, and two language testers. We would ask them, working individually, to evaluate the likely effectiveness of the item type for its intended purpose and recommend any improvements that may be made to the design. Once they have done this we may bring them together to discuss their reactions so that item designers could focus on areas where the expert judges agree that there are design faults.

Here is some sample feedback on this item type from an experienced teacher of English who has also written test items and prepared students to take language tests.

What do you think the items are supposed to test?

You could only make very general inferences because you have a variety of item types. If they got all of these right we'd be dealing with an advanced student of English generally. But not academic English or anything like that.

What knowledge, skills or abilities would a learner need to answer each of these items correctly?

Number 4 involves schematic knowledge: we associate 'pot', 'pan' and 'wok' with the kitchen, but this may not be the case in other cultures. In some cultures the word 'wok' might be a problem if they aren't familiar with Chinese cooking.

Cultural knowledge is needed in items 1, 3, 4 and 5, although 3 requires less cultural knowledge than the others because it's likely to be more familiar.

Number 2 requires not just the knowledge of an idiomatic expression but also linguistic knowledge when we're talking about student types. It would be a certain type of person who can do crosswords and think laterally who would be able to do number 2.

The fifth one requires the ability to remember the meanings of specific words out of context, to be able to access a definition in your mind.

Do you think there are any problems with these items? If so, what?

The answer to 2 is 'elephant' for a native speaker, but for a non-native speaker 'take' would be equally correct because it is the only verb. We're also expecting the students to be able to recognize idiomatic expressions. This involves complex processes of association.

Number 5 is a problem where there isn't any context because there are difficulties with formality and register. Recalling the meaning of a word out of context doesn't really test if the words are in active vocabulary anyway. A lot of native speakers would have a problem giving definitions for the four of them and being able to identify the correct one without any kind of context. It's difficult to say which is the odd one out. The choice for number 5 would depend very much on collocation.

There is also the problem that someone may know all the words but doesn't know the criteria of the person who set the task for the odd one out. In the case of number 3 it would be selecting the superordinate.

This type of task is one that more advanced students are likely to find frustrating because they're able to see that there is more than one that's likely to be the odd one out. It's likely to create negative washback.

Can you suggest how these items could be improved?

When you've got an odd one out item there is almost always a way you can select another one and find some kind of reason for it. For example, you could select 'sofa' in 3 and argue that a sofa doesn't have legs.

This teacher has raised some serious questions about this item type. We will list some of the most interesting points raised below.

Cultural content. This was specifically designed into the items as a variable that would influence item difficulty, but it had not been hypothesized that cultural references may have a variable impact upon test takers. If the teacher is correct and cultural references may make an item more difficult for test takers from one culture than another, we may be in danger of introducing bias into some of the items. However, if understanding culture-rich items from Anglo-British environments is part of our construct definition, we may still decide to retain such items if they do disadvantage learners who are unfamiliar with cultural and idiomatic language usages.

Construct-irrelevant processes. The teacher says that only certain types of people would be able to answer the second item correctly – those who would also be good at crosswords. This is not what the item is intended to test. This is an interesting observation that needs to be investigated empirically; if the item survives alpha testing this would be an appropriate research question to take forward to beta testing.

Context. The teacher points out that all the words are presented out of context, something that was not considered to be particularly relevant when the item type was originally conceived during brainstorming sessions. However, she goes on to say that this requires learners to access definitions in their minds, or operate as if they were a dictionary. This raises a particularly interesting question about how second-language learners construct a mental lexicon and access this to use words productively in speech, a point which the teacher also makes. If item 5 turns out to be far too difficult for even advanced learners of English it may be that the process the item writers thought would be activated by the item (elimination of a word that does not occur in a lexical set) could not be, because this is not how items are stored in the mental lexicon.

Correct responses and linguistic sophistication. Although these items were constructed to have only one correct response according to the linguistic theory of chains and sets, it is argued that there are alternative correct responses. Further, it is argued that, the more sophisticated (and advanced) the learner, the more likely they would be to create a context for the use of an incorrect word that would make it the odd one out, thus leading learners with a larger and richer lexicon to answer more items incorrectly. If correct, this hypothesis would result in the item type being rejected from a test immediately. Any item that systematically disadvantages test takers who have 'more' of the construct the items are designed to test is by definition a poor item that does not provide useful information from which inferences can be drawn.

★ Task A6.3

➤ Show this item to others and see what they think about it. Can you think of anything else that you would add to the list above?

➤ What changes would you be likely to make to these items before taking them forward to beta testing? Or would you discard them at this point and look for alternative item types to test textual competence? What alternative item types can you think of?

We can see that for very little cost we have collected a great deal of valuable data that helps us to think about how useful our items or tasks are. We have the opportunity to revise them before taking them forward to the next stage.

The second stage of rapid prototyping is beta testing, which is the external test of preproduction items. The purpose is to test the items or tasks for all the functions identified, with actual test takers or second-language learners. At this stage we may test a range of hypotheses, both those that have been developed by the test designers and those that have arisen from alpha testing. It is now critical to realize that *the design process itself has generated a research agenda that we are only just beginning to address.* We will attempt to list the questions that we must start to address with our prototypes in order to decide if they are worth retaining in any form at all after beta testing, or if the expense of field testing is justified. And we must realize that for those items that are retained, the results of our research will begin to form the evidentiary basis of the score meaning for the resulting test.

Claim we wish to make

Correct responses to the items will allow us to make meaningful statements about students' textual competence in the specific area of fluent and automatic word recognition skills, size of recognition vocabulary and ability to recognize common word combinations.

Expected difficulty drivers

Are collocation or set items more difficult?

Are items with superordinates as the key more difficult than options with hyponyms only?

Does the inclusion of cultural/idiomatic references make the item more difficult?

Does word frequency make the item more difficult?

Are items with abstract nouns more difficult than other items?

Assumptions

Do responses to items correlate with reading speed?

Do responses to items correlate with estimates of vocabulary size?

Can learners at different ability levels access relevant meanings for words taken out of context? (alpha testing)

Does the reasoning for the selection of a key become more problematic with increasing linguistic sophistication? (alpha testing)

Format and presentation

Can test takers understand the instructions easily?

Do the font size and spacing impede responding to the item?

Construct-irrelevant variance

Do items with cultural or idiomatic references disadvantage sub-groups of the test taking population? (alpha testing)

Do collocation items test cognitive ('crossword') abilities unrelated to textual competence? (alpha testing)

In beta testing we are not able to generate item difficulty statistics for our prototypes. The reason for this is that in rapid prototyping we use only small numbers of test takers who try out small numbers of each of the item types that we have designed.

Usually this is no more than five in a group. This is not unlike the process used in testing an interface for a computer-based test in order to ensure that the presentation model does not interfere with the test-taking process. Fulcher (2003b) describes this process, which is in part applicable to the beta testing of test items.

The group selected should be as representative as possible of the future test-taking population, but with only five members this may not be possible; however, there are sometimes reasons for selecting particular individuals. In order to see if good readers have more difficulty identifying the key in these items because they are able to create a context in which each of the options may be correct, we would need a group made up of better readers. In this way, small groups of approximately five test takers would attempt the items at a time and provide verbal feedback both individually and in a group on what they are doing while answering the items, what they find problematic and the reasons for their decisions. This process is iterative, and should be carried out as many times as necessary with new groups of learners who are representative of the population or sub-sets of the population, until the amount of information that is being provided and recorded by the researchers becomes insignificant.

Asking second-language learners to do this cannot be undertaken without preparation. Setting up situations in which students provide verbal protocols as they actually undertake test tasks, or after they have completed test tasks (in the case of speaking tests, for example), needs to be done with care (see extended discussions in Gass and Mackey, 2000; Green, 1998). What is most important is that the participants should be able to provide valuable information on the processes they are using in responding to the test items, for this provides *substantive validity evidence* that supports or weakens the hypotheses of the designers about why the test takers are responding in the way they do.

★ Task A6.4

Look again at the list of research questions that we have formulated above. From the last reflective activity you may have generated a number of research questions of your own.

➤ Which of these questions can be investigated during beta testing?

In prototyping, the approach to addressing our research questions is mostly qualitative. Protocol analysis is ideal for addressing substantive validity questions, but interviews, questionnaires and focus groups are also useful. For production tasks in the assessment of speaking and writing, discourse analysis is also extremely valuable (see Lazaraton, 2002, for an extensive discussion of qualitative approaches to test validation with speaking tests). This is because with so few test takers and rapidly changing and evolving task types, it is impossible to have sample sizes (N-sizes) large enough to calculate useful statistics.

We should note that at the time of writing the authors are not aware of any data or evidence in the public domain relating to rapid prototyping activities from any major test development agency. This is not surprising either in the world of manufacturing or in language testing (perhaps with the exception of the automobile industry – the prototype 'concept car'), because the processes lead to design documents that are the blueprints of the product. The more research and development that goes into design, the higher the quality of the end product. Much of the design information therefore remains proprietary to the company. However, many testing agencies do not have such information because the test design processes are very much ad hoc and not based upon research that would enhance product quality, and quality information (such as reliability and validity evidence) is not available.

A6.4 FIELD TESTING

Field testing is often described as *product use testing* with users from the target market. At this stage the prototypes have been extensively tested and refined in alpha and beta testing, but this does not mean that there are no further changes to be made, or that some items or tasks will not be eliminated from the mix at this point. However, taking tasks to field testing implies that initial decisions have been taken about the range and number of task types that should be included on a *prototype test*, rather than the prototyping individual task or item types. In field testing, the items and tasks are still under investigation, but they are considered in the context of the larger product of which they are a component part.

In the development of the TOEFL Internet-based test iBT that was launched in late 2005, we can see the process of design through prototyping to field testing as it was conceived five years earlier in Cumming et al. (2000). This document considers the constructs to be measured and the variables that the researchers thought could be operationalized in a set of tasks for which difficulty drivers could be established. A task model and reader–writer model are laid out briefly, and a research agenda set for prototyping and field testing. One of the new task types developed for the TOEFL iBT was the integrated academic reading–writing task, which was hypothesized to have significant washback on the academic writing classroom (ibid.: 28). Some of the questions on this research agenda are:

■ Investigating construct-irrelevant influences on score meaning

 ■ Studying internal test structure
 ■ Is it necessary to have a minimum reading ability before it is possible to perform on writing tasks?
 ■ Do the writing tasks relate to one another in theoretically anticipated ways?
 ■ Do integrated tasks relate in expected ways to independent tasks?

- Studying external relations

  - What is the relationship of the new TOEFL to its predecessors?
  - *What is the relationship between new writing measures and qualities in writing that experienced markers and teachers value?*

- Group comparisons, or the differences between performance of

  - graduate versus undergraduate students
  - native versus non-native writers
  - skilled versus less skilled writers
  - students before and after instruction.

In Unit B6 you will read a study conducted by Cumming et al. (2005) which was conducted as part of a field study of the prototype writing tasks that survived prototyping. This study addresses three key research questions:

1 Do the prototype tasks represent the domain of academic English needed for study in North American colleges?
2 Do they elicit performances that are similar to performances in regular writing classes?
3 Can the teachers understand the evidence claims upon which the tasks had been designed?

This study therefore addresses a key element of the external relations between prototype tasks and what writing instructors value, as well as addressing the substantive issue of whether experienced instructors could recognize from the task types the constructs and claims upon which the tasks had been designed.

We can see that in field testing we have access to a much larger number of informants, and we are able to give a prototype test to groups of test takers who are representative of the target test-taking population. This allows the designers to collect statistical information on the performance of items and tasks in addition to the qualitative feedback that primarily informs rapid prototyping. Typically, item statistics can be calculated, and we are able to begin to investigate the internal structure of the test. This is valuable if we have theoretical reasons to suppose that there are particular relationships between sets of items that are designed to test the same construct, or different constructs. We would expect the correlations between these sets to converge if they were designed to test the same construct, and diverge if they were designed to test different constructs. Initial studies can be done also to start to investigate the assembly model, in which we might ask questions like how long it may take for test takers to answer particular sub-tests, as well as the entire test, in so far as we understand its overall structure at this point. This will now begin to affect how we see the shape of the test and how many items or tasks of particular types we can use. As we know that test length and reliability are closely related, we are now able to begin to estimate how reliable our final test is likely to be, given the configurations we can put together.

Further activities that investigate these aspects of field testing will be presented in Unit C6. Here, however, we will simply look at some item statistics associated with the item types that we have presented as potentially being useful in the measurement of textual competence. Although it is unlikely that each of our sample items would have survived to field testing, let us assume that they have; let us assume that the designers were so keen on these items that they wished to collect statistical information on their performance and see whether they were of value in a complete test. That is, does the item contribute to score meaning? Does it discriminate well between test takers who are 'stronger' and 'weaker' on the construct of interest? Are our difficulty drivers and assumptions correct?

The calculation of item-level statistics is easy to do, and is explained in Unit A7 and in most standard language testing texts, such as Alderson et al. (1995) and Bachman (2004). We gave our five items to fourteen students who were representative of a pre-university reading and vocabulary improvement course for whom the test was initially designed. In Table A6.1 we have presented some of the basic item statistics that are helpful in further evaluating the usefulness of these items. Each item is listed in the left-hand column, and each of the options across the top. The value in each of the cells tells us how many students in our sample selected that option, and the correct option (the key) is marked with an asterisk. The FV column stands for the facility value, which is nothing more than the proportion of test takers who selected the key. This gives an indication of how difficult the item is for the target test takers. Finally, the DI or discrimination index is a measure of how well the item discriminates between test takers who scored higher on the whole prototype test and those who scored lower on the whole test.

We can see from the facility values that all of these items are difficult for the intended test-taking population, with the exception of item 4. The pattern of responses to items also indicates that some of the questions raised by our expert commentator in alpha testing were highly relevant. In item 2, for example, it appears that most test takers are selecting option 1. If this is because it is the only verb in the group, the purpose of our item design has been subverted!

Table A6.1 Basic item statistics for five items included on a prototype test of textual competence

	Option 1	Option 2	Option 3	Option 4	FV	DI
Item 1	2	9	0	3*	0.21	0.00
Item 2	9	3*	2	0	0.21	0.29
Item 3	0	10	3*	1	0.21	0.43
Item 4	10*	1	1	2	0.71	0.46
Item 5	1	2	7	4*	0.29	0.29

Task A6.5

➤ Examine the responses across these items focusing on the most and least pop-ular choices. What might this tell us about how the test takers are interpreting the items? Does this lead to any further hypotheses about the processes that are being used to answer these items?

We will now repeat the set of questions that we generated regarding the drivers of item difficulties that arose from the design process and alpha testing, and place tentative answers next to each:

Are collocation or set items more difficult?

Set items appear to be easier when all the options are hyponyms.

Are items with superordinates as the key more difficult than options with hyponyms only?

Yes.

Does the inclusion of cultural or idiomatic references make the item more difficult?

Yes

Does word frequency make the item more difficult?

It may not, as all items are equally difficult for this group of test takers (see the facility value of item 5).

Are items with abstract nouns more difficult than other items?

Yes.

For this group of test takers it appears clear that apart from the set item with noun-phrase hyponyms as options, the item type is inappropriate and too difficult. This can further be investigated by looking at the extent to which our sample items are related to general vocabulary knowledge and reading ability. In an ideal world we would like to administer separate tests, but we can also look at the correlation between each individual item and test total, which gives an indication of how well a particular item discriminates between test takers. In our small batch of items only items 3 and 4 discriminate well, but item 3 is too difficult on the whole for this group of students.

Task A6.6

We have investigated some of the research questions that were posed in relation to our prototype items. Mounting evidence in relation to difficulty drivers suggests that these items should not be included on the final test.

➤ Can you think of studies that you could design to further investigate those questions that we earlier labelled as being related to 'assumptions'?

A6.5 THE ITERATIVE NATURE OF THE PROCESS

The first field test is not the end of the process. Information from each stage in test design and its associated research feeds back into the design process. Items need to be revised and re-designed, test specifications change and develop, and prototype tests are piloted to discover the mix of tasks and items that best provide the evidence needed to generate scores from which inferences are made. The design process should be recorded. Each decision and its reasons constitute *validity evidence.*

In this process the test specs (see Unit A4) become more and more precise, until the point at which the designers have the evidence and the confidence to address the 'go/no-go' decision. In language test development we should therefore think of any processes being not linear or fixed but iterative and dynamic. The process goes on until the very moment at which we decide we have reached the optimal design to release a working, crafted product, suitable for its intended purpose.

In this Unit we have discussed how we create a new test. This is very different from writing new items or tasks for a test that already exists, and which is the topic of most other texts on language testing. We are concerned about the creation of the first form of a test. Other forms are then generated from the test specifications.

Summary

We have compared the test creation process with the design of products in the world of manufacturing. As part of the design process, prototypes are created. These are used in rapid prototyping to discover whether the parts will work well within the larger product that is being developed. If this is done before the product goes into production, much money is usually saved through not manufacturing large numbers of something that may not work and therefore may not sell. In language testing there is no point in manufacturing many forms of a test that is unreliable or not valid for its intended purpose. However, this is not to say that there are no test designers who produce tests of poor quality, sell them, but fail to tell their customers of the potential faults of the product.

Keeping a record of the process of test design, including all the decisions taken, with the reasons for those decisions, is very important. Decisions may sometimes be made on practical grounds and at other times research may be commissioned to address design questions to which we do not know the answers. However, the record constitutes validity evidence that may be appealed to in a validity argument (see Unit A.10). It is quite possible that the entire record cannot be placed in the public domain, especially if the test has been designed by a company that has rivals with whom they would not like to share design secrets. But the entire record should be available for inspection by external experts, and key research or findings should be made available in documents that customers can consult to ensure that this is the right product for them.

Unit A7
Scoring language tests and assessments

A7.1 INTRODUCTION

Models and frameworks (see Unit A3) describe the *what* of language testing, the constructs to which we wish to make inferences and the domains to which we wish to make predictions. The tasks (see Units A4 and A5) tell us about the *how* of language testing, the methods by which we elicit the evidence that we need.

Scoring is concerned with the *how much* or *how good* of language testing. We may say that we wish to draw inferences from performance on a task to the ability to manage turn taking in social interaction, and we may have designed tasks to elicit evidence, but this does not tell us how much evidence is necessary, or how much of the ability is present. How we score is the link between the evidence we elicit from the task on the one hand, and the construct and domain on the other.

We can also put it like this: a model or framework is descriptive and horizontal, while the scoring model is vertical (Figure A7.1). The score and how it is arrived at are very important. The purpose of some tests may be to give detailed, explicit feedback to learners (a diagnostic test), where no (alpha)numeric score is necessary. This is likely to be in the case of local classroom assessments or very low-stakes tests. In other cases the evidence is summarized in a score, which is then used as the basis of inference and prediction.

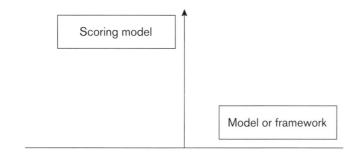

Figure A7.1 The *what* and *how much/how good* of language testing

In the case of the TOEFL iBT, for example, the information produced for test takers and score users states that:

> Each institution sets its own requirements for TOEFL iBT scores. Test takers taking the new TOEFL test to fulfill an admissions requirement should ask their target institutions for score requirements.
>
> (ETS, 2005)

This approach places the onus for score interpretation – whether or not a particular score is appropriate for admission to higher education – on to the receiving institution. But we know that in practice certain scores soon have meaning attached to them. University admissions officers in the United Kingdom believe that they know what an IELTS 6.0 means, in the same way that their US counterparts interpret TOEFL 550 on the paper-based test, TOEFL 213 on the computer-based test and TOEFL iBT 80. These users can be seen as *score consumers*, and they exert a very powerful influence on test providers. ETS (2005: 54–58) provides a concordance table that relates ranges of scores across the three TOEFL tests because the meaning of particular scores for these consumers has become embedded in consciousness and practice. Any suggestion that the meaning of the score may change is potentially damaging to the test provider, just as changing the taste of tomato ketchup would be to Heinz, or the introduction of the new and improved blue taxicab to New York.

⭐ Task A7.1

> ➤ Look at two or three websites maintained by test providers. What, if anything, do they say about score meaning? Does the site provide any caveat to this interpretation, or is it 'absolute'?

Yet the reality is that score meaning does change. When IELTS replaced ELTS there was no discussion of any potential change in score meaning even though the test had changed significantly in order to incorporate enhancements that had grown out of research on the older test (see Criper and Davies, 1988; Hughes et al., 1988; Alderson, 1990). Similarly, ETS (2005: 55) adds the note under the concordance table that the paper-based test did not include a writing score, and the paper-based and computer-based tests did not include a speaking score. However, ETS (2005: 53) goes further in stating that:

> Although score comparisons can be useful in understanding the relationship between scores on the three versions of the TOEFL test, it is important to note that differences among the tests make it difficult to draw exact comparisons.

While this is accurate, it is also an understatement. The construct definition underlying the TOEFL iBT is radically different from that in the paper-based and computer-based tests; the evidence model and scoring procedures have changed; the task types used to generate the evidence have been expanded and altered. Score meaning is different, even if it is possible to say through criterion studies that learners who tend to get 550 on the paper and pencil test tend to get 79–80 on TOEFL iBT.

This discussion of how we attach meaning to test scores shows just how they can become iconic. When scores achieve this status their meaning tends to become fixed. But we have argued that the meaning of a score derives from its function in linking evidence generated in performance, to the claims we wish to make about underlying ability and the likelihood of success within a defined domain that is related to test purpose. How we arrive at a score and the meaning we invest in the score are therefore extremely important.

A7.2 DEFINING THE QUALITY OF LANGUAGE

Task A7.2

➤ If score meaning cannot be arrived at solely through comparison between two different tests, does it make sense to compare the meaning of scores from two tests by comparing them to a model such as the Common European Framework of Reference?

➤ Assess the value of the interpretation of score meaning implied by the *Manual for Relating Language Examinations to the Common European Framework of Reference for Languages: Learning, Teaching, Assessment* (CEF) (North et al., 2003). This document is available online at http://www.coe.int/T/DG4/Portfolio/?L=E&M =/documents_intro/Manual.html.

The earliest attempts to invest language test scores with meaning that could be related to an ability to perform in a 'real world' domain were made within the United States military (see Fulcher, 1997, 2003a, 2007). Language educators within the military were using tests that did not adequately predict the ability of military personnel to perform in the field, and it was assumed that this was hampering the war effort. Kaulfers (1944: 137) argued:

> The urgency of the world situation does not permit of erudite theorizing in English about the grammatical structure of the language for two years before attempting to converse or to understand telephone conversations . . . The nature of the individual test items should be such as to provide specific, recognizable evidence of the examinee's readiness to perform in a life-situation, where lack of ability to understand and speak extemporaneously might be a serious handicap to safety and comfort, or to the effective execution of military responsibilities.

The most recognizable outcome of this realization was what we now know as the *scoring rubric* (US terminology) or the *rating scale* which contains *band/level descriptors* (UK terminology). These were attempts to address the question: how good does language have to be for this particular purpose and domain? Rubrics or descriptors therefore draw on those elements of a model of communicative competence that have been selected for the domain-specific framework, but do so in a hierarchical fashion. The earliest rating scales were simple semantic differentials like this one from the Foreign Service Institute (FSI) that was in use for the assessment of language skills in the US military from the early 1950s. Used in the context of a speaking test, each test taker was rated on five constructs. The rater placed a mark on the line that was judged to best reflect the ability of the speaker. We should note that there are no definitions of the central options, and it is also very difficult to know what we mean by the terms 'foreign' or 'adequate' for any particular speech sample.

Accent	foreign	_ : _ : _ : _ : _ : _	native
Grammar	inaccurate	_ : _ : _ : _ : _ : _	accurate
Vocabulary	inadequate	_ : _ : _ : _ : _ : _	adequate
Fluency	uneven	_ : _ : _ : _ : _ : _	even
Comprehension	incomplete	_ : _ : _ : _ : _ : _	complete

★ Task A7.3

➤ In Unit A1 we considered the nature of constructs. Now consider the terminology used in the FSI rating scale above. Is it possible to give meaningful descriptions for any of these terms?

However, such simple ways of arriving at a score soon evolved into more complex systems, containing levels with definitions. These definitions were designed to tell the rater more about what constituted 'more of' the ability in which we are interested. The following is one of the first attempts to do this, produced by the Foreign Service Institute in 1958, and has served as a template for many rating scales produced since then. It assumes that learners have something termed 'proficiency' that starts at an elementary level, proceeds through three intermediate levels and culminates in bilingual or native proficiency: the ability to do anything with the language that would be expected of an 'educated native speaker'. This criterion at the top end of the scale was used as the ultimate yardstick in the measurement of language proficiency until very recently.

The definitions of each level are written intuitively and may not characterize actual language use, and it is difficult (if not impossible) to define what a 'native speaker' might be (see Davies, 1991; Fulcher, 2003a: 93–95). Using this intuitively obvious category as a 'peg' upon which to hang the descriptors further down the scale has also led to claims that these tests were in fact *norm-referenced*, rather than *criterion-referenced* (Lantolf and Frawley, 1985; 1988). That is, awarding a score amounts to deciding which test taker is 'the best', placing him or her in band 5, and spreading the rest out across the other bands in the scale – whereas scoring of this type should involve matching each performance to a descriptor without reference to any other test taker.

Level 1: Elementary Proficiency. Able to satisfy routine travel needs and minimum courtesy requirements.

Can ask and answer questions on topics very familiar to him; within the scope of his very limited language experience can understand simple questions and statements, allowing for slowed speech, repetition or paraphrase; speaking vocabulary inadequate to express anything but the most elementary needs; errors in pronunciation and grammar are frequent, but can be understood by a native speaker used to dealing with foreigners attempting to speak his language; while topics which are 'very familiar' and elementary needs vary considerably from individual to individual, any person at Level 1 should be able to order a simple meal, ask for shelter or lodging, ask and give simple directions, make purchases, and tell time.

Level 2: Limited Working Proficiency. Able to satisfy routine social demands and limited work requirements.

Can handle with confidence but not with facility most social situations including introductions and casual conversations about current events, as well as work, family and autobiographical information; can handle limited work requirements, needing help in handling any complications or difficulties; can get the gist of most conversations on non-technical subjects (i.e., topics which require no specialized knowledge) and has a speaking vocabulary sufficient to express himself simply with some circumlocutions; accent, though often quite faulty, is intelligible; can usually handle elementary constructions quite accurately but does not have thorough or confident control of the grammar.

Level 3: Minimum Professional Proficiency. Able to speak the language with sufficient structural accuracy and vocabulary to participate effectively in most formal and informal conversations on practical, social, and professional topics.

Can discuss particular interests and special fields of competence with reasonable ease; comprehension is quite complete for a normal rate of speech; vocabulary is broad enough that he rarely has to grope for a word; accent may be obviously foreign; control of grammar good; errors never interfere with understanding and rarely disturb the native speaker.

Level 4: Full Professional Proficiency. Able to use the language fluently and accurately on all levels normally pertinent to professional needs.

Can understand and participate in any conversation within the range of his experience with a high degree of fluency and precision of vocabulary; would rarely be taken for a native speaker, but can respond appropriately even in unfamiliar situations; errors of pronunciation and grammar quite rare; can handle informal interpreting from and into the language.

Level 5: Native or Bilingual Proficiency. Speaking proficiency equivalent to that of an educated native speaker.

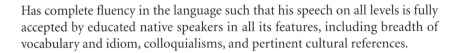

Has complete fluency in the language such that his speech on all levels is fully accepted by educated native speakers in all its features, including breadth of vocabulary and idiom, colloquialisms, and pertinent cultural references.

What is clear is that these descriptors are exceptionally general, and it is frequently difficult to match specific examples of performance (evidence) to a descriptor. In other words, the link between the evidence and the score is difficult to establish clearly.

 Task A7.4

➤ Take a sample of student speech from an oral proficiency interview. Try to match it to one of the descriptors in the 1958 FSI scale and justify why the descriptor is the most appropriate for that sample. Do you find this process easy?

In speaking tests this approach was extended throughout the US military during the 1960s (Lowe, 1987) and as the Interagency Language Roundtable is still in use today. In the 1980s this approach was also adopted for use in schools and colleges, and in the form of the American Council on Teaching Foreign Languages Guidelines (1999) the scales are the de facto framework for the scoring of language samples in both education and workplace assessment (Swender, 2003).

A7.3 DEVELOPING SCORING SYSTEMS

The two examples of rating scales for speaking provided above are *holistic*. A speech sample is awarded a single number, and the meaning of that number is intended to generalize to a large number of other possible speaking tasks. Holistic scales have typically been generated on *a priori* grounds, that is, by a committee of experts that attempts to define the construct of interest, and sits down to write definitions that can be placed into a predetermined number of levels. These are perhaps the most common types of scales because this was how the FSI was developed. For example, Wilds (1975: 35) writes that the FSI is

very much an in-house system which depends heavily on having all inter-viewers under one roof . . . It [the system] is most apt to break down when interviewers are isolated by spending long periods away from home base, by testing a language no one else knows, or by testing so infrequently or so independently that they evolve their own system.

In this kind of evaluation the argument that the score adequately summarizes the evidence depends upon the acceptance of a collective understanding of the meaning of the descriptors. There must be a group of people whose ability to place language samples into categories has evolved over time, and into which newcomers can be socialized. Lowe (1986) refers to this as becoming an 'adept', and this is indeed apt. For being able to classify new samples systematically into the levels on the scale involves becoming part of a community of people who behave in the same way and believe in the word. Validity is the acceptance of the word and participation in the community of practitioners, as Lowe (1986: 392) argues: 'The essence of the AEI proficiency lies not in verbal descriptions of it, but in its thirty-year-long tradition of practice – making training in AEI proficiency testing a desideratum.'

Weigle (2002: 114), while applauding holistic scoring for its ease of use, suggests that one of its disadvantages is 'its focus on achieving high inter-rater reliability at the expense of validity'. But within the community of practice, it is precisely the agreement between trained practitioners that *is* the validity argument.

This does not mean to say that holistic scales could not be developed in other ways, or claim to link evidence to construct in other ways. It is just that such differences are not common.

Primary trait scoring also allocates a single score to a performance, but the scoring procedure is designed for each individual task, or class of tasks. Weigle (2002: 110) lists the components of a primary trait scoring guide as follows:

- a description of the task
- a statement of the primary trait (construct) to be measured
- a rating scale with level descriptors
- samples of performance to illustrate each level
- explanations of why each sample was graded in the way it was.

As a rating scale is required for each task or task type, the development process is much longer and more complex. There are multiple scales that have to be used by raters if they are to assess more than one task type, thus making the rating process more difficult. However, primary trait scoring benefits from the requirement that there have to be very careful and explicit statements linking evidence to claims. This means that samples have to be judged by many experts, and the key features that make one performance better than another have to be laid out so that other experts would be likely to come to the same judgments as the test developers.

Note, however, that the score tells us only about the ability of the student to perform on a specific task, or a specific species of tasks, rather than tasks in general. What we gain in explicitness and a stronger validity claim has to be offset against a reduction in the generalizability of the meaning we may wish to invest in the score.

Multiple-trait scoring may be either general (as in holistic scoring) or task specific (as in primary trait scoring), but instead of awarding a single score to a performance, multiple scores are awarded. Each score represents a separate claim about the relationship between the evidence and the multiple underlying constructs. The method of constructing multiple-trait scoring systems may be through either expert committee judgment or the analysis of samples. This is also the case with *analytic scoring*, which requires the counting of something (e.g. errors) in order to arrive at a score.

Task A7.5

➤ Look at the rating scales you use in your institution to grade speaking or writing. What kinds of scales are they? Do you find them easy or difficult to use? Why?

A7.4 INTUITION AND DATA

Although it may not be entirely fair to say that scoring systems not based on data are *intuitive*, because the latter are based on shared experience and theory, it is scoring systems developed in this way that have come under most criticism. Data-based approaches differ in that they use multiple language samples to extract the criteria necessary to arrive at summaries of qualities. This can be done through the direct analysis of language samples (spoken or written), using techniques of discourse or conversational analysis to describe samples (see Fulcher, 1996; 2003a: 97–104). Alternatively, samples may be judged 'poorer' or 'better' by sets of judges, who then say which features in the samples lead them to make these distinctions. The resulting scales are known as empirically derived, binary choice, boundary definition scales (see Upshur and Turner, 1995; Fulcher, 2003a: 104–107).

Task A7.6

➤ Take two scripts written in response to the same prompt from a writing class. With a colleague, decide which one is 'better' than the other, and why. Is it possible to link the features that help you to make your decision to student abilities (constructs)?

➤ Now add a third script. Where would you place it in relation to the first and second scripts? Do you need to take into account additional features in order to place it in sequence?

A7.5 PROBLEMS WITH SCALES

The Common European Framework of Reference scales contain 'can do statements' that have been put in sequence and divided into levels on the basis of teacher judgments of perceived difficulty. The can do statements themselves have been drawn from previously existing scales, although these have been altered in order to cover any perceived gaps in the proficiency continuum.

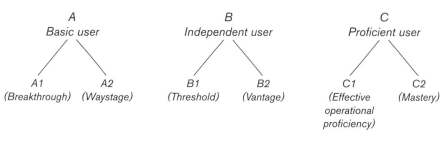

Figure A7.2 The structure of the CEF

Below is the CEF Overall Spoken Interaction Scale (Council of Europe, 2001: 74), divided into the six levels according to the classificatory scheme in Figure A7.2.

C2 Has a good command of idiomatic expressions and colloquialisms with awareness of connotative levels of meaning. Can convey finer shades of meaning precisely by using, with reasonable accuracy, a wide range of modification devices. Can backtrack and restructure around a difficulty so smoothly the interlocutor is hardly aware of it.

C1 Can express himself or herself fluently and spontaneously, almost effort-lessly. Has a good command of a broad lexical repertoire allowing gaps to be readily overcome with circumlocutions. There is little obvious searching for expressions or avoidance strategies; only a conceptually difficult subject can hinder a natural, smooth flow of language.

B2 Can use the language fluently, accurately and effectively on a wide range of general, academic, vocational or leisure topics, marking clearly the relationships between ideas. Can communicate spontaneously with good grammatical control without much sign of having to restrict what he or she wants to say, adopting a level of formality appropriate to the circumstances. Can interact with a degree of fluency and spontaneity that makes regular interaction, and sustained relationships with native speakers quite possible without imposing strain on either party. Can highlight the personal significance of events and experiences, account for and sustain views clearly by providing relevant explanations and arguments.

B1 Can communicate with some confidence on familiar routine and non-routine matters related to his or her interests and professional field. Can exchange, check and confirm information, deal with less routine situa-tions and explain why something is a problem. Can express thoughts on more abstract, cultural topics such as films, books, music etc. Can exploit a wide range of simple language to deal with most situations likely to arise whilst travelling. Can enter unprepared into conversation on familiar topics, express personal opinions and exchange information on topics that are familiar, of personal interest or pertinent to everyday life (e.g. family, hobbies, work, travel and current events).

A2   Can interact with reasonable ease in structured situations and short conversations, provided the other person helps if necessary. Can manage simple, routine exchanges without undue effort; can ask and answer questions and exchange ideas and information on familiar topics in predictable everyday situations. Can communicate in simple and routine tasks requiring a simple and direct exchange of information on familiar and routine matters to do with work and free time. Can handle very short social exchanges but is rarely able to understand enough to keep conversation going of his or her own accord.

A1   Can interact in a simple way but communication is totally dependent on repetition at a slower rate of speech, rephrasing and repair. Can ask and answer simple questions, initiate and respond to simple statements in areas of immediate need or on very familiar topics.

The first thing to notice is that the 'can do' statements define the different levels in the scheme, but we can do the things mentioned with different degrees of accuracy and effectiveness. It is possible that we are able to do some things well, and others not so well. However, the assumption underlying this scale is that all individuals progress up the scale in a uniform manner, so that it would be impossible to achieve a 'can do' statement in a higher level and not achieve a 'can do' statement at a lower level for another ability.

There is a general problem with level definition using can do statements of this kind. How many of the 'can dos' must we be able to do before we are in a level? That is, how can a single level summarize our performance? This problem is compounded by the fact that levels tend to be either under- or over-defined. If under-defined they do not contain enough information for us to match samples to the level, and if over-defined no single sample is defined by just one level. Given the number of levels, it is often the case that we end up with statements like 'on average an individual would fit into level x rather than y'. But the levels are not discrete enough for making a more certain claim.

In Unit A3 we also saw that some scales include performance conditions. These ground scales in context rather than containing allusions to notions of how 'common' or 'usual' topics might be. However, this has the effect of making the scale usable only in relation to specific tasks.

⭐ Task A7.7

➤ Look again at the rating scale you selected for the last reflective activity. How do you think this rating scale could be improved? What research might you have to do in order to make the changes you propose?

A7.6 SCORING IN CLASSICAL TEST THEORY

When we are dealing with samples of speech or writing we have to design methods of assessing their quality in a way that leads to a summary of that quality as a number or letter. When we have other item types on a test, like multiple choice, it is much more common to score these as simply *correct* or *incorrect*. A test, or part of a test, may be made up of a cluster of individual items that look something like the following:

2 Gary _____ his car to the mechanic before he leaves for Montana.

  a. will take *
  b. is taking
  c. has taken
  d. had taken

(from Davidson and Lynch, 2002: 56)

Each test taker responds to each item in the sequence. If a test taker selects the *key*, a score of 1 is awarded. If a test taker selects a *distractor* from the *options*, a score of 0 is awarded. In order to arrive at a score, the number of correct answers is summed and reported, or transformed in some way. Consider Table A7.1, which shows the responses of twenty test takers to ten items.

Table A7.1 Responses of twenty test takers to ten test items

Item	Item 1	Item 2	Item 3	Item 4	Item 5	Item 6	Item 7	Item 8	Item 9	Item 10	Total
A	B	C	D	E	F	G	H	I	J	K	L
P1	1	1	1	0	1	1	1	0	0	1	7
P2	0	1	1	1	1	0	0	1	0	1	6
P3	1	1	1	1	0	1	0	0	0	0	5
P4	0	0	0	0	0	0	0	1	0	0	1
P5	1	0	0	0	1	1	0	0	0	1	4
P6	1	1	1	1	1	1	1	1	1	1	10
P7	1	1	1	1	0	1	1	1	1	1	9
P8	1	0	0	0	0	0	1	0	0	0	2
P9	1	0	1	1	1	0	0	1	0	0	5
P10	0	1	0	0	0	0	1	0	0	0	2
P11	1	1	1	0	1	0	1	1	0	0	6
P12	0	1	1	0	1	1	1	1	1	1	8
P13	1	0	1	0	1	0	0	0	0	1	4
P14	1	1	1	1	1	1	1	1	1	1	10
P15	1	1	1	0	0	1	0	0	0	0	4
P16	1	0	0	0	1	0	0	0	0	1	3
P17	0	1	1	0	1	1	1	1	0	1	7
P18	1	1	1	1	1	0	0	1	1	1	8
P19	1	1	1	1	1	0	0	1	0	1	7
P20	1	0	0	0	1	1	0	1	0	1	5
Total	15	13	14	8	14	10	9	12	5	13	

We assume that it is possible to add together correct responses, and the sum of the correct responses tells us something about the ability of each test taker on the construct that the items were designed to measure. In order to make this assumption we have to rely on two arguments: firstly, that the items do in fact test the construct to which we wish to make a claim; and secondly, that all the items we add together measure the same construct. The second of these arguments is frequently referred to as the assumption that tests are *unidimensional* (Baker, 1997: 13).

In order to defend this approach to scoring responses to test items, language testers have relied on a number of statistics that help to shape the test scores. These are described briefly below.

A7.6.1 Difficulty (item facility)

This is defined simply as the proportion of test takers who answer an item correctly. If we look at item 1 in Table A7.1, we see that fifteen test takers have answered item 1 correctly. That is, 75 per cent of the test takers got the item correct, and so the item difficulty or item facility value is 0.75. Item 9 in our table is the most difficult. Only five test takers answered this item correctly, and so the facility value is 0.25.

It is generally assumed that items should not be too easy or too difficult for the population for whom the test has been designed. Items with facility values around 0.5 are therefore considered to be ideal, with an acceptable range being from around 0.3 to 0.7 (Henning, 1987: 50).

While this is referred to as *item difficulty*, we should note that the proportion correct is actually dependent not only on the difficulty of the item itself but on the ability of the test takers who are used in calculating the value. Technically, this is known as the *sample dependence* of the statistic. Another way to put this is that with a different sample of test takers, the value could be different. It is for this reason that the sample upon which the statistic is calculated should be genuinely representative of the

Table A7.2 Item facility values

Item	Number correct	Facility value
Item 1	15	0.750
Item 2	13	0.650
Item 3	14	0.700
Item 4	8	0.400
Item 5	14	0.700
Item 6	10	0.500
Item 7	9	0.450
Item 8	12	0.600
Item 9	5	0.250
Item 10	13	0.650

population of test takers for whom the test is designed. Unless this is the case, score meaning is compromised. Similarly, score meaning is compromised if the test is used for a purpose or population for which it was not originally intended. Table A7.2 provides the facility values for the items in Table A7.1.

Task A7.8

➤ Are there ever cases where we would deliberately wish to include items on a test that are easier or more difficult than other items?

A7.6.2 Discrimination

We also assume that the responses to individual items are capable of discriminating between *higher ability* and *lower ability* test takers. Although talk of *discrimination* is now pejorative,[2] the ability to discriminate is important in an approach to scoring that assumes that getting more correct answers is directly related to more of the ability in question, and that getting fewer correct answers is directly related to less of the ability in question.

The most commonly used method of calculating item discrimination is the point biserial correlation. This is a measure of the association between responses to any specific item (i.e. a 0 or a 1) and the score on the whole test (a continuous rather than a binary variable). In the case of our example, we would have ten point biserial correlations between the responses to each test item and the total score that the test takers got on the test.

The point biserial correlation can easily be calculated by hand. The formula is:

$$r_{pbi} = \frac{\overline{X}_p - \overline{X}_q}{S_x} \sqrt{pq}$$

where

r_{pbi} = point biserial correlation

$\overline{X}_p$ = mean score on the test for those who get the item correct

$\overline{X}_q$ = mean score on the test for those who get the item incorrect

S_x = standard deviation of test scores

p = the proportion of test takers who get the item correct (facility value)

q = the proportion of test takers who get the item incorrect.

In our example the point biserial correlations for each of the ten items are presented in Table A7.3. Generally speaking, items with an r_{pbi} of 0.25 or greater are considered acceptable, while those with a lower value would be rewritten or excluded from the test (Henning, 1987: 52–53). From our test, item number 1 does not adequately discriminate between the more and less able test takers, and would be a cause for concern.

Table A7.3 Point biserial correlations

	Total
Item 1	0.192
Item 2	0.638
Item 3	0.722
Item 4	0.591
Item 5	0.465
Item 6	0.489
Item 7	0.399
Item 8	0.567
Item 9	0.757
Item 10	0.597

As with item difficulty, measures of discrimination are sensitive to the size of the sample used in the calculation, and the range of ability represented in the sample. If the sample used in the field trials of items is not large and representative, the statistics could be very misleading.

A7.7 RELIABILITY

In tests constructed of items that can be scored correct or incorrect, each item should provide additional information about the ability of a test taker on the construct in question. By ensuring that responses to individual items are not dependent upon the responses to other items, that they have good facility values and discrimination, and that we have enough items, we can ensure that such tests have the quality of *reliability*:

> Whenever a test is administered, the test user would like some assurance that the results could be replicated if the same individuals were tested again under similar circumstances. This desired consistency (or reproducibility) of test scores is called reliability.
>
> (Crocker and Algina, 1986: 105)

In other words, it is assumed that for a score to be meaningful and interpretable, the sum of the parts should be reproducible. The classical formulation of this was put by the British psychologist Charles Spearman in his work on correlation between 1907 and 1913. He argued that an observed score on any test was a composite of two components: a true score and an error component:

$$X = T + E$$

If we asked an individual to take a test many times, the observed score would be slightly different each time. The error is the extent to which the observed score differs from a hypothetical true score for some reason other than the ability of the individual on the construct of interest. Spearman assumed that all error was random. That is, the observed score was only an estimate of the true score because random influences changed the observed score. These might be fluctuations in the environment, such as changes in test administration. Or they might be temporary psychological or physiological changes, such as tiredness or sickness.

Task A7.9

➤ Try to create a list of random influences that might affect observed test scores on any particular administration of a test.

Methods of computing reliability therefore try to estimate the extent to which an observed score is near to a true score, for it is only if the observed score is a good estimate of a true score that we can draw sound inferences from the score to the construct. Interestingly, as Ennis (1999) points out, concepts like 'true score' do not usually enter the public discussions about testing, where the parent term (reliability) dominates.

A7.7.1 Test–retest

The same test is administered twice and a correlation calculated between the scores on each administration. This assumes that no learning takes place between the two administrations, and that there is no practice effect from taking the test on the first administration on the scores from the second administration.

A7.7.2 Parallel forms

Two forms of the same test are produced, such that they test the same construct and have similar means and variances. The correlation between the scores on the two forms is taken as a measure of reliability.

A7.7.3 Split halves

From the administration of a single test, half of the items are taken to represent one form of the test and correlated with the items in the other half of the test. The correlation coefficient is taken as a measure of reliability.

Task A7.10

➤ What do you think are the advantages and disadvantages of each of these methods?

In practice, most tests report measures of internal consistency as reliability coefficients. These measures are simply a measure of mean inter-item correlation, or how well items correlate with each other. This is one definition of *consistency*. However, internal reliability coefficients are also affected by other factors:

- *Number of items on the test*: increasing the number of test items will increase reliability.
- *Variation in item difficulty*: items should be of equal difficulty to increase reliability, while if items have a range of facility values, reliability will decrease.
- *Dispersion of scores*: If the sample upon which the test is field-tested is homogeneous (there is not a spread of scores), reliability will decrease.
- *Level of item difficulty*: items with facility values of 0.5 maximize item variance, and so increase test reliability.[3]

We will consider two measures of reliability that are easy to calculate by hand.

A7.7.4 Kuder–Richardson formula 21

Perhaps the easiest reliability formula to calculate is KR-21. This is:

$$R = \frac{k}{k-1} \left\{ \frac{\bar{X}(k - \bar{X})}{ks^2} \right\}$$

where

k = number of items on the test
$\bar{X}$ = mean of the test scores, and
s^2 = the estimate of the variance of test scores.

For the ten-item test in our example, $k = 10$, $\bar{X} = 5.65$ and $s^2 = 6.86$.[4] Placing these into the formula, we have:

$$R = \frac{10}{10-1} \left\{ \frac{5.65(10 - 5.65)}{10 \times 6.86} \right\}$$

$$R = 0.40$$

Tests that do not achieve reliabilities of 0.7 are normally considered to be too unreliable for use, and high-stakes tests are generally expected to have reliability estimates in excess of 0.8 or even 0.9.

A7.7.5 Kuder–Richardson formula 20

Similar to another common reliability coefficient called Cronbach's alpha, KR-20 is an estimate of all possible split halves for a test made up of independently scored items. KR-21 is a quick estimate of KR-20, and usually produces a value somewhat lower than KR-20. It can be significantly lower if small samples or small numbers of items are involved.

The formula for KR-20 is:

$$R = \frac{k}{k-1}\left\{\frac{s^2 - \Sigma pq}{s^2}\right\}$$

where

> k = number of items on the test
> s^2 = the estimate of the variance of test scores, and
> Σpq = the sum of the variances of all items.

For our ten-item example, KR-20 = 0.75, which is higher than for the quick KR-21 estimate.

Once we know how reliable a test is, we can easily calculate the *standard error of measurement* – that is, the extent to which an observed score might differ from the true score. The formula for the standard error of measurement is:

$$se = sd \sqrt{1 - R}$$

where

> se = standard error
> sd = standard deviation of scores
> R = reliability coefficient.

If we use the KR-20 reliability coefficient for our ten-item test, the standard error of measurement is:

$$se = 2.62 \sqrt{1 - 0.75}$$
$$se = 1.31$$

We can use the standard error to calculate a confidence interval for a test score, as we know from the normal distribution that 68 per cent of the time a score will fall within + or − 1 standard error of measurement, that 95 per cent of the time it will fall within + or − 1.96, and 99 per cent of the time it will fall within + or − 2.58 standard error of measurement. These are the estimates for the position of the true score, about which the observed scores would form a normal distribution.

For each of these probabilities we can now form a probability estimate that the observed score of a test taker is near to his or her true score.

> 68 per cent confidence interval: 1.31
> 95 per cent confidence interval: 2.57
> 99 per cent confidence interval: 3.38

The practical value of this is the following. If a test taker gets a score of 5 on our ten-item test, as persons 3, 9 and 20 did, we could be 95 per cent certain that their true score lies between 5 + or − 2.57; that is, in the range 2.43 < 5 < 7.57. This is critical for our interpretation of score meaning within this paradigm, because we cannot be entirely sure that an observed score is equivalent to the assumed true value for any individual on the ability we believe we are measuring. If we can be certain only that the true score could be anywhere within a range of 5 (from a total of 10), we should not make any serious decisions on the basis of the score without further evidence to support our inferences about student ability.

A7.8   SCORE TRANSFORMATIONS

It is not always the case that we report raw scores from a test. Frequently the scores are subjected to a transformation process so that they are interpretable in terms of the normal distribution. Raw scores can be transformed so that they are expressed as standard deviations, thus giving information on the probability of getting any particular score. T-scores are the most common form of transformation.

Firstly, for each score we calculate a deviation score. This is simply the observed score minus the mean score on the test. If we take person 1 and person 20 from our example, we have two observed scores of 7 and 5 respectively. The mean score on the test is 5.65. The deviation scores (x) are then:

> 7 − 5.65 = 1.35
> 5 − 5.65 = −0.65

We then transform these into z scores, or standard deviation scores, using the following formula:

$$Z = \frac{x}{Sd}$$

For our two scores we now have:

$$1.35/2.62 = 0.52$$
$$-0.65/2.62 = -0.25$$

z scores have a mean of 0 and a standard deviation of 1, creating an interval scale that is very easy to interpret. However, it is not common to present such low scores, or give test takers negative scores. T-scores are therefore calculated, which have an arbitrary mean of 50 and a standard deviation of 10. In order to achieve this, each z score is multiplied by the required standard deviation and the arbitrary mean added to the number. For our two scores, this would give us:

$$0.52 \times 10 + 50 = 55.2$$
$$-0.25 \times 10 + 50 = 47.5$$

A7.9   ITEM RESPONSE THEORY

Since the 1960s there has been a growing interest in item response theory (IRT), a term which covers a range of models used to score tests. All of these models assume that a test is unidimensional, as described above. Further, they assume that an observed score is indicative of a person's ability on an underlying construct, which is often referred to as a *latent trait*. The trait is assumed to be a continuous, unobservable variable.

Using item response theory test designers can create a scale, usually scaled from around -4 to $+4$, upon which all items or tasks can be placed, and the value on the scale is the item difficulty. Test takers who take the items can be placed on to the same scale, and their scores are interpreted as person ability. As such, there is a direct connection between ability and difficulty.

All models assume that when student ability = item difficulty, the probability of a test taker getting the item correct will be 0.5. On a scale, therefore, some items would have lower values (be easier), and the probability of more able students passing the item would be very high. As the difficulty value of the item rises, a test taker must be more able to have a chance of getting the item correct.

For our ten items, the difficulty estimates produced by an analysis using a one-parameter *Rasch model* are shown in Table A7.4. The first thing to notice is that each estimate of difficulty has its own standard error, something that is not possible in classical test theory. This additional information is also provided in the estimate of person ability. The problem in classical test theory is that the standard error of measurement is more accurate at the test mean, but, as scores diverge from the mean, we know that measurement error increases. Consider Table A7.5, which gives ability estimates for our twenty test takers. You will notice that as the score moves further from the mean (which is zero), the standard error of measurement increases.

Table A7.4 Rasch difficulty estimates for ten items

Item	Fitted difficulty	Standard error
Item 1	−1.07	0.59
Item 2	−0.47	0.55
Item 3	−0.76	0.57
Item 4	0.88	0.56
Item 5	−0.76	0.57
Item 6	0.33	0.54
Item 7	0.60	0.55
Item 8	−0.20	0.54
Item 9	1.92	0.66
Item 10	−0.47	0.55

Table A7.5 Ability estimates for twenty test takers

Person	Fitted ability	Standard error
P1	0.96	0.75
P2	0.44	0.70
P3	−0.04	0.68
P4	−2.45	1.07
P5	−0.51	0.69
P6	misfit	
P7	misfit	
P8	−1.59	0.83
P9	−0.04	0.68
P10	−1.59	0.83
P11	0.44	0.70
P12	1.60	0.86
P13	−0.51	0.69
P14	misfit	
P15	−0.51	0.69
P16	−1.01	0.73
P17	0.96	0.75
P18	1.60	0.86
P19	0.96	0.75
P20	−0.04	0.68

Where a person is labelled as a *misfit* this is not pejorative. IRT applies a probabilistic model to the actual data. If the model cannot account for the data, a person or item is flagged as *misfitting*. What this means is that 'an instance of person misfit can usually be attributed to anomalous test-taking behaviour of some kind' (Baker, 1997: 41). Such 'anomalous behaviour' may include cheating. In our case, two persons had the maximum score of 10 and therefore could not be modelled, and one person got an item wrong that a person of his ability would have been expected to get correct.

Apart from the advantage of providing multiple error terms, IRT is also sample-free. That is, the item difficulty estimates are not dependent upon the sample used to generate them. As long as the sample was drawn from the population of interest, the estimates should be independent of the sample used (Crocker and Algina, 1986: 363). This also means that it is not necessary for every test taker to take every item in a pool in order to ensure that the item statistics are meaningful. Because of these properties, IRT has become the scoring method of choice for computer-based and computer-adaptive tests, where new items are selected according to difficulty on the basis of the current estimate of test taker ability (see Fulcher, 2000b).

A7.10 ENDOWING A SCORE WITH SPECIAL MEANING

Sometimes the users of language tests endow a score with special meaning. We have already seen the iconic status that was attached to TOEFL 550 on the pencil and paper test, and how that has conditioned the need to provide score concordance tables even as the test and score meaning have changed. It achieved this status because it became associated with the decision point to admit applicants to North American universities and colleges. Within Europe, level B2 on the Common European Framework is being interpreted as the level required for immigration, even though the research needed to validate such an interpretation has not been undertaken.

Nevertheless, it is frequently the case that we do wish to endow a score with a special meaning for the purposes of decision making. But when we do this we should be very aware of the fact that there is always error in measurement, and we need to realize the chances that a score just below or just above an established cut point may in fact be a point estimate of a true score that falls at the other side of the cut point.

Setting cut scores must also be done with sensitivity, and associated warnings about their interpretation. Following are two of the most common approaches to setting cut scores.

A7.10.1 A test-centred method: the Angoff approach

As the name suggests, this approach was developed by Angoff (1984), and relies on the use of expert judges. The approach consists of five steps:

- *Step 1.* Form a group of judges who are experts in the content area of the test (e.g. language learning, reading, etc.).
- *Step 2.* Ask the judges to review the test and estimate the score at which they would begin to say that students were 'competent'.
- *Step 3.* Present the judges with *each item* on the test in sequence. Ask the judges to estimate the probability that a student who is *minimally competent* will answer the item correctly. That is, if a student is just into the master category, what is the chance that he or she will answer item 1, item 2, item 3, etc. correctly? Each item will be assigned a different probability estimate.

- *Step 4.* Add up the probability estimates for each judge on each item and divide by the number of test items, thus providing a percentage cut score for each individual judge.
- *Step 5.* Establish the final cut by averaging the cut score of each individual judge.

Advantages: It uses the averaged judgments of people who are seen as experts in the field to establish a cut score (a standard) that defines a 'minimally competent master'. The assumption underlying this method is that professionals are capable of making these judgments on test items and tasks. Angoff studies are also relatively easy to carry out, and do not require a large amount of time.

Disadvantages: The method described here can be used only on dichotomously scored items (i.e. items that are either 'right' or 'wrong'). Note also that test-centred approaches do not use student performance data. The judges merely examine the test content and are asked to make judgments about a 'typical' minimally competent student. When using this approach it is therefore critical to discover whether and to what extent there is disagreement among the judges (i.e. a source of unreliability), even though the averaging process in step 5 is designed to 'average out' individual error-related variance. Over the years such studies have found that judges differ widely in their decisions regarding individual items, and this is a threat to the validity of the cut score.

A7.10.2 A student-centred method: Zieky and Livingston's contrasting group approach

While our first example required judgments about a test, the second concentrates on making judgments about students (Zieky and Livingston, 1977), and contains six steps:

- *Step 1.* Identify a group of students drawn from the population of interest, and a group of professional experts who are familiar with the students to act as judges.
- *Step 2.* Ask the judges to define 'good', 'borderline' and 'inadequate' performances on the test. These should be written down as explicitly as possible.
- *Step 3.* Ask each of the judges to decide if each student is in the 'good', the 'borderline' or the 'inadequate' category.
- *Step 4.* Give the test to the students.
- *Step 5.* Look at the distributions of the students in the 'good' and 'inadequate' categories separately, to see how greatly they differ (especially in terms of means and standard deviations). Plotting the distribution of scores is useful.
- *Step 6.* Make a decision regarding the 'best' cut score that separates out the two groups, defined as masters and non-masters.

The final step (step 6) is not quite as straightforward as it sounds, and is discussed extensively in Brown and Hudson (2002). Let us consider a specific example represented in Figure A7.3.

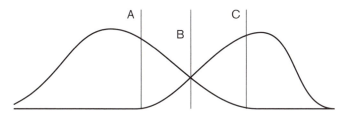

Figure A7.3 Three possible cut scores

The left-hand curve represents the score distribution of the students defined as 'inadequate' in Step 3 of the Zieky and Livingston method. The right-hand curve is the score distribution of students defined as 'good', 'competent' or 'masters'. When we come to step 6 there are (at least) three possible cut scores: A, B and C.

Cut score B. This cut score is arrived at because it is the point at which the two distributions cross. It is the point that best separates the 'masters' and the 'non-masters'. But notice that the curve for the masters starts at point A, and the curve for the non-masters finishes at point C. There will be some non-masters who are classified as masters (false positives) and some masters who will be classified as non-masters (false negatives).

Cut score A. This cut score is the start of the distribution of the 'masters'. If we use this as the cut score there will be no false negatives: all masters will be correctly classified as masters. The trade-off is that the number of false positives will significantly increase. If our test were being used to judge success on a programme, would it be acceptable for so many learners who have not actually achieved the criterion to 'pass' in order to be fair to *all* the students who have genuinely 'passed'?

Cut score C. This cut score is at the end of the distribution of the 'non-masters'. If we use this cut score there will be no false negatives: all the non-masters will be correctly classified as non-masters. But now what happens is that the number of false negatives increases significantly. Many learners who have achieved the criterion will be classified as non-masters. Are we prepared to live with this in order to stop learners who are not 'masters' from 'passing' the test?

Task A7.11

➤ Which cut score would you use (A, B or C) in the following situations, and why?

1   an academic reading class in which passing the test leads to joining the first year of graduate studies
2   a test of listening for readiness for air traffic control duties
3   a test of social English to be used as part of a decision to grant immigration
4   a university admissions test

5   a medical English test to allow qualified nurses to practise in an English-medium health service

6   a classroom quiz designed to help teachers decide if material needs to be recycled in the next semester

7   an exit test for language majors wishing to graduate

8   a technical reading test for engineers who maintain helicopters at a military airbase

Summary

In this Unit we have seen that the scoring procedures for tests are associated with asking questions about how much a test taker knows, or how well something can be done. When considering performance tests that require the production of speech or writing we are primarily concerned with the evaluation of the quality of the work product. For this we usually design rating scales against which samples of performance can be matched. When a test contains closed response items the scoring normally involves counting the number of correct responses followed by some procedure to transform the raw score into a scale score that is more meaningful.

Historically, one of the primary concerns of educational assessment and testing has been reliability. The science of modelling item statistics to produce high test reliabilities is one of the most developed in testing practice. Reliability is still extremely important in large-scale testing because we have known for a long time that all measurement includes error. If there is error, relying on a single cut score for decision making can lead us to 'pass' those who undeservingly get a score higher than the cut score; similarly, there will be those who deserve to 'pass' who get a score lower than the cut score, just because of measurement error (Edgeworth, 1888, 1890). Because error will always be present in the use of any test, it is essential that we build the expectation of error in to decision-making procedures.

Scoring is therefore very important. How we decide to score, and the values that we place upon particular scores, need careful thought. We need to convince others that the scores can be used to make inferences about learners to the knowledge, skills or abilities being tested. And we need to ensure that the use of the scores for decision making is undertaken with a full awareness of the possibility that a mistake could be made. The former concern is one of validity, and the latter one of fairness (see Unit A9).

Unit A8
Administration and training

A8.1 INTRODUCTION

The delivery of tests requires an infrastructure, and a set of procedures that are usually followed. In Unit A6 we used the analogy of rapid prototyping from manufacturing to describe the initial process of item design, a technique that is used before machines are tooled to produce the final product. Tooling machines to make final parts is expensive. The factory is set up to produce the product, after which any changes are expensive to make. Raw materials have to be sourced and delivered. Once made, the components have to be assembled and delivered. Responses have to be collected, processed and stored. The accuracy of data needs to be checked. Outcomes must be communicated to test takers or other score users, and summary reports written. The administration of large-scale tests is therefore exceptionally complex, but the administration of local tests also needs careful thought and planning.

Task A8.1

➤ When you give a test in your institution, what are the processes that you go through? List them, step by step, including such tedious tasks as photocopying any test and answer papers, who takes them to the room where the test is going to take place, and who hands them out and collects them. Not forgetting who books the rooms!

The whole process of test administration is important not just because we expect everything to run smoothly – although we certainly do want this. There are theoretical reasons for considering all aspects of administration carefully. In this book we have constantly emphasized the importance of validity, or how we ensure that the inferences we make from test scores are meaningful and can be supported. Any mistakes, inconsistencies or abnormalities at any stage in the test administration process can threaten validity.

In order to understand this we will consider four examples.

1   An item writer does not follow the test specifications when writing items.
2   The usher at one test centre who shows students to their seats is rude and aggressive.

3   Five venues are selected for a speaking test during the summer. One of these is next to a major road where extensive roadworks have just begun.
4   Students on vacation are hired to add grades together from four sub-tests on a paper-based test to form a composite score and record this on a computer. They aren't paid very much and do the work as quickly as possible.

In each case there is the very real possibility that the score awarded will not mean what we intend it to mean. In the first example there is a problem with the construction of some parts of the machine. We may have items on some tests that introduce variable elements that are not intended to be part of the test. In the second case it is highly likely that coming into contact with such an individual is going to result in stress. When students arrive to take tests they are usually quite nervous at best. We try to put students at their ease so that when they come to take the test they are performing as well as they are able. If stress interferes with taking the test, the lower score that they get may well reflect this stress and not their ability on the intended construct. The third example involves non-human factors in the test-taking process that require considerable foresight and planning. During the test there may be significant noise from the road that distracts students, something that we know to have an impact on test scores (see Powers et al., 2002). Alternatively, the test administrator may close all the windows and increase the temperature in the room to a level that also causes discomfort. As there are five venues, we have the additional problem of fairness to all students. One group of students has been treated differently and, if they are at a disadvantage compared with others, also unfairly. Finally, we see that a test provider uses students to do what it thinks are mundane tasks like adding up scores and creating data files. The conditions of their employment make it likely that mistakes will be made and incorrect scores issued. The processes employed appear to threaten principles of data handling (see Davidson, 1996).

Any non-standard practice in the administration of testing is a potential threat to validity. We should therefore think in terms of the quality assurance procedures that we could put in place to protect the value of the product for the customer, in very much the same way that would be done in manufacturing. Research to address non-standard practice is rare. One exceptional case is the investigation into the threat to score meaning on speaking tests conducted in Hong Kong during the SARS epidemic (Coniam, 2005). All test takers and interlocutors were required to wear masks; the question that arose was whether these test takers were treated differently to those who were tested when wearing a mask was not compulsory. If wearing the mask impeded communication it may also have impacted negatively on test scores.

★   **Task A8.2**

➤   Take each of the four examples above. What administrative systems would you put in place to avoid these problems occurring again in the future?

A8.2 GETTING THINGS DONE

The brief description of test administration in the first paragraph conceals a lot of detail. In what follows we are going to treat our test administration as one run by a testing organization of some size. However, from the descriptions it will be possible to see how many of the activities are also related to how an educational institution might organize its testing activities.

Assuming that a test has been designed, piloted, field-tested, test specifications have been agreed, and a 'go-decision' (see Unit A4) has been made, what are the essential things that need to be considered?

A8.2.1 Construction systems

The test specifications and the first set of items will not be enough for multiple administrations. In large-scale testing there may be a requirement for hundreds of forms (versions) of the test each year. Even for institutional testing there may be a need for more than one form of the test, especially if testing is to take place at different times. The most obvious reason why we need multiple forms is *test security*.

A8.2.2 Sourcing and collecting raw materials

Many tests require material in addition to the prompt. These materials may include reading passages that will support questions, or listening texts that must be recorded on to tape or CD. Graphs, illustrations or charts may be required to create information transfer items. The range of possible prompt and item types is defined in the test specifications (see Unit A4), and during prototyping test designers should consider the expense that will be needed to generate many items of the same type.

If texts are required as input (spoken or written), we also need to specify difficulty level, length, delivery speed, topic, and so on. People are needed to generate the necessary number of texts, either by finding copyright-free material that meets the specifications, buying the copyright to material, or creating the material. For listening material we may require sophisticated recording equipment to get the necessary quality, and actors may have to be hired to record each prompt.

Task A8.3

➤ What are the advantages of having a library of sources that can be used for item generation, rather than having to find new source material every time a new test has to be written?

A8.2.3 Item writing and review

Writing test items is a difficult task. Writers need to be trained to follow the test specifications and supplied with item-writing templates. Some testing agencies employ professional item writers whose sole task is to generate standard items and tasks for its tests. Other agencies employ teachers on a 'piecework' basis, in a similar way to the textile industry of the late eighteenth century.[5] Ensuring that the items meet the specifications is much more problematic in the latter case.

But for both these scenarios it is essential that the quality of the work is checked. Each piece must meet the company specifications, and have the necessary statistical qualities to make it usable in an operational test. This means that each item must be reviewed. Item or task review is an absolutely critical part of the quality assurance process. This usually consists of four sub-processes:

- *Content review*: ensuring that the item matches the specification.
- *Key check*: ensuring that the answer is correct, that distractors in multiple-choice items are not likely to be correct, and that the suggested answers to any constructed response items (the marking script or guide) are feasible.
- *Bias or sensitivity review*: giving serious consideration to whether an item or its wording is likely to result in bias against a particular group of test takers, upset some test takers or cause offence.
- *Editorial review*: check each item or task to ensure that there are no spelling mistakes, faulty grammar or other errors that may make it difficult to process the language of the prompt.

In large testing organizations each of these processes is likely to involve a committee rather than an individual. It is always possible for individuals to make mistakes. For example, in a bias or sensitivity review it is essential that the committee considering each item is made up of individuals with a range of first-hand experience of the cultures of the intended test takers. In smaller organizations, teams of teachers should review items produced by each other.

Task A8.4

➤ Do you have item or task quality control procedures in your institution? Are they similar to or different from those listed above?

A8.2.4 Item banking

All items or tasks that survive review need to be banked, or stored, in a format that allows easy retrieval according to any number of search criteria that may be used as identifiers. These criteria are usually those used in describing tasks for test specifications (see Unit A5). However, the item bank should also contain any statistical data that are associated with an item or task, such as its facility value, discrimination index or IRT difficulty estimate. This allows test assemblers to find items that meet specific criteria.

Item banking is usually done electronically so that searching through the bank is done easily. This means that it is necessary to have the computer technicians maintain the system and update the database with new items and tasks as they are produced and approved for operational use.

Task A8.5

➤ In your institution do you have item banks, or do you write tests as and when you need them? What are the advantages and disadvantages of these two different methods of test production?

A8.2.5 Test assembly

Finally in this section, we consider the assembly of a test that is going to be delivered operationally. In a computer adaptive test, where a computer selects the next item for any individual test taker, test assembly is automatic. The item bank is the basis for the selection of items based on the current student model, or the best estimate of student ability based on responses to items already encountered. The algorithms in the system control test assembly, which varies for each individual.

However, most tests are linear. They are given in paper and pencil format, or the computer delivers a set of items that is the same for each test taker. The TOEFL computer-based test was adaptive, but this was found to be far too expensive to maintain because of the number of items needed for the bank if test security was to be preserved. Since 2005, when the TOEFL iBT was introduced, large-scale computer-based language testing has reverted to linear forms that are much easier to construct and keep secure (Fulcher, 2005). In linear tests, items or tasks must be extracted from the bank according to test assembly rules, and combined to make the linear form. Test assembly rules tell the creator how many items of certain types are to be used, what content coverage must be achieved, which sections they are to be placed in and what the intended measurement properties are.

Once a form has been assembled according to the rules, the expected reliability of the form must be calculated, and its equivalence to all other possible forms evaluated. For it is assumed that any possible test form that we might generate is equivalent to any other test form; the principle is that it should be a matter of indifference to the test taker which test form he or she takes. Given measurement error (see Unit A7), the scores should in principle be the same.

★ **Task A8.6**

➤ Writing test assembly rules may seem like a great deal of work. However, it leads to many savings in time and resources. Can you think what these might be?

A8.2.6 Preparation and dispatch

Presentation

The presentation of a test should be uniform across forms. When a test taker opens a paper it should resemble previous forms. If the medium of delivery is electronic, the computer interface should be the same as that for other test takers. All instructions should be standardized, and presented in the same font type, style and size. In order for this standardization to be implemented from form to form and year to year, the definition of the appearance of the test needs to be written and stored. Ideally, templates should be created so that new content is simply dropped into a standard layout. Once again, the reason for this standardization is that there is no construct-irrelevant variation that impacts upon test taker performance.

Designing the presentation may involve the use of graphic designers, especially if it is necessary to include institutional branding into a language test. Logos have sometimes found to be distracting to test takers. In addition, some institutional colour schemes are not suitable for printing on test papers because of the impact they have on colour-blind test takers. Whether graphic designers are used or not, it is always important to ensure that the presentation (the interface) does not interfere with test taking. In computer delivery of tests this is particularly important, where graphics, colours or operations (e.g. scrolling) may interfere (see Fulcher, 2003b).

★ **Task A8.7**

➤ Look for an on-line language test. When you have found one, look at how it is presented (the interface). Is it easy to navigate? How much non-test-related reading do you have to do? What aspects of the interface would be distracting for your students?

Printing and duplication

Making copies of test papers, answer papers or multiple copies of tapes or CDs is not a problem in computer-based testing. In all other testing situations it is necessary to have the correct numbers for the expected testing *volume*. Volume is an important concept, and *volume planning* is critical in a testing operation of any size. Expected numbers of test takers will dictate the number of copies to be made of any given test form. The forms need to be sent to printers or duplicators in a secure manner, and all copies returned securely for storage. If test content is leaked, the test is useless, and the associated expense extremely high.

Storage systems

While individual items can be stored in electronic format, complete paper-based forms need to be stored in secure rooms within institutions or in warehouses for large testing agencies. It should be remembered that most testing agencies are planning for the delivery of tests two to three years ahead. This involves a large number of forms and millions of individual test papers. The cost of the forms, the individual papers and the storage is often extremely high. So once again, security is absolutely critical. In large testing agencies guards are required, and the storage facilities are treated like high-security banks.

Task A8.8

➤ Where do you store copies of tests?

➤ Are these places secure?

➤ Who has access to the tests?

Record keeping

With the type of complex organization we are describing it is essential to take record keeping very seriously. The forms need to be referenced according to the intended place and time of use, and each test paper accounted for from the moment it is printed to the moment it is returned to storage after use, or destroyed. This may involve using bar codes on each paper so that its movements can be tracked and accounted for. Even within educational institutions it is important to know precisely how many copies of each component of a test are made, and where they are, especially if any items or prompts are likely to be reused in the future.

A8.2.7 Distribution systems

Paper-based tests and physical test components need to be extracted from storage and dispatched by secure means to test centres. Receipt of materials needs to be confirmed. The number of tests dispatched needs to match the number of test takers registered. Some testing agencies employ courier firms to distribute components to local test centres. This outsourcing has to be carefully managed to ensure reliable and secure services.

A8.2.8 Delivery systems

Rather surprisingly, when texts on language testing discuss test administration, they are usually concerned only with delivery systems. These are most often dealt with in terms of the test-taking process and/or the physical environment of the test (Alderson et al., 1995: 115–118; Bachman and Palmer, 1996: 231ff; Hughes, 2003: 215–217). This is not to say that this is not important, because it is. However, it should be recognized that this is only the most obvious and visible part of the test administration process because it deals with 'what happens on the day'.

Any *materials and equipment* should be checked and ready for use. Test components need to be transferred securely to and from the rooms in which tests are to be conducted. If recording, playback or computer systems need to be used, these should be checked in advance. Replacements should be available, and technicians on hand in the event of problems.

Processes are also critical. All invigilators need to be trained to operate equipment, deal with unforeseen eventualities and be able to write reports on events that they cannot control. Further, they need to be trained in how to deal with test takers. This will include checking the identity of test takers, and giving instructions. They must also be aware of the kind and amount of help that can be given in response to questions after the start of the test. They also need to be informed how to deal with late arrivals, disruptive test takers, potential cheaters, those who wish to finish early and those who may need to use the rest room. Training for a potential emergency should not be overlooked, especially to deal with any medical help that may be needed during the test. Distribution and collection of test materials should also be standardized, and precise time-keeping is required. If spoken instructions are necessary, invigilators should read these as directed from pre-prepared cards.

The *test environment* is also very important. It is generally accepted that rooms should be protected from noise, and large enough to host the number of test takers with plenty of space between individuals so that copying is unlikely. Rooms should be laid out well in advance, be clean and well aired. This means that janitors need to be available on the day of the test and be present throughout the event. If a listening test is involved, rooms must have adequate acoustic properties.

★ Task A8.9

In some countries test volume has grown faster than the availability of suitable accommodation for speaking tests. Some testing agencies have begun to use hotel bedrooms as alternatives to more traditional sites for conducting tests. Sometimes the rooms are stripped of furniture other than that recommended, but at other times the room is simply a hotel bedroom, and may also be the room in which the interlocutor or rater is staying.

One teacher with considerable experience working in such conditions wrote: 'This happened a lot. I remember having to do interviews in a room that was so small I had to climb across the bed to let the next candidate in. It was very embarrassing for them and I'm sure that it had an impact on performance.'

➤ What effects might this 'alternative environment' have on performance? Are you aware of other 'alternative environments' that are used because of lack of space and poor volume planning?

➤ Do you think there are any other issues, legal or ethical, in the use of 'alternative environments'?

A room plan is necessary, clearly indicating where each test taker is to sit. This makes it possible to check the identity of test takers and make a record of absent test takers so that any unused answer papers can be accounted for.

A8.2.9 Environment security

When large-scale testing is involved, the management of the local test administration site is normally the role of a local agent. Responsibility for the overall security of the site nevertheless remains with the testing agency. It is important that a member of the agency, or a local representative trained and certified by the agency, is responsible for the overall performance of all personnel involved in the testing. The responsibility of the site manager extends to site security beyond the immediate rooms used for test taking.

It is not uncommon for publishers' representatives or owners of school chains to wait outside test venues and interview students on test content as soon as they leave the rooms. Within hours of one test ending, test content can be available for purchase on the Internet, or as training material in a preparatory school. While it is impossible to stop test takers from engaging in these activities once they have left the site, it remains the responsibility of the site manager to reduce contact between test takers and the public for a reasonable period of time after the end of the actual test.

This requires the use of secure areas in which test takers can wait under the supervision of site staff. This is particularly the case if test takers are waiting to take individual or small-group speaking tests and so are able to pass on information to, or collect information from, test takers who have already taken a test. Maintaining this kind of security becomes almost impossible in test sites such as hotels where guests and others mix freely with test takers in public areas such as the lobby.

⭐ **Task A8.10**

You have been asked to organize a testing session at the Ethelynn Institute, which is the local agent for a well-known international test provider. You have fifty students registered for the test. The format of the day is as follows:

1   Students arrive at 9.00 for identity check before the test starts
2   Reading and listening test 9.30–10.30
3   Break 10.30–11.00
4   Writing test 11.00–12.30
5   Lunch 12.30–13.30
6   Individual speaking tests 13.30–16.00

The following staff are available 8.30–15.00:

Employed by the school:

   One centre manager
   One janitor
   One technician
   Three invigilators or proctors

Employed by the testing agency and brought in for the event:

   Five interlocutors (speaking test)
   Five raters (speaking test)

➤ For each of the six activities during the day decide how you would deploy the staff within the school. Mark their positions on the plan of the Institute (overleaf) and decide what their duties would be. You may need to photocopy the plan to complete this activity.

A8.2.10 Interlocutors and raters

Perhaps even more discussed than the processes or physical environment of the test are the interlocutors and raters needed for the administration of speaking tests. Speaking tests are unusual in that they need multiple secure, noise-free rooms. Each room needs to accommodate an interlocutor, one to three test takers, and a second rater. And while the physical resources demand significant investment and management, the human resources are even more challenging. Testing agencies need to recruit enough interlocutors and raters to process the expected volume, and also need to train them in advance. Rater training is a large task in itself and so we will consider this topic separately below.

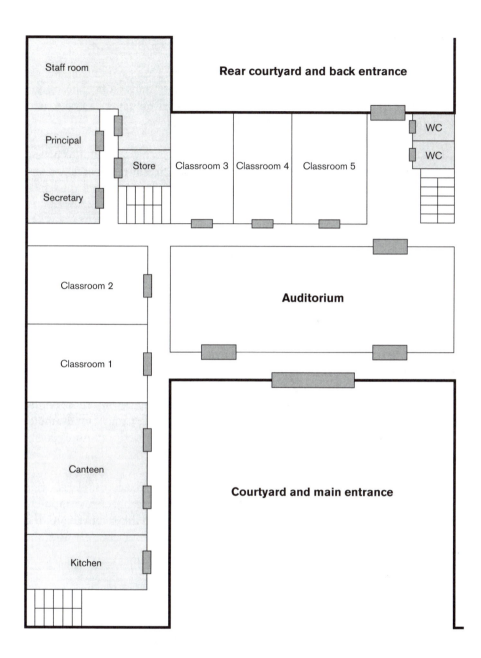

A8.2.11 Retrieval systems

As soon as a test is over, all test components must be collected. Scripts must be posted (or transmitted electronically) for scoring. Confidential materials that cannot be reused must be shredded, and reusable materials returned to storage. In computer-based tests all responses must be stored on servers.

A8.2.12 Scoring systems

Scripts or speech samples are sent to raters unless these are scored during the test itself. In many speaking tests the interaction is recorded for third rating if necessary, and the recordings need to be safely stored. If responses on paper can be scored automatically, bubble sheets need to be fed into computers.

For constructed response items on computer-based tests it is essential to have a distribution system that sends scripts or speech samples directly to raters. The raters score the scripts and then return them electronically to the server, where the scores are uploaded into student files.

Scores from the various sections of the test need to be compiled into the student files. If these are composite scores the rules for adding scores and awarding final grades are then applied.

A8.2.13 Feedback systems

Once scores are stored in student files, reports are generated for various users. Individual test takers need to be notified of outcomes. If the test is for university entry or employment, the score users (e.g. admissions officers) are sent separate reports. Finally, in many cases it is necessary to produce an aggregate report on the performance of test takers in a particular context. In the United States, for example, all test results must be reported by racial background in order to monitor social mobility.

It is rare for individuals or teachers to receive diagnostic feedback from large-scale speaking tests. However, it is much easier to give this kind of feedback in computer-based testing. One on-line testing system that attempts to do this is DIALANG, the Diagnostic Language Test that allows you to estimate your proficiency in one of the languages taught in the European Union.

 Task A8.11

➤ Take the DIALANG test in a language which you speak. URL: http://www.dialang.org/english/index.htm. Is the feedback provided useful?

A8.3 QUALITY MANAGEMENT SYSTEMS

Test administration is about doing things consistently, in ways that are prescribed. We refer to this as *standardization*. Whatever Dilbert thinks about ISO 9000 on the one hand, or Aldous Huxley believes about the impossibility of achieving consistency on the other, consistency in language testing is about avoiding any variation in procedure that could threaten score meaning. The International Organization for Standardization (ISO) has argued since 1946 that quality in manufacturing and services is dependent upon consistency, which leads to 'dependability'. The ISO 9000 label requires companies to:

- document the methods and procedures used to define dependability characteristics
- document the methods and procedures used to control dependability characteristics
- document the methods and procedures used to evaluate dependability characteristics.

For language testing, part of a validity claim is that the test administration and all the processes used by the testing agency are done according to standardized procedures. Consider the following quotation from Beeston (2000) about the University of Cambridge ESL tests:

> Many organisations now endeavour to practise Total Quality Management by which they mean that they adopt a comprehensive approach to achieving quality in every aspect of their work. For UCLES EFL, this starts with ensuring that we know all about the different kinds of people who take our examinations and exactly what it is they need and expect when they enter an examination. Not surprisingly, we have identified issues of fairness and the usefulness of our qualifications as key requirements of our examinations. Part of what fairness in language testing means is making

sure that procedures for every stage in the testing process are well planned and carefully managed, including the way each test is produced, and the way it is administered, marked and graded. Our approach to item banking addresses the way the test is produced by guaranteeing that all test material goes through a series of specific quality control checks before a completed test is constructed and administered.

Also look at the following quotation from ETS (2002: 49–50):

Give the people who administer assessments information about the

- purpose of the assessment, the population to be tested, and the information needed to respond to expected questions from test takers;
- qualifications required to administer the assessments;
- required identifying information for test takers, admittance procedures, timing and directions;
- materials, aids, or tools that are required, optional or prohibited;
- maintenance of appropriate security procedures;
- actions to take if irregularities are observed;
- operation of equipment and software as needed for the administration;
- provision of approved accommodation to test takers with disabilities; and
- resolution of problems that may delay or disrupt testing.

★ Task A8.12

One of the most important aspects of monitoring the quality of test administration is identifying key stages in the process. For each key stage we describe what needs to be done, and to what standards. These need to be documented.

➤ Identify the key stages in test administration at your own institution. How could test administration be improved?

A8.4 CONSTRAINTS

All testing systems work within constraints. It is very important to spell these out at a very early stage in deciding how a test can be administered. Constraints are limitations on any of the resources that are necessary for successful test administration. These can occur with regard to:

- people
- skills
- equipment
- accommodation

- security
- information technology
- money.

Task A8.13

➤ What are the major constraints that affect testing in your own institutional context?

A8.5 TEST ADMINISTRATION WITHIN THE ECD DELIVERY MODEL

We first introduced the concept of evidence-centred design in Unit A5. Within that model we noticed in Figure A5.1 that all processes were enclosed within a *delivery model*. While this concept is not as broadly conceived as what we have dealt with in this Unit, it is nevertheless important to return to the ECD model at this point. Mislevy (2003a: 56) refers to the four processes that impact upon a test delivery system as:

- *Activity selection*: the selection of the next task in a test from a task or evidence library. This library contains all the information that is stored on tasks, as discussed in Units A4 and A5.
- *Presentation*: the presentation of the prompt or stimulus material to the test taker to generate evidence, or a work product.
- *Evidence identification*: the process of collecting evidence from the student for scoring.
- *Evidence accumulation*: updating information on the student so that we continue to develop a student model for the individual test taker being assessed.

Mislevy et al. (2003: 13–15) see these four processes as guiding thinking about what happens during the part of test administration that contains what we think of as the 'test itself'. First is what we are going to ask the test takers to do, and second how we handle the interaction with the test taker. Built into this is the presentation model. Third is the processing of responses, which may be immediate or delayed. Fourth is how we accumulate evidence across tasks. Feedback is then given either at the task level or, more usually, as a summary of general performance for a group or individual. This four-process model is represented graphically in Figure A8.1.

Here is an example of a paired speaking test:

- *Activity selection*: interlocutor conducts the warm-up and then selects an information gap activity from a library of ten used in any single test administration.

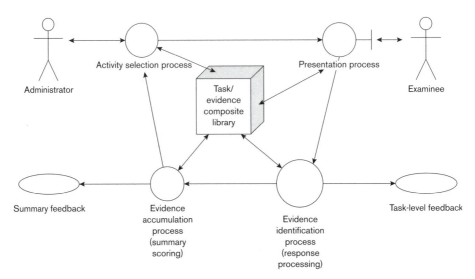

Figure A8.1 Four-process delivery model (Almond et al., 2001: 11)

After the use of a task the interlocutor engages in a common wind-down activity that provides a final opportunity to check grades awarded.

■ *Presentation process*: cards with different pieces of information are handed to each of the two test takers, who are invited to spend one minute reading the instructions and the information.

■ *Evidence identification*: the interlocutor and a rater who takes no part in the interaction listen to the exchanges of the pair of test takers. The contributions of each test taker are individually matched to a rating scale that draws the attention of the interlocutor and rater to key features of the discourse to be rated.

■ *Evidence accumulation*: a holistic score is awarded to each individual after their second contribution to the conversation. This score is altered with each new contribution after the second until the interlocutor and rater are separately satisfied that the score descriptor adequately describes the performance. These scores are confirmed or altered by up to one level during the wind-down.

 Task A8.14

Try to write down the details of a four-stage delivery process for an academic writing test and a reading test separately.

➤ Do you find being this explicit helpful?

➤ Why do you find it helpful or unhelpful?

A8.6   RATER AND INTERLOCUTOR TRAINING

The training of all staff who administer tests is important. But probably the most discussed area of test administration is the training of interlocutors for speaking tests, and raters for speaking and writing tests. Rater training probably has the longest history. It has been acknowledged since the beginning of what used to be called 'subjectively scored' tests that it should be *a matter of indifference to a test taker who scores the performance.* If the score is likely to change depending upon the rater, the question arises as to whether it is the rater's own personal views that impact on the score, rather than the ability of the test taker. In technical terms, variability by rater is seen as a source of *construct-irrelevant variance* (see Unit A1).

This has frequently been the reason why some large-scale language tests have not contained tests of speaking, even if speaking has been considered extremely important. Lado (1961: 331) for example, says that:

> instability or unreliability of test scores may be caused by scorer fluctuation or even examiner fluctuation . . . In various production tests and essay or long response tests, scorer fluctuation can be a major factor of the unreliability of a test.

Lado recommended the use of rating scales that raters are trained to use, so that

> as soon as an examiner begins to listen carefully for speaking ability he notices differences in the various elements of speech which he can grade more accurately than the over-all impression of speaking or the desirable but elusive criterion of intelligibility.
>
> (Lado, 1961: 241)

The need to ensure that a grade meant the same thing despite the person awarding it has also been of primary concern in the United Kingdom, usually expressed as different examiners applying the same 'standards' to the assessment of written and spoken production. With the spread of speaking tests during the Second World War, Roach (1945: 4) set up a series of studies to address:

> (a) How far it is possible to coordinate the standards of oral examiners in modern languages by means of joint examining, and (b) whether standards could be defined, for examiners both near and far, by some more positive means than rather sketchy and abstract instructions.

The use of more detailed rating scales (see Unit A7) and the training of raters to use those scales according to established norms and practices have now become the key elements in maintaining a consistent approach to grading. Nevertheless, Alderson et al. (1995: 118–127, 136–145) show that many examination boards in the United Kingdom did not have appropriate procedures in place for training and monitoring raters. Nor do all testing agencies calculate the degree to which raters agree with each other when rating the same performances (*inter-rater reliability*) or the degree to which each individual rater agrees with himself or herself over time when rating the same performance (*intra-rater reliability*). In other cases, reports on such problems have led to changes in practice (see, for example, Davidson and Bachman, 1990: 35; Bachman et al., 1995: 63).

★ **Task A8.15**

➤ What procedures are used in your institution to ensure the agreement of raters who are asked to score writing samples or speech samples? Do you think that these are adequate, or can you list steps you would take to improve consistency?

The training of interlocutors is a much more recent phenomenon. It had merely been assumed that interlocutors could engage test takers in conversation using the input associated with the tasks, and score the resulting performance of the test taker. Since the development of the notion of interactional competence this view has been challenged. We are now much more aware of the fact that discourse is co-constructed (see Unit A3), and so the performance of the test taker is in part dependent upon the performance of the interlocutor.

The response to this realization has taken a number of forms. On the one hand, some test developers have taken this to be a new argument in favour of the use of indirect tests that are tape-mediated and have no interactive interlocutor (see O'Laughlin, 2001). Some examination boards now provide interlocutors with interlocutor scripts (see Fulcher, 2003a: 74–77 for examples) that restrict the freedom of the interlocutor to interact with the test taker. Others would argue that this realization enriches our understanding of the construct definition (Chalhoub-Deville, 2003; Jacoby and McNamara, 1999; Jacoby and Ochs, 1995), but we may lack the ability to score co-constructed performances adequately as we now understand them.

★ **Task A8.16**

➤ Do you train interlocutors in your institution?

➤ What do you think are the main effects an interlocutor may have on the performance of a test taker?

A8.7 SECURITY

As we noted in Unit A2, collaboration in the classroom is generally seen as something to be encouraged. In a test, it is seen as 'cheating'. Surprisingly, there is no definition of 'cheating' in the *Dictionary of Language Testing* (Davies et al., 1999). However, we should be aware that cheating will always be a concern in testing generally. The problem may be expected to become more acute as the decisions to be made on the basis of the outcomes become more serious. High-stakes testing, as it has come to be known, will always be the target for attempts to cheat.

The *Standards for Educational and Psychological Testing* (AERA et al., 1999: 64) do contain one standard that helps to explicate matters:

Standard 5.6

Reasonable efforts should be made to assure the integrity of test scores by eliminating opportunities for test takers to attain scores by fraudulent means.

Specific elements of concern listed by the *Standards* include 'stipulating requirements for':

- identification of test takers
- creating seating charts
- assigning test takers to seats
- the space between seats
- providing continuous monitoring of test taking
- reporting on instances of irregularities.

ETS (2002: 51) lists similar elements, but adds that the space between seats should be such that copying is not possible. This implies that if a test taker copies the work of another and presents it as his or her own, this is cheating. From the first bullet point above, we can also infer that if a test taker employs or persuades someone else to impersonate them during the test, this also constitutes cheating. But we are not told what else might constitute cheating.

From this short discussion, 'cheating' may be taken to be any behaviour that might result in a test taker getting a higher (and also presumably a lower) score through *fraudulent* means, which might include identity switching or passing off the responses of someone else as one's own. Consider the following definition of *fraud*:

All multifarious means which human ingenuity can devise, and which are resorted to by one individual to get an advantage over another by false suggestions or suppression of the truth. It includes all surprises, tricks, cunning or dissembling, and any unfair way in which another is cheated.

(*Black's Law Dictionary*, 5th ed., 1979)

In high-stakes tests the results are highly likely to advantage or disadvantage some individual with regard to opportunities in education or employment (see Spolsky, 1995: 15–22). Using fraudulent methods to gain higher test scores is therefore likely to disadvantage decision makers in those institutions, or even competitors for places or advancement.

⭐ **Task A8.17**

➤ What types of fraudulent activities have you come across in your teaching career?

➤ What new types of cheating are possible with access to micro-technology, such as mobile phones with digital cameras, or digital recording equipment?

Institutions are also actively involved in encouraging fraudulent activity for profit. This may involve attempts to clone active test materials or develop on-line profiles of interlocutor styles which can be sold or used to attract students to test-preparation courses. With writing tests it has sometimes become practice to release all writing prompts in advance of tests, and it has been demonstrated that knowledge of the prompts does not result in improved test scores (Powers and Fowles, 1997). However, this is not likely to be the case with tests other than writing. Restricting attempts to copy and sell confidential test information normally requires monitoring and controlling the activities of these institutions.

⭐ **Task A8.18**

➤ How is it possible to restrict the activities of institutions that are able to profit from engaging in fraudulent activities relating to the testing industry?

We have already mentioned that invigilators or proctors require training, and that part of this training should prepare them to deal with unexpected circumstances. Obviously, one such circumstance is cheating. The first problem is that anyone accused of cheating is likely to deny it. We should therefore be as clear as possible about the grounds for action.

■ *Intent.* Cheating does not happen by accident. Therefore it is a requirement that an accusation of cheating is associated with evidence of the intention to cheat. If test takers are provided in advance of the test with a clear list of activities that are not allowed and would be interpreted as evidence of intention to cheat, the possibility of misunderstandings is significantly reduced.
■ *Repetition.* Evidence of intent is strengthened if it is repeated. Holding up a number of fingers to indicate the answer to a multiple-choice question may be reducing cramp the first time it is done, but not the fifth.
■ *Witness statements.* If the instances of cheating have been observed by the invigilators or proctors and others, reports should be written and signed.

The final problem is what to do if evidence suggests that an individual or an institution is guilty of any kind of fraudulent practice. For an individual this may be making the outcome of the test null and void, and banning that person from taking tests for a period of time in the future. What can be done about an institution is much more problematic and may need recourse to the law of the country in which the test is being held.

Task A8.19

➤ How does the institution in which you work deal with individuals found guilty of fraudulent behaviour? Do you consider the penalties to be too harsh or too lenient?

A8.8 TEST ADMINISTRATION FOR DISABLED PEOPLE

Institutions that use tests – whether these are large testing organizations or local educational institutions – need to consider how they are going to make it possible for disabled people to take tests. If a disabled person is excluded from the potential advantages that are to be gained from taking a test, it is classed as discrimination in many countries around the world. The kinds of disabilities that need to be considered are physical, such as blindness or deafness. But they also include psychological disorders and learning disabilities. This requires the test provider to introduce *test accommodations* that allow reasonable *access* to the disabled. Typical accommodations include:

- the provision of additional testing time
- provision of additional breaks
- readers to read textual prompts or explain graphical input
- sign language interpreters
- Braille texts
- large-print copies of texts
- modified response formats
- provision of special furniture or physical equipment
- amanuenses.

Test providers need to discover if there are likely to be disabled test takers in the population for whom their test is designed. If there are, accommodations need to be incorporated into test design if litigation is to be avoided under, for example, the Americans with Disabilities Act.

Task A8.20

➤ Using the Internet, discover what legislation affects access to educational provision by disabled people in your country. Does the institution for which you work take this legislation into account when designing and implementing language tests?

➤ If yes, how does it do this? If it does not, what are the potential consequences for the institution?

Looking at accommodations for the disabled highlights some of the most fascinating validity questions that language testers wrestle with. Consider the following situations, all of which relate to the administration of a reading test:

1. Blind test takers are allowed access to a Braille text and may respond to the questions verbally.
2. In a computer-based test the visually impaired may access large-font texts and/or magnify the screen.
3. Dyslexic students are granted access to a dictionary with auditory information on words contained in the text.
4. Learners with serious visual disabilities who do not read Braille are provided with a synthesized speech function.

In the first situation it would appear that all we are doing is allowing blind students to take a test from which they would otherwise be excluded. In other words, we are extending access and therefore fairness. The second case is slightly more complex, and requires us to ask two questions. The first is whether alternative font sizes should be available to the non-visually impaired. That is, should altering the text size be a feature of the test for everyone? It seems unlikely that allowing the non-impaired to read in larger fonts would enable them to increase their test score just because they can use larger fonts – but this is at least a question that should be addressed in a research study. The second question we need to ask is whether increasing font size or screen magnification introduces scrolling or other non-intended manipulation of the computer or mouse that would interfere with the speed or dexterity with which the visually impaired might undertake the test. If this were the case, the accommodation itself might introduce other sources of construct-irrelevant variance.

The third and fourth situations are even more complex. At first glance it looks as if the accommodations provide extended access. However, it could be argued that providing these accommodations violates the test construct. Perhaps a reading test *should* discriminate (in the testing sense introduced in Unit A7) between dyslexic and non-dyslexic readers. It may even be that part of the validity argument for the meaning of scores from a reading test is that test takers with reading disabilities gain lower scores. Similarly, if text in a reading test is read aloud for some test takers, is this a test of *reading*? Perhaps it is just that they cannot read, even if this is because of a disability. In situations 3 and 4 it may be argued that the accommodation interferes with the construct that the test is intended to measure. The task has been altered in ways that mean the evidence is no longer relevant to the inferences that we wish to make (see Hansen et al., 2005: 110).

When we make tests accessible for the disabled we therefore have to consider the issue of access on the one hand, and the possibility that an accommodation is a threat to construct validity on the other. This is not only an ethical but also a legal matter. Getting the balance wrong can, and often has, landed test providers in court.

Task A8.21

➤ Does your institution provide accommodations for learners with disabilities?

➤ If you don't have learners with disabilities, what is the general attitude to educational opportunities for people with disabilities in the culture where you work?

Summary

In this Unit we have argued that the administration of language testing is of much more importance than it is usually afforded in the language testing literature. Generally, it has been placed under the catch-all term of 'test practicality', but not treated in any detail, even if its centrality to questions of validity has been recognized. Davies (1990: 6) writes:

> It is important to remember (and to recall) that testing is possible only if it is practicable. A good test . . . may in practice be unusable because in the situation for which it is intended it would take up too much time, too much skilled manpower, or it might require expensive or elaborate media systems or scoring arrangements, and so on. How then (it might be asked) does one know that it is both valid and reliable? That is a very fair question, and on one interpretation of 'valid' it would have to be admitted, that if it is not practical it must lack validity because it is unusable on its target population.

Davies (ibid.: 25) saw all of these practical matters as issues or constraints that needed to be taken into account at the time of test design, particularly with regard to 'time, cash and patience'. This is certainly true. However, we hope that we have shown not only that practical matters of test administration are critical to maintaining the validity of test scores but that considerations of test administration can also raise some of the most interesting validity questions that pertain to fairness, ethics, the law and how different cultures view testing and test takers.

In Unit A9 we will turn to these issues and look at how language testers have addressed ethics and fairness in their work.

Unit A9
Fairness, ethics and standards

A9.1 INTRODUCTION

Looking at fairness and ethics in language testing is not as easy as it appears at first glance. One of the initial problems we have is actually defining the terms. But even once this is done, there are many different views about the role that tests play in society, and even whether they can be fair at all.

We believe along with Shohamy (2001: 160–2) that tests 'are here to stay', and that, despite the potentiality for their misuse, ethical and democratic approaches to testing provide opportunities and access to education and employment. And with Davies (1997b: 333, see B9) we argue that 'the professional response of language testers as a collective has to be that testing is a valid activity'. Shohamy states that the message in her book on the power of language tests 'should not be interpreted in anarchistic terms' but seen as 'a call for the practice of quality tests . . . Such testing requires shared authority, collaboration, involvement of different stakeholders – test takers included – as well as meeting the various criteria of validity.'

At the heart of an ethical approach to language testing that is designed to achieve fairness is the concept of *professionalism* as developed by Davies (1997a; 1997b; 2004), and we agree that 'What a professional morality does . . . is to provide a contract for the profession and the individual with the public, thereby safeguarding all three' (Davies, 1997b: 333). This contract normally takes the form of a Code of Ethics, Code of Practice, or Standards document, introduced by a professional association, and to which individual members subscribe as an act of becoming a member of that profession.

A9.2 PROFESSIONALISM AS A COMMUNITY OF PRACTITIONERS

Each individual language tester counts himself or herself as part of a *community of practitioners*, and therefore *engages* in discussion, debate and research that leads to *progress*. At any given point in time the community knows that with the hindsight of the future its current position may be seen as incorrect, or, as Rorty (1999: 82) says:

Long after you are dead, better informed and more sophisticated people may judge your action to have been a tragic mistake, just as they may judge your scientific beliefs as intelligible only by reference to an obsolete paradigm.

Collective understanding among the community helps determine what it feels to be *true*, or to be *right*. In Unit A5 we considered Peirce's characterization of the four bases for believing something to be true: tenacity, authority, *a priori* reasoning and the scientific method. Regarding the latter, Peirce (1877: 154–155) argues that if members of a community who share a commitment to certain goals and methods pursue their investigations:

> They may at first obtain different results, but, as each perfects his method and his processes, the results will move steadily together toward a destined center. So with all scientific research. Different minds may set out with the most antagonistic views, but the progress of investigation carries them by a force outside of themselves to one and the same conclusion . . . The opinion that is fated to be ultimately agreed to by all who investigate, is what we mean by the truth, and the object represented in this opinion is the real. That is the way I would explain reality.

Peirce was not a fatalist. Rather, as an empiricist he did not want to appeal to some metaphysical conception to justify his view of what constituted truth. He argued that as a community continues to grow and develop, what is ultimately 'real' is that which, given a hypothetically indefinite period of time, the community would ultimately agree upon (see the discussion in Unit A1). This is not dependent upon the belief of any individual in the community, or even the community itself. Rather, 'the reality of that which is real does depend on the real fact that investigation is destined to lead, at last if continued long enough, to a belief in it' (Peirce, 1877: 155).

This position does not seem unreasonable. If we look at the history of testing and assessment there are many issues that are now settled in the sense that the community agrees unanimously that a practice was unethical, or that a line of enquiry has proved unfruitful (see the example provided in Unit A10). Recounting one of these shows just how unacceptable, even alien, some past practices now seem to us.

A9.2.1 Case study 1: Intelligence testing

In 1905 the psychologist Alfred Binet produced the first intelligence test. The purpose of the test was to classify children into mental levels with the explicit purpose of providing additional help for those with low scores. Binet believed that intelligence was linked to environment, and that with additional help children could improve their scores and become 'more intelligent'.

In the United States H. H. Goddard translated the Binet intelligence tests from French into English and used them to classify some of the test takers as 'feeble-minded'. If a test taker fell into this category, he or she could be further classified as an idiot, an imbecile or a moron (Goddard, 1919: 60). The latter were termed 'higher grade defectives'. The tests were used at Ellis Island immigration centre, where it was found that between 40 and 60 per cent of immigrants could be designated as feeble-minded. Using these and more sophisticated tests, similar results were claimed among the black population, the poor, and enlisted men in the First World War. Goddard and his colleagues argued on the basis of this research that intelligence was hereditary. The poor were poor because they had less intelligence than the rich, and certain racial groups (Aryan) were inherently more intelligent than others (Black, 2003: 76–80).

At the time, the heredity argument was generally accepted by society. In order to protect society from a steady deterioration in mean intelligence, strict immigration laws directed at 'less intelligent' races were proposed, and enacted in 1924. For the 'defectives' already in the country, it was suggested that:

> If both parents are feeble-minded all the children will be feeble-minded. It is obvious that such matings should not be allowed. It is perfectly clear that no feeble-minded person should ever be allowed to marry or to become a parent. It is obvious that if this rule is to be carried out the intelligent part of society must enforce it.
>
> (Goddard, 1914: 561)

In some states test scores were required for the issuing of marriage licences, and in many others the feeble-minded were incarcerated or subjected to forcible sterilization (Gould, 1996: 188–204; Black, 2003: 87–123). Poor test scores for people from certain backgrounds or regions were not treated as evidence that social reform was necessary to introduce policies for improvement. Rather, they were held to provide further evidence of the hereditary lack of intelligence for which solutions needed to be sought.

The professional educational testing and assessment community is now agreed unanimously that these beliefs and uses of the tests were unethical, unfair and empirically unfounded.

A9.2.2 Individuality and participation

This leads us to consider the role of the individual within the community. Within the view of ethics that we are presenting, the individual has a critical and pivotal role to constantly challenge the community to question its own currently accepted position. In other words, the mark of an ethical community and ethical practice is the constant exercise of self-questioning and open debate. Ethical practice involves listening to and considering seriously contrary views and new evidence.

This is completely in keeping with Peirce's view of the nature of a scientific community, and balances the freedom of the individual with the collective progress of the profession. 'All silencing of discussion is an assumption of infallibility,' wrote Mill (1858: 22), adding that:

> There must be discussion, to show how experience is to be interpreted. Wrong opinions and practices gradually yield to fact and argument: but facts and arguments, to produce any effect on the mind, must be brought before it. Very few facts are able to tell their own story, without comments to bring out their meaning.
>
> (Mill, 1859: 25)

Mill proceeds to argue that only by challenging every view from every angle, and listening to the opinions of all, can we make progress.

Task A9.1

➤ In current language testing debates there is a call to include all 'stakeholders' in the discussion of test uses. In your own working context who would be the key stakeholders? How might soliciting their opinions lead to 'fairer' testing practices?

A9.3 PROFESSIONALISM AND DEMOCRACY

This approach to the definition of ethical practice in language testing does not presuppose any absolutes. On the other hand, neither is it prey to relativism (see below). It avoids these extremes because it is essentially a *democratic* approach, which holds that the ultimate good consists in the highest possible development of both society and the individual. The individual language tester therefore has a responsibility to the professional community and to the society within which he or she works, being neither subservient to the community or society nor independent from them. Rather, within this view, individualism:

> is an individualism of freedom, of responsibility, of initiative to and for the ethical ideal, not an individualism of lawlessness. In one word, democracy means that personality is the first and final reality. It admits that the full significance of personality can be learned by the individual only as it is already presented to him in objective form in society . . . It holds that the spirit of personality indwells in every individual and that the choice to develop it must proceed from that individual. From this central position of personality result the other notes of democracy, liberty, equality, fraternity, – words which are not mere words to catch the mob, but symbols of the highest ethical idea which humanity has yet reached – the idea that

personality is the one thing of permanent and abiding worth, and that in every human individual there lies personality.

(Dewey, 1888: 191)

This position mediates between those who believe that an ethical position can be justified only in terms of ahistorical concepts, on the one hand, and those who believe that there are no moral codes other than those that can be identified with a particular historical context, culture or community, on the other. The problem here is that what seems 'agreeable to reason' (Kant, 1785) differs from culture to culture. Only in a democracy can we operate the scientific method of enquiry rather than rely on tenacity, authority or what is agreeable to reason. As Putnam (1990: 190) puts it:

> For Dewey, the scientific method is simply the method of experimental enquiry combined with free and full discussion – which means, in the case of social problems, the maximum use of the capacities of citizens for proposing courses of action, for testing them, and for evaluating the results.

This is the same conclusion as that reached by Shohamy (2001: 161) where she calls for 'continuous examination' of testing. Silence about testing is the real enemy, not the testing practice itself. Shohamy advised: 'Do it, but do it with care.' We would alter that advice: 'Do it, but do it with care, and no matter what happens, don't stop talking and writing about it.'

A9.4 CONSEQUENTIALISM

We have extended the notion of professionalism to include engagement with a democratic community of professionals. The value of our activity as professionals can be judged by the extent to which our work contributes to the opportunities which our tests open up to all the citizens of our society.

This extended definition is essentially pragmatic. However, it does not take account of one of the standard criticisms of pragmatism, namely, how we decide on the ethicality of the decision of an individual taken at a particular point in time. The answer lies in the consideration of the consequences that we expect our present decisions and actions to entail. The intention of a decision should be to maximize the good for the democratic society in which we live, and *all* the individuals within that society. As we saw in Unit A1, Messick (1989) introduced the notion of con-sequential validity to educational testing and assessment, and it has become a central notion in language testing:

> The central question is whether the proposed testing should serve as the means to the intended end, in light of other ends it might inadvertently serve and in consideration of the place of the intended end in the pluralistic framework of social choices.

(Messick, 1989: 85)

Positive consequence is best achieved through distributive justice, which Messick described as follows:

> The concept of distributive justice deals with the appropriateness of access to the conditions and goods that affect individual well-being, which is broadly conceived to include psychological, physiological, economic, and social aspects. Any sense of injustice with respect to the allocation of resources or goods is usually directed at the rules of distribution, whereas the actual source of discontent may also (or instead) derive from the social values underlying the rules, from the ways in which the rules are implemented, or from the nature of the decision-making process itself. In selection systems, we are thus faced with multiple sources of potential injustice – injustice in values, of rules, or implementation, and of decision-making procedures – any combination of which may be salient in a particular selection setting. And it must be remembered that 'the whole selection system is to be justified, not the test alone'.
>
> (Messick, 1989: 86)

We can combine distributive justice with a new definition of what a test is if we re-conceive the problem of ethical test use in terms of the consequences of its use. Doing so takes new advantage of the pragmatic maxim (Peirce, 1877: 146; see the discussion of pragmatic validity in Unit A1):

> Consider what effects, that might conceivably have practical bearings, we conceive the object of our conception to have. Then, our conception of these effects is the whole of our conception of the object.

That is, the nature of a thing is its impact or effect on the world. This, we believe, is also true for any testing or assessment procedure. As such, we may define any test as its consequences.

Task A9.2

➤ Do you think that it is possible to say that the TOEFL test *is* the influence that it renders on acceptance or rejection by American universities? Or do you argue that TOEFL is defined by the tasks and items it contains? Could there not be an alternative collection of tasks and items that would still yield the same value to score users – American universities?

➤ Select one other large-scale test with which you are familiar. What is its influence upon whom? Does it seem reasonable to define these other tests as their influence, as well?

The logic of our argument is that if we design a test with its impact in mind, then the best results are more likely to follow. From this stance we are able to address the charge that we are not able to make an ethical decision at any particular point in the test design or implementation process. 'Ethical' or 'fair' decisions are those which address the test's effect at every step of the way during the test development process. The criterion against which we measure the success of the enterprise is acceptance by the community of professionals and the stakeholders. Putnam (1990: 196) cites James:

> The 'absolutely' true, meaning what no farther experience will ever alter, is that ideal vanishing-point towards which we imagine that all our temporary truths will some day converge . . . Meanwhile we have to live to-day by what truth we can get to-day, and be ready to-morrow to call it falsehood . . . When new experiences lead to retrospective judgments, using the past tense, what these judgments utter was true, even tho no past thinker had been led there. *We live forwards, a Danish thinker*[6] *has said, but we understand backwards.* The present sheds a backward light on the world's previous processes.
>
> (James, 1907: 98, italics added)

The task for the ethical language tester is to look into the future, to picture the effect the test is intended to have, and to structure the test development to achieve that effect. This is what we refer to as *effect-driven testing*.

A9.5 ON POWER AND PESSIMISM

In a famous commentary on tests, Foucault (1975: 184) claims that all examinations are symbols of power and control:

> The examination combines the technique of an observing hierarchy and those of normalizing judgment. It is a normalizing gaze, a surveillance that makes it possible to quantify, classify, and punish. It establishes over individuals a visibility through which one differentiates and judges them. That is why, in all the mechanisms of discipline, the examination is highly ritualized.

This is a very different perspective on the 'consistency' in the rituals of administration that we presented in Unit A8, and is (of course) very different from the position that we take in this book. For Foucault, the evolution of the test in education is a form of control, in which the test takers are turned into objects to be measured and classified. The whole notion of 'knowledge' is a construct, used by the powerful to oppress the weak and keep them under control. This postmodern re-working of a Marxist view of knowledge is deeply embedded in a philosophy of ethical relativism, where the rules, values and modes of behaviour that are encouraged are those which privilege the powerful. For postmodern thinkers, talk of ethics and fairness is simply that – talk. It is lodged within a discourse that is created within specific societies or groups in order to normalize behaviour. As the language of ethics is local or regional, this philosophy is at its very heart a celebration of relativism, which Davies (1997b: 334) cannot accept: 'My own view is that such relativist approaches are untenable since they would also allow for more extreme practices (for example, cannibalism, torture, slavery) to be accorded a relativist sanction.' Nevertheless, the relativist position has deeply influenced language testing practice at the national, institutional and personal levels.

In Unit A8 we referred to the quality management systems (QMS) that have been introduced by the Association of Language Testers in Europe (ALTE), which is an association of test-providing organizations rather than individuals. This approach to consistency of practice from test creation, through delivery, to the reporting of results is very much perceived by the organization as ensuring 'fairness' through the equal treatment of test takers (Van Avermaet et al., 2004). Yet they argue that standards cannot be imposed, merely used to encourage best practice and the maintenance of minimally acceptable standards among their own members. In a postmodern society they argue that one has to be cautious about setting standards because 'the attraction of those "in power" or who have the most prestige in the eyes of the other members of the group' (ibid.: 146–147) needs to be counteracted. The discourse of social and cultural diversity is used to explain why standards cannot be imposed upon the members of the organization. The acceptance of a relativistic paradigm means that QMS cannot be implemented within a single organization unless the individual members 'buy into' the systems.

Similarly, in the first decade of the twenty-first century, the International Language Testing Association (ILTA) has tried to develop a Code of Practice that will guide language testing practice around the world, building upon the successful acceptance of its Code of Ethics (2000) (previously referred to as a Code of Practice – see Davies, 1997b, and Unit B9). The search for agreement on principles has been in vain, even though many local language testing organizations have been able to develop their own Codes of Practice (Thrasher, 2004). The primary reason for this appears to be that a Code of Ethics can contain very broad and vague principles upon which there can be general agreement. If these become too specific or if the content places constraints upon actual practice, or what Thrasher (ibid.: 159) refers to as the 'minimum requirements for practice in the profession', agreement becomes much more difficult. If there can be no agreement on the values that we place on key concepts such as 'validity', it is unlikely that agreement could ever be reached on what constitutes 'best practice'.

Task A9.3

➤ Read the ILTA Code of Ethics. You can download this document from the ILTA website at www.iltaonline.com/code.pdf. Does this contain any principles with which you would disagree? Can you imagine any language professional from countries where you have worked disagreeing with any of these principles?

The question being asked in the ALTE and the ILTA examples cited above is: who sets the standards? This question is translated directly into: who wields 'power'? Postmodern thought merely reflects the crisis that views Western intellectual paradigms (including validity theory) as a new form of imperialism intent on world domination (Pennycook, 1994: 45). What right do we have to force our modes of thought or Anglo-American practices on other cultures or societies when they use tests?

The problem of power takes us back to one of the oldest and most fundamental debates in the history of thought, and it impacts upon language testing practice today. Foucault's critique of testing echoes the debate between Plato and the Sophists, primarily explored in the *Theaetetus*. In this text the Sophists are allowed to put forward their view that morality is merely a set of rules invented by the powerful to subjugate the weak, and that ethical behaviour is but a relative social contract to guide behaviour. The greatest advocate of this position was Protagoras (480–411 BC).

There are two sides to every question.

Of all things the measure is Man, of the things that are, that they are, and of the things that are not, that they are not.

Socrates characterized this position as 'what seems true to anyone is true for him to whom it seems so' (*Theaetetus*, 170a).

Nietzsche (1887) argued that history and culture determine our view of what is right and wrong, even though we like to think of ourselves as independent individuals. Rather, moral codes are imposed with threats of discipline and punishment (hence Foucault's title) until the individual conscience is nothing more than the internalization of the rules of a specific society. Like the existentialists, Nietzsche believes that we *make* values rather than discover them. But he is even more radically relativist, for 'Facts are precisely what there is not, only interpretations' (Nietzsche, 1906: 481).[7]

⭐ **Task A9.4**

> Culture both liberates and constrains. It liberates by investing the randomness of nature with meaning, order, and rationality, and by providing safeguards against chaos; it constrains by imposing a structure on nature and by limiting the range of possible meanings created by the individual.
> (Kramsch, 1998: 10)

➤ Can you think of a cultural way of thinking that might bring a test taker into conflict with any of the 'rules and regulations' of an essentially Western examination system as described in Unit A8?

Read these two quotations:

> The master said, 'I transmit but do not innovate. I am truthful in what I say and devoted to antiquity.
>
>> (Confucius, quoted in Scollon, 1999: 16, from the *Analects* VII.2)

> It is certainly possible to identify values and practices among certain groups of multilingual students which contradict established notions of plagiarism in the West.
>
>> (Sowden, 2005: 226)

➤ What problem does this raise for the conventions of Western testing?

We believe that a focus on relativism and power leads to a dead end in the discussion of how to be fair to test takers. A more efficient ethical solution is pragmatic, effect-driven test development that is democratic and that openly values dialogue among all stakeholders. In the next section we hope to show why this is so.

A9.5.1 Relativism and power

Hamp-Lyons (1997a: 324) argues that the growing interest in ethics is related to the fact that language testers have had a positivist approach to their discipline; that 'the object of our enquiry really exists'. She argues that this is not the case. She anchors processes from test design to interpretation, from research to score use, firmly within the exercise of power, as all 'language testing is a political act' (ibid.: 325). Hamp-Lyons (2000a: 581) expands upon this, with an explicit statement of what 'ethical language testing' is under postmodernism:

> Under the influence of postmodernism, we cannot avoid acknowledging the contingent nature of knowledge nor the fact that different stakeholder groups will have competing goals and values. The combination of expanded views of stakeholders and accountability with growing acceptance that the truth is not 'out there' but in us has made many language testing professionals question what they do and how they do it: this is what I mean when I refer to 'ethical language testing.'

Hamp-Lyons (2000a: 589) also writes: 'I do suspect that what is considered ethically acceptable varies from country to country, culture to culture.'

Hamp-Lyons takes a postmodern perspective because it opens up an awareness and sensitivity to difference and variety, creating a concern for the minority and the under-represented in society. This insight we would call ethical even from a pragmatic position. The real question is whether the epistemology that underpins this kind of postmodern compassion deprives us of the ability to set ethical standards across cultures. Thus, when it comes to posing questions about whether test developers are responsible for test uses that are not within their original stated purpose, Fulcher (1999b) has argued that there can be no answer within a post-modern paradigm, because there are different ethics for different societies.

We contend that effect-driven testing – as defined above – provides a feasible resolution: the test development team and all its stakeholders should never be prohibited from discussing any aspect of testing, and, provided that they keep the test effect in mind, we believe they have done their job. Relativism will enter – naturally, we believe – into such test design discussions.

⭐ **Task A9.5**

> No man ever looks at the world with pristine eyes. He sees it edited by a definite set of customs and institutions and ways of thinking. Even in his philosophical probings he cannot go behind these stereotypes . . . The life-history of the individual is first and foremost an accommodation to the patterns and standards traditionally handed down in his community. From the moment of his birth the customs into which he is born shape his experience and behaviour. By the time he can talk, he is the little creature of his culture, and by the time he is grown and able to take part in its activities, its habits are his habits, its beliefs his beliefs, its impossibilities his impossibilities. Every child that is born into his group will share them with him, and no child born into one on the opposite side of the globe can ever achieve the thousandth part.
>
> (Benedict, 1934: 2–3)

> Truth gains more even by the errors of one who, with due study and preparation, thinks for himself, than by the true opinions of those who only hold them because they do not suffer themselves to think. Not that it is solely, or chiefly, to form great thinkers, that freedom of thinking is required. On the contrary, it is as much and even more indispensable, to enable average human beings to attain the mental stature which they are capable of.
>
> (Mill, 1859: 39)

➤ These two quotations represent radically opposed views of human nature. Which one are you most sympathetic towards?

➤ Would one view more than the other seem to admit of the possibility of cross-cultural agreement on fairness in testing practice and validation?

We have already agreed with Davies (1997b: 334) that relativism opens up the doors to practices that we would consider to be unethical. However, this does assume that we are in a position to decide that certain practices *are* unethical by appeal to an absolute standard. Such a standard is denied to us if we do not adopt a rationalist position such as that of Bishop (2004). However, we do not need to do this. For the proponents of relativism are also the primary critics of applied linguistics and the practice of language testing. The language of power is used to argue that Western applied linguists or language testers do not have the right to impose their views and practices on others. Thus, as cited above, even a European organization (ALTE) does not think that the values of one (dominant) organization can do anything other than encourage partners to consider the issue of minimum standards. Putnam (1990: 186) lays such thinking bare:

> One argument that is often used to justify a relativistic standpoint is virtually identical to an argument that is used by reactionaries in our own culture, and it is surprising that these social scientists fail to see this. At bottom, the idea is that people in traditional societies are 'content' – they are not asking for changes and we have no right to say that they should be asking for changes, because in so doing we are simply imposing a morality that comes from a different social world.

Putnam agrees with Dewey that paternalistic intervention is certainly misguided and can only lead to rejection. Furthermore, there has to be 'active cooperation both in forming aims and carrying them out'. But the argument that others should not change because they are *satisfied* with their present condition or practices is flawed:

> The fact that someone feels satisfied with a situation means little if the person has no information or false information concerning either her own capacities or the existence of available alternatives to her present way of life . . . One of Dewey's fundamental assumptions is that people value growth more than pleasure. To keep the oppressed from learning so that they remain 'satisfied' is, in a phrase originated by Peirce, to 'block the path of inquiry.' What the radical social scientists are in fact proposing is an 'immunizing strategy,' a strategy by which the rationales of oppression in other cultures can be protected from criticism.
>
> (Putnam, 1990: 187)

In language testing terms, if some European test producers do not design tests to acceptable minimum standards (as acknowledged implicitly by Van Avermaet et al., 2004), this implies that scores on tests may fluctuate for many reasons that are unrelated to the abilities that the tests are designed to measure. These may be design, measurement or administrative reasons. Further, there is no dissatisfaction because this is not known by test takers. Additionally, society does not question the value and authority of the test and its producers. But while all concerned are 'satisfied', by maintaining the status quo in the name of respect for other societies and cultures we are in fact allowing the perpetuation of systems that block opportunities for individual growth.

⭐ **Task A9.6**

The first standard that governs the practice of language testing (AERA, 1999: 17) is:

Standard 1.1

A rationale should be presented for each recommended interpretation and use of test scores, together with a comprehensive summary of the evidence and theory bearing on the intended use or interpretation.

There is an associated comment that contains the following: 'Test developers have the responsibility to provide support for their own recommendations, but test users are responsible for evaluating the quality of the validity evidence provided and its relevance to the local situation.'

➤ Do you think it would be 'fair' for the International Language Testing Association (ILTA) to say that this standard should be universally applied, and that any testing organization that did not adhere to this standard should be named as not complying with professional standards?

A9.5.2 Taking power into account

The preceding discussion does not imply that tests are not used to maintain the power of sections of society. Nor does it imply that tests are not misused. We can agree with Hamp-Lyons (1997a: 325) that testing is a political act and an instance of the exercise of power. However, this can equally be for the good of the individual test takers and society. Shohamy (2001) has explored this aspect of the ethics of language testing further than anyone else. Taking Foucault as her starting point, Shohamy (2001: 20–24) argues that tests are instruments of power because of six factors:

1   Tests are administered by powerful institutions. Test takers take tests that are set by organizations that have complete control over the type and content of the tests that are set. These tests prioritize what is considered to be important by educational systems, governments or society; failure to get the appropriate grades can therefore lead to fewer educational or work opportunities.
2   Tests use the language of science. The use of statistics and the presentation of tests and examinations in scientific terms gives the process authority, so that the public make an assumption that testing systems are 'fair' and 'trustworthy' even if they are not.
3   Tests use the language of numbers. The use of numbers is endemic in society and the media. Quoting numbers in a report, even if these are questionable, gives the report an air of authority.
4   Tests use written forms of communication. Introducing the written test in which there is no communication increases the sense that the process was

scientific. Test takers are required to demonstrate the knowledge that is valued without being able to interpret that knowledge.

5   Reliance on documentation. Test results can be recorded and documented, so that each individual has a file that can be used for comparison with others, as well as classifying and judging the individual. A permanent record of the person is created that exists forever.

6   Tests use objective formats. The 'truth' is contained in the test, as most tests contain items to which there is a 'correct' response. This is even the case with some constructed response items or tasks (as in writing and speaking tests) where the format and scoring procedure limit what can be said and what can be valued.

Within centralized educational systems, Shohamy (ibid.: 29) argues that these features allow exceptional levels of control when state-level high-stakes tests can be introduced. This control can include access to higher education, and the ability to impose a national curriculum on all schools and colleges. In many countries tests are also used to monitor teacher effectiveness, produce school league tables and intervene to remove teachers from post. They may even be used to close schools when test scores are not considered to meet some externally set bureaucratic target. Shohamy (2001) discusses a number of tests introduced at national levels, and interprets them in Foucault's terms: as an act of authority that introduces *sur-veillance*, in order to *quantify* compliance, *classify* into failing and non-failing, and *punish* the failing. Tests are therefore used to ensure the pre-eminence of the knowledge valued by society's elite, thus maintaining the status quo.

Task A9.7

Consider the following standard, Standard 7.9 (AERA, 1999: 83)

> When tests or assessments are proposed for use as instruments of social, educational, or public policy, the test developers or users proposing the test should fully and accurately inform policymakers of the characteristics of the tests as well as any relevant and credible information that may be available concerning the likely consequences of test use.

➤   This standard has been accepted within the United States, which has a legal system to govern the uses of tests. Is it likely that this standard would be accepted in other cultures with which you are familiar?

➤   Does the wording of this standard hide any ethical problems? Consider the following two hypothetical circumstances:

(a)   A test is introduced by a Ministry of Education with the intention of forcing language teachers to change their teaching methodology to one that is more 'communicative'. An unforeseen effect is to put additional stress on learners who feel that they are not prepared for the test, and there is a rise in absenteeism and associated medical problems.

(b) The Immigration Office selects a general language test from a large international language test provider for administration to all potential immigrants. It sets its own cut score for admission to the country at a level that will reduce the current immigration level.

➤ Does the standard address either of these situations? What are the ethical issues at stake?

Of course, this is not what tests are supposed to be for. When tests were first embedded into society the purpose was precisely to challenge the position of society's elite. Before the existence of tests, entry into certain educational institutions or careers was limited to those of wealth or social standing in ages when social mobility was not possible. The introduction of tests in 1858 for access to the British colonial service was one measure that opened up opportunities for many to whom they had previously been denied (Spolsky, 1997: 243). It was recognized that tests were not infallible for their intended purposes, but the test was seen 'as a species of sortition infinitely preferable to the ancient method of casting lots' (Edgeworth, 1888: 626). As Spolsky (1995: 17–22) has shown, the ideal for a test is to introduce liberty, equality and opportunity.

A9.5.3 Case study 2: Language testing in gatekeeping

Many countries around the world use language testing as a method of controlling immigration. This is done because the countries would be accused of racism if the controls were to be openly imposed without some pretext. As Davies (1997c) makes clear, the argument put forward by the countries concerned is that a certain level of English (and other transferable skills) is necessary for an immigrant to integrate with society and find gainful employment. It is not only English-speaking countries that are engaged in this kind of gatekeeping; it is now common across the European Union (Fulcher, 2003c). The practice of using tests in this way appears to have little to do with language skills necessary for employment, but rather 'whether they can claim cultural identity with the host country' (Davies, 1987c: 82).

The archetypal example of this practice is the Australian dictation test (Davies, 1987c: 79–80; Hawthorne, 1997). This was introduced as part of the Immigration Restriction Act of 1901, which was the first major piece of legislation of the newly independent country. At the time, Australia was experiencing significant immigration from Asia, and the number of immigrants had begun to alarm white workers, who feared for their jobs. Pressure had grown on politicians to limit the number of immigrants, but this could not be done openly. Britain still had considerable influence over Australia, and Japan was Britain's main ally in the East. Any Immigration Act in a Commonwealth country could not therefore specifically target immigration from Asia. In order to overcome this problem a dictation test was introduced that allowed officials to exclude individuals on the basis of race without race being the explicit reason for the decision. The dictation tests were to be of fifty words or more in length, and at a level of difficulty that would result in failure.

The texts were selected by the Department of External Affairs and changed every two weeks in order to avoid the possibility that a test taker might 'cheat' by learning a text by heart. These texts were then distributed to immigration officials who would administer the texts. An example of a text from 1932:

> The tiger is sleeker, and so lithe and graceful that he does not show to the same appalling advantage as his cousin, the lion, with the roar that shakes the earth. Both are cats, cousins of our amiable purring friend of the hearthrug, but the tiger is king of the family.
>
> Perhaps the native will one day show fight, and endeavour to deprive his terrible enemy of its prey. Then the tiger, in rage or self-defence, attacks him, and the spell is broken. The flesh-eater finds that there is no magic protecting the guardian of the cattle, and thenceforth becomes a man-slayer.
>
> Tigers have been known to depopulate villages. One was known to exist in this way for several years, taking eighty human lives a year before it was hunted down and slain. When matters become too terrible to be borne, the natives pack up and move to another part of the country.

In a memorandum of 1927 from the Home and Territories Department to the Collector of Customs in Fremantle, the purpose of the test was made even more explicit:

> (a) Test, when applied, to be effective: As indicated in I.A.I.56, the test when applied to an immigrant, is intended to serve as an absolute bar to such person's entry into Australia, or as a means of depriving him of the right to remain in the Commonwealth if he has landed. The test should therefore be applied in a language with which the immigrant is not sufficiently acquainted to be able to write out at dictation.
> (b) Languages: Section 3, paragraph (a), of the Act requires that the test applied shall consist of not less than fifty words in any prescribed language. No languages have yet been specially prescribed by Regulation, but the Act permits of any European language being used, as authorized by Section 3 of the Principal Act.

That these instructions were put into effect is well documented, as the following extract confirms:

> A German subject . . . was released last week from Maitland prison and by commonwealth authorities in Newcastle submitted to a test in the Greek

language although he speaks German, English and French. As he could not pass the test, he was sentenced in Newcastle to six months imprisonment for being a prohibited immigrant.

> (Telegram from Paul Von Bari (German Consul General)
> to Governor-General (Hopetoun), 8 December 1903,
> Australian Archives A6662/1 200)

Davies (1997c) comments that this 'is reminiscent of those fairy tales in which the prince is given an impossible task to perform, but the difference of course is that in the fairy tales the prince always succeeds'. In the dictation test, if by chance a test taker was familiar with the language selected, the immigration officer administering the test could select another text for dictation in a language with which he or she was not familiar.

A9.5.4 Language tests for immigration

The use of tests as instruments of immigration policy in Australia has not abated. Hawthorne (1997) relates the story of the *access: test*, developed in the 1990s to limit the flow of skilled migrants to Australia. Although the test was designed to high technical standards its political role was made particularly clear in 1996 when the government wished to reduce immigration and achieved this by raising the pass mark on the test (ibid.: 251). Conversely, the development of the STEP (Special Test of English Proficiency) was developed in the mid-1990s to assist the Australian government in accepting larger numbers of immigrants without appearing to be letting anyone into the country without any kind of control (Davies, 1997c; Hawthorne, 1997: 253). In short, Australia found that a large number of immigrants from China were not returning following the events in Tiananmen Square in 1989 and their claims to remain in Australia had become a drain on court time and national resources. The STEP test was designed to allow the immigrants to pass, so that, as Hawthorne (ibid.: 258) says, 'STEP had a capacity to deliver the Australian government a solution which was timely, cheap and administratively simple – almost wholly on a user-pays basis'.

Bishop (2004) highlights two problems language testers have with issues of immigration. Firstly, the work of language test developers may be used for purposes which are not obvious to us either at the time the test is designed or subsequently. Secondly, even if we believe that the use of a test to restrict (or enable) immigration is unethical, there are likely to be others in the professional community who would disagree. As Davies (1997c) says, there may be benefits to ensuring that those who enter a country are either culturally compatible with the host nation or are likely to wish to integrate. This is the argument of cultural stability, which should not be confused with xenophobia. Or we may simply take the view that relying on language tests in this fashion is unethical because it allows liberal democracies to take decisions that could not be admitted in public.

Task A9.8

➤ Is there an ethical difference between using a test to deliberately exclude immigrants, and using a test to deliberately accept them?

➤ Are test designers responsible for the political uses of their tests?

➤ Does the ILTA Code of Ethics provide any guidance in such situations?

A9.6 PROFESSIONAL CONDUCT: STANDARDS FOR PRACTICE

The ILTA Code of Ethics sets out broad ethical principles, but does not constrain or prescribe practice at all. Standards, on the other hand, provide much more detailed guidelines for professional conduct. Davidson et al. (1997: 303) outline the different meanings that 'standard' can have in language testing. Here, we are concerned with the first of their definitions:

A standard can refer to a guideline for good practice; for example, an important standard for educational tests is that their developers should demonstrate evidence of test validity. This meaning equates 'standards' (in the plural) with a code of professional practice or set of professional guidelines which could cover all stages of test development, from initial construction, through trialling, and on to operational use.

Davidson et al. (1995) undertook a large-scale survey of standards by contacting agencies around the world involved in language testing. They received responses from 110 agencies, and reported that only 53.7 per cent of respondents were able to send relevant documents. They report that within this percentage there was significant variability with regard to the quality of the documentation and the understanding of what professional standards are. Nevertheless, a clear link has been made between practising as a professional and adherence to some form of professional standards (Stansfield, 1993; Davies, 1997b, 2004). We will focus on the best-known standards, those of AERA et al. (1999). The *Standards for Educational and Psychological Testing* are probably the most frequently cited standards available, although the *Code of Fair Testing Practices* (1988) is also widely used.

We have already reproduced a number of the standards from these documents in this Unit. Here we will select one standard from each of a number of sections that relate to themes that we have covered so far in this book and then ask you to evaluate the value of asking professionals to adhere to standards of this type.

For reliability and errors of measurement (see Unit A8):

Standard 2.1. For each total score, subscore, or combination of scores that is to be interpreted, estimates of relevant reliabilities and standard errors of measurement or test information functions should be reported.

For fairness in testing and test use (see above):

Standard 7.1. When credible research reports that test scores differ in meaning across examinee subgroups for the type of test in question, then to the extent feasible, the same forms of validity evidence collected for the examinee population as a whole should also be collected for each relevant subgroup . . .

Annotation: . . . Relevant examinee subgroups may be defined by race or ethnicity, culture, language, gender, disability, age, socioeconomic status, or other classifications.

For testing individuals with disabilities (see Unit A8):

Standard 10.1. In testing individuals with disabilities, test developers, test administrators, and test users should take steps to ensure that the test score inferences accurately reflect the intended construct rather than any disabilities and their associated characteristics extraneous to the intent of the measurement.

For testing in programme evaluation and public policy (see immigration above):

Standard 15.1. When the same test is designed or used to serve multiple purposes, evidence of technical quality for each purpose should be provided.

★ Task A9.9

➤ Messick (1989: 91–92) points out that professional judgment is required in applying standards. What kinds of judgments might we have to make in the interpretation of each of these standards?

A9.7 RESPONSIBILITIES OF LANGUAGE TESTERS AND THEIR LIMITATIONS

A critical question is the extent of the responsibility of language testers for the use of the tests that they create. On the one hand are those who extend the responsibility for both intended and unintended test use to society in general (Hamp-Lyons, 1997b: 302; 2000a, 2001). On the other hand, there are those who would limit the responsibility to 'within reasonable limits' (Davies, 1997a: 238), which is a common limitation within professional codes of practice. Shohamy (2000; 2001: 147–148) advocates the development of shared responsibility by involving all stakeholders in the decision-making process, a stance with which we strongly agree.

Task A9.10

Stansfield (1993: 199–200) contains a rare discussion of 'cost versus quality'. He recounts a story of a test development project in which he was asked to develop a test and refused to undertake the contract because he did not believe the figure on offer was enough to do the work to meet professional standards. The contract was given to a company that was prepared to work within the funds available, and the test was ultimately not usable for its stated purpose.

➤ Should a test developer agree to take on a test design project with insufficient funding to meet professional standards on the grounds that 'if we don't do it, someone else with fewer professional skills will'?

One thing that all language testers are now agreed upon is that positive washback (see Unit A2) is something that language testers should plan for, even if there is no clear evidence for how this can be planned (Messick, 1996; Hamp-Lyons, 1997b; Wall, 1997, 2000).

A9.8 ACCOUNTABILITY

The *Standards* (AERA et al., 1999) have been cited in US court cases (Davidson et al., 1997: 309), which also make them relevant to issues of *accountability* to test takers (Norton, 1997). This becomes an issue in a jurisdiction where equal protection legislation of any kind has been introduced (Kunnan, 2000: 8), and therefore a perception of unfair treatment can lead to legal action. Fulcher and Bamford (1996) review key legal cases involving testing, primarily in the United States. These mainly involve cases where discrimination against sub-groups of the population has to be established, particularly discrimination by race, gender or disability. In these cases it is necessary to establish that the outcomes of the testing have led to differential treatment and/or the reduction in opportunities for the group or an individual from this group.

Task A9.11

Consider the two following critical court cases:

Golden Rule Insurance Company versus *Mathias*. Hood and Parker (1991: 611) report that as a result of this case all test results in the United States should be reported and analysed by race in order to show that there is no bias in test scores.

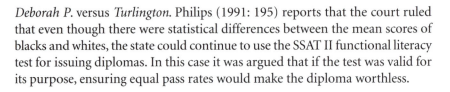

Deborah P. versus *Turlington.* Philips (1991: 195) reports that the court ruled that even though there were statistical differences between the mean scores of blacks and whites, the state could continue to use the SSAT II functional literacy test for issuing diplomas. In this case it was argued that if the test was valid for its purpose, ensuring equal pass rates would make the diploma worthless.

➤   How might you go about establishing that a difference between two groups was as a result of a real difference in the ability of interest, rather than a difference that could be traced to membership of a specific minority group?

Summary

We have argued that a postmodern perspective on ethics and fairness in language testing leads to relativism, which is a counsel of despair. On the other hand, we cannot find a basis for fairness in absolutism. Such a position would force us to seek for universally agreed principles of action that lie in a universe that is not unfolding like our own but exists separately and eternally, in what James (1907: 113) refers to as the *edition de luxe.* The problem is that each culture (and religion) has a radically different view on what the deluxe edition contains. The basis for international professional practice, like democracy, cannot therefore lie in another world.

Our solution to this problem lies in the pragmatic maxim of Peirce, which translates into: design a test with its best future effects in mind.

When they are asked, 'better by what criterion?', they have no detailed answer, any more than the first mammals could specify in what respects they were better than the dying dinosaurs.

(Rorty, 1999: 27)

Rather, we then have to appeal to the notion of engagement with the professional community, which will lead us in a direction that we cannot as yet predict, but we believe will be better, just as our current practice is better than that which led to the practice of mass sterilization, incarceration and ultimately the death camps of the Nazis (Black, 2003: 270–277).

Unit A10
Arguments and evidence in test validation and use

A10.1 INTRODUCTION

In Unit A1 we showed that Cronbach and Meehl (1955) argued for a view of validity that was based around a research programme that collected evidence to support specific interpretations of test scores. This should be done in order for a community of researchers and other stakeholders to evaluate public claims. The evidence may provide more confidence in a theory or interpretation, but new evidence may render the theory obsolete. We can therefore talk about validity as a process of argument for the meaning and use of test scores. This process is fundamentally empirical, and requires us not only to seek evidence that supports intended or current test use but also to investigate alternative interpretations of score meaning and test use (Messick, 1989; and Unit A1 above).

It is this notion of presenting an *argument* and the collection of evidence to support that argument that provides a constant in the discussion of construct validity from the first introduction of the term in 1955 until the present. Stating that a score carries certain meaning, or that a test can be used for an intended purpose, is a *claim* that must be supported through the argument. Consider this quotation from Cronbach and Meehl (1955: 290, reproduced in Unit B1):

> Construct validation takes place when an investigator believes that his instrument reflects a particular construct, to which are attached certain meanings. The proposed interpretation generates specific testable hypotheses, which are a means of confirming or disconfirming the *claim*. [emphasis added]

The view of validation as argument has to some extent been established in the latest edition of the *Standards for Educational and Psychological Testing* (AERA et al., 1999: 9), which explains validation in this way:

> Validation can be viewed as developing a scientifically sound validity argument to support the intended interpretation of test scores and their relevance to the proposed use. The conceptual framework points to the kinds of evidence that might be collected to evaluate the proposed interpretation in light of the purposes of testing. As validation proceeds and

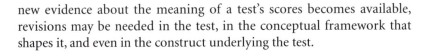

new evidence about the meaning of a test's scores becomes available, revisions may be needed in the test, in the conceptual framework that shapes it, and even in the construct underlying the test.

Validation is therefore a process, but it is also a process that does not stop. It is an activity that continues throughout the life of a test. When we make a claim about the meaning and use of a test, we are obliged to present a supporting argument. This argument may be challenged in a variety of ways, and further evidence then needs to be collected to investigate the threat to the current interpretation. In other words, we do the best that we can to test our arguments and claims. The best we can hope for is that the validity argument and the evidence will provide enough assurance in the strength of our claim for us to use the test for its intended purpose.

This brings us to the issue of certainty. We can never reach the point at which we can say 'Test X is valid for Y purpose'. Rather, our claim should be that, at the present time, the evidence and arguments (including theoretical rationales) suggest that the claims we make for the interpretation and use of the test scores are valid.

Validity research thus hopes to achieve two ends. Firstly, the reduction of doubt surrounding a claim: 'The trouble with aiming at truth is that you would not know when you had reached it, even if you had in fact reached it. But you *can* aim at ever more justification, the assuagement of ever more doubt' (Rorty, 1999: 82). Secondly, the growth in assurance that a claim is justified, so that test use may continue for its stated purpose: 'There is no such thing as absolute certainty, but there is assurance sufficient for the purposes of human life' (Mill, 1859: 24).

The assuagement of doubt is undertaken by conducting studies that consider alternative hypotheses for score meaning, particularly those that target the effect of construct-irrelevant factors. Increasing the assurances that we have for test use involves investigating the nature and strength of our own claims, which we hope are sound enough for the purpose of testing.

The discussions of *argument* in this Unit were prefigured in Dewey (1938), as we noted in Unit A1. His use of the phrase *warranted assertability* established a connection between enquiry and establishing what warrants an assertion or claim. Like Toulmin (2003), he focuses upon the nature of warrants and claims, and the conditions of enquiry under which a claim can be justifiably asserted. A true assertion is not determined so much by the effects of believing as by stating the conditions of enquiry that warrant an assertion. In research, we look for assertions that seem more plausible because repeated investigations tend to produce similar results under the same conditions. Dewey's notion of warranted assertability is also a probabilistic approach to justifying claims, as was Peirce's notion of the ultimate acceptability of a claim to the community of investigators. Both are also thoroughly empirical in nature. The formalism of substantial arguments (Toulmin, 2003) reflects all of these features.

Task A10.1

In the 1980s there was disagreement in the language testing community that led to debate, and to the collection and reinterpretation of evidence, relating to an argument that supported a claim for test use. Some researchers argued that language proficiency was a unitary concept, rather than a divisible concept in the way we have presented in Unit A3. Oller and Hinofotis (1980: 13) put it like this:

> Hypothesis 1 (H1) claims that language skill is separable into components related either to linguistically defined categories or the traditionally recognized skills . . . Another possibility (H2) is that second language ability may be a more unitary factor such that once the common variance on a variety of language tasks is explained, essentially no meaningful unique variance attributable to separate components will remain.

If evidence suggested that H2 is correct, Oller (1979) claimed that this in part supported the use of cloze tests as the best general language proficiency measures of the single underlying language ability (named 'g'). Just a few years later Oller (1983a: 352) could write: 'We may begin with the observation that *the strongest form of the unitary hypothesis was wrong.*' Yet when asking what 'g' is, he also states:

> it is not a unitary and exhaustive factor encompassing all the variance generated by tests that engage language abilities. On the other hand, arguments that 'g' is just a statistical artifact, or an illusory mirage of maturation, seem less than fully persuasive. If there were no 'general' language factor associated with 'knowing a language natively' or with 'communicative competence' then why would it make any sense to speak of such things as if they had some kind of coherence, unity even, or at least integrity? Or, putting it differently, isn't it possible that some type of 'general' factor will be necessary to a theory of language proficiency? Or to a theory of the capacities underlying language use?
>
> (Oller, 1983b: 35–36)

➤ What do you think led to the growing doubt that caused Oller to abandon the strong version of the unitary competence hypothesis (UCH)?

➤ What evidence do you think may strengthen the view that apart from different abilities underlying language use (see Unit A3) there is also a 'general' language ability?

A10.2 ARGUMENTATION AS SOLUTION

Those who have studied the role of arguments in scientific enquiry have done so because they wish to avoid absolutist positions on the one hand, and relativist positions on the other (see Unit A9). Jonsen and Toulmin (1988) distinguish between *substantial* and *analytic* arguments. An analytic argument, like a syllogism, derives its conclusion from its premises. It therefore relies on eternal principles. A substantial argument is one that requires inference from evidence to a conclusion, and therefore has to involve itself with the specific and temporal details of a case. It is also thoroughly empirical in its requirements. Yet a substantial argument does not admit a relativist position; it falls squarely within the pragmatic position that we have presented in Unit A9. As Toulmin (1972: 23) states:

> The absolutist reaction to the diversity of our concepts, thus emancipates itself from the complexities of history and anthropology only at the price of irrelevance . . . [while the relativistic reaction] takes good care to avoid the defects of historical relevance, but in doing so (as we shall see) it ends in equal difficulties by denying itself any impartial standpoint for rational judgment.

As we have already argued, absolutist claims place groups who disagree in positions where all they can do is restate their case ad infinitum, or come into conflict. Relativists have no case to put, and no reasons for disagreement, other than distaste for the practice of others. Looking at validity in terms of an argument to support a claim releases us from the two extremes and provides a practical and pragmatic solution to the problem.

A substantial argument is an attempt to justify a claim. It does not do this by appeal to some reality beyond the evidence, but it does assume that a claim may be justified according to some level of probability that can be agreed upon by subjecting the argument to criticism and testing, as in a court of law (Toulmin, 2003: 8). This position is consonant with Messick's (1989) view that validity is about investigating alternative arguments, Peirce's (1877) conception of the community of investigators constantly striving to reach agreement by challenging and questioning claims, and Davies's (1997b) notion of professionalism.

It is therefore not surprising that Toulmin (1972) criticized Kuhn's (1970) view that advances occur when new paradigms replace older paradigms when the latter are no longer capable of dealing with new evidence (scientific revolutions). In a revolution two opposing groups believe in absolute principles and usually cannot see or accept the view of the other group. True advancement, Toulmin (1972: 140) argues, takes place through evolution that is caused by rational argumentation about competing ideas within a 'forum of competition', which includes the professional organizations set up for this purpose. Progress is in fact much smoother, as newer theories evolve from older ones, incorporating what was useful from the older theories and adding new ones to better explain the facts to hand. In educational testing and assessment, Kane (1992; Unit B10; 2002; Kane et al. 1999) employs 'practical arguments' in the investigation of test validity, showing how we use evidence to formulate the most 'convincing' or 'plausible' validity argument that we can.

Kane (2001: 329) has termed this approach 'validity as argument', following an earlier proposal by Cronbach (1988). In accordance with Kane, the process of developing a validity argument would proceed as follows:

- State an interpretive argument clearly, laying out the 'network of inferences leading from the test scores to the conclusions to be drawn and any decisions to be based on these conclusions'.
- The validity argument is created by 'assembling all available evidence relevant to the inferences and assumptions in the interpretive argument'.
- The 'most problematic assumptions' in the argument are then evaluated, perhaps by investigating existing evidence or developing new lines of research.
- The argument is then restated in a more plausible form and further investigated, or is rejected.

Looking at validity as argument has a number of major advantages over other approaches to validity.

The first is that each validity argument must be developed in relation to specific claims about the meaning and use of scores from a test developed for a particular purpose. It forces us to acknowledge that no test can be used in any or every situation, but this is often what is assumed by test developers. For example, Swender (1999) claims that 'the applications of the OPI [oral proficiency interview] are limitless' in academic, professional and research contexts. Chalhoub-Deville and Fulcher (2003: 502) argue that 'a test that suits all purposes creates validation chaos. In such a situation, it is not clear what research evidence should be targeted or given priority'. Indeed, validation research becomes impossible because the validity claim is unmanageable.

The second major advantage follows from this. As Kane (2001: 331) puts it:

> A major strength of this argument-based approach to validation is the guidance it provides in allocating research effort and in deciding on the kinds of validity evidence that are needed. The kinds of validity evidence that are most relevant are those that evaluate the main inferences and assumptions in the interpretive argument, particularly those that are the most problematic. The weakest parts of the argument are to be the focus of the analysis.

The third advantage is that this approach allows us to detect sleight of hand. It has become more and more common for test users to search for existing tests to fulfil new purposes for which they were not designed. These are 'off-the-peg solutions' that reduce the need to develop new tests or conduct validity studies, which saves a great deal of money. However, *retrofitting* tests to new purposes, while not necessarily an illegitimate enterprise, requires the development of a new validity argument for its new context. The onus is on the test provider as well as the test user to undertake this work, rather than simply agree to the new uses of tests for commercial reasons.

★ Task A10.2

➤ Visit the websites of three or four testing agencies. Can you detect evidence of (1) claims of universal relevance, (2) validity claims and/or evidence for the main purpose of the test, or (3) retrofitting?

A10.3 THE FORM OF AN ARGUMENT

Toulmin (2003: 8) states that 'A sound argument, a well-grounded or firmly backed claim, is one which will stand up to criticism, one for which a case can be presented coming up to the standard required if it is to deserve a favourable verdict'. In order to present a sound argument it is necessary to be explicit about claims (what Kane would call the interpretive argument) and the evidence that is used to support it (Kane's validity argument).

Toulmin first distinguishes between the force of an argument and the criteria for evaluating an argument. The force of an argument is the probability that we wish to associate with the claim, which Toulmin refers to as modal terms. These are words such as 'certainly, probably, may, or never'. The criteria are the standards by which a claim may be evaluated, and these will differ from field to field. In language testing, the criteria are generally agreed to be those laid out in the *Standards* (AERA, 1999). The concept of force is therefore 'field invariant', whereas criteria are 'field dependent' (Toulmin, 2003: 36).

Field-dependent arguments vary in the formality required, the precision expected by practitioners, and the modes of resolution that are set in place for settling arguments. However, the format of an argument is considered to be field-invariant. The format has three basic components and three modifying components.

■ *Basic components*

  ■ Claim: The claim is the conclusion of the argument that we seek to justify.
  ■ Grounds: The grounds are the facts, evidence, data or information that we have available.
  ■ Warrant: The warrant is the justification of the claim using the grounds. In other words, it is the link between the grounds and the claim.

■ *Modifying components*

- ■ Backing: The backing is any support that is required for the warrant, which may take the form of theoretical models, previous research, or supporting data.
- ■ Modal term: The model term indicates the strength of the warrant.
- ■ Rebuttal: The rebuttal is a counter-claim that the warrant does not justify the step from the grounds to the claim. In language testing these would most likely constitute claims of construct-irrelevant variance or construct under-representation (see Unit A1).

Figure A10.1 provides the basic form of an argument as outlined by Toulmin (2003: 97). Before we investigate the form of a validity argument within language testing, we will present the simple example used by Toulmin in order to show how it can be used in a legal domain.

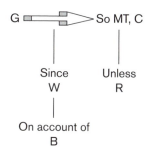

Figure A10.1 The basic form of an argument

Toulmin (ibid.: 97) puts forward the claim that Harry is a British subject. The grounds that support this claim consist of evidence to show that Harry was born in Bermuda. The warrant that supports this claim is that people born in Bermuda are *generally* British citizens. The force of the claim is therefore that Harry is *presumably* a British citizen. The rebuttal is that he would not be a British citizen if either (1) both his parents were aliens, or (2) he had become a naturalized citizen of another country. Rebuttals therefore require an alternative claim and may or may not have additional evidence attached to them. The backing for the warrant would take the form of laws regarding the nationality of persons born in British colonies. The form of this specific argument is presented in Figure A10.2.

If the warrant is challenged in this argument, the backing provides the evidence to refute the challenge. The weakest part of the argument is the assumption that because Harry was born in Bermuda he must be a British citizen, because there are two conditions under which this would not be the case. Research would therefore focus on the nationality of Harry's parents, and on seeking evidence about any naturalization proceedings in another country.

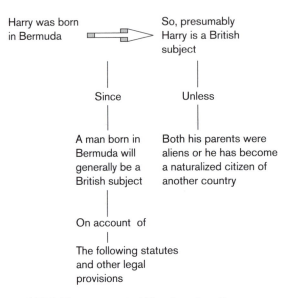

Figure A10.2 The argument of Harry's nationality

The kind of warrant that is presented will depend upon the field. In this case, Toulmin (ibid.: 96) makes it clear that 'A Bermudan will be (*in the eyes of the law*) a Briton' – in other words, the warrant that links grounds to claim appeals to the legal system. 'A whale will be (i.e. *is classifiable as*) a mammal' relates the warrant to a taxonomical system, whereas 'A Saudi Arabian will be (*found to be*) a Muslim' appeals to 'statistics which record how religious beliefs are distributed among people of different nationalities'. Thus, an analysis of the nature of the warrant gives direct insights about the kind of evidence that needs to be amassed to investigate the claim. Toulmin (ibid.: 98) explicitly states that warrants 'are hypothetical, bridgelike statements' that are the focus of an argument.

Although Toulmin does not make any reference to pragmatism, this approach to argument sits easily with our exposition of ethics in Unit A9. 'Truth', so far as it can be established, is not the property of a belief (here a claim), or the facts (here the grounds, or data), but rather the link between them (here the warrant). The connection of belief to facts, or the warrant, constitutes that which is true or not true, or somewhere in between (De Waal, 2005: 50). As James (1907: 99) says:

> In the realm of truth-processes facts come independently and determine our beliefs provisionally. But these beliefs make us act, and as fast as they do so, they bring into sight or into existence new facts which re-determine the beliefs accordingly. So the whole coil and ball of truth, as it rolls up, is the product of a double influence. Truths emerge from facts; but they dip forward into facts again and add to them; which facts again create or reveal new truth (the word is indifferent) and so on indefinitely. The 'facts' themselves meanwhile are not *true*. They simply *are*. Truth is the function of the beliefs that start and terminate among them.

This echoes Mill's (1859: 25) earlier argument that 'Very few facts are able to tell their own story, without comments to bring out their meaning'.

A10.4 ARGUMENT IN EVIDENCE-CENTRED DESIGN

Not surprisingly, Toulmin's approach to argument is also at the centre of evidence-centred design (ECD) as discussed in Unit A5 (Mislevy, 2003a, 2003b). There we introduced the concept of *evidentiary reasoning*, which is an argument designed to support a claim about a test taker from what that person does in a test, or their *work product*. Mislevy (2003a: 12) provides an example of how this could be operationalized in an English test, which we adapt in Figure A10.3.

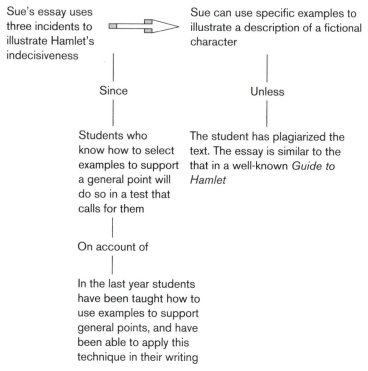

Figure A10.3 Mislevy's language testing example

The simple claim involved in this argument also prioritizes particular pieces of research that need to be undertaken to assuage our doubt about the claimed meaning of the score. These might include group difference studies between students who have been taught to use examples in this kind of writing and those who have not. The supposition that memorizing and reproducing essays from study guides might be a major problem in this kind of test would also need to be investigated, perhaps leading to regular electronic checking of test samples against known examples.

⭐ **Task A10.3**

➤ Think of a test that you use on a regular basis in your class or institution. Identify the claim that is made about students taking the test, the data used as the grounds for the claim, and the warrant(s) that link the grounds to the claim. Draw a simple Toulmin diagram like that in Figure 10.3.

A10.5 ARGUMENTS IN LANGUAGE TESTING

In language testing an argument may be constructed at a number of different levels. We may construct an argument for the use of a particular item type in a test that would be useful in test design and prototyping (see Unit A6), or for a complete test. We can also construct an argument to support test use for its stated purpose.

A10.5.1 An item-level argument to guide prototyping

At the level of the item, we will once again consider our discredited lexical items from Units A5 and A6, which we reproduce below once more. It will be remembered that these items were designed for prototyping because it was hypothesized that they would test three features of the 'good reader', namely fluent and automatic word recognition, the ability to recognize collocations, and having a large recognition vocabulary. These features were drawn from theory and previous research, which led us to construct items that tested words in collocation and sets, the former being more or less culturally fixed and the latter as superordinates or co-hyponyms.

Identify the odd word out by drawing a circle around it.

1	dog	walk	lead	fish
2	take	elephant	horns	bull
3	chair	stool	furniture	sofa
4	bath	pot	pan	wok
5	impudent	insolent	audacious	pompous

We then saw in Unit A6 that these items were challenged during prototyping. An argument for this item type may look that in Figure A10.4.

As we saw in Unit A6, some of the challenges to the argument may be addressed with data that were collected as a matter of course to support score meaning, but other challenges may require the collection and analysis of new data. If mounting data suggest that the validity argument is unsound, we are obliged to abandon our item type.

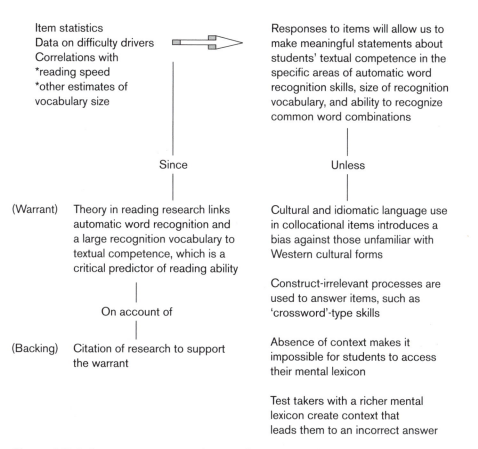

Figure A10.4 An argument structure for textual competence items

A10.5.2 A test-level argument

The same argument structure can be used for the claims made for specific tests or for claims about test types. Earlier in this Unit we considered the widely held view that the cloze test was a valid measure of general language ability. This is a claim which was supported by data that showed that cloze tests correlated highly with integrative measures of language proficiency, but had low correlations with discrete point tests of language elements such as grammar. From the grounds, we are invited to draw the inference that cloze is a valid measure of general language proficiency. The argument would look something like Figure A10.5.

The warrant in this argument is that cloze tests are a valid integrative measure of general language proficiency. This links the grounds to the claim in a way that is empirically testable, and this is precisely what happened in the 1980s. The rebuttal took the form of four challenges, three directed at the warrant and the fourth at the backing. In the first three, Alderson (1983) questioned the warrant on the grounds that scores on cloze tests varied according to text chosen, the method of scoring the

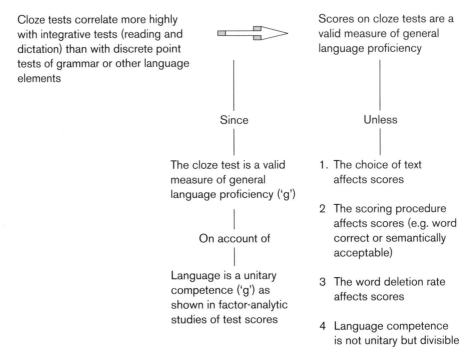

Cloze tests correlate more highly with integrative tests (reading and dictation) than with discrete point tests of grammar or other language elements

Scores on cloze tests are a valid measure of general language proficiency

Since

Unless

The cloze test is a valid measure of general language proficiency ('g')

1. The choice of text affects scores

On account of

2 The scoring procedure affects scores (e.g. word correct or semantically acceptable)

Language is a unitary competence ('g') as shown in factor-analytic studies of test scores

3 The word deletion rate affects scores

4 Language competence is not unitary but divisible

Figure A10.5 The cloze argument

test, and the word deletion rate. He showed that scores varied along each of these three method parameters, thus demonstrating that scores on cloze tests vary by factors other than language proficiency (construct-irrelevant variance). In the final rebuttal, Bachman and Palmer (1982) were among the first to provide evidence to suggest that language competence was indeed componential, and Vollmer and Sang (1983) started to find flaws in the factor-analytic studies that supported the unitary competence hypothesis. As we saw in our reflective task earlier in this Unit, the rebuttal was ultimately so well supported that the strong form of the unitary competence hypothesis had to be abandoned, and with it the claim that the cloze test was valid as a general test of proficiency whenever it was used.

While the challenges to items should grow out of the test development process through alpha, beta and field testing, challenges to complete tests are considered in field testing and once the test becomes operational. Challenges or rebuttals to a claim made in a validity argument may involve any aspect of the test architecture. Using the ECD model (see Unit A5), these may include:

Student model in the framework

- is inappropriate for the domain of inference
- is under-specified
- is under-represented

Evidence model

- work products are not related to a student model
- work products are not sufficiently large to bear intended inferences
- evidence rules do not link observed variables to constructs
- the scoring model is inappropriate or confused

Task model

- presentation material (input or prompts) does not generate expected work products
- presentation material introduces construct-irrelevant variance
- work products are not related to the presentation material
- task variables are under-defined for the creation of parallel forms

Presentation model

- work products vary according to presentation
- scores vary according to presentation

Assembly model

- targets: the test is unreliable
- constraints: test specifications are poor and so test content varies from form to form. Therefore the test does not adequately represent the specified domain in relation to test purpose

Delivery model

- timing (speed) affects test scores
- test content is not secure
- any aspect of test administration (see Unit A8) affects work products or scores

With reference to the example of the cloze test we can see that the four rebuttals or challenges to the argument can be explained by reference to these potential challenges.

1. Choice of text affects scores. This is a task model challenge, that the choice of presentation material or input affects scores. In other words, scores vary depending upon the text chosen, which is not predicted by the claim.

2. Scoring procedure affects scores. This is an evidence model challenge, that the scoring procedure is either inappropriate or confused. Two scoring procedures have been developed for cloze tests: the correct word method, where only the original word from the text is scored correctly, or the semantically acceptable word method, where any appropriate word is scored correctly. The claim relies on test scores being the same whichever method is chosen, but this was shown not to be the case.

3. Word deletion rate affects scores. This is a task model challenge, that the task variables are under-defined for the creation of parallel forms. The claim suggests that cloze tests should be parallel even with different word deletion rates, but research showed that different deletion rates produced different scores for the same individuals.

4. Language competence is not unitary but divisible. This is a student model challenge, that the model under-represents the construct. In this case, the construct is as broad as 'language ability', and treating this as a single ability does not account for what it means to know a language.

We note here that research effort was directed at what were considered to be the weakest parts of the validity argument, which is precisely what is recommended in any argument-based research agenda.

Task A10.4

➤ Look again at the Toulmin diagram you drew for the last reflective activity. Can you now add potential rebuttals or counter-claims that would help guide a validity research agenda?

A10.5.3 A test use argument

Bachman (2005) follows Kane (2001, 2002) in suggesting that a validity argument can be supplemented by a distinct argument for test use, which Bachman terms a 'utilization argument'. He achieves this by fusing the Toulmin argument model with Messick's (1989) view that two types of evidence are required to support test use: the relevance and usefulness of the score meaning for the intended decision. To these are added Messick's notion of the intended consequences of test use (as unintended consequences cannot be foreseen), and the concept of 'sufficiency' (Bachman, 2005: 14). By extending the use of argument to test use in this way, Messick's concern for the social consequences of test use is addressed (see McNamara, 2006).

In a test use argument the claim from a validity argument would become the grounds (or data), and the new claim would be the decision to be made on the basis of the validity claim. Bachman suggests an argument structure similar to that presented in Figure A10.6. The warrant types and required backing are explained as follows.

The *relevance* of the score to the decision being made is supported by evidence that shows that the ability being tested is required for the activity in the real-world

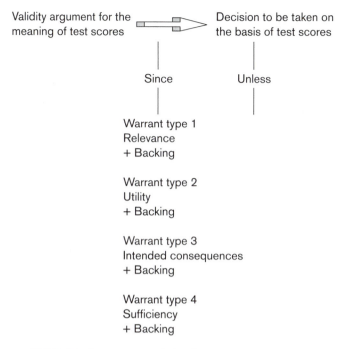

Figure A10.6 A test use argument structure

context about which a decision is being made. Such evidence might, for example, include needs analyses or comparisons of the real-world tasks and the test tasks.

The *utility* of the score for the decision being made relates to whether or not using the test score (even if it is relevant) is useful in that it 'increases the probability of making appropriate decisions' (Bachman, 2005: 19). If it does not do this, other relevant assessment processes should be used instead.

The *intended consequences* is a statement of the benefits which might accrue to the test taker, the test user or any of the other stakeholders through the use of the test.

Sufficiency concerns whether the information provided by the test is in itself sufficient for making a decision, or whether additional information would be required in addition to the test score. In job-related language tests, for example, it may also be necessary to have assessments of subject-specific knowledge or skills in order to make a decision for employment or promotion purposes (Bachman, 2005: 20; Douglas, 2000). We also add that in Messick's (1989: 67–69) terms this also concerns the representativeness of test method and content in relation to the domain to which we wish to make predictions.

What is not clear is what would constitute a rebuttal, or counter-claim. Bachman (2005: 21) suggests that these might be (1) reasons for not making the intended decision, or (2) the unintended consequences of using the test. The examples provided are in the context of a language test for hiring in the hotel industry. For (1), Bachman suggests that a test taker with a low score might still be hired because he was the son of the hotel owner, and for (2), that the test taker 'has friends in cement and explosives and knows where the owner of the company lives' (ibid.). This is to misunderstand the nature of the rebuttal or counter-claim. Toulmin (2003: 94) makes it clear that the rebuttal indicates 'circumstances in which the general authority of the warrant would have to be set aside'. That is, rebuttals are generally focused on warrants in order to challenge the argument. A counter-claim would therefore take one of four general forms, namely that (1) the ability being questioned is not relevant to the decision being made, (2) the test score is not useful to making the decision (it could be made without any test, or using some other instrument more reliably), (3) the intended consequences are not in fact beneficial, or (4) the test score is being used as a sufficient condition when in fact it is not. This interpretation may also be primarily what Messick (1989: 86) had in mind when discussing the use of counter-hypotheses to challenge arguments for test use.

Unintended consequences, including the impact upon individuals and society, may be generated through sources of score invalidity (Messick, 1989: 84–85; 1994), but may also derive from the unintended impact of outcomes on individuals and the unintended use of test scores. It appears that Bachman is treating the first of these two as potential rebuttals within an argument. We will briefly treat each separately.

Unintended impact on individuals

Bachman provides an excellent example of how it would be impossible to predict the effect of test use on each individual who might take the test. As such, these cannot be the basis for evaluating a test use argument. However, it may be that we can predict an unintended impact of using the test on a collection of individuals. For example, in a society that places exceptionally high value on educational achievement as reflected in test scores, the introduction of a new high-stakes test may have the unintended consequence of increasing suicide rates. This unintended consequence would indeed constitute a challenge to the test use argument, but this would take the form of a challenge to the intended consequences. That is, the actual consequences are not the beneficial consequences that were intended.

★ Task A10.5

Consider this story extracted from a BBC report predicting the unintended consequences of introducing new tests to the United Kingdom.

Mr Roberts said he believed children were already showing signs of neurosis – nervousness, worry, panic, anxiety – 'not behaving like kids'.

Recalling a holiday job he had once had in a battery chicken farm, he said there was a pecking order in force – with pressure from the government onto schools inspectors, from them to head teachers, to teachers, 'and the poor pupils at the bottom'.

'It's time to end factory farming and give our kids a bit of free range,' he said.

In Japan there had been cases of children committing suicide under the relentless pressure to do well in exams.

Last year there were 192 cases of under-16s killing themselves in Japan, a 44% rise on the previous year and the highest figure for 12 years.

Mr Roberts said he believed England was heading the same way.

'The route this government is treading is the route to child suicide . . . because of the intolerable hothouse pressures put on children's learning.'
(From http://news.bbc.co.uk/1/hi/in_depth/
education/2000/unions_2000/717723.stm)

➤ How can concerns over such unintended consequences be considered within a test use argument prior to the implementation of the test?

Unintended use of test scores

The intended use of test scores is included in the test use argument, and should be contained in all test documentation, including the specifications. Any unintended use of the scores is therefore any use that is not so specified. Such an unintended use may take one of two forms: (1) an unintended use that the test developers do not know about, or do not approve of, or (2) an unintended use that the test developers know about and approve of. Neither of these can be included as a rebuttal in a test use argument because they do not relate to the argument at all. Both cases are instances of retrofitting a test to a new purpose that was not intended at the time of design. Both are equally invalid unless a new argument is constructed for the new testing purpose and evidence collected to show that the retrofitting is valid, so that the same test may be shown to be useful in a new decision-making context. In other words, retrofitting test purpose without the construction and investigation of a new validity and utilization argument constitutes an implicit claim that any test can be used for any purpose, which is to introduce validity chaos.

Task A10.6

➤ Consider the potential use of a general language test being adopted by a government for immigration purposes, as described in Unit A9. Can you draft a claim, warrants and rebuttals that might guide the process of retrofitting the test to the new purpose?

A10.6 ARGUMENTS AND FEASIBILITY

Haertel (1999: 6) suggests that there are a number of advantages to looking at validity as argument, rather than considering it to be a matter of collecting information according to a 'checklist' of things to do, a process that we might engage in if we were to work our way through the *Standards* (AERA et al., 1999) and apply each standard to the development and implementation of a new test. The first, he says, is that in the application of checklists the tendency is to look for evidence that supports the validity or test use claim, whereas in an argument approach we are forced to focus on disconfirming evidence. This brings us back to the major focus of validity, which is the evaluation of alternative interpretations. Secondly, an argument focuses our attention on the validity questions that are relevant to a particular test and its purpose. Time and resources are therefore not wasted on collecting evidence that has no bearing upon specific warrants or rebuttals. Both Haertel and Bachman point out that this is especially useful when there is limited time or resources for validation studies. And at the heart of this, 'we are asked to embrace the scientific ideal of striving to understand and disclose the weaknesses as well as the strengths of our tests and testing practices' (Haertel, 1999: 6).

A10.7 ARGUMENT, EVIDENCE AND ETHICS

There is nevertheless a seductive danger that lurks behind the metaphor of validity and test use as argument. It is revealed in the extensive use of the legal metaphor in Toulmin (2003), which comes across into language testing in texts such as this:

> The empirical validation in language testing is to ensure the defensibility and fairness of interpretations based on test performance. In the case of both legal and assessment settings, the focus of investigation is on the procedures used. If the procedures are faulty, then the conclusions about particular individuals will most likely be unsound. The scrutiny of such procedures will involve both reasoning and examination of the facts.
>
> (McNamara, 2006: 32)

Menand provides an explanation for why there is a modern tendency to rely on procedures that are supported by professional standards:

In societies bent on transforming the past, and on treating nature itself as a process of ceaseless transformation, how do we trust the claim that a particular state of affairs is legitimate? The solution has been to shift the totem of legitimacy from premises to procedures. We know an outcome is right not because it was derived from immutable principles, but because it was reached by following the correct procedures. Science became modern when it was conceived not as an empirical confirmation of truths derived from an independent source, divine revelation, but as simply whatever followed from the pursuit of scientific methods of inquiry. If those methods were scientific, the result must be science. The modern conception of law is similar: if the legal process was adhered to, the outcome is just. Justice does not preexist the case at hand; justice is whatever result just procedures have led to.

(Menand, 2001: 432)

Procedures are important. As we have seen in this book, there are ways of doing things and getting things done in language testing that have come to be accepted by the language-testing community, in research and practice. Many more procedures relating to practice (see Unit A8) have come to be accepted by society as a fair way of distributing limited opportunities to members of society, despite postmodern critiques of testing. But correct procedure in itself cannot ensure that the meaning of test scores and their uses are fair, any more than following strict legal procedures will result in just outcomes. Even Holmes (1919: 180), the legal arch-proceduralist, eventually had to use a theory to decide a case brought under the Sedition Act of 1789, when he ruled that freedom of speech is essential on the grounds that 'the best test of truth is the power of the thought to get itself accepted'.

The notion of validity as argument, indeed as *ongoing argument*, brings together two traditions. The first is to have agreed procedures both in research and in practice, even if these change and evolve over time. The second is to establish the pragmatic principle in language testing that the test *is* its effect. Negative effects may be shown through (1) successfully challenging the warrants for test use, or (2) demonstrating that the use of a test does not have an associated argument. Effect-driven testing is a blending of procedure with fundamental virtue, and the fundamental virtue is simple: think about intended beneficial impact as the test is built, and be willing to knock it down when things change. We illustrate this with an extended task in Unit C10, a task that shows how the formalism of validational reasoning is manageable, if test developers work – always – with effect in mind.

Designing an argument for test validity and use that focuses on the weakest part of the confirmatory bias in the warrants, and exploring alternative interpretations of data, allow us to assuage doubt and create a space in which we may have enough certainty to test. For as Mill (1859: 25) says:

The steady habit of correcting and completing his own opinion by collating it with those of others, so far from causing doubt and hesitation in carrying it into practice, is the only stable foundation for a just reliance on it: for, being cognizant of all that can, at least obviously, be said against him, and having take up his position against all gainsayers – knowing that he has sought for objections and difficulties, instead of avoiding them, and has shut out no light which can be thrown upon the subject from any quarter – he has a right to think his judgement better than that of any person, or any multitude, who have not gone through a similar process.

Summary

This Unit has primarily been concerned with the metaphor of validity as argument. A validity argument can be constructed in a formal way that lays out the claims we wish to make about the meaning of test scores and how those claims may be supported by evidence. The formal validity argument also provides the infrastructure of a research agenda for us to test alternative interpretations in the on-going process of assuaging doubt.

We have argued that this approach to validity has a number of major advantages. The creation of validity arguments inextricably links validity claims to stated test purpose and therefore guides research. This is an efficient and effective way for allocating resources to the tasks that require the most attention. The approach also shows us that retrofitting test purpose, while not always illegitimate, cannot be undertaken without extensive validation efforts.

Above all, seeing validity as argument provides a framework within which we can conduct validity research in a principled way that allows the professional community to decide upon whether claims are satisfactorily established given our current state of knowledge. Or as Dewey (1938: 56–57) says:

The 'truth' of any present proposition is, by definition subject to the outcome of continued inquiries; *its* 'truth' if the word must be used, is provisional; as *near* the truth as inquiry has *as yet* come, a matter determined *not* by a guess at some future belief but by the care and pains with which inquiry has been conducted up to the present time.

SECTION B
Extension

Unit B1
Construct validity

The importance of the work of Cronbach and Meehl on construct validity cannot be overestimated. It was their seminal paper of 1955 that introduced the term to educational and psychological testing, and was immediately incorporated into the American Psychological Association's official documentation (APA, 1955, 1966). Although written from a particular philosophical perspective, it contains all the ideas that have led to our expanded understanding of validity, including Messick's (1989) unified concept of validity, and even validity as an argument to support claims. Shavelson et al. (2002: 5–6) write of Cronbach:

> His work on validity theory – the extent to which an interpretation of a test is conceptually and empirically warranted – was no less significant. With Paul Meehl, he placed this idea at the center of psychological, education, and social testing. Just as in other areas of science, for Lee [Cronbach] validation was a process of theory building and testing. Validation, a never-ending process, examined a proposed test interpretation – a construct – by testing it logically and empirically against counterinterpretations. Moreover, what was validated, according to Lee, was not the test itself, for a test could be used for many purposes (e.g., predication, diagnosis, placement). Rather, what was validated was a proposed interpretation.

Task B1.1

➤ Why do you think Cronbach argued that validation was 'a never ending process'?

The paper in this Unit represents at least two landmarks in testing and assessment. The first is that it introduces a strong theoretical component where the meaning of a test score needs to be established. Before this, validity was seen primarily as establishing a relationship between the test score and some external criterion using correlational methods. Secondly, it claims that variation in test scores is *caused* by the relative presence or absence of unobservable constructs in the test-taking population.

Text B1 L. J.
Cronbach and
P. E. Meehl

Lee J. Cronbach and Paul E. Meehl (1955) 'Construct validity in psychological tests.' *Psychological Bulletin* **52, 281–302.**

Four types of validation

The categories into which the *Recommendations* divide validity studies are: predictive validity, concurrent validity, content validity, and construct validity. The first two of these may be considered together as *criterion-oriented* validation procedures.

The pattern of a criterion-oriented study is familiar. The investigator is primarily interested in some criterion which he wishes to predict. He administers the test, obtains an independent criterion measure on the same subjects, and computes a correlation. If the criterion is obtained some time after the test is given, he is studying *predictive validity*. If the test score and criterion score are determined at essentially the same time, he is studying *concurrent validity*. Concurrent validity is studied when one test is proposed as a substitute for another (for example, when a multiple-choice form of spelling test is substituted for taking dictation), or a test is shown to correlate with some contemporary criterion.

Content validity is established by showing that the test items are a sample of a universe in which the investigator is interested. Content validity is ordinarily to be established deductively, by defining a universe of items and sampling systematically within this universe to establish the test.

Construct validation is involved whenever a test is to be interpreted as a measure of some attribute or quality which is not 'operationally defined.' The problem faced by the investigator is, 'What constructs account for variance in test performance?' Construct validity calls for no new scientific approach. [. . .] Construct validity is not to be identified solely by particular investigative procedures, but by the orientation of the investigator [. . .] When an investigator believes that no criterion available to him is fully valid, he perforce becomes interested in construct validity because this is the only way to avoid the 'infinite frustration' of relating every criterion to some more ultimate standard. In content validation, *acceptance* of the universe of content as defining the variable to be measured is essential. Construct validity must be investigated whenever no criterion or universe of content is accepted as entirely adequate to define the quality to be measured.

⭐ **Task B1.2**

Moss (1995) argues that one of the reasons for the impact of the notion of construct validity was the difficulty of finding an appropriate criterion or defining the 'universe of content'.

Search on-line for a language test for a particular profession. This may be a test of medical, legal or business English, for example. Ask yourself two questions:

➤ What would be an appropriate criterion with which this test could be correlated to provide validity evidence?

> From a brief inspection of the test content, could it be said that this is 'representative' of the communication and language use that one would expect within this domain?

We can distinguish among the four types of validity by noting that each involves a different emphasis on the criterion. In predictive or concurrent validity, the criterion behavior is of concern to the tester, and he may have no concern whatsoever with the type of behavior exhibited in the test. (An employer does not care if a worker can manipulate blocks, but the score on the block test may predict something he cares about.) Content validity is studied when the tester *is* concerned with the type of behavior involved in the test performance. Indeed, if the test is a work sample, the behavior represented in the test may be an end in itself. Construct validity is ordinarily studied when the tester has no definite criterion measure of the quality with which he is concerned, and must use indirect measures. Here the trait or quality underlying the test is of central importance, rather than either the test behavior or the scores on the criteria.

L. J. Cronbach and P. E. Meehl

Task B1.3

Performance tests, particularly those that involve simulation, are said to have grown out of the 'work sample' or 'job evaluation' approach to testing. In such tests we ask learners to actually do what they are expected to do in the 'real world'. The meaning of the test score can therefore only be generalized to the same tasks in a non-test context.

> Is it possible to recreate 'real world' performance in any test? Imagine one particular 'real world' activity. List the variables that might impact upon performance (sometimes called 'performance conditions').

> How many of these might you be able to include in a test?

Example of construct validation procedure. Suppose measure X correlates .50 with Y, the amount of palmar sweating induced when we tell a student that he has failed a Psychology I exam. Predictive validity of X for Y is adequately described by the coefficient, and a statement of the experimental and sampling conditions. If someone were to ask, 'Isn't there perhaps another way to interpret this correlation?' or 'What other kinds of evidence can you bring to support your interpretation?', we would hardly understand what he was asking because no interpretation has been made. These questions become relevant when the correlation is advanced as evidence that 'test X measures anxiety proneness.' Alternative interpretations are possible; e.g., perhaps the test measures 'academic aspiration,' in which case we will expect different results if we induce palmar sweating by economic threat. It is then reasonable to inquire about other *kinds* of evidence.

Add these facts from further studies: Test X correlates .45 with fraternity brothers' ratings on 'tenseness.' Test X correlates .55 with amount of intellectual inefficiency induced by painful electric shock, and .68 with the Taylor Anxiety scale. Mean X score decreases among four diagnosed groups in this order: anxiety state, reactive

L. J. Cronbach and P. E. Meehl

L. J. Cronbach
and P. E. Meehl

depression, 'normal,' and psychopathic personality. And palmar sweat under threat of failure in Psychology I correlates .60 with threat of failure in mathematics. Negative results eliminate competing explanations of the X score; thus, findings of negligible correlations between X and social class, vocational aim, and value-orientation make it fairly safe to reject the suggestion that X measures 'academic aspiration.' We can have substantial confidence that X does measure anxiety proneness if the current theory of anxiety can embrace the variables which yield positive correlations, and does not predict correlations where we found none.

[. . .]

The practical user of tests must rely on constructs of some generality to make predictions about new situations. Text X could be used to predict palmer sweating in the face of failure without invoking any construct, but a counselor is more likely to be asked to forecast behavior in diverse or even unique situations for which the correlation of test X is unknown. Significant predictions rely on knowledge accumulated around the generalized construct of anxiety.

★ Task B1.4

➤ Notice the use of the words 'generality' and 'generalized' in the preceding extract. What does the use of these words tell us about Cronbach and Meehl's view about score meaning in a test that is based on a construct interpretation?

Applied linguistics and language testing make use of many generalized constructs. Two of the most famous are 'fluency' and 'accuracy' (Brumfit, 1984).

➤ Would you expect 'fluency scores' to increase as 'accuracy scores' increase? Or would you expect there to be an inverse relationship? Why?

➤ How would you expect fluency and accuracy scores to relate to anxiety? Why?

L. J. Cronbach
and P. E. Meehl

Experimentation to investigate construct validity

Validation procedures

We can use many methods in construct validation [. . .]

Group differences. If our understanding of a construct leads us to expect two groups to differ on the test, this expectation may be tested directly. Thus Thurstone and Chave validated the Scale for Measuring Attitude Toward the Church by showing score differences between church members and nonchurchgoers. Churchgoing is not *the* criterion of attitude, for the purpose of the test is to measure something other than the crude sociological fact of church attendance; on the other hand, failure to find a difference would have seriously challenged the test.

[. . .]

Correlation matrices and factor analysis. If two tests are presumed to measure the same construct, a correlation between them is predicted. [. . .] If the obtained correlation departs from the expectation, however, there is no way to know whether the fault lies

L. J. Cronbach
and P. E. Meehl

in test A, test B, or the formulation of the construct. A matrix of intercorrelations often points out profitable ways of dividing the construct into more meaningful parts, factor analysis being a useful computational method in such studies.

[. . .]

Studies of internal structure. For many constructs, evidence of homogeneity within the test is relevant in judging validity. If a trait such as *dominance* is hypothesized, and the items inquire about behaviors subsumed under this label, then the hypothesis appears to require that these items be generally intercorrelated. Even low correlations, if consistent, would support the argument that people may be fruitfully described in terms of a generalized tendency to dominate or not dominate. The general quality would have power to predict behavior in a variety of situations represented by the specific items. Item-test correlations and certain reliability formulas describe internal consistency.

It is unwise to list uninterpreted data of this sort under the heading 'validity' in test manuals, as some authors have done. High internal consistency may *lower* validity. Only if the underlying theory of the trait being measured calls for high item intercorrelations do the correlations support construct validity. Negative item-test correlations may support construct validity, provided that the items with negative correlations are believed irrelevant to the postulated construct and serve as suppressor variables.

[. . .]

Studies of change over occasions. The stability of test scores ('retest reliability,' Cattell's 'N-technique') may be relevant to construct validation. Whether a high degree of stability is encouraging or discouraging for the proposed interpretation depends upon the theory defining the construct.

More powerful than the retest after uncontrolled intervening experiences is the retest with experimental intervention. If a transient influence swings test scores over a wide range, there are definite limits on the extent to which a test result can be interpreted as reflecting the typical behavior of the individual. These are examples of experiments which have indicated upper limits to test validity: studies of differences associated with the examiner in projective testing, of change of score under alternative directions ('tell the truth' vs. 'make yourself look good to an employer'), and of coachability of mental tests. We may recall Gulliksen's distinction: When the coaching is of a sort that improves the pupil's intellectual functioning in school, the test which is affected by the coaching has validity as a measure of intellectual functioning; if the coaching improves test taking but not school performance, the test which responds to the coaching has poor validity as a measure of this construct.

[. . .]

Studies of process. One of the best ways of determining informally what accounts for variability on a test is the observation of the person's process of performance. If it is supposed, for example, that a test measures mathematical competence, and yet observation of students' errors shows that erroneous reading of the question is common, the implications of a low score are altered.

[. . .]

Task B1.5

➤ Discuss each of the methods mentioned by Cronbach and Meehl to ensure that you understand what kind of study each would imply.

➤ For each method consider a study that you might conduct to investigate the construct validity of a test with which you are familiar.

L. J. Cronbach and P. E. Meehl

The logic of construct validation

Construct validation takes place when an investigator believes that his instrument reflects a particular construct, to which are attached certain meanings. The proposed interpretation generates specific testable hypotheses, which are a means of confirming or disconfirming the claim. The philosophy of science which we believe does most justice to actual scientific practice will now be briefly and dogmatically set forth [. . .]

The nomological net

The fundamental principles are these:

1   Scientifically speaking, to 'make clear what something *is*' means to set forth the laws in which it occurs. We shall refer to the interlocking system of laws which constitute a theory as a *nomological network*.
2   The laws in a nomological network may relate (*a*) observable properties or quantities to each other; or (*b*) theoretical constructs to observables; or (*c*) different theoretical constructs to one another. These 'laws' may be statistical or deterministic.
3   A necessary condition for a construct to be scientifically admissible is that it occur in a nomological net, at least *some* of whose laws involve observables. Admissible constructs may be remote from observation, i.e., a long derivation may intervene between the nomologicals which implicitly define the construct, and the (derived) nomologicals of type *a*. These latter propositions permit predictions about events. The construct is not 'reduced' to the observations, but only combined with other constructs in the net to make predictions about observables.
4   'Learning more about' a theoretical construct is a matter of elaborating the nomological network in which it occurs, or of increasing the definiteness of the components. At least in the early history of a construct the network will be limited, and the construct will as yet have few connections.
5   An enrichment of the net such as adding a construct or a relation to theory is justified if it generates nomologicals that are confirmed by observation or if it reduces the number of nomologicals required to predict the same observations. When observations will not fit into the network as it stands, the scientist has a certain freedom in selecting where to modify the network. That is, there may be alternative constructs or ways of organizing the net which for the time being are equally defensible.
6   We can say that 'operations' which are qualitatively very different 'overlap' or 'measure the same thing' if their positions in the nomological net tie them to the same construct variable.
    [. . .]

L. J. Cronbach
and P. E. Meehl

The preceding guide rules should reassure the 'toughminded,' who fear that allowing construct validation opens the door to nonconfirmable test claims. *The answer is that unless the network makes contact with observations, and exhibits explicit, public steps of inference, construct validation cannot be claimed.* An admissible psychological construct must be behavior-relevant. For most tests intended to measure constructs, adequate criteria do not exist. This being the case, many such tests have been left unvalidated, or a fine-spun network of rationalizations has been offered as if it were validation. Rationalization is not construct validation. One who claims that his test reflects a construct cannot maintain his claim in the face of recurrent negative results because these results show that his construct is too loosely defined to yield verifiable inferences.

A rigorous (though perhaps probabilistic) chain of inference is required to establish a test as a measure of a construct. To validate a claim that a test measures a construct, a nomological net surrounding the concept must exist. When a construct is fairly new, there may be few specifiable associations by which to pin down the concept. As research proceeds, the construct sends out roots in many directions, which attach it to more and more facts or other constructs. [. . .]

'Acceptance,' which was critical in criterion-oriented and content validities, has now appeared in construct validity. Unless substantially the same nomological net is accepted by the several users of the construct, public validation is impossible. If A uses *aggressiveness* to mean overt assault on others, and B's usage includes repressed hostile reactions, evidence which convinces B that a test measures *aggressiveness* convinces A that the test does not. Hence, the investigator who proposes to establish a test as a measure of a construct must specify his network or theory sufficiently clearly that others can accept or reject it.

Task B1.6

A study by Ely (1986) (extensively discussed in Johnson, 1993) posed the research question: 'What affective factors are associated with oral participation in the classroom?' In this piece of research Ely created an explicit nomological net, as shown.

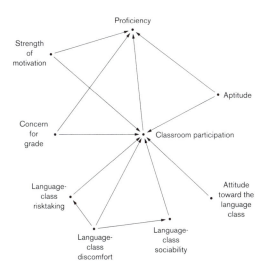

L. J. Cronbach
and P. E. Meehl

➤ For each arrow in the nomological network, suggest what the relationship between the constructs might be. Provide a reason for your decision. For example:

[concern for grade ──────────▶ proficiency]

As a learner's concern for getting higher grades increases, we would expect an increase/decrease in proficiency because . . .

 Task B1.7

➤ How would you measure 'classroom participation'?

➤ Select three or four other constructs from the nomological network and decide what *observable variables* would be associated with each construct.

L. J. Cronbach
and P. E. Meehl

Conclusions regarding the network after experimentation

[. . .] The network . . . generates a testable prediction about the relation of the tests scores to certain other variables, and the investigator gathers data. If prediction and result are in harmony, he can retain his belief that the test measures the construct. The construct is at best adopted, never demonstrated to be 'correct.'
  [. . .]
In any probable inductive type of inference from a pattern of observations, we examine the relation between the total network of theory and observations. The system involves propositions relating test to construct, construct to other constructs, and finally relating some of these constructs to observables. In ongoing research the chain of inference is very complicated . . . A predicted empirical relationship permits us to test all the propositions leading to that prediction.
  [. . .]

Implications of negative evidence

The investigator whose prediction and data are discordant must make strategic decisions. His result can be interpreted in three ways:

1. The test does not measure the construct variable.
2. The theoretical network which generated the hypothesis is incorrect.
3. The experimental design failed to test the hypothesis properly. [. . .]

  For further research. If a specific fault of procedure makes the third a reasonable possibility, his proper response is to perform an adequate study, meanwhile making no report. When faced with the other two alternatives, he may decide that his test does not measure the construct adequately. Following that decision, he will perhaps prepare and validate a new test. Any rescoring or new interpretative procedure for the original instrument, like a new test, requires validation *by means of a fresh body of data.*

L. J. Cronbach
and P. E. Meehl

[. . .]

The choice among alternatives, like any strategic decision, is a gamble as to which course of action is the best investment of effort. Is it wise to modify the theory? That depends on how well the system is confirmed by prior data, and how well the modifications fit available observations. Is it worth while to modify the test in the hope that it will fit the construct? That depends on how much evidence there is – apart from this abortive experiment – to support the hope, and also on how much it is worth to the investigator's ego to salvage the test. The choice among alternatives is a matter of research planning.

For practical use of the test. The consumer can accept a test as a measure of a construct only when there is a strong positive fit between predictions and subsequent data. When the evidence from a proper investigation of a published test is essentially negative, it should be reported as a stop sign to discourage use of the test pending a reconciliation of test and construct, or final abandonment of the test. If the test has not been published, it should be restricted to research use until some degree of validity is established. The consumer can await the results of the investigator's gamble with confidence that proper application of the scientific method will ultimately tell whether the test has value. Until the evidence is in, he has no justification for employing the test as a basis for terminal decisions.

Task B1.8

Think of a time when you have had to abandon a test before it came into use.

➤ What were the reasons for taking this decision?

➤ What did you do as a result?

Reporting of positive results

L. J. Cronbach
and P. E. Meehl

[. . .] The proper goals in reporting construct validation are to make clear (*a*) what interpretation is proposed, (*b*) how adequately the writer believes this interpretation is substantiated, and (*c*) what evidence and reasoning lead him to this belief. Without *a* the construct validity of the test is of no use to the consumer. Without *b* the consumer must carry the entire burden of evaluating the test research. Without *c* the consumer or reviewer is being asked to take *a* and *b* on faith. The test manual cannot always present an exhaustive statement on these points, but it should summarize and indicate where complete statements may be found.

[. . .]

To evaluate evidence calls for a statement like the conclusions from a program of research, noting what is well substantiated and what alternative interpretations have been considered and rejected. The writer must note what portions of his proposed interpretation are speculations, extrapolations, or conclusions from insufficient data. The author has an ethical responsibility to prevent unsubstantiated interpretations from appearing as truths. A claim is unsubstantiated unless the evidence for the claim is public, so that other scientists may review the evidence, criticize the conclusions, and offer alternative interpretations.

**L. J. Cronbach
and P. E. Meehl**

The report of evidence in a test manual must be as complete as any research report, except where adequate public reports can be cited. Reference to something 'observed by the writer in many clinical cases' is worthless as evidence. Full case reports, on the other hand, may be a valuable source of evidence so long as these cases are representative and negative instances receive due attention. The report of evidence must be interpreted with reference to the theoretical network in such a manner that the reader sees why the author regards a particular correlation or experiment as confirming (or throwing doubt upon) the proposed interpretation. Evidence collected by others must be taken fairly into account.

[. . .]

Confidence in a theory is increased as more relevant evidence confirms it, but it is always possible that tomorrow's investigation will render the theory obsolete.

★ Task B1.9

Consider again the test you selected for investigation in Task A1.8. Look at the website and any other test documentation that you have. Is there a test manual? Evaluate the documentation in terms of the coverage of:

➤ what interpretation is proposed

➤ how adequately the writer believes this interpretation is substantiated, and

➤ what evidence and reasoning lead him or her to this belief.

Summary

Cronbach and Meehl set out a theory of construct validity that impacts upon the way we think about and do testing today. As we have observed in Unit A1, they wrote as empirical realists; that is, they believed that the constructs they were attempting to describe were *real* – that they existed in the heads of the test takers. And they were empiricists because they argued that claims for construct validity could be made only on the basis of evidence. Even if researchers now hold that constructs are precisely that – something constructed in order to make the best interpretation of test scores possible – it does not detract from their achievement and legacy.

Note that throughout the text they use the word *claim* when talking about what we think test scores mean. We make such *claims* and then construct *arguments* to support those claims. We return to this topic in Unit B10, after we have looked at all the kinds of evidence and thinking that may contribute to an argument, which we consider in the units in between.

We conclude this Unit with another quotation from Cronbach (1984: 149):

Construct validity is a fluid, creative process. The test constructor or any subsequent investigator works to develop an interpretation, persuade others of its soundness, and revise it as inadequacies are recognized. The interpretation has scientific aspects, but it often embodies policies and suggests practical actions. This complexity means that validation cannot be reduced to rules, and no interpretation can be considered the final word, established for all time.

Unit B2
Pedagogic assessment

In recent years the applicability of validity theory to the classroom has been questioned. This does not mean that the basic principles may not be applicable, but that the extensive theory building and empirical investigation are not appropriate within the classroom. Furthermore, most classroom teachers do not have the time to invest in this kind of test development.

Rather, what is needed for the classroom is an approach to evaluation that is judged in terms of the consequences of the decisions made. These consequences are perceived in terms of improved learning outcomes for the individual students. Decisions within the classroom are primarily pedagogic. This does not mean that validity theory associated with large-scale testing is not relevant to the classroom. Some classroom assessment takes place in order to demonstrate that learning is aligned with external standards, or that students are achieving the goals laid out in a curriculum imposed by a national agency. This is the twilight zone, where classroom assessment and large-scale assessment meet. Teachers need to co-operate with others, perhaps in a local school district, a state, or nationally, to standardize assessment in such a way that any claims to have achieved external standards can be justified.

⭐ Task B2.1

➤ Is there an external curriculum that you have to teach to? Are there other 'standards' of achievement that your students have to meet?

➤ If there are, how does this affect your assessment practices?

The text in this Unit is by Pamela Moss from the University of Michigan. Over many years she has questioned the value of the validity paradigm in large-scale testing for other contexts. In the article that follows she considers one of her own classes in which she teaches research methodology, and asks whether the assumptions of validity theory hold.

She shows that teachers are able to look at their own aims and objectives within a particular learning context, and ask what would constitute 'valid assessment' for that context. We should not be slaves to the most dominant models of validity, or readily accept borrowed criteria. As we will see, this does not mean that there is a 'validity free-for-all', but that defensible criteria need to be creatively developed and implemented for local instructional needs.

As we follow Moss's description of her own class, you will be asked to describe and reflect on one of your own, in order to see how you are able to assess without frequent recourse to formal tests.

P. Moss (2003) 'Reconceptualizing validity for classroom assessment.' *Educational Measurement: Issues and Practice* 22, 4, 13–25

Text B2
P. Moss

A theory of validity, like any theory, provides us with an intellectual framework or set of conceptual tools that shape both our understanding (We 'use it to think with') and our actions. It illuminates some aspects of social phenomena for consideration and leaves others in the background. As Bernstein notes, an intellectual framework 'lend[s] weight to a sense of what are the important issues, the fruitful lines of research to pursue, the proper way of putting the issues.' Or, as the 1999 *Standards* puts it: 'it provides a frame of reference to assure that the relevant issues are addressed' (AERA et al., 1999, p. 2). The question I consider in this article is to what extent does our understanding of validity in the measurement profession 'assure that the relevant issues are addressed' in classroom assessment and what role might other theoretical perspectives play in providing a more robust validity framework to guide thinking and action?

Although I could certainly frame what I'm doing as a teacher in conventional psychometric validity terms – focusing on particular assessment-based interpretations and their uses; considering the propositions (Kane, 1992), aspects of validity (Messick, 1989), or categories of evidence (AERA et al., 1999) useful or necessary to evaluate the interpretation; and building my validity 'argument' (Cronbach, 1988) accordingly – this approach does not provide the most relevant general heuristic for designing and evaluating my assessment practice. While it is, at times, useful and relevant, it does not, I will argue, adequately illuminate or guide me in addressing a number of important issues. Other theoretical resources, both conceptions of validity and of how people learn, that derive from *interpretive* conceptions of social science have proven more broadly useful to me.

Task B2.2

In Units A1, A2 and A3 we look in some detail at validity theory.

➤ Is there any particular approach that you would find valuable within the context of the classroom? Explain why.

Assumptions of validity theory and alternative perspectives

P. Moss

. . . In addition to what I have learned from psychometrics, my thinking about my classroom assessment is increasingly informed by a sociocultural perspective on the nature of teaching and learning. Psychometric characterizations of learning – which infer learning from observed changes in individuals' performances over time – have been criticized for viewing learning only as something that takes place 'inside the head of the learner' and typically up through a vertical hierarchy of increasingly generalized and abstract knowledge and skills. From a sociocultural perspective, learning is perceived through changing relationships among the learner, the other human participants, and the tools (material and symbolic) available in a given context. Thus learning involves not only acquiring new knowledge and skill, but taking on a new identity and social position within a particular discourse or community of practice. As Wenger (1998) puts it, learning 'changes who we are' (p. 5) 'by changing our ability to participate, to belong' (p. 227) and 'to experience our life and the world as meaningful' (p. 5). This understanding has important implications for the design of a learning environment, including those aspects that we might distinguish as assessment.

[. . .]

Validity issues in one case of classroom assessment practice

The context of the class

Qualitative Methods in Educational Research is intended as a general introduction for doctoral students to various traditions of 'qualitative research.'

Our goals for the course are to provide: (a) a conceptual overview of a range of research traditions that have been associated with qualitative methods (including ethnography, critical discourse analysis, feminist poststructural research, and an etic version of qualitative research more congenial to quantitative social science; (b) the opportunity to produce an individual research proposal, reflecting each student's personal research interest, that is similar to what one might write for a small grant; (c) hands-on experience with particular qualitative methods each practiced from within the perspective of one of the research traditions studied; and (d) the opportunity to engage in ongoing critical reflection about different research practices and perspectives that highlight the validity, ethics, and consequences of the choices we make as researchers.

[. . .]

Each of the following sections begins with an explanation of the source of the 'assumption' from conventional validity theory, offers an alternative perspective from sociocultural and/or interpretive theory, and illustrates both by drawing on our experience in the qualitative research methods class.

Task B2.3

➤ Select a class that you currently teach. Describe the goals of the course as Moss does. Also describe the participants in the course, and what *they* wish to achieve from attending the course in addition to the goals that *you* set.

Conception of assessment: 'Assessment is a discrete activity'

P. Moss

Our very discipline, educational measurement, is predicated on the assumption that assessment can and should be considered as a discrete aspect of the context in which it is used – in this case, the context of learning and teaching . . . The conception of assessment as distinct from teaching and learning has consequences for the design of a learning environment. While from time to time I bring 'assessment' to the fore-ground as a discrete issue, I find it is artificial for me to separate out particular activities as 'assessment' when I design a learning environment and put it into motion.

When I design a course, I think about the kinds of *'practices'* that are important in the research *'communities'* for which I am preparing students to participate, the kinds of experiences they are likely to bring with them to the class, and the kinds of experiences I want them to have in class to provide resources for their learning.

[. . .]

In the qualitative research class, there are two major interrelated projects which are designed to engage students in the practices of qualitative research and learning about qualitative research: an individual research proposal and a collaborative research project where students study the process of developing research proposals. Each of these projects is broken down into a series of smaller activities that builds on the previous activities and introduces a new challenge. While these experiences provide rich opportunities for assessment, they are much more than that: they provide the focus around which learning is organized.

The *individual proposal* describes plans for a research project that draws on qualitative research methods located within a well articulated research perspective of their own choosing. We intend it to further each student's personal research agenda. The development of the proposal is scaffolded throughout the course: in the readings, in interim writing assignments, in class/lab time devoted to work within research support groups, and in individual conferences with the instructors. For the *collaborative research project*, students study the processes through which the individual proposals are developed, focusing especially on how individuals work with the resources and con-straints they experience within and beyond the class. We have designed a set of interrelated activities that give hands-on experience with four methods of qualitative research: analyzing open-ended surveys; conducting and analyzing interviews; taking, elaborating, and analyzing field-notes; and recording, transcribing, and analyzing group discourse, each practiced from within one of the research traditions explored in the course. These activities provide students with the crucial experience of being the subjects of research as well. Students finish the class with a small group pre-sentation regarding what they have learned about how novice researchers develop research proposals.

Certainly these activities serve purposes conventionally associated with assessment – informing instructional decisions, providing opportunities for self-assessment and feedback from others, monitoring learning, holding students accountable, and so on; equally importantly, they also provide students with opportunities to engage in the practice of qualitative research, not just as a learning exercise, but as an activity that can have purpose and meaning within and beyond the class. The activities generate the need for information that the readings provide and they generate problems that become the focus of class discussion about validity and ethics. The evidence-based conclusions that students develop from the group research project provide additional resources for teaching and learning. In Wenger's terms they allow students to build 'complex social relationships around meaningful activities . . . in which taking charge of learning becomes the enterprise of a community' (Wenger, p. 272). And they engage the classroom community 'in activities that |can| have consequences beyond their boundaries, so that students may learn what it takes to become effective in the world' (Wenger, p. 274). Thus, in this class at least, assessment becomes not so much a discrete set of activities, but rather a way of looking at the evidence available from the learning activities that focus students' 'practice' as learners and researchers.

Task B2.4

For the class that you described in Task B2.3, make a list of the types of tasks and activities that you ask the students to undertake.

➤ How does each task or activity relate to your goals?

➤ How do you observe the activities you have listed in order to:

- ■ inform instructional decisions?
- ■ provide opportunities for self-assessment and feedback from others?
- ■ monitor learning?
- ■ hold students accountable?

Focus of validity: 'The focus of validity theory is on an assessment based interpretation and use'

Conventionally, validity is conceptualized as referring to an inference or interpretation, and a use or action based on a test score. The 1999 *Standards* defines validity as 'the degree to which evidence and theory support the interpretations of test scores entailed by proposed uses of tests' (p. 9). As the authors of the standards assert: 'a rationale should be presented for *each* recommended interpretation and use of test scores, together with a comprehensive summary of the evidence and theory bearing on the intended use or interpretation' (p. 17, italics mine). Similarly Messick, defines validity as 'an integrated evaluative judgment of the degree to which empirical evidence and theoretical rationales support the adequacy and appropriateness of inferences and actions based on test scores or other modes of assessment' (1989, p. 13). Thus the validity argument (or judgment) focuses on *an* interpretation or action based on *an* instrument. While this focus is at times relevant and useful, it is both too small and too large for most of the decisions I need to make.

For much of what I do, I have no need to draw and warrant fixed interpretations of students' capabilities; rather, it is my job to help them make those interpretations obsolete. What I need to do is make decisions – moment-to-moment, day-to-day, course-to-course – that help students learn, as individuals and as members of learning communities and to study the effects of my decisions.

[. . .]

As mentioned previously, when I first design a class, I think in terms of the overall shape of the activities in the course rather than about single assessment instruments and the particular interpretation I can draw from them. And so, the focus on a single assessment activity is in this way too small to inform what I do. The validity of any particular assessment practice has to do with how it fits with the other assessment practices, in progression, to support (and illuminate) learning. And while each of these activities provides opportunities for us and the students to assess progress, each also serves the multiple purposes that I described.

In one very real sense, assessment is always ongoing: any time I interact with my students is an opportunity for me (and them) to learn about what they are learning and about the quality and effects of my own teaching. In fact, every move I make as a teacher responds to or anticipates a move by students, whether consciously or not. Even if I focus on the major assignments that students are required to turn in (four different components of the collaborative research project and four drafts of the individual proposal), the interpretations I draw are (hopefully) ephemeral and intended to inform next steps for them and for me.

My goal is to interact with students about their work in a way that supports their learning. This occurs in different ways for different assignments. For the components of the collaborative research project, we give relatively detailed written feedback, much like an editor would, inserted into lines of a draft and write summary comments that highlight what we perceive as strengths and areas in need of work. I keep a working list of issues that I want to be sure to address, but the feedback is not otherwise standardized; it responds to the unique features of each paper . . . For the research proposal, we meet with the students one on one (except for the final draft where written feedback is given in the manner described above). Here, we find the 'feedback' most needed is a conversation that helps draw out what they want to accomplish, that points them toward resources tailored to their interests, that helps brainstorm ways to accomplish their goals or imagine new goals, and/or that suggests ways to manage what seems like an overwhelming task. We keep written notes from these conversations to inform the next meeting. While we intend the feedback to promote rigorous standards of high-quality work, we do not give a grade or otherwise rank the papers into ordinal categories (more on this later). We also ask students to respond to one another's assignments in groups, usually with a series of questions as prompts, to give one another feedback. While I might be able to develop sounder interpretations, in a situation in which time is limited and evidence is continually available, it would be a relatively unproductive use of time to maximize the quality of any single interpretation.

Task B2.5

What kind of feedback do you give to students in your class?

➤ Do you give grades? If yes, why do you do this? Give good reasons to defend this practice.

➤ Do your students get feedback on their work from others? Who else could be involved in providing feeback? How might this be beneficial to your students?

P. Moss

Unit of analysis: 'The unit of analysis for an assessment is the individual'

The methods of educational measurement are most typically used to develop interpretations that characterize individuals, or rather, classes of individuals with the same scores. Group level interpretations are typically based on aggregates of individuals' scores. While other units of analysis could certainly be used, the most common unit of analysis is the individual. Whatever the unit of analysis, the associated scores must be comparable across units and contexts in which the assessment is used. This leads us to standardized assessment. To enhance comparability of scores, we attempt to control the influence of context through standardization – in essence, we attempt to *fix* the context – so that each individual experiences essentially the same test and contexts of administration. Thus context is treated as separable from inferences about the individual. And we typically make untested assumptions about the generalizability of students' performances from the testing situation to other contexts. As Messick notes, 'It is important to recognize that the *intrusion of context* raises issues more of generalizability than of interpretive validity. It gives testimony more to the ubiquity of interactions than to the fragility of score meaning' (Messick, 1989, pp. 14–15, italics mine). This emphasis on individual scores masks the complex role of the social context in shaping those scores and the interpretations they entail.

For the work students undertake in our classroom, the sort of standardization that enables comparability of scores is not feasible, nor would it be pedagogically sound to alter the tasks to make it so . . . Such standardization is not consistent with what students would experience doing qualitative work outside this class as competent members of a community of qualitative researchers. It does not allow students to build 'complex social relationships around meaningful activities' (Wenger, p. 272).

Even if we focus on the formal assignments in the qualitative methods class, students' experience of them is necessarily and appropriately complex, varied, and partially unique. While students' performances are shaped by the written descriptions of these assignments, which all students see, they are also shaped by a myriad of factors, including the choices students make (e.g., about how to focus their research proposal), by the always partially unique data they encounter in the collaborative project, by the particular class readings and the readings students locate on their own; by their ongoing interactions about their work with other students in the class, with us as instructors, and with their advisors (who often become actively involved in the research proposal); and by more formal feedback from the instructors which is itself tailored to the unique features of each paper. And, of course it is shaped by students' interpretations of the task which, in turn, is shaped by all the perspectives and practices that students bring with them to class from their own experiences outside of class. A change in any one of these features may well affect (a little or a lot) the nature of the 'assessment' for a single student, a group of students, or the entire class. In order to interpret and/or evaluate a student's performance, I need to understand the influence of the contexts in which it was produced and to understand the factors that shape that performance.

Consistent with a sociocultural perspective, the most appropriate unit of analysis is the *social situation* – which entails the recursive relationship between person and context (including the actions of other people, available resources, and larger social structures in which they are encountered) – and claims about individuals must be grounded in *interaction*. Understanding students' performance in context is also crucial to enhancing fairness with more and less standardized assessments.

Task B2.6

➤ How do you take account of individual variability in your classroom assessment?

➤ Can you list the factors that are 'standardized' in a formal test, which we do not consider when evaluating learners in a classroom context?

Combining evidence: 'Interpretations are constructed by aggregating judgments from discrete pieces of evidence to form an interpretable overall score'

P. Moss

Having multiple sources/pieces of evidence to inform a consequential interpretation/decision is a fundamental feature of the epistemology and ethics in any of the social science perspectives that I have encountered. Similarly, although it is framed in different ways in different social science disciplines, illuminating and challenging (disabling) biases is also fundamental. The practices of educational measurement are flush with techniques for aggregating evidence to an overall score, with associated standard error(s), from which interpretations/decisions can be made; however, they have very little to offer when aggregation is not possible or desirable. Thus while certain types and combinations of evidence lend themselves well to measurement perspectives, others do not. Aggregation entails that (at least categorical) judgments be made about discrete pieces of information so that once an assessment system is developed, these judgments can be algorithmically combined (weighted and accumulated) to form a 'score' that has a predetermined interpretation associated with it. The very definition of validity in the testing *Standards* associates it with test scores. 'Validity refers to the degree to which evidence and theory support the interpretations of test scores entailed by proposed uses of tests' (AERA et al., 1999, p. 9). The AFT, NCME, and NEA *Standards for Teacher Competence in Educational Assessment of Students* asserts that 'teachers should be skilled in administering, scoring and interpreting the results of . . . teacher produced assessment methods' which includes 'being able to use guides for scoring essay questions and projects, stencils for scoring response choice questions, and scales for rating performance assessments . . . [to] produce consistent results.' That assessment items are 'scored' (i.e., result in at least categorical judgments) seems to be taken for granted. I have at least two concerns about this assumption and the methodological advice associated with it: (a) it is inadequate to inform a large part of my practice as a teacher and (b) it risks shaping my practice to conform to its vision of assessment. Where conventional psychometric tools fit, I would certainly use them; where they do not, I need other sorts of advice.
[. . .]
In the qualitative methods class, there are many sources of evidence and conceptual lenses for analyzing them that could inform my interpretation of each student's practice and trajectory toward becoming a competent researcher (and my own progress toward becoming a better teacher). These include not only what students have produced in response to the multiple formal assignments, but how they engaged the tasks as evidenced through successful drafts, ongoing conversations, and observations of their interactions with others, and my knowledge of what resource they had available to them to support this work. The appropriateness of using these different sources of evidence depends on the purposes to which the interpretations are put.

P. Moss

[. . .]

Having multiple sources of evidence gathered across time and situation enhances the validity of an interpretation. If I do not have enough evidence to address an issue that I believe needs to be addressed, I can seek additional evidence. The vigorous attempt to discover problems with the proposed interpretation – the search for disconfirmatory evidence and for alternative interpretations that account for the same evidence – is central to the development of well warranted interpretations. The interpretation and supporting evidence are best presented in such a way that the reader (or listener), including the student, can evaluate the interpretations and supporting evidence for himself or herself and be allowed to offer counter interpretations and counter examples . . . valid interpretations are justified, not imposed, on the person(s) about whom they are made. Having multiple readers (interpreters) contributes to the strength of the validity of the interpretation. This can involve an independent evaluation of the same evidence or an audit of the trail of evidence leading to the conclusions. While agreement among readers may be a welcome outcome, disagreement is also a validity resource.

★ Task B2.7

Moss takes the view that judgments about learner progress should be based in multiple sources of evidence, often evaluated by a number of different people in order to counteract the bias that may be present if just one person makes a judgment. If these people do not agree, it is a source for debate and discussion that throws further light upon the judgments being made. Furthermore, the learner is involved in the process.

➤ How realistic would this be in your educational setting?

P. Moss

Role of consequences: 'Consequences are an aspect of validity only if they can be traced to a source of construct underrepresentation or construct irrelevant variance'

The relationship between validity and consequences remains controversial within the field of educational measurement. The perspective characterized above, which sees a limited role for consequences in the understanding of validity, can be traced to Messick (1989) and the testing *Standards* . . . Others see a larger role for consequences in their conception of validity, focusing on whether the test serves the purpose it was intended to serve and on unintended (positive and negative) consequences.

Whatever one's definition of validity, with classroom assessment, understanding these effects is crucial to sound practice. I might go so far as to argue that validity in classroom assessment – where the focus is on enhancing students' learning – is primarily about consequences. Assuming interpretations are intended to inform instructional decisions and that instructional decisions entail interpretations about students' learning, it is on evidence of their (immediate, long-range, and cumulative) effects on which their validity primarily rests. The insistence on interactional evidence at various grain sizes – for understanding an action in the context in which it was produced and received – also highlights the central role of consequences in validity.

[. . .]

Informal consideration of interactional evidence [. . .] helped me make the decision to abandon grades, whenever possible. I had always found the giving of grades to require a substantial commitment of time to develop a meaningful rubric and assign scores fairly – time that took me away from tasks that seemed to have a higher pedagogical value. I began to attend more explicitly to how they shaped my inter-actions with students about their work, both before and after the assignment of the grade. Conversations too frequently focused on what I wanted, on what I (could specify I) considered necessary for an A, or on the way a higher grade than the one I had assigned was fair. When I gave students opportunities to revise their work to improve the grade or I postponed the giving of a grade until revised versions were turned in, I found the revision typically accomplished just what I had asked for and nothing more. As Shepard (2003) notes: 'competitive grading practices seem to be so pervasive in U.S. classrooms that the purpose of rubrics has been corrupted from criteria that make the features of excellent work accessible into a point system used for defending and quarrelling over grades' (p. 176). I don't want the capital in my classroom to be grades or even my approval; it will not sustain students (as professionals) outside the class-room. I want it to be doing something that is meaningful and useful within the context of classroom and the relevant research communities.

Task B2.8

★

➤ How are grades used in your teaching situation?

➤ Are these uses valuable in an educational setting?

➤ Who wants grades? What are the arguments for keeping them?

The role of cases in validity theory

P. Moss

The most basic question underlying this article is what role cases of assessment practice should play in the development and/or representation of validity theory and assessment pedagogy? A straightforward answer is that the principles are necessarily general and that we need cases to illustrate how they can be instantiated in practice.

[. . .]

In the context of classroom assessment and of validity research more generally, we need to develop and maintain a rich repertoire of cases: not just those that illustrate how our guiding principles can be thoughtfully applied but, equally important, those that have not already been shaped by our principles so that we can learn about their limitations . . . These cases provide us with vicarious experiences of how successful teachers create learning environments and evaluate their students' work using evidence based in interaction. Moreover, they position us (productively), not as the experts whose role it is to reshape these environments in our own images of what constitutes good assessment, but as fellow learners who can think with teachers and teacher educators about how to conceptualize validity to be of use in particular contexts of assessment.

[. . .]

P. Moss

Careful consideration of concrete cases and of alternative conceptions of validity, taken together with the willingness to risk our own preconceptions, can only strengthen the epistemological moorings of our profession and our ability to be of use to others.

★ Task B2.9

➤ Write up your responses to the other tasks in this Unit as a case study. Add a conclusion to your case study explaining what your own practice tells you about the meaning of validity within that particular context.

Summary

Moss provides a reflective commentary on her own teaching practice. This is a case study of one particular course and how she combines assessment with teaching. She argues that the paradigm of large-scale assessment does not provide a useful context for the goals and philosophy of her classroom, and as a result arrives at some radical decisions such as not issuing grades at all.

However, Moss takes the concept of *validity* very seriously. She still has to make inferences about what the students in her class can do, and this involves collecting evidence for what they can do. But as the focus is on learning, the interpretation of the evidence involves the learner and other judges who discuss the evidence and inferences for the purpose of learning. Within this paradigm the notion of standardizing assessment practices (see Unit A8) is not only irrelevant but potentially harmful.

From a strong theoretical perspective, Moss makes us aware that while there is a place for large-scale testing, its theory and practice, these should not be uncritically imported into the classroom

Unit B3
Investigating communicative competence

The excerpts in this Unit come from an extremely influential paper in both the testing and teaching of languages, Canale and Swain's 1980 discussion of theoretical models of language ability. Prior to this paper, language teaching (and testing) was dominated by a fairly narrow vision of linguistic ability. The paper opened the door to a wider array of language skills as viable elements of classrooms and of tests.

Task B3.1

➤ Why do you think it is important to expand our view of language as a human ability? Certainly, human language is a complex mental system, but what of Ockham's Razor (see p. 20) – all else being equal, are simpler explanations of complex phenomena better than complicated and detailed models?

For perhaps the only time in our book, we will go out on a limb and answer one of our own tasks – but only in part. We believe that the previous question has no correct answer. The real challenge is in thorough exploration of both extremes: complex versus simple models of mental phenomena.

M. Canale and M. Swain (1980) 'Theoretical bases of communicative approaches to second language teaching and testing.' *Applied Linguistics* 1, 1, 1–47

Text B3
M. Canale and
M. Swain

[. . .]

Grammatical and communicative approaches

For our purposes it is useful to make a general distinction between grammatical (or grammar-based) and communicative (or communication-based) approaches to second language teaching. In choosing these particular terms we hope to avoid the confusion that has resulted from use of the more inclusive terms 'formal' and 'functional' (cf. Stern 1978 for discussion). By a grammatical approach we mean one that is organized on the basis of linguistic, or what we will call grammatical forms (i.e. phonological forms, morphological forms, syntactic patterns, lexical items) and emphasizes the ways in which these forms may be combined to form grammatical

M. Canale and
M. Swain

sentences. Most teaching materials currently in use in general second language courses are organized along these lines: for example, the Lado English series and the series Le français international. A communicative (or functional/notional) approach on the other hand is organized on the basis of communicative functions (e.g. apologizing, describing, inviting, promising) that a given learner or group of learners needs to know and emphasizes the ways in which particular grammatical forms may be used to express these functions appropriately. Second language textbooks developed within this framework, such as the Challenges series (Abbs et al. 1978) and the series Communicate (Johnson and Morrow 1978), have begun to appear but are in general limited to English as a second language.

A third approach referred to quite often in recent work on second language teaching is the situational syllabus (cf. Morrow 1977, Munby 1978, Wilkins 1976). This approach is organized primarily with reference to the particular settings (or situations) in which the learner may need to perform in the second language. Ockenden's (1972) *Situational dialogues* is cited frequently as an example of teaching material developed from this perspective. While it is clear that the three approaches are logically distinct, in this paper situational syllabuses will simply be subsumed under either the grammatical or communicative approach. There are two reasons for this decision. First, as has been pointed out by Morrow (1977), grammatical syllabuses often present the grammatical forms under study in dialogues or contexts that are labelled 'situations'. However, to the extent that the basis of syllabus organization is the grammatical forms and not the situations themselves, the approach is essentially a grammatical one. Second, to the extent that the main reasons for including a given situation in a situational syllabus are to respond to the learner's sociocultural needs and to generate appropriate language, there seems to be sufficient overlap in objectives between situational approaches and communicative approaches to justify relaxing the distinction. The work of Johnson and Morrow (1978) illustrates this point quite clearly.

Other types of approaches are of course possible and have surfaced in second language research and materials (cf. Candlin 1977 and Cook 1978 for discussion). Again, although we think that these approaches are all logically distinct, we will not distinguish them here in view of the overlap of their main objectives and those of the grammatical or communicative approaches.

The brief descriptions of grammatical and communicative approaches provided above are intended to serve as general working definitions throughout the rest of this paper. Also, although it should be clear, it is important to note that the term 'approach' is used here to refer to principles of syllabus construction and not to actual classroom teaching materials and methods (cf. Wilkins 1978 for such a use of this term).

★ **Task B3.2**

A syllabus is an ordered sequence of study for use in (typically) a time-limited teaching setting: a sixteen-week academic term, for instance, with three class meetings per week. The syllabus of that class sets forth the manner and order of activities and goals by which the teaching will proceed.

➤ Above – and very early in their article – Canale and Swain discuss syllabus organization, teaching approaches, and various decisions made on what shall and shall not enter into the classroom: for example, dialogues, situations and grammatical forms. Why do you think a discussion of syllabus design is in this paper, and early on?

Canale and Swain do proceed to outline a theory of communicative competence, in a segment of the paper that has achieved bedrock status among the literature in language studies.

[. . .]

M. Canale and M. Swain

Toward an adequate theory of communicative competence

In this section we will first present a set of guiding principles for a communicative approach to second language teaching, then outline a theory of communicative competence adequate to support such an approach, and finally sketch some of the implications of such a theory for second language teaching and testing.

Guiding principles for a communicative approach

Based primarily on the discussion so far in this paper, there seem to be five important principles that must guide the development of a communicative approach for a general second language programme.

1. Communicative competence is composed minimally of grammatical competence, sociolinguistic competence, and communication strategies, or what we will refer to as strategic competence . . . There is no strong theoretical or empirical motivation for the view that grammatical competence is any more or less crucial to successful communication than is sociolinguistic competence or strategic competence. The primary goal of a communicative approach must be to facilitate the integration of these types of knowledge for the learner, an outcome that is not likely to result from overemphasis on one form of competence over the others throughout a second language programme.

2. A communicative approach must be based on and respond to the learner's communication needs. These needs must be specified with respect to grammatical competence (e.g. the levels of grammatical accuracy that are required in oral and written communication), sociolinguistic competence (e.g. needs relating to setting, topic, communicative functions), and strategic competence (e.g. the compensatory communication strategies to be used when there is a breakdown in one of the other competencies).

3. The second language learner must have the opportunity to take part in meaningful communicative interaction with highly competent speakers of the language, i.e. to respond to genuine communicative needs in realistic second language situations. This principle is a challenging one to teachers and programme designers, but is motivated strongly by the theoretical distinction between communicative competence and communicative performance. It is significant not only with respect to classroom activities but to testing as well. J. B. Carroll (1961) has argued for testing in more realistic communicative settings (i.e. performance) as follows:

> If we limit ourselves to testing only one point at a time, more time is ordinarily allowed for reflection than would occur in a normal communication situation, no matter how rapidly the discrete items are presented.
>
> (p. 34)

We think that exposure to realistic communication situations is crucial if communicative competence is to lead to communicative confidence.

4. Particularly at the early stages of second language learning, optimal use must be made of those aspects of communicative competence that the learner has developed through acquisition and use of the native language and that are common to those communication skills required in the second language. It is especially important that the more arbitrary and less universal aspects of communication in the second language (e.g. certain features of the grammatical code) be presented and practiced in the context of less arbitrary and more universal aspects (e.g. the fundamental appropriateness conditions in making a request, the basic rules of discourse involved in greeting a peer).

5. The primary objective of a communication-oriented second language programme must be to provide the learners with the information, practice, and much of the experience needed to meet their communicative needs in the second language. In addition, the learners should be taught about language primarily (although not exclusively) in the first language programme, i.e. taught, for example, about grammatical categories, communicative functions, appropriateness conditions, rules of discourse, and registers. The learners should also be taught about the second language culture primarily (although not exclusively) through the social studies programme in order to provide them with the sociocultural knowledge of the second language group that is necessary in drawing inferences about the social meanings or values of utterances (cf. Widdowson 1978 for discussion of these points). It is felt that such a curriculum-wide approach to the development of communicative competence in the second language may also facilitate (and perhaps encourage – cf. Savignon 1972) continued study of this language (cf. Van Ek 1976 on this point).

A proposed theoretical framework for communicative competence

Our own tentative theory of communicative competence minimally includes three main competencies: grammatical competence, sociolinguistic competence, and strategic competence. The purpose of this section is to briefly outline the contents and boundaries of each of these areas of competence.

[. . .]

Grammatical competence. This type of competence will be understood to include knowledge of lexical items and of rules of morphology, syntax, sentence-grammar semantics, and phonology. It is not clear that any particular theory of grammar can at present be selected over others to characterize this grammatical competence, nor in what ways a theory of grammar is directly relevant for second language pedagogy (cf. Chomsky 1973 on this point), although the interface between the two has been addressed in recent work on pedagogical grammars (cf. Allen and Widdowson 1974 for example). Nonetheless, grammatical competence will be an important concern for any communicative approach whose goals include providing learners with the knowledge of how to determine and express accurately the literal meaning of utterances.

Sociolinguistic competence. This component is made up of two sets of rules; sociocultural rules of use and rules of discourse. Knowledge of these rules will be crucial in interpreting utterances for social meaning, particularly when there is a low level of transparency between the literal meaning of an utterance and the speaker's intention.

Sociocultural rules of use will specify the ways in which utterances are produced and understood appropriately with respect to the components of communicative events outlined by Hymes (1967, 1968). The primary focus of these rules is on the extent to which certain propositions and communicative functions are appropriate within a given sociocultural context depending on contextual factors such as topic, role of participants, setting, and norms of interaction. A secondary concern of such rules is the extent to which appropriate attitude and register or style are conveyed by a particular grammatical form within a given sociocultural context. For example, it would generally be inappropriate for a waiter in a restaurant to actually command a client to order a certain menu item, regardless of how the proposition and communicative function were expressed grammatically; likewise, inappropriate attitude and register would be expressed if a waiter in a tasteful restaurant were to ask, 'O.K., chump, what are you and this broad gonna eat?' in taking an order. It should be emphasized that it is not clear that all of the components of speech events that Hymes and others have proposed are always necessary to account for the appropriateness of utterances or that these are always the only components that need to be considered.

Until more clear-cut theoretical statements about rules of discourse emerge, it is perhaps most useful to think of these rules in terms of the cohesion (i.e. grammatical links) and coherence (i.e. appropriate combination of communicative functions) of groups of utterances (cf. Halliday and Hasan 1976 and Widdowson 1978 for discussion). It is not altogether clear to us that rules of discourse will differ substantively from grammatical rules (with respect to cohesion) and sociocultural rules (with respect to coherence). However, the focus of rules of discourse in our framework is the combination of utterance and communicative functions and not the grammatical well-formedness of single utterance nor the sociocultural appropriateness of a set of proposition and communicative functions in a given context. Also, rules of discourse will presumably make reference to notions such as topic and comment (in the strict linguistic sense of these terms) whereas grammatical rules and sociocultural rules will not necessarily do so (cf. Widdowson 1978).

Strategic competence. This component will be made up of verbal and non-verbal communication strategies that may be called into action to compensate for breakdowns in communication due to performance variables or to insufficient competence. Such strategies will be of two main types: those that relate primarily to grammatical competence (e.g. how to paraphrase grammatical forms that one has not mastered or cannot recall momentarily) and those that relate more to sociolinguistic competence (e.g. various role-playing strategies, how to address strangers when unsure of their social status). Knowledge of how to use such strategies may be particularly helpful at the beginning stages of second language learning, and it is to be expected that the need for certain strategies may change as a function of age and second language proficiency. Furthermore, as Stern (1978) has pointed out, such 'coping' strategies are most likely to be acquired through experience in real-life communication situations but not through classroom practice that involves no meaningful communication.

Task B3.3

★

The excerpt above is the heart of the paper. It is a splendid example of a salient moment in history at which a new perspective is presented. Arguably, it is the

M. Canale and
M. Swain

birth of a paradigm. Certainly, this is theory-building at its most challenging and exciting.

➤ Re-read the paragraph beginning 'Until more clear-cut . . .' The authors mention the existence of one area of language ability (discourse) but they defer discussion of it in the 1980 paper.

Canale wrote a subsequent paper (1983b) in which he set forth a model of discourse competence. As we show in Unit A3, the 'Canale and Swain model' is often portrayed as containing four components: grammatical, sociolinguistic, strategic and discourse competencies. However, the fourth one took a few more years to work out.

➤ Why do you suppose that happened? Think about discourse control of language ability in languages that you teach or have studied. Consider matters of extended control of the language – across long arcs of conversation, or through long stretches of written discourse. What are the particular challenges to describing that ability, and how do those challenges reflect the paragraph ('Until more clear-cut . . .') of interest here?

Our book is not about syllabus design, nor is it about modelling language ability. It is about testing. While the above excerpt is the heart of theory in Canale and Swain's paper, later they turn to testing.

M. Canale and
M. Swain

[. . .]

Implications for a communicative testing programme

Two important general implications of our theoretical framework for testing communication in a second language are the following.

First, . . . communicative testing must be devoted not only to what the learner knows about the second language and about how to use it (competence) but also to what extent the learner is able to actually demonstrate this knowledge in a meaningful communicative situation (performance). It has been emphasized quite frequently (e.g. by J. B. Carroll 1961, Clark 1972, Jones 1977, Morrow 1977, Oller 1976) that pencil-and-paper tests now in use do not necessarily give a valid indication of second language learners' skills in performing in actual communicative situations. Our theoretical framework suggests the general boundaries and contents of communicative competence that are necessary and important for this type of performance. We think that it is important to empirically study the extent to which competence-oriented tests are valid indicators of learners' success in handling actual performance. However, actual performance tasks such as those dealt with in the FSI Oral Proficiency Interview or those developed by Savignon (1972) would seem to have more face validity with respect to communication skills in that such tasks correspond more directly to normal language use where an integration of these skills is required with little time to reflect on and monitor language input and output (as noted by J. B. Carroll 1961 and mentioned above). One would thus not want to ignore performance tests completely in a

M. Canale and
M. Swain

communicative testing programme even if more competence-oriented tests that correlated highly with actual performance were developed (cf. Clark 1972 – quoted above – on this point). However, one might wish to make more use of performance test (tasks) informally in the classroom and perhaps at stages other than the initial ones in second language study so as not to risk frustrating the beginner (cf. Morrow 1977 and the findings on integrative motivation presented by Savignon 1972 [. . .]).

Second, although it has been argued that integrative type tests must be used to measure communicative competence (e.g. Oller 1976), it seems that discrete-point tests will also be used in our proposed communicative approach. This is because such tests may be more effective than integrative tests in making the learner aware of and in assessing the learner's control of the separate components and elements of communicative competence. This type of test would also seem to be easier to administer and score in a reliable manner than is a more integrative type of test. While it also seems that discrete-point tests may be more suitable for assessing communicative competence and integrative ones more suitable for assessing actual communicative performance, this may not necessarily be a rigid division of labour. For example, a test designed to assess grammatical accuracy might be considered to have more of a discrete-point orientation if it consisted of items such as (1).

(1) Select the correct preposition to complete the following sentence:
     We went __ the store by car.
     (a) at; (b) on; (C) for; (d) to.

but more of an integrative orientation if it were composed of items such as (2).

(2) The sentence underlined below may be either grammatically correct or incorrect. If you think it is correct, go on to the next item; if you think it is incorrect, correct it by changing, adding, or deleting only one of its elements.

     We went at the store by car.

That is, it is possible to view the discrete-point versus integrative distinction as a continuum along which tests of communicative competence and tests of actual communicative performance may be arranged (cf. Davies 1975 for discussion of this point).

Aside from these general implications, a more elaborate and fine-grained description of our theoretical framework will also guide selection of evaluation criteria and acceptable levels of proficiency at different stages of second language study. Such selection will be informed primarily by the specification and sequencing of behavioural objectives, cognitive-semantic notions, grammatical forms, communicative functions, and sociolinguistic variables. Work in these areas . . . seems quite promising, and should be of help in fleshing out our theoretical framework and its implications.

There are, of course, several aspects of test development for which our theoretical framework has less than obvious implications. For example, it is not clear how reliable scoring procedures are to be established with respect to the appropriateness of utterances in various sociocultural and discourse contexts. Also, there is no obvious basis for generalizing attested performance in a given context to expected performance in another context or for weighting different aspects of the theoretical framework or different evaluation criteria. Nor is it clear that criterion-referenced testing is to be

M. Canale and
M. Swain

preferred to norm-referenced testing on the basis of this framework; we suspect that this is a separate issue [. . .]

Task B3.4

This is a particularly fascinating excerpt, especially given the years that have elapsed since the paper's publication. Canale and Swain are concerned about the implications of their model for testing, and in particular, they point to certain dilemmas such as 'how reliable scoring procedures are to be established'.

➤ Consider our book, which you are currently studying. Consider your experience as a language learner. Consider your experience teaching languages and developing language tests.

➤ Then list out all the concerns (like scoring reliability) which Canale and Swain detail in their excerpts along with definite proposals that they make (such as their claim that discrete-point tests would survive a theory like theirs).

➤ What actually has come to pass? Draw from your own experiences. Alternatively – and this could yield a publishable paper, we believe – do a literature review and a study of existing language test manuals and websites. What influence did Canale and Swain actually have on the subsequent quarter-century?

Canale and Swain do not limit themselves to suggestions about test development. They close the paper with a closely articulated research agenda, and one item (in particular) is of interest given modern testing's concern with washback (which we discuss elsewhere, see Units A5 and B5). It is a single paragraph, but it is one we feel remains quite strikingly relevant even today.

M. Canale and
M. Swain

Finally, it must be determined whether or not and to what extent a communicative approach increases learners' motivation to learn, and teachers' motivation to teach the second language (as suggested by Palmer 1978). We think that it is likely that both learners and teachers will find the task of learning/teaching such communicative functions as how to greet someone more useful and enjoyable than the task of learning/teaching different grammatical points such as verb tenses. Of course, such grammatical points will be covered in the classroom, but only to the extent that they are necessary to carry out a given communicative function; in this sense a communicative approach may be likened somewhat to the coating on the pill. It is also important to remember that without motivation, learners who have an adequate level of communicative competence may not have the desire to perform well in the second language; thus such students may do quite well on more competence-oriented communicative tests but quite poorly on more performance-oriented ones. In our view, sustained learner and teacher motivation may be the single most important factor in determining the success of a communicative approach relative to a grammatical one, perhaps important enough to compensate to a large extent for the various short-comings of communicative approaches that we have tried to identify.

Task B3.5

➤ If communicative language teaching necessitates a broader view of language performance as well as language competence, and if such a broader view should help to motivate students, then is it also the case that a broad test that covers many competencies should cause better washback? Put another way, when applied to test design, does the Canale and Swain model improve washback? At the end of the above excerpt, they seem to take a more nuanced view of the matter. They note that 'students may do quite well on competence-oriented communicative tests but quite poorly on more performance-oriented ones'. Does positive washback depend on test success, or could washback be enhanced even on a communicative performance test, one where some students would score 'quite poorly'? Finally, bear in mind that 'washback' did not exist in the scholarly literature at the time of the Canale and Swain paper. Do you think that Canale and Swain would have written something different had they had that concept at hand?

Summary

This unit explores excerpts from a major, influential paper in second-language education and testing. Our tasks were designed to engage critically some of the claims and discussion in the paper and to relate it to newer concepts that have emerged since its writing (e.g. washback). Of greatest importance is the historical role now assumed by the work of Canale and Swain. We suspect that terms like 'strategic competence' have become part of your daily professional lexicon.

Unit B4
Optimal specification design

The unifying theme for the excerpted readings here is the question: what is the optimal design for a test specification? What should it include? Should all specs have common elements, or should the design of the spec reflect vexations that arise as the specs are written?

 Task B4.1

➤ Before studying the excerpts here, pull some tests from your archives. These can be tests that you developed yourself or assessments developed in collaboration with others. Look across several seemingly different tests. Try to re-live the debates that followed – within yourself or with colleagues: can you identify any similar debates across different tests? For example, did you grapple with the clarity of the instructions? With the choice of item type? Make notes of the problems that you encountered, and as you read through the material below, see if any of them relate to the problems posed by Davidson and Lynch, beginning with what is maybe an original vexation of all test creation – the distinction between that which is given to a test taker (a prompt) and whatever the test taker is expected to do as a result (a response).

Text B4
F. Davidson and
B. K. Lynch

F. Davidson and B. K. Lynch (2002) *Testcraft: A Teacher's Guide to Writing and Using Language Test Specifications*. **New Haven and London: Yale University Press. Chapter 3, 'Problems and issues in specification writing', pp. 34–59**

The difference between the PA and the RA

At the heart of all human behavioral assessment is the contrast between a 'prompt' and a 'response'. The former is the input to the examinee: whatever he or she sees or hears. The latter is what the examinee does as a result. In this section, our examples and discussions concern this prompt/response contrast, and we emphasize that it is not always easy to detect. Our exercises below focus on that detection . . . our general model of test specification is derived from Popham's work and uses the terms 'PA' (Prompt Attributes) and 'RA' (Response Attributes) for the distinction at issue here. Spec writers should describe fully the input material in the PA and then describe fully the criterion response in the RA. There are many other ways to phrase this distinction,

F. Davidson and
B. K. Lynch

for example 'characteristics of the input' versus 'characteristics of the expected response' (Bachman and Palmer 1996). But at the core of any workable spec is the input/response distinction – it must be specified somehow.

A very simple case of the PA/RA distinction concerns any multiple-choice question. Suppose the examinee faces an item like this after reading some text, for example, a newspaper editorial, in which the author takes sides on an issue:

> Clearly, the author disagrees with the majority viewpoint. It is also clear that the author is open to a change of perspective. How do we know this?
>
> a. The author states precisely a willingness to change.
> b. The phrase in line 10 'there may be some value to the opposing view if . . .' suggests a willingness to change.
> c. The title suggests a willingness to change.
> d. The comment near the end indicates a willingness to change: 'I may be persuaded if . . .'

The RA for the item above might simply read:

> The student will select the correct answer from among the choices given.

If that were the case, then the spec writer has decided on a rather minimalist approach to the PA/RA distinction. The only use of the RA is to indicate the actual physical action which the examinee will perform. An alternative RA might read like this:

> RA
> The student will study all four choices. He or she will reread the passage as needed to eliminate any choices given. If a particular choice references a particular line in the passage, the student will study that line carefully. Then the student will select the correct answer from among the choices given.

This RA specifies a multiple-choice process. Either of these RAs could work in conjunction with a PA something like the following:

> PA (excerpt)
> The item stem will pose a direct or indirect question about the author's own beliefs or viewpoints. The stem will also require inference from that belief/ viewpoint. Choices a, b, and d will be incorrect because they will attribute to the passage some remark or comment that the author did in fact not make, or which the author made but which is taken out of context and misinterpreted. Choice a will refer generically to some comment the author made, without actual reference to a line number, paragraph, or quotation. Choices b and d will refer specifically to some part of the text, either by citing a paragraph or by citing some other location feature (e.g., a line number if the passage has them, a header, a title, and so forth). Choice c will be the correct response; it may use any of the locator features given above (line number, header, title), or it can simply attribute the passage directly. Note: for all items constructed from this spec, the order of the four choices must be randomized before use in any actual test.

F. Davidson and
B. K. Lynch

The PA above is relatively long by necessity. It specifies in detail how to write the incorrect and correct choices. In addition, it gives quite a bit of information about the item stem – the question or statement above the four choices.

The PA/RA formula shown above – regardless of which RA is used – is a classical model of specification for multiple-choice items. In this formula, all guidelines about the item are in the PA: the entire description of its stem, its choices, and why the incorrect choices are incorrect (and why the key is correct) is considered to be part of the prompt and not the response.

But what does an examinee actually do? What actually happens when answering an item such as the one given above? Perhaps the examinee sees the correct choice immediately. If the examinee does not, then the item demands a trial-and-error or choose-and-eliminate cognitive process. The choices themselves seem to be part of the examinee's thinking. In the above item, for example, the examinee will probably double-check whether the author did indeed say what is claimed in line 10 or near the end and if so, whether it is being interpreted correctly. In effect, the item itself is a kind of outline of the examinee's answering strategy – a layout of the response. Does that necessarily mean that stem and choice characteristics should be in the RA instead of the PA? Perhaps, though as we have noted here, tradition usually puts it in the description of the 'prompt.'

It is not always clear whether a particular testing behavior is part of the prompt or the response. Let's consider a more striking example of this dilemma. Suppose we have a spec for an oral interview, which by its nature is interactive. The response by the examinee depends on the language of the examiner, and vice versa. Guidance to the examiner about how to construct the interview might include suggestions such as the following:

PA (excerpt)
The interviewer will create utterances which maximally utilize the language of the examinee; that is, the interviewer's language should reference and build on the examinee's language.

An oral interview so constructed might yield the following dialog between an interviewer (I) and an examinee (E):

I: I'm sorry. What did you say?
E: Uh, that I wasn't sure what to do.
I: About what your friend said?
E: Yes, that's right.
I: Ok, so what happened then?
E: Well, uh, I guess because I wasn't sure what to say about what he said and not to offend him, I changed the subject.

In the above excerpt, the examinee is reporting a prior conversation he or she had with a friend. The interesting issue is what the interviewer does: note that his or her questions depend exactly upon what the examinee says. The interviewer builds on what the examinee has to say, and, in turn, the examinee responds to the interviewer's questions. What exactly is the interviewer doing? Is the interviewer's speech actually part of the test 'prompt'? It does prompt the examinee to respond and continue; however, the interviewer chooses what to say based on what the examinee says, so in a roundabout way, the examinee is also serving as a prompt.

F. Davidson and
B. K. Lynch

One way to resolve the PA/RA contrast is to simply ensure that a test specification provides adequate guidance about both the prompt and the response, regardless of what that guidance is labeled. It is possible to fuse the PA and RA and simply give clear specification guidance on both, simultaneously; in effect, you could create a new spec element (the 'PARA') and put all this guidance there. Alternatively, spec writers might wish to commit and go on record that a particular behavior is to be considered a 'prompt.' Doing so has some advantages, chief of those being that the 'response' is then more isolated and, because the response is the primary location of the criterion being measured, the creation of a valid measure is facilitated. Regardless how the spec writing team solves dilemmas like this, the distinction between the PA and RA is one of the fundamental issues that will surface during the crafting of a specification.

Task B4.2

➤ Locate a collection or file of language tests with a wide variety of item types: open-ended, multiple-choice, matching, oral interview protocols, instruction sheets for writing exams, and so forth – perhaps it is the collection you pulled for Task B4.1. Analyse the tasks for the problem that Davidson and Lynch discuss – can you really describe the difference between 'prompt' and 'response'? In later teaching – since the publication of that book – Davidson and his students have migrated to the jargon used here in Unit A4: 'guiding language'. It seems that the only fundamental element of all spec design is to produce samples of the things to be produced and to produce the guiding language that talks about those samples. Guiding language and samples, alone, constitute a true minimalist definition of a 'specification', one born of the vexation of trying to tease apart prompt from response. Do you like that new minimalism? Or are there other universals of test design that always need clarity and formal exposition? Later in the same chapter and excerpted below, Davidson and Lynch discuss another frequently vexing issue in spec-driven testing: the distinction between an 'event' and a 'procedure'. And a bit later, they introduce another possible design universal: specplates, which we also excerpt for your consideration.

The event versus the procedure

F. Davidson and
B. K. Lynch

A useful distinction that can be made for educational tests is that of an 'event' versus a 'procedure.' A testing event we shall define as a single task or test item. We use 'event' in a very restricted sense and do not consider the day of the test as an event. A 'procedure' is a set of events or tasks. For example, a multiple-choice item is an event. An oral interview is a procedure, as would be a portfolio assessment or a protocol for teacher observation of student classroom performance.

If many events are collected into a single test, that too is a type of a procedure. Students take the test by answering all the items; they go through the procedure of the test. Test developers often organize items into a contiguous test by use of a 'table of specifications' (this is a very particular use of the word 'specification,' which we discuss in Chapter 4). A table of specs presents information, at a very global level: How

F. Davidson and
B. K. Lynch

many of each item type are needed? How many of each skill? What special materials are required to develop or administer the test? Questions like these are helpful but do not provide information in sufficient detail to actually write items or tasks. That is, this test probably needs a spec for each unique item type.

Specplates

Specs are built by the consensus of a team of interested parties over time, and gradually specs achieve an operational generative livelihood. In this section, we would like to discuss a way to improve the efficiency of spec-driven testing: the specplate.

A 'specplate' is a combination of the words 'specification' and 'template.' It is a model for a specification, a generative blueprint which itself produces a blueprint. Specplates evolve naturally in spec-driven testing, as design similarities emerge between specifications.

Elsewhere in this chapter . . . we discuss the level-of-generality problem in crafting specifications. Over time, as specs are created and evolve, it may be that certain specifications themselves fuse into a higher-order specification. The best level of generality for a specification might increase such that a wider and wider array of test tasks is generated by the spec.

In this section, we deal with something rather different. We pose this situation: suppose you have a number of specifications which are or must be retained as distinct. That is, suppose that the specs have achieved the best level of generality. Suppose, also, that on examining these specs you discover that, even though each addresses a distinct criterion skill to be tested, they share much in common . . . A specplate is a guide tool to ensure that the new specifications meet a common standard established by the existing specs. One type of information that might appear in a specplate is guidance on item/task type. For example, a PA for a multiple-choice task on verb tense and agreement might include the following language:

> Sample 1
> PA (excerpt)
> Each incorrect choice (distracter) in the item must be incorrect according to the focus of the item. One distracter should be incorrect in tense, another incorrect in voice, and the third incorrect in both tense and voice.

Consider also the following excerpted PA for an item on pronoun–coreferent agreement.

> Sample 2
> PA (excerpt)
> Each incorrect choice (distracter) in the Item must be incorrect according to the focus of the item. One distracter should be incorrect because it refers to the wrong coreferent anaphorically (before the pronoun being tested). Another distracter should be incorrect because it refers to the wrong coreferent cataphorically (after the pronoun being tested). The third distracter should be incorrect because it refers to the wrong coreferent exophorically (outside the lexicon of the passage but within the topical domain of the passage).

A specplate for generation of specs similar to these two might read as follows:

F. Davidson and
B. K. Lynch

Sample 3

PA Specplate (excerpt)

When specifying the distracters, the PA should contain the following language 'Each incorrect choke (distracter) in the item must be incorrect according to the focus of the item.' Immediately following that sentence, the PA should clearly specify how each of the three distracters is incorrect.

Samples 1 and 2 are excerpts from specifications. Sample 3 is the kind of language one might find in a specplate for similar specifications. Sample 3 provides some precise guidance in the crafting of the spec by giving a precise sentence that should be included in the spec ('Each incorrect choice . . .'). It also allows some flexibility and creativity; it specifies only loosely how the distracters should be formed.

Now consider the specplate excerpt in Sample 4, which is a variation on Sample 3:

Sample 4 (an alternative to Sample 3)

PA Specplate (excerpt)

When specifying the distracters, the PA should contain the following language: 'Each incorrect choice (distracter) in the item must be incorrect according to the focus of the item.' Immediately following that sentence, the PA should clearly specify how each of the three distracters is incorrect. You are encouraged to employ (if feasible) the dual-feature model of multiple-choice item creation, namely:

Correct choice/key: both of two features of the item are correct

Distracter: one of two key features of the item is incorrect

Distracter: the other of two key features of the item is incorrect

Distracter: both of two key features of the item are incorrect

Here, the specplate is highly suggestive of a time-honored 'magic formula' model of multiple-choice item creation: craft an item for which, in order to get the item right, you must do two things correctly. The correct choice has both features right. The three distracters can be easily crafted by altering one, then the other, then both of these features. We see this classical formula in the tense/voice spec excerpt shown in Sample 1. Both Samples 1 and 2 fit the specplate shown both in Sample 3 and in Sample 4. Sample 4 does not require the spec author to use this classical two-feature model; it merely suggests that it be done.

Over the long term, spec-driven testing benefits greatly from whatever design shortcuts you can implement to speed up not only item construction but also spec construction. Specs are themselves a way to do the former; spec-driven testing is itself a foundational efficiency in test development. Specplates are a logical extension of that same efficiency which should help in the crafting of specs in much the same way that specs themselves help to craft items. Once the specplate has been written, capturing important and recurring spec design features, it can serve as the starting point for new specs that require those features. Rather than starting from scratch each time, the specplate generates the specification shell and important details follow somewhat automatically.

In effect, the choice between a 'specification' (which generates test tasks) and a 'specplate' (which generates specs) is a special case of the level of generality problem. As things evolve, you can peg your test design at the most efficient level.

⭐ **Task B4.3**

➤ What is your opinion of the minimalist version of specs, now that you have read Davidson and Lynch's discussion of specplates and of the event/procedure distinction? Do those two design features always need to be clearly delineated in a test spec, or are they (but) examples of possible problems that may arise?

Davidson and Lynch go on to point out another interesting problem that may arise, one that has both a practical and a human overtone: ownership.

**F. Davidson and
B. K. Lynch**

Ownership

A well-crafted test is the product of many minds. It is the result of consensus among many interested parties. In this section, we discuss some logistical and technical issues of ownership of specifications and tests. We acknowledge the natural human tendency to feel ownership, but at the same time a spec is never really owned by a single individual. We conclude that a simple historical record of contributions is the best way to attribute a spec to its various authors.

Why is ownership an issue? In part it is due to the natural group dynamics of a testcraft team. [. . .] Ownership is also a technical issue of the spec building process because it necessitates a historical record, and so deserves mention in this chapter. That is, ownership can be thought of as a process that needs to be worked through, and documented, as a part of test design.

We have noted in our experience with test specs that a rather contrary force often interferes with our team-driven testcrafting philosophy, particularly if the team grows larger or begins to include persons not previously involved. Human nature includes a sense of ownership. A teacher 'teaches from my lesson plan.' A school principal 'governs according to my philosophy.' A researcher investigates 'using my strategies.' There also is a sense of investment in the testcrafting process, a sense of the time and effort that a single individual expends as creating a link between them and the testcraft product.

For example, suppose that a particular elementary school wishes to align its testing with newly produced national standards or guidelines, in which there is specific mention of acquisition of reading in integration with other language skills. There is a debate at this school about how best to assess second language reading in children to align with the national call for integration of language skills. Some teachers believe that the reading should be 'scaffolded'; that is, some teachers think that each reading task in their tests should build on other items and tasks in the test so that the child has the best opportunity to understand a particular reading passage. Other teachers feel that it is better to assess reading in isolation; they believe that the best reading assessment is that which stands by itself, and for which no other 'clue' is presented elsewhere in the test. This second group of teachers reasons that children must demonstrate the ability to read before they can demonstrate the ability to integrate reading with other skills. As time passes, these two camps come together and craft a new reading test – a compromise between the two positions. Some of the items are scaffolded to other parts of the test. Some of the items are isolated. There is consensus that the faculty will observe the test in action and decide in a year or two whether more changes are needed.

F. Davidson and
B. K. Lynch

Let us assume (budgets being what they are) that teacher and test development energy gets diverted from this project. Let us also assume (human nature being what it is) that some teachers leave the school. A few years later somebody remembers: 'We were supposed to revise that reading test, weren't we?' An ad hoc group of teachers forms to revisit the test, and the specification is located and brought out for discussion again.

These teachers should now feel free and comfortable to change the specification. Some of the teachers are new to the spec, and their newness should not prohibit them from providing input. Some of the teachers worked on the specification originally, and their input should be vital and valued but not deterministic. These teachers and this school will make the best decision (about scaffolding the reading test) if they are comfortable with changing the specification, and they can best decide whether and how to change it if they have historical information about its genesis and ongoing use. If one teacher or one small group of teachers digs in and demands authority and ownership, the process and evolution of the spec will be thwarted.

A successful test specification has no 'author' in the classical academic sense of that term. It does have authorial 'voice.' It resonates the consensus of the many educators who have (so far) helped to craft it. The best and the most that can be done as a spec is crafted into operational life is to simply record its history and contributors. To attribute the spec to one individual would be to deny historical fact. Not to attribute it at all would also deny historical fact and possibly irritate those who did contribute to its evolution.

Thus, in terms of the design of a spec, ownership involves decisions about what gets recorded. Ultimately, this will be a judgment call, but one that needs to be worked into the spec writing process. One way of doing this is to have an overt category or section of the spec that narrates the origin and history of its development. In deciding what gets written down and who gets mentioned, the spec crafting team will need to come to a consensus about individual versus group investment and contributions.

Following is an excerpt of historical record from a specification in the hypothetical reading test situation above:

Origin/History: This specification originated among a group of nine teachers here in the mid-1990s. The group felt it was necessary to induce a new second language reading test, because the new national standards for second language teaching had just been issued. The group noted (in particular) that the new standards made specific mention of scaffolding as a valid component of instruction and assessment in reading, and this point caused some debate. The result was a spec that can produce two types of tasks: those that are scaffolded to input elsewhere in the test, and those that are not. It was agreed that the school administration and faculty would review results of the test over its first few years of life and specifically monitor and compare these two item types. In that way, we could come to a better understanding of the role of scaffolding in our tests and curricula.

The names of the original test development team are given in the Specification Supplement.

Task B4.4

➤ What is your opinion about test ownership? Who really owns the tests at your institution – and what value might be gained if your specs included an 'origin/ history' section, such as suggested here? Do you think that such a spec element as 'origin/history' should be a routine part of test specs, or is it also just a problem that may – or may not – arise?

Summary

The focus of the excerpts in this unit is the nature of a test spec: its elements. There are many designs of specs in the literature, perhaps as many as there are testing textbooks that mention specs at all. We raise the question: what are the essential minimum components to specs beyond the bare minimum of guiding language and samples?

Unit B5
Washback

'Washback is generally defined as the influence of testing on teaching and learning' (Bailey, 1996: 259). The concept of washback is therefore part of what Messick (1989) calls *consequential validity*. As part of consequential validity, Messick (1996: 241) says that:

> Washback refers to the extent to which the introduction and use of a test influences language teachers and learners to do things that they would not otherwise do that promote or inhibit language learning.

The focus of washback study has therefore been on those things that we do in the classroom because of the test, but 'would not otherwise do'. If the concept of washback is to have any meaning, it is necessary to identify what changes in learning or teaching can be directly attributed to the use of the test in that context. Traditionally, this has meant creating an empirical link between a negative consequence and a source of invalidity. Messick (1996: 252) reiterates this with regard to washback:

> The primary measurement concern with respect to adverse consequences is that negative washback or, indeed, any negative impact on individuals or groups should not derive from any source of test invalidity such as construct under-representation or construct-irrelevant variance.

The argument would be that unless negative washback can be traced to such sources of test invalidity, it is not possible to ask the test designer to take responsibility for the negative washback (also see Unit A9). Alderson (2004: xi) has partially come to accept this view, while also forcefully arguing that language testers cannot disengage from understanding the forces of washback on what happens within the classroom, as an interaction effect from test, society, educational system, schools, and the individuals involved in decision making (Wall, 1996, 1997, 2000).

Task B5.1

➤ Do you prepare students to take a particular test?

➤ Which one?

➤ Does the test provider make any claim about the advantages to students of preparing for this particular test?

The following paper by Alderson and Wall was the first to critically investigate the concept of washback. Before 1993 it had merely been assumed that (1) tests did have an effect on teaching, and (2) the effect was largely negative. By framing the 'washback hypothesis' Alderson and Wall made it possible for washback to be studied empirically, and the simplistic nature of the original concept was soon turned into a conceptually rich source of theory and research.

Text B5
J. C. Alderson
and D. Wall

J. C. Alderson and D. Wall (1993) 'Does washback exist?' *Applied Linguistics* 14, 2, 115–129

Introduction

The notion that testing influences teaching is commonplace in the educational and applied linguistics literature . . . Many educationalists have written about the power of examinations over what takes place in the classroom. Pearson, for example, says: 'It is generally accepted that public examinations influence the attitudes, behaviour, and motivation of teachers, learners, and parents' (1988: 98). This influence is often seen as negative: Vernon (1956: 166) claimed that examinations 'distort the curriculum'. He felt that teachers tended to ignore subjects and activities which did not contribute directly to passing the exam, and lamented what he considered to be excessive coaching for exams. Others, however, see washback in a more positive way. Morris (1972: 75) considers examinations necessary to ensure that the curriculum is put into effect, Swain (1985: 42–4) recommends that test developers 'bias for best' and 'work for washback', while Alderson (1986: 104) argues for innovations in the language curriculum through innovations in language testing.
 [. . .]
Some writers have even gone so far as to suggest that a test's validity should be measured by the degree to which it has had a beneficial influence on teaching. Morrow (1986) coined the term 'washback validity' to denote the quality of the relationship between a test and associated teaching. The notion presumably means something like: 'this test is valid when it has good washback'; and conversely, 'this test is invalid when it has negative washback'. He says: 'The first validity criterion that I would . . . put forward for [these examinations] would be a measure of how far the intended washback effect was actually being met in practice' (Morrow 1986: 6). He admits, however: 'I am not sure at this stage how it could be measured', although he then goes on to claim: 'In essence an examination of washback validity would take testing researchers into the classroom in order to observe the effect of their tests in action.' He cites Wilkins, Widdowson, and others as asserting that direct tests of language performance will be 'most beneficial in terms of washback effect', and argues that communicative tests like the former Royal Society of Arts Examination in the Communicative Use of English as a Foreign Language should have a 'powerful and positive washback effect into the classroom'.

Task B5.2

➤ Look at the task or item types in a number of tests with which you are familiar, or in sample tests that you can access from the websites of test providers.

(a) Select two or three task or item types that you *would* use for classroom teaching and learning. How would you use them in your classroom?
(b) Select two or three task/item types that you *would not* use for classroom teaching and learning. Why do you think they are unsuitable?

➤ Do you think there are any principles that help us to distinguish between task/item types that would be useful in either a teaching or a testing context, but not in the other?

Frederiksen and Collins (1989) introduce a concept similar to washback validity. They use the term 'systemic validity', which they define as follows:

J. C. Alderson
and D. Wall

> A systemically valid test is one that induces in the education system curricular and instructional changes that foster the development of the cognitive skills that the test is designed to measure. Evidence for systemic validity would be an improvement in those skills after the test has been in place within the educational system for a period of time.
>
> (1989: 27)

However, to our knowledge, this form of validity has never been demonstrated, or indeed investigated, nor have proposals been made as to how it could be established empirically rather than asserted. Moreover, it is not at all clear that if a test does not have the desired washback this is necessarily due to a lack of validity of the test, as Morrow and Frederiksen and Collins simplistically imply. It is surely conceivable that other forces exist within society, education, and schools that might prevent washback from appearing, or that might affect the nature of washback despite the 'communicative' quality of a test. This can then hardly be attributed to a problem with the test. Whereas validity is a property of a test, in relation to its use, we argue that washback, if it exists – which has yet to be established – is likely to be a complex phenomenon which cannot be related directly to a test's validity.

It seems to us to be important to investigate the nature of washback first, and the conditions under which it operates. Only once we are able to describe what actually happens, will we be in a position to explore what 'causes' these effects. And only after we have established causal relationships will we be in a position to explore whether we are justified in relating washback to a test's validity. Thus, talk of washback or systemic validity is at best premature, and at worst ill-conceived.

★ **Task B5.3**

➤ What 'forces' might have an effect on washback from:

- society?
- education more generally?
- and schools?

**J. C. Alderson
and D. Wall**

Exploring the concept of washback

The term 'washback' is itself a neutral one, and can be related to 'influence'. If the test is 'poor', then the washback may be felt to be negative. But if the Washback Hypothesis holds, then good tests should have good effects (as yet undefined) rather than negative effects.

If we consider these beliefs briefly, we can see that other possibilities also hold. The Washback Hypothesis seems to assume that teachers and learners do *things they would not necessarily otherwise do* because of the test. Hence the notion of influence. But this also implies that a 'poor' test could conceivably have a 'good' effect if it made teachers and learners do 'good' things they would not otherwise do: for example, prepare lessons more thoroughly, do their homework, take the subject being tested more seriously, and so on. And indeed, teachers are often said to use tests to get their students to do things they would not otherwise do: to pay attention to the lesson, to prepare more thoroughly, to learn by heart, and so on. To the extent that these activities are in some sense desirable – hard work is presumably more 'desirable' than no work at all, and extrinsic motivation might be better than no motivation at all – then any test, good or bad, can be said to be having beneficial washback if it increases such activity or motivation.

★ **Task B5.4**

➤ How does your teaching change when you engage in test preparation?

➤ Is the way you select and use teaching material different when you are preparing students to take a test?

**J. C. Alderson
and D. Wall**

Alternatively, one might wish to consider the possibility of a test, good or bad, having negative effects. The most obvious such effect is anxiety in the learner brought about by having to take a test of whatever nature, and, if not anxiety, then at least concern in teachers, if they believe that some consequence will follow on poor performance by the pupils. The argument would go like this: any learner who is obliged to do something under pressure will perform abnormally and may therefore experience anxiety. Thus pressure produces abnormal performance, the fear of which produces anxiety. In addition, the fear of the consequences of particular performances produces anxiety which will influence those performances. Similarly for teachers, the fear of poor results, and the associated guilt, shame, or embarrassment, might lead to the desire for their pupils to achieve high scores in whatever way seems possible. This might lead to 'teaching to the test', with an undesirable 'narrowing of the curriculum'.

We may also wish to consider the possibility of a test *reinforcing* some behaviour or attitude rather than bringing about an otherwise unlikely behaviour. Thus students may already work hard, and a test may simply motivate them to work harder. A learner may constantly self-evaluate against internal or external criteria, and the test may provide very useful additional criteria for this kind of comparison. Thus the relationship between a test and its impact, positive or negative, might be less simple than at first sight appears to be the case. The quality of the washback might be independent of the quality of the test.

Task B5.5

➤ How do your students react to tests and test preparation?

➤ Does this cause 'anxiety' or other reactions?

The question arises as to whether 'washback' is the same as 'influence' or whether the term refers solely to some sorts of influence and not others? We might not want to use the term 'washback' for the anxiety caused by having to take a test, but might well want to apply it to syllabus or textbook design specifically based on a test.
[...]
Even if we were to use the term 'washback' to refer to the test's effect on textbook design, we would probably need to distinguish between pedagogic material which is directly related to a specific test in terms of content or method ... and material which is intended to help students get ready for an exam in some more general way – for example, study skills courses which claim they give students skills relevant to taking a test of English for Academic Purposes like the International English Language Testing System (IELTS). Given these complexities, we may wish to restrict the use of the term 'washback' to classroom behaviours of teachers and learners rather than to the nature of printed and other pedagogic material. It is not clear from the literature, however, that writers do indeed make these distinctions.

J. C. Alderson
and D. Wall

Task B5.6

Look at a commercial test preparation package for a major test. This may be for an ETS or Cambridge ESOL test, or that of some other test provider.

➤ What is the content of the test preparation package?

➤ How does the package assume teachers will use it in the classroom? What effect would it have on teaching and learning if you used the package in this way?

Another aspect of the notion of washback that needs to be explored is its deterministic nature. How directly, according to the Washback Hypothesis, do tests bring about change in teaching and learning? A naïve deterministic view (which is often implicit

J. C. Alderson
and D. Wall

J. C. Alderson
and D. Wall

in the complaints about TOEFL, for example, or even in the claim that tests can be used as 'levers for change') would assume that the fact of a test having a set of qualities is sufficient in itself, by virtue of the importance of tests in most societies, to bring about change. However, this takes little account of other factors in the environment which may also influence teaching: the teachers' basic competence, their understanding of the principles underlying the test, levels of resourcing within the school system, etc.

Most discussions of washback tend to assume that the existence of a test brings about some change in motivation and thus in behaviour. In fact, the relationship between motivation and performance is a very complex matter, beyond the scope of this discussion. However, a thorough study of washback must surely take account of research findings in this area. In fact, there appear to be conflicting results, as Fransson's brief review (1984) indicates. Fransson points out that an increase in level of motivation is accompanied by an increase in learning, up to an optimal point. However, beyond that point an increase in motivation seems to have negative effects and performance declines (the so-called 'Yerkes–Dodson Law'). The position of the optimal point, Fransson suggests, depends upon the difficulty of the task. However, it may well also relate to the consequences of the task (in our case, the test), as well as to other factors within the performer such as that person's need for achievement (nAch). This may be the result of two opposed tendencies: the motivation to succeed and the motivation to avoid failure. These, in their turn, may relate to the person's expectations of success (or failure), the value of the task as an incentive, and the person's orientation toward success or toward avoidance of failure.

As if this were not sufficiently complicated, McDonough goes on to review a further theoretical position, that of attribution theory, which describes motivated behaviour in terms of 'the causes to which the individuals attribute or ascribe their own and other people's performance: their own ability, effort, intention or others' ability, effort and intention, luck and so on'.

It may be, however, that the key factor is not motivation but anxiety, both 'state anxiety' – the condition associated with performing a task – and 'trait anxiety' – one's habitual response to stress. Furthermore, it may be important to distinguish two sorts of anxiety: debilitating and facilitating. Which of these is aroused in a particular learner or teacher may depend on personality factors (for example, extroversion/introversion, need for achievement, fear of failure, and so on) as well as the consequences (and the learners' perception of those consequences) of particular performances.

 Task B5.7

➤ Alderson and Wall set out some of the many variables that might affect the washback of a test on learners. What might some of the teacher variables be that would impact on how they might adapt their teaching and classroom materials when preparing students for a test?

J. C. Alderson
and D. Wall

The Washback Hypothesis

It might help to clarify our thinking if we attempt to state the Washback Hypothesis explicitly. From a reading of the literature on language testing generally, and from

J. C. Alderson
and D. Wall

our experience of talking to teachers about their teaching and testing, it is possible to develop different hypotheses, from the most general and vague to the somewhat more refined, which take account of different factors.

Some possible *Washback* Hypotheses

(1) A *test will influence teaching*. This is the Washback Hypothesis at its most general. However, a second partly different hypothesis follows by implication from this first one, on the assumption that teaching and learning are related, but not identical:

(2) A *test will influence learning*. Since it is possible, at least in principle, to separate the content of teaching from its methodology, then we need to distinguish the influence of a test on the content of the teaching from its influence on the methodology. Thus:

(3) A *test will influence* **what** *teachers teach*; and

(4) A *test will influence* **how** *teachers teach*; and therefore by extension from (2) above:

(5) A *test will influence* **what** *learners learn*; and

(6) A *test will influence* **how** *learners learn*.

However, perhaps we need to be somewhat more precise about teaching and learning, in order to consider how quickly and in what order teachers teach and learners learn. Hence:

(7) A *test will influence the* **rate and sequence** *of teaching*; and

(8) A *test will influence the* **rate and sequence** *of learning*.

Similarly, we may wish to consider explicitly both the quality and the quantity of teaching and learning:

(9) A *test will influence the* **degree and depth** *of teaching*; and

(10) A *test will influence the* **degree and depth** *of learning*.

If washback relates to attitudes as well as to behaviours, then:

(11) A *test will influence attitudes to the content, method, etc. of teaching and learning.*

In the above, however, no consideration has been given to the nature of the test, or to the uses to which scores will be put. Yet it seems not unreasonable to hypothesize:

(12) *Tests that have important consequences will have washback*; and conversely

(13) *Tests that do not have important consequences will have no washback.*

J. C. Alderson
and D. Wall

It may be the case that:

(14) *Tests will have washback on **all** learners and teachers.*

However, given what we know about differences among people, it is surely likely that:

(15) *Tests will have washback effects for **some** learners and **some** teachers, but **not** for others.*

Clearly, we are complicating what was initially a simple assumption. Is this justified? Is washback a concept to be taken seriously, or simply a metaphor which is useful in that it encourages us to explore the role of tests in learning and the relationship between teaching and testing? We are not sure at present, but we suspect that if it is a metaphor, it needs to be articulated somewhat more precisely if it is to throw light on teaching and testing, or indeed on the nature of innovation and change. And if it is a concept to be taken seriously, then we need to examine it critically, and see what evidence there might be that could help us in this examination.

We need in either case to identify and examine cases where washback is thought to have occurred, and to see how and why it did or did not occur.

[. . .]

What this amounts to is a long-term and relatively complex research programme. We believe that this is both inevitable and desirable. What is undesirable is a continuation of our state of ignorance about a phenomenon on whose importance all seem to be agreed. Equally undesirable is a continuation of naïve assertions about washback on the part of applied linguists in general and materials writers, syllabus designers, and language teachers in particular, as well as language testers, until some empirical investigations have been undertaken.

★ **Task B5.8**

➤ How do you think we could 'measure' washback?

➤ After the introduction of a new test, what data might you collect in order to discover whether the test has had an impact? Make a list, using the hypotheses above to help you.

➤ Why might you have to collect 'baseline data' before the new test is introduced and you begin to study washback?

Summary

Alderson (2004: ix) writes:

I believe there is no longer any doubt that washback does indeed exist. But we now know that the phenomenon is a hugely complex matter, and very far from being a simple case of tests having negative impact on teaching. The question today is not 'does washback exist?' but much rather what does washback look like? What brings washback about? Why does washback exist?

Empirical research carried out since 1993 has shown that we cannot always expect to find what we predict. Indeed, preparation for TOEFL does not always lead to poor teaching and learning, and teachers approach their task in very different ways (Alderson and Hamp-Lyons, 1996). And similar findings have been discovered for other tests (Cheng and Watanabe, 2004).

It seems that there is no way to generalize about washback at the present time. Teaching and learning will be impacted in many different ways depending upon the variables at play in specific contexts. What these variables are, how they are to be weighted, and whether we can discover patterns of interaction that may hold steady across contexts, is a matter for ongoing research. In the meantime, we need to investigate washback for every context in which test use is hypothesized to impact upon the process and content of teaching and learning.

Unit B6
Researching prototype tasks

As we discuss in Unit A6, test development and research on testing often work together. Developing a test involves problems of basic research, whether such problems are identified early in the test development or – as with some of our Unit C6 samples – they emerge along the way.

 Task B6.1

➤ Text B6 is presented with few deletions in order to explore fully the rationale and procedures of a test development research report. As you progress through this text, please use your skills of critical reading: are the authors' intentions clear? Can you find the research objectives? Are the procedures easy to follow? Do the results seem well-argued? And do the final discussions follow from the paper in a logical manner?

Text B6
A. Cumming,
L. Grant,
P. Mulcahy-
Ernt and
D. Powers

A. Cumming, L. Grant, P. Mulcahy-Ernt and D. Powers (2005) *A Teacher-Verification Study of Speaking and Writing Prototype Tasks for a New TOEFL*. **TOEFL Monograph Series 26. Princeton, NJ: Educational Testing Service**

Abstract

This study was undertaken, in conjunction with other studies field-testing prototype tasks for a new Test of English as a Foreign Language™ (TOEFL®), to evaluate the content validity, perceived authenticity, and educational appropriateness of these prototype tasks. We interviewed 7 highly experienced instructors of English as a second language (ESL) at 3 universities, asking them to rate their students' abilities in English and to review samples of their students' performance to determine whether they thought 7 prototype speaking and writing tasks being field-tested for a new version of the TOEFL test (a) represented the domain of academic English required for studies at English-medium universities or colleges in North America, (b) elicited performance from their adult ESL students that corresponded to their usual performance in ESL classes and course assignments, and (c) realized the evidence claims on which the tasks had been designed. The instructors thought that most of their students' performances on the prototype test tasks were equivalent to or better than their usual performances in classes. The instructors viewed positively the new prototype tasks that required students to write or to speak in reference to reading or listening source texts, but they observed certain problems with these novel tasks and suggested ways that the content and presentation might be improved for the formative development of these tasks.

Task B6.2

> What are the elements of a good research abstract? Do you think this abstract follows those elements? Suppose the abstract had to stand on its own – in a bibliographic database (for example): after you read the rest of the paper, does the abstract adequately capture what was done?

Introduction

A. Cumming,
L. Grant,
P. Mulcahy-
Ernt and
D. Powers

The present study was one of many coordinated studies aimed at developing new task types for the Test of English as a Foreign Language™ (TOEFL®) following the conceptual foundations for new integrated reading, writing, listening, and speaking tasks with communicative, academic orientations for the test outlined in Jamieson, Jones, Kirsch, Mosenthal, and Taylor (2000) and elaborated in more detail for each mode of communication in Bejar, Douglas, Jamieson, Nissan, and Turner (2000, for listening); Butler, Eignor, Jones, McNamara, and Suomi (2000, for speaking); Cumming, Kantor, Powers, Santos, and Taylor (2000, for writing); and Enright et al. (2000, for reading). Specifically, the present study was coordinated with field tests of prototype tasks for the new TOEFL in the autumn of 2000 that involved 475 ESL students in Australia, Canada, Hong Kong, Taiwan, and the United States (described in Enright & Cline, 2002). The present study supplemented this larger field test by gathering in-depth data from a small sample of highly experienced English as a second language (ESL) instructors, whom we interviewed about their perceptions of the prototype tasks and of their students' performance on these tasks in the field test. The present research complemented other studies of student performance on the field test, such as analyses of the difficulty, score reliability, and consistency of measurements of the tasks (Enright & Cline, 2002) or analyses of the relationship of scores on the field tests to external criteria, including placement in ESL classes, scores on other ESL tests, teachers' ratings of students' English proficiency, and students' self-ratings of their English proficiency (Bridgeman, Cline, & Powers, 2002).

The purpose of the present study was primarily formative. The research was undertaken to inform decisions about the content validity, authenticity, and educational appropriateness of the prototype tasks under consideration for a new version of the TOEFL test. In addition to verifying these qualities of the prototype tasks, we aimed to produce findings that could help to guide revisions to certain task types or decisions about deleting some of them from the pool of task types under consideration for the new test. We looked to experienced ESL instructors to provide information that would help to answer the following research questions:

Is the content of the prototype tasks being field-tested for the new TOEFL perceived to assess the domain of academic English required for studies at an English-medium university in North America?

Is the performance of ESL students on the prototype tasks field-tested for the new TOEFL perceived to correspond authentically to the performance of these students in their ESL classes?

A. Cumming,
L. Grant,
P. Mulcahy-
Ernt and
D. Powers

Are the prototype tasks being field-tested for the new TOEFL perceived to realize the evidence claims on which the tasks were designed?

The research questions address the concepts of content validity, authenticity, and educational relevance. These concepts have been principal foci of criticisms about the task types in the current TOEFL test. They have therefore formed a major impetus for revisions to the test that are now underway. They have also formed the basis for new definitions of the constructs to guide the design of a new version of the test (Jamieson et al., 2000). For example, Chapelle, Grabe, and Berns (1997) argued that the content and format of the TOEFL needed to be revised substantively to reflect contemporary concepts of communicative competence and practices of language teaching and learning. Likewise, Hamp-Lyons and Kroll (1997) and Raimes (1990) criticized the current writing component of the TOEFL (or the Test of Written English™) for not assessing the types of writing that students realistically need to perform at universities in North America and for the test not having educationally relevant definitions of the construct of writing ability in a second language. Because the current TOEFL does not engage examinees in actually speaking English in any way, various arguments have been made to add a component to the test that assesses speaking abilities directly (Butler et al., 2000). Perhaps the strongest criticism of the task types in the current TOEFL is that many items focus on discrete knowledge about the forms of the English language (such as multiple-choice items about grammar or vocabulary) that can easily be coached or can have a negative washback on learning and teaching English by directing students' attention to learning such items rather than developing their abilities to communicate proficiently (Alderson & Hamp-Lyons, 1996; Bailey, 1999).

The design of prototype tasks for the new TOEFL test has tried to address these concerns by creating a range of new task types for the assessment of writing and speaking, by defining precisely the constructs that these tasks are intended to assess, and by integrating the modalities for language production (i.e., writing and speaking) with tasks that involve examinees reading or listening to source texts, as they would in real academic tasks in English.

Task B6.3

➤ Please pause to reflect on the authors' discussion of prototyping, immediately above. Compare it to the discussion of prototypes in A6. What particular value did these authors obtain from prototyping? How did prototyping help their project, or conversely, what would have happened if no prototypes were produced?

A. Cumming,
L. Grant,
P. Mulcahy-
Ernt and
D. Powers

The rationale for the present study also follows from recent, expanded conceptualizations of the centrality of construct validity in test development, requiring diverse kinds of evidence from multiple relevant sources about the interpretation of test scores and the uses to which test results are put (e.g., as argued by Messick, 1989; Moss, 1992). This view has proved to be as important for language testing as for other domains of assessment (Bachman, 2000; Cumming, 1996; Fulcher, 1999a; Kunnan, 1998). For instance, many educators have argued that the content of tests in education should relate integrally to curriculum standards as well as to students' typical achievements and performance requirements. This perspective has promoted the use of task types for assessments that authentically resemble the tasks that students

A. Cumming,
L. Grant,
P. Mulcahy-
Ernt and
D. Powers

actually need to perform in their academic studies (Darling-Hammond, 1994; Freedman, 1991; Gipps, 1994; Linn, Baker, & Dunbar, 1991). For tests of language abilities, many theorists have recently argued that assessment tasks need to 'somehow capture or recreate . . . the essence of language use' (Bachman, 1990, p. 300), urging that authenticity should be a fundamental criterion for the validity of tasks that aim to evaluate how well people can really communicate in a language (Bachman & Palmer, 1996; Lewkowicz, 2000; Spence-Brown, 2001; Spolsky, 1985). In turn, to achieve educational relevance, test tasks should elicit performance that is congruent with instructors' perceptions of their students' abilities, as numerous different inquiries in second language assessment have recently emphasized and demonstrated (e.g., Brindley, 1998, 2000; Chalhoub-Deville, 1995; Elder, 1993; Epp & Stawychny, 2001; Grant, 1997; North, 1995, 2000; Stansfield & Kenyon, 1996; O'Sullivan, Weir, & Saville, 2002).

With these ideas in mind, we initiated this study to explore how a small group of highly experienced ESL instructors might evaluate the content of the prototype tasks being field-tested for the new TOEFL, judge the authenticity of their students' performance on these prototype tasks, and evaluate whether the prototype tasks appropriately fulfilled the purposes for which they had been designed.

Method

Participants

The participants in this research were four instructors at the University of Toronto, two instructors at Central Michigan University, and one instructor at the University of Bridgeport.

Task B6.4

➤ Is sufficient information given about the participants in the study?

Interviews

A. Cumming,
L. Grant,
P. Mulcahy-
Ernt and
D. Powers

We interviewed instructors shortly after their ESL courses were completed in either December 2000 or early January 2001, once data on their students' performance on the prototype tasks (from the autumn of 2000) had been processed and made available to us in CD-ROM form. All instructors were interviewed individually except for Francis and Tyler, who met for their interview together because they had taught the same students and had complementary perspectives on either the oral or the literate abilities of the same ESL students. Each interview lasted from 2.5 to 4 hours, was audiotaped, and was later transcribed in full. Bob returned for a second interview to complete the descriptions of the performance of the 10 students he had taught.

Each interview followed a common format. Instructors were asked to describe the ESL course they had been teaching, the sample of students' work they had brought to the interview, as well as the ratings they had given previously (as part of the larger prototype study in the autumn of 2000; see Enright & Cline, 2002) to the writing and speaking abilities of the focal students they had selected from their classes. Then, for each of the focal students, the instructor either read or listened to the student's writing

A. Cumming,
L. Grant,
P. Mulcahy-
Ernt and
D. Powers

or speaking performance on the prototype TOEFL tasks, commenting on how representative they thought the performance was for the student, based on their knowledge of that student and the person's typical performance in class and in course assignments. Each student's performance was provided on a CD-ROM from ETS; when students had written by hand, photocopies of their writing were given to the instructors to review. In the final part of the interview, the instructors individually completed the profile questionnaire shown in the appendix.

Questionnaire

We developed, piloted, and then refined a questionnaire (shown in the appendix to this report), which asked each instructor to evaluate the effectiveness (on a scale from 1 = not effective to 5 = very effective) of each of the prototype task types; then to explain briefly why the instructors considered each task type effective or not; then to rate how well they thought the tasks 'represent the domain of academic English required for studies at an English-medium university' and to explain why which tasks do this best, and what might be missing from the tasks. The final section of the questionnaire asked the instructors to profile themselves, their teaching and assessment experiences, and their knowledge of the ESL students they had been teaching.

⭐ Task B6.5

➤ It is very typical to present research instruments in an appendix. Please skip ahead and look at the questionnaire (p. 245). Taken together with the above paragraph, is it clear what the questionnaire was intended to measure?

A. Cumming,
L. Grant,
P. Mulcahy-
Ernt and
D. Powers

Samples of students' performances

To keep each interview to a reasonable duration (i.e., no more than 2 hours per instructor), we decided in advance that we would have to sample from among a total of the 13 integrated tasks (i.e., tasks involving more than a single language modality) and 6 independent tasks (i.e., those that involved a single modality) that were administered in the field test, focusing particularly on tasks that we collectively had decided might best display students' abilities. The seven tasks (and the constructs they were intended to evaluate in students' performance, that is, the evidence claims for the tasks) we considered were

- independent writing (TOEFL essay), intended to assess writing about personal experiences and opinions;
- academic writing in response to a lecture (on plate tectonics), intended to assess writing about academic topics;
- academic writing in response to a reading passage (on dance), intended to assess writing about academic topics;
- independent speaking, intended to assess speaking about personal experiences and opinions;
- speaking in response to a lecture (on ground water), intended to assess speaking about academic topics;

- speaking in response to a conversation (about student housing), intended to assess speaking in academic contexts; and
- speaking in response to a reading passage (about innate vs. learned abilities), intended to assess speaking about academic topics.

A. Cumming, L. Grant, P. Mulcahy-Ernt and D. Powers

This selection of tasks from among the many prototype tasks that were field-tested provided a range of one of each of the three different types of writing and the four different speaking types of tasks. But the sample of tasks was not sufficient to permit our analyses to be able to distinguish between the task type, the stimuli material, or the topic. We have not included descriptions of these tasks here for two reasons: (a) test security and (b) most of the tasks are being revised substantively, on the basis of analyses from the present and other field tests, so we would not want, by publishing them here, to mislead future users of the test about what the content or format of the tasks will be in the new TOEFL. Parallel to these prototype tasks, the instructors also provided ratings (as part of the larger prototype study), using a scale from 1 ('is clearly insufficient') to 5 ('is highly developed, will not be a barrier to success'), of each of the focal students' abilities in 'writing about personal experiences and opinions,' 'writing about academic topics,' 'speaking about personal experiences and opinions,' and 'speaking about academic topics' (i.e., corresponding to the evidence claims for these tasks). We only considered the students' performance on writing and speaking tasks (most of which included tasks that involved reading and listening stimuli), because these provided holistic samples of students' performance in extended discourse.

Task B6.6

➤ We discuss test specifications elsewhere in this book, in Units A4 and C4 (and to a lesser extent in Units A5 and C5). Can you envision a spec for any of the seven task types? Is sufficient information given here to do so?

Analyses

A. Cumming, L. Grant, P. Mulcahy-Ernt and D. Powers

To answer our research questions, we developed a common framework for tallying and reviewing the data from the questionnaire and transcribed interviews. We then conducted initial analyses individually at each site (i.e., by the interviewer who had conducted the original interview), preparing three separate reports for each of the three sites. Then we shared among ourselves the full set of data and our respective interpretations, synthesizing these interpretations into the present, common report. For items where the instructors had made numerical evaluations, we tallied these. But most of the data involved open-ended responses either to questionnaire items or to the questions posed in the standard interview schedule. We interpreted these using a constant-comparative method (Miles & Huberman, 1994), reviewing the data to identify trends and themes and then crosschecking them (against the data and with each other's interpretations of them).

⭐ **Task B6.7**

Miles and Huberman (1994) is a methodology reference. Rather than describe the 'constant-comparative method', the authors send you to that reference.

➤ What is your opinion of this tactic in writing a research paper? Should the authors describe their approaches in greater detail? Might doing so make the paper too long? What if Miles and Huberman is a widely cited source, and thus the authors are relying that their readership are familiar with it?

➤ Moving forward, please note how the authors detail the methodology associated with each research question, one by one. This is an important component of a classically designed empirical paper. Is it clear?

A. Cumming,
L. Grant,
P. Mulcahy-
Ernt and
D. Powers

To answer our first research question (Is the content of the prototype tasks being field-tested for the new TOEFL perceived to assess the domain of academic English required for studies at an English-medium university in North America?), we analyzed the instructors' responses to Item I.3 in the questionnaire (see the appendix). To answer our second research question (Is the performance of ESL students on the prototype tasks field-tested for the new TOEFL perceived to correspond authentically to the performance of these students in their ESL classes?), we categorized and analyzed the instructors' spoken judgments of whether they thought their students' performance on the various task types corresponded to their usual performance in classes, identifying trends in their stated impressions about how well or poorly their students had performed.

For the third research question (Are the prototype tasks being field-tested for the new TOEFL perceived to realize the evidence claims on which the tasks were designed?), we analyzed the instructors' responses to Items 1 and 2 (and their corresponding subsections) on the questionnaire, distinguishing between the instructors' evaluations of the various kinds of writing and speaking tasks. We also calculated Spearman's rank-order correlations (rho) between (a) the ratings by the seven instructors of their students' speaking and writing abilities in English (i.e., according to the evidence claims cited above) and (b) the scores these students received in the field test . . . on the seven prototype tasks that intended to measure the constructs corresponding to the abilities that the instructors had rated. These items on the questionnaire and the separate ratings by teachers followed the definitions of the constructs for reading and writing tasks specified in Rosenfeld, Leung, and Oltman (2001) as well as in the frameworks prepared by Butler et al. (2000, for speaking) and Cumming et al. (2000, for writing). For these analyses, in addition to p values, we estimated effect sizes using the Aaron–Kromrey–Ferron formula, appropriate to this small, disparate sample.[1] As described above, data were missing for numerous task performances for certain students, so the number of cases varied for each correlation; we omitted the missing data from the correlation analyses.

1 Aaron, Kromrey, and Ferron's (1998) formula produces an index of effect size (r) accounting for variance (rather than just standardizing mean differences) through the formula: $r = d / [(d2 + [N2 - 2N) / (n1\ n2)]].5$ where $N = n1 + n2$. This indicator of effect size is appropriate for nonexperimental studies when 'total sample size is small or group sizes are disparate' (Thompson, 2000, p. 2). The interpretation of r is that 0 is a trivial effect, 0.2 is a small effect, 0.6 is a moderate effect, 1.2 is a large effect, 2.0 is a very large effect, and 4.0 is a nearly perfect effect.

Task B6.8

Following on to the previous task, the Spearman coefficient is a very old and well-established statistic dating back nearly ninety years. It is no longer common to cite Spearman's original work or publications, because the coefficient has entered into common usage.

➤ How do you suppose this happens? How much common citation do you think is necessary for a statistic or procedure for citation of the original work no longer to be necessary?

Task B6.9

➤ The previous page contains a footnote. Do you think the footnote was necessary?

Research question 1: Content validity

A. Cumming, L. Grant, P. Mulcahy-Ernt and D. Powers

In considering the prototype tasks overall, all of the instructors expressed in their questionnaire responses (after hearing samples of their students' speech and reading samples of their writing on the seven tasks) that they thought these tasks represented quite well (i.e., mostly ratings of 4 out of 5) the domain of academic English required for studies at an English-medium university. The integrated nature and realistic academic content of the reading, listening, speaking, and writing tasks were the chief reasons the instructors cited. For example, one instructor observed, 'If a student can read/listen to a fairly complicated text and respond clearly, it seems like a good indication they'll be able to do academic work.' Another instructor noted, 'They all seem to be typical academic tasks, as realistic as can be in a testing situation.' Another wrote in her overall evaluation, 'Both the simulated lectures and the readings were close to real university-level material.' Likewise, another instructor judged that the tasks 'cover skills needed by students, i.e., attending to lectures, writing essays, exams, interpreting lectures/text books.' One instructor, however, rated the tasks a bit lower, giving an overall rating of 3 out of 5. She noted that the tasks might be appropriate for undergraduate students, but she was concerned about graduate students: 'However, for graduate students, they would not necessarily have the language ability needed to deal with these topics, but might have the language ability needed to succeed in their particular fields.' The instructor who taught solely at the graduate level, though, rated the tasks overall as 5 but indicated he would like to see more open-ended choices 'based on individuals' preferences, interests, and inclinations.'

When asked which tasks best represent the domain of academic English required for university studies, five of the seven instructors indicated the written and spoken responses to the readings and lectures. One instructor said she found the spoken responses were 'less representative' than written responses of university studies; and one liked the idea of spoken responses to the lecture, but felt the content of the lectures (and readings) was difficult.

In addition to these positive comments, the instructors expressed some reservations about the content of the prototype tasks, particularly when asked what they thought might be 'missing' from the tasks. Several instructors suggested they thought

A. Cumming,
L. Grant,
P. Mulcahy-
Ernt and
D. Powers

the tasks could be more cognitively or intellectually challenging or complex. For instance, one instructor thought the tasks 'reflect stressful (e.g., exam) situations, but don't allow for the application of some study skills and strategies which take time or relaxation.' In a similar vein, another instructor observed that the tasks 'don't include anything requiring the students to apply or extend – i.e., think about, around, or beyond – the material.' A third instructor similarly suggested that 'some tasks could ask a student to expand on a topic and/or provide analogies/contrasts to the theories or information presented.' The brief time allocated to do the tasks was a concern for several of the instructors, though they acknowledged the difficulties of overcoming this in the context of a standardized test. One teacher noted (as described above) the difficulty that graduate students might have with 'general interest' topics, such as geology, dance, and ecology, and suggested 'incorporating a wider variety of discipline-specific topics (e.g., business topics).' Another instructor likewise thought there should be more choices for the examinees to write about based on their individual preferences or interests. One instructor also observed that the processes of conversation in classroom situations, such as 'interacting, interrupting, holding the floor,' were not assessed. Two instructors pointed out that visual material, such as graphs, pictures, and outlines, was limited in the lectures and readings. One comment suggested that if the prompts for the reading passages were presented both prior to and after the reading tasks, this would approximate conditions for reading in academic contexts.

Research question 2: Authenticity of performance on the prototype tasks

The instructors verified during their interviews that most of their students' performances on the prototype TOEFL tasks corresponded closely to how these students usually performed on classroom tasks or course assignments in their ESL courses. For the 208 performances of their students on the prototype tasks that the instructors evaluated, they stated 70% of the time that students' performances were equivalent to how the students usually spoke or wrote English in their ESL classes. Moreover, for an additional 8% of the ratings the instructors thought the students did better than they usually did in their ESL classes. But for 22% of the ratings the instructors thought the students did worse than they usually did in classes. These percentages were relatively consistent across the seven instructors and the three sites. Most of the estimates of the students performing worse on the prototype types involved three tasks, suggesting that these tasks might usefully be revised for or deleted from future field tests: the reading–writing task on dance, the listening–writing task on plate tectonics, and the reading–speaking task on innate versus learned behavior. The listening–writing task on plate tectonics was seemingly the most problematic of these tasks, as 46% of the students were perceived to perform worse on this task than they usually did in their classes.

The interview transcripts were full of expressions that attest to the instructors' perceptions that the prototype tasks tended to elicit performances from their students that they readily recognized as typical of these individual learners' performances in English. For instance, in the independent speaking or writing tasks:

> That's our student. That's typical of him at his best. He can be very articulate
> and quite forceful, and a strong speaker, and he knows what he wants to say,

A. Cumming,
L. Grant,
P. Mulcahy-
Ernt and
D. Powers

quite often. That's more like what we usually saw, as I say, when he was on his best form.

(Francis, student 130075, Independent speaking task)

Such remarks also abounded as the instructors commented on the match between a student's performance on the prototype tasks that integrate language modalities and the instructor's knowledge of the student's language abilities. For example:

I think that sample really demonstrated her ability well. Uh, she answered the prompt so well and identified all the parts and gave a lot of details from the lecture, and I thought it was really good the way the she connected the ideas together using transitions. Uh, so she was not just repeating facts, but making a synthesis of the ideas. So I think that sample was really good; it represented her well.

(Ann, student 240022, Groundwater listening speaking task)

Such correspondences were also evident for individual students across the various task types. For instance, Tracy consistently observed that the performances of student 130005 on several of the prototype tasks matched closely what she had seen him do in tasks in her class:

That is a classic example. That is bang on the way he always speaks in class and out of class. Perhaps a tad slower. He will often speak very quickly. He doesn't hesitate much unless he's thinking of something to say. There was for me, or for a nonarchitect, some vagueness in what he was referring to. It makes perfect sense if you know architecture and deconstructivism, but if you don't, he doesn't clarify, but he would do the same thing in his first language. So that's exactly the way he speaks. It's a perfect sample.

(Tracy, student 130005, Independent speaking task)

Task B6.10

➤ Many of the results here are reported in the actual voice of the research participants. Do you enjoy reading such data? Is it particularly persuasive? Why and/or why not?

Research question 3: Fulfillment of evidence claims for the prototype tasks

A. Cumming,
L. Grant,
P. Mulcahy-
Ernt and
D. Powers

Two types of information were solicited to address this research question. First, the seven instructors provided, in their questionnaire responses, impressionistic evaluations of the prototype tasks in view of the constructs that each task was intended to realize as well as the performances that their students had demonstrated on these tasks. Second, we correlated the independent ratings that the instructors had given of their students' abilities to perform the kinds of speaking and writing that were supposed to be represented in these tasks with the scores that the students were given on these tasks in the field tests.

A. Cumming,
L. Grant,
P. Mulcahy-
Ernt and
D. Powers

Writing tasks. The instructors' evaluations of the independent writing task (i.e., TOEFL essay about personal experiences and opinions) ranged from 'very effective' (ratings of 4 or 5 from four instructors) to middling (ratings of 3 from three instructors). The flexible opportunities this task offered for personal expression were mostly cited as its chief virtue. Tracy was positive about this task because 'students have freedom to explore a wide variety of experiences they've discussed and/or written about before.' Tyler similarly observed how students were 'able to respond to situations with which they were familiar.' Bob thought the 'open-ended prompts lead to individual inter-pretations.' Steve noted that 'everyone was able to write about these topics.' Ann stated, 'The topics to choose from were general enough to enable various proficiency levels of students to write their ideas.'

Francis expressed a contrary view, remarking that 'many students are very reluctant, for personal and/or cultural reasons, to freely express themselves in this area,' observing that the effectiveness of the independent writing task was variable: 'it worked better for some of our students than for others.' Sara contrasted this writing task with the other ones that involved reading or listening, claiming she thought the TOEFL essay was a 'better test of their writing' because the students 'didn't need to under-stand a reading/listening' passage prior to writing. At the same time, Sara criticized the time limit on this essay task and called it 'formulaic.'

The instructors' evaluations of the prototype writing tasks that involved responses to reading or listening materials were similarly positive (ratings of 4 or 5 on the scale of 5 for four instructors) to middling (ratings of 2 or 3 for three instructors). Six instructors praised the authenticity of these tasks, particularly for their correspondence to real texts and performance in academic settings. For example, 'The lectures were good simulations of real academic situations'; 'Typical of material they would encounter in university settings'; 'seems to be a true academic task'; 'it is an authentic type task (one that would be expected in an academic class)'; 'lecturers paraphrased and gave examples in an authentic way'; and 'they dealt with analysis and theory as academic texts do.'

Sara, however, judged these tasks less positively, observing that her students' writing performance was heavily dependent on their comprehension of the reading or listening source materials they had to write about. As she put it, 'They had to understand the lecture. It's very hard to write clearly when you don't know what you're writing about.' The limitations the other instructors observed about these tasks focused on two concerns. One concern was about bias or unfamiliarity in the topics: 'previous experi-ence and background cultural knowledge (especially Western culture) would predispose a student to do well'; 'Asians may not be familiar with ballet as an art form – the topic seems to be somewhat culturally biased'; 'outside of area of interest'; 'the lecture topic was perhaps unfamiliar to many students'; 'choices of different topics are recommended within that framework of delivery'; 'I think that more business-oriented or social science/education/public administration topics should be considered for readings and lectures. Many students starting graduate school in the U.S. are going to be studying in these areas (more so than dance or plate tectonics type subjects).' The other concern related to the presentation of the stimulus materials: 'they spoke slowly and paused much more than lecturers at university tend to'; 'the lectures were very short.' In the interests of facilitating examinees' comprehension of the stimulus materials, Steve recommended 'an outline or other visual aids,' and Ann suggested that 'PowerPoint-type slides (nonmoving visuals) or diagrams/pictures would be useful visuals.'

Speaking tasks. The instructors rated the prototype speaking tasks positively overall (ratings of 4 or 5), except for Sara, who rated the speaking tasks in response to readings

A. Cumming,
L. Grant,
P. Mulcahy-
Ernt and
D. Powers

or lectures as limited in their effectiveness (giving these ratings of 2). As with the comparable writing tasks, Sara felt her students did not perform well if they had not fully understood the stimulus materials they had to speak about.

The independent speaking task was rated positively by all the instructors (all rating it 5 out of 5 except for Francis, who rated it 3). They praised its 'straightforward questions and situation'; 'freedom to explore topics of interest'; 'a topic that most students could speak on'; 'real life tasks'; 'many opportunities for students to recall their past experiences and to use their basic communicative skills'; and the 'clear sample' of students' speech obtained. These comments resembled those that the instructors gave to the independent writing task. Limitations the instructors observed in this task related to its time constraints and the affective states of students speaking independently into a microphone ('anxiety can be a barrier to effective performance'; 'some students won't/can't respond to this sort of task'; 'seemed too short; not time for development') or the formulaic nature of the students' speech ('they may have given this speech before in ESL classes'; 'doesn't necessarily elicit abstract ideas').

Some of the instructors evaluated more positively the speaking tasks that involved responding to listening materials (ratings of 4 or 5 for all instructors) than the tasks that involved speaking about written texts (which three people rated as 2 or 3 out of 5). They praised these speaking tasks for the opportunities they presented to students: 'forces students to speak about abstract topics'; 'being put on the spot to orally explain what one has heard in class is a skill students require and one which they often lack'; 'students encounter such situations in classrooms and need more experience and exposure.' Likewise, the instructors praised the realism of the stimulus texts, particularly the lecture ('the lectures balanced theory and abstract thought with examples and concrete detail in a realistic mix'; 'lecture was clear; the topic not too specialized'; 'visuals, vocabulary, geographical location were identified to reinforce the oral presentation') and the conversation ('very typical conversation – realistic exchanges'; 'idioms and natural miscommunications or vagueness were included in the conversations'), and in some instances also the reading stimuli ('the range of texts used was revealing – pointed towards the importance of contextual understanding in reading comprehension'; 'good task, but . . .').

The limitations the instructors observed in these tasks likewise concerned qualities of the stimulus materials: 'the passages were dense; students may have had trouble remembering information under pressure'; 'the speakers spoke slowly and repeated ideas more frequently than normal. There was no background noise'; 'the conversation-based task used with our students was not academic in its nature/topic'; 'Most but not all students here are familiar with the background. If not, would it go over their heads?' Some instructors also queried the abilities that students demonstrated in these integrated tasks: 'memorization and repetition of the lecture passages may have taken place'; 'Asian speakers . . . were less confident'; 'wide range of skills and abilities in the class and therefore difficult to get [an] accurate reflection' [of their abilities].' This criticism focused particularly on the task that required speaking about a reading text: 'Reading text and topic were tough. I noticed only the very high-level students handled it as well as their ability really was. Weaker students didn't seem to stand a chance.'; 'Too technical? Many students just quoted parts of the text.'

Instructors' ratings and scores on the field test. The instructors' ratings of the students' abilities to speak about personal experiences and opinions correlated significantly, showing a large effect size, with the students' scores on the independent speaking task: rho = .48 (p < .01), r = 1.1, n = 28. None of the other ratings of the students' abilities by the instructors correlated significantly with the students' scores

A. Cumming,
L. Grant,
P. Mulcahy-
Ernt and
D. Powers

on the prototype tasks that were designed to assess corresponding constructs. The only other correlation to be statistically significant and to show a large effect size was the correlation between the two writing tasks that involved writing from sources (i.e., the listening–writing task about plate tectonics and the reading–writing task about dance): rho = .50 (p < .01), r = 1.2, n = 41. It should be noted, of course, that because individual test items or tasks are typically of marginal reliability (when compared to the reliability of a complete test), the correlations of individual task performance with instructors' ratings can be expected to be relatively low. However, some of these correlations did show small effect sizes, indicating that a larger sample of teachers and students might have produced significant correlations among the variables.

Discussion

Although exploratory and small in scale, this study provides considerable qualitative information that demonstrates the educational relevance, authenticity, and content validity of the prototype tasks being field-tested for a new version of the TOEFL test. At the same time, these findings point toward revisions that might usefully be undertaken on certain aspects of the prototype tasks being field-tested for the new TOEFL.

★ Task B6.11

We often see an apologia like this in research papers in testing: 'Although exploratory and small in scale . . .'

➤ Do you think this paper was too small in scope? Regardless, do you find the paper persuasive?

A. Cumming,
L. Grant,
P. Mulcahy-
Ernt and
D. Powers

Considering tasks that (a) involve independent writing or speaking and (b) involve writing or speaking in response to reading or listening materials, seven highly experienced ESL instructors expressed positive impressions of the prototype tasks, judging them to be realistic and appropriate in their simulation of academic content and situations, in the skills they required students to perform, and in the opportunities they provided for students to demonstrate their abilities in English. Importantly, the instructors thought the prototype tasks permitted the majority of their students to perform in English in the test contexts in ways that corresponded closely to the performance those students usually demonstrated in their ESL classes and course assignments. As such, the present results contribute some limited evidence for the construct validity of these prototype tasks, suggesting that the prototype tasks field-tested here have the potential for positive washback on educational practices. In instances where certain tasks were not, the findings suggest ways in which these tasks might be improved in further field trials.

The instructors' impressions of the prototype tasks and of their students' performances on them support the inclusion on the new TOEFL of the two principal types of tasks field-tested here: (a) independent writing and speaking tasks that permit students to choose how they express themselves in English, and (b) tasks that integrate students' reading of or listening to specific academic texts then either writing

A. Cumming,
L. Grant,
P. Mulcahy-
Ernt and
D. Powers

or speaking about them. The instructors had few criticisms to make of the independent writing or speaking tasks, apart from observing that they tended to invite rhetorically formulaic kinds of language production. Although familiar with the independent writing task (as the TOEFL essay or the Test of Written English), the instructors appeared to welcome the parallel version of it in the form of the independent speaking task, and to find their students performed well on it. The instructors praised the new integrated tasks for their authenticity with respect to the demands of academic studies in English, but they also raised numerous criticisms that suggest how such tasks might be optimally designed.

The most prevalent problem observed in the integrated tasks was that students with lower proficiency in English were hampered in their speaking or writing performance if they did not comprehend the ideas, vocabulary, or background context of the reading or listening stimulus texts. This problem of task dependencies, which was anticipated from the outset of task development, has commonly been observed as a limitation in language tests that use interpretive texts as the basis for language production tasks (e.g., Clapham, 1996). To this end, several instructors suggested that topics be selected for such texts that most students would be fairly familiar with and interested in; visual or schematic materials be appended to guide examinees' inter-pretations of the principal content in and rhetorical organization of the texts (cf. prototype tasks analyzed by Ginther, 2001); and examinees need to be familiar with and practiced in the task types and their prompts. At the same time, the instructors praised characteristics of the prototype tasks – such as their authenticity, natural language, and academic orientation – suggesting these characteristics be retained as primary features of the tasks. Indeed, some instructors thought the tasks might be made even more challenging in terms of their cognitive or intellectual demands. In turn, many of the instructors' remarks about their students' performance on the prototype tasks indicate that the limitations that some students experienced in comprehending the content, vocabulary, or significance of the stimulus materials realistically reflected limitations in their abilities in English. Given that the sample of ESL students here included a range of students who were studying English just prior to attending, or who had just been admitted into their first year of, universities in the United States or Canada, this tendency indicates that the present prototype tasks may be pitched at a level that might demarcate distinctly between students who do have, or do not yet have, the requisite proficiency in English for academic studies. Students lacking abilities to read or listen to academic texts then write or speak about them in English might simply not be able to fare well in this new version of the test until they have acquired such abilities. Orientation or other educational materials could help such students determine their readiness for the test and to prepare themselves for it.

Interpreting the correlations between the instructors' ratings of their students' abilities and the students' performance on the prototype tasks is difficult for several reasons: Only a small number of teachers (and small samples of their respective students) participated in the study; over half the data from speaking tasks were lost in transmission from the field test sites; and the number of tasks that could reasonably be considered in an interview was too small to be able to distinguish between the construct of the task and the topics and prompts through which each task was realized. Moreover, as mentioned earlier, because individual tasks can be expected to be of only modest reliability when compared with the reliability of a complete test, correlations were necessarily restricted. We were therefore not able to demonstrate, as evidence for construct validation, that scores on the prototype tasks corresponded

A. Cumming,
L. Grant,
P. Mulcahy-
Ernt and
D. Powers

to teachers' judgments about relevant aspects of their students' abilities. Nonetheless, many suggestive directions arise from these results.

The most striking quantitative result was that scores on the independent speaking task correlated with the instructors' ratings of their students' usual abilities to speak about personal experiences and opinions. This finding seems to verify the worth and relevance of this task type, which has not previously appeared on the TOEFL test. Likewise, the correlations between the two tasks that required students to write about either reading or listening passages suggest these tasks may be assessing similar constructs. But the lack of correlations between the instructors' ratings of their students' abilities and the students' scores on the prototype tasks is puzzling (apart from the empirical constraints outlined in the preceding paragraph).

One possible interpretation of this pattern of findings is Cummins's hypothesis about teachers' abilities to distinguish between their students' basic interpersonal communicative skills (BICS) and cognitive-academic language proficiency (CALP) (e.g., articulated in Cummins, 1984, and refined in subsequent publications). Cummins's research suggests that ESL teachers are able, from frequently observing their students' oral performance in classes, to make relatively accurate judgments about their students' BICS, but that they seldom have access to information about their ESL students' CALP because that is usually exercised mentally and privately in the context of tests, reading, or studying, so teachers have difficulties evaluating these abilities. This tendency may have applied to the present instructors as well. But given their focus on teaching writing and academic skills to their students, and their claims to have known their students' abilities in these domains very well, this is a speculative interpretation at best. Another possible interpretation is that the prototype writing tasks differed from the types of writing the students usually did in their courses (i.e., the prototype tasks were single drafts written under strict time constraints, rather than multiple-draft compositions revised at students' leisure between classes), as Sara remarked in her interviews, so the instructors' ratings may have referred to different conditions for writing than in a test context. In this regard, regular university professors, rather than ESL instructors, may be informative judges of the content validity of prototype test tasks, as demonstrated by Elder (1993) or for the new TOEFL by Rosenfeld et al. (2001). Moreover, the instructors themselves may have differed from each other in their standards for assessing students' writing because they each taught different courses and worked at different institutions. Alternative explanations may well be considered within the scoring schemes for the prototype tasks and the nature of the tasks themselves, which would appear to warrant refinements, particularly the three tasks (i.e., on plate tectonics, dance, and innate vs. learned behavior) that elicited numerous performances that the instructors judged to be worse than their students usually did in classes. Such tasks did not appear to have a high-level schematic organization to their presentation of information that students could easily grasp in their comprehension or convey in their writing or speaking, suggesting that a basic level of rhetorical, schematic organization of information might be required in reading or listening to source texts to make them viable for integrated tasks on a test like the TOEFL.

Task B6.12

➤ The authors close with a discussion of some difficulties in interpretation. What do you think of their resolution of those difficulties? Do you agree, and/or can you come up with alternative interpretations?

Task B6.13

➤ With the information at hand in this report, including the appendices below, could you replicate the research?

➤ Why is replication important? Were you to re-do this study, would you pursue any different procedures – perhaps different (or more) prototyping? Why or why not? Is there a way to change the procedures in order to address some of the concluding difficulties that the authors discuss?

Appendix Profile Questionnaire

A. Cumming,
L. Grant,
P. Mulcahy-
Ernt and
D. Powers

The purpose of this questionnaire is to gather background information about you and your overall impressions of the prototype tasks for the project, A Teacher-Verification Study of TOEFL Prototype Tasks. As with other data generated for this project, your identity will remain confidential.

The pseudonym I would like to use is: _____

Date of completing this questionnaire: _____

I.   The Prototype Tasks
1.   Overall, how well do you think the prototype tasks elicited the performance of the students from your class? For each skill, please circle the number that best corresponds to your answer. Circle 0 if you can't tell.

	Not Effective				Very Effective	
Writing	1	2	3	4	5	0
A. About personal experiences and opinions	1	2	3	4	5	0
B. About academic topics						
1. in response to lectures	1	2	3	4	5	0
2. in response to reading text	1	2	3	4	5	0
Speaking	1	2	3	4	5	0
A. About personal experiences and opinions	1	2	3	4	5	0
B. About academic topics						
1. in response to lectures	1	2	3	4	5	0
2. in response to conversations	1	2	3	4	5	0
3. in response to reading text	1	2	3	4	5	0

A. Cumming,
L. Grant,
P. Mulcahy-
Ernt and
D. Powers

Extension

2. For each of the tasks, please indicate the ways, if any, in which they were effective and also the ways, if any, in which they were not effective. If there were any specific tasks that you felt were effective or not effective, please describe which tasks.

Writing

A. About personal experiences and opinions

Effective because _____

Not effective because_____

B. About academic topics
1. In response to lectures

Effective because _____

Not effective because_____

2. In response to reading text

Effective because _____

Not effective because_____

Speaking

A. About personal experiences and opinions

Effective because _____

Not effective because_____

B. About academic topics

1. In response to lectures

Effective because _____

Not effective because_____

2. In response to conversations

Effective because _____

Not effective because_____

3. In response to reading text

Effective because _____

Not effective because _____

3. Overall, how well do you think the tasks represent the domain of academic English required for studies at an English-medium university?

Not well				Very well	
1	2	3	4	5	0

Why?_____

_____

Which tasks do this best? _____

_____

What do you think is missing?_____

_____

A. Cumming,
L. Grant,
P. Mulcahy-
Ernt and
D. Powers

II. Personal Profile

1. My gender is: Male _____ Female _____

2. My age is: _____

3. I have taught English for _____ years.

III. Current Teaching Situation

1. My current role is: Assessor _____ Instructor _____ Administrator _____
    Student _____ Researcher _____ Other (specify) _____

2. The context(s) I have mostly worked in is: English (mother tongue) _____ ESL ___
    EFL _____ ESP _____ Other (specify) _____

3. I have taught the present students for _____ weeks.

4. I know their abilities in English:

	Not well				Very well	
Writing	1	2	3	4	5	0
Speaking	1	2	3	4	5	0
Reading	1	2	3	4	5	0
Listening	1	2	3	4	5	0

IV. Language(s)

1. My first language is: _____

2. My dominant language at home at present is: _____

3. My dominant language at the workplace is: _____

V. Educational History

Please describe your educational background in terms of:

	Degree/diploma/ certificate	Subject area	Language of education
1. Undergraduate studies			
2. Postgraduate studies			
3. Professional certification			
4. Any specialized training related to assessment			

VI. Experiences Teaching and/or Assessing English

1. Please describe any significant teaching and/or assessment experiences that might have influenced
    your assessments of the ESL students' abilities in the present research project. _____
    _____
    _____

2. How would you describe your own skill in assessing English as a second language?
    _____ Expert _____ Competent _____ Novice

3. How many years' experience do you have in assessing ESL? _____

Extension

A. Cumming,
L. Grant,
P. Mulcahy-
Ernt and
D. Powers

4. Have you given any training courses in assessing language performance or administered such programs? If so, please describe these briefly._____

_____

Thank you for this information!

Summary

This reading is an entire data-driven research paper. Our focus has been twofold: to engage critical reading skills for empirical articles, and to explore the topic of Unit A6: test development stages such as prototyping and field trials. As we noted, the B6 text is both a research article and the write-up of a test development project, and so it reflects our contention in *How to use this book*:

> In a sense, therefore, each section of this book is about the practical aspects of *doing* and of *creating*. And so each section has a research implication; no section is concerned purely with exposition. Research ideas may be made explicit in the *Exploration* section, but they are implicit throughout the book; put another way, the creative drive of language testing makes it a research enterprise, we think, at all times.

Unit B7
Scoring performance tests

Assessing writing and speaking samples has always been considered important for two main reasons. Firstly, the view has often been expressed that the best way of predicting writing or speaking performance in 'the real world' is to get students to write or speak in a test. Secondly, it has been assumed that only by including writing and speaking in a test will the test have the required washback on the classroom (see Unit B5). But we realize that this is a simplistic view of testing and of the impact that testing may have on teaching practice.

The first problem that we encounter is defining 'the real world', and trying to recreate that in the test (Unit A5). Then comes the problem of how to score the limited sample that we are able to collect in the test, so that the score carries meaning for the target domain and is relevant to any instructional context that is preparing learners to become competent communicators within that domain.

When judges look at a piece of writing or a sample of speech they must focus on a particular part of what is written or said. The judges' reaction, whether presented as a score, summary or comment, is an abstraction. One of the key tasks is to ensure that the abstractions we create are the most useful for test purpose.

Task B7.1

➤ In your teaching context, how do you score writing and speaking samples?

➤ Did you develop the tools you use within the institution or adapt them from an external source?

➤ Describe the development process, or explain the rationale for the selection and adaptation of the tools.

In this Unit we will work with a text that argues for the use of multiple-trait scoring in English as a second language contexts. Hamp-Lyons was among the first to distinguish between the different types of rating scales that could be used to score sample performances from test prompts, clearly identifying three basic types of scales that we still work with today. While the text does not deal with scale construction methodology or the more recent concern with performance conditions, it remains one of the clearest published arguments for the use of a particular type of scale for testing writing in a specific context.

Text B7
L. Hamp-Lyons

L. Hamp-Lyons (1991) 'Scoring procedures for ESL contexts.' In L. Hamp-Lyons (ed.) *Assessing Second Language Writing in Academic Contexts.* Norwood, NJ: Ablex, 241–276

ESL writing: a different context

While all writers would benefit from sensitive and detailed feedback on their writing, ESL writers have a special need for scoring procedures that go beyond the mere provision of a single number score. First . . . ESL writers often acquire different components of written control at different rates. Every instructor of second language writers has encountered those students who have fluency without accuracy and those with accuracy but little fluency. We also sometimes see writers who have mastered a wide vocabulary but markedly less syntactic control; or syntactic control not matched by rhetorical control; and so on. With second language writers who already have some mastery of a specialized discipline, it is quite common to encounter texts that show very strong content while grammatical and textual competence lag far behind. It may be that as ESL writers advance, the strands of competence in their writing converge until at the highest levels unity (that is, an equal measure of competence in all areas) is achieved . . . Few L1 writing assessment measures provide the level of detail that would allow such disparities to emerge.

Another reason there is a need for a special kind of scoring in ESL writing assessment contexts is to help ensure that scores reflect the salient facets of writing in a balanced way. The tendency of many raters is to respond negatively to the large number of grammatical errors found in many second language texts, and not to reward the strength of ideas and experiences the writer discusses. Or, when the assessment emphasizes ideas and formal argument structures, readers may not attend sufficiently to language errors that would be seriously damaging in an academic course context. In order to reach a reasonable balance among all the essential elements of good writing, readers need to pay conscious attention to all those elements. A detailed scoring procedure requiring the readers to attend to the multidimensionality of ESL writing is needed.

But even more important, the chances of significant improvement in writing are greater for ESL writers than for most L1 writers. By the time they reach college most first language writers have achieved most of their writing skills. Writing courses may appear to move them forward, but this movement may prove temporary . . . Second language learners, on the other hand, are *in the process* of developing their language skills, of acquiring new areas of control and expanding their confidence in areas where they already have some control. ESL writing teachers have the joy of seeing their students make real progress, often in rather short periods of instruction. The potential for using writing assessment instruments to measure the real language gain of second language learners over a course of instruction (that is, achievement testing) is very real, but once again this means that a detailed scoring procedure is needed.

A carefully constructed writing proficiency test with detailed score reporting is not only of great use for large-scale proficiency assessment of writing and for the program evaluation application of evaluating change in writing. It also offers the potential for providing information that can be used in language instruction programs for making fine-grained initial placements or needs diagnosis. A writer whose score information suggests she is weak on syntactic structure but strong in vocabulary might be placed in a grammar class as well as at the appropriate level of the writing course sequence; another writer, whose score information suggests he has strong grammatical skills but has little of substance to say may be placed into a reading course in addition to the appropriate level of the writing course sequence. However, to be able to do this, more than a single score is needed. I return to this later, but first I describe holistic methods of writing assessment in general, and holistic scoring and primary trait scoring in particular.

Task B7.2

Hamp-Lyons argues that many second-language learners may have progressed further in one area of competence than another. She later terms this 'a marked profile.'

➤ Is this true in your teaching experience?

➤ Which competences do your own students develop first, and in which do they 'lag behind'?

Holistic scoring

In holistic scoring, each reader of a piece of writing reads the text rather quickly (typically one minute or less per handwritten page) and assigns the text a single score for its writing quality. This may be done wholly subjectively, or (and more commonly nowadays) by reference to a scoring guide or rubric, in which case it is often known as 'focused holistic scoring.'
[. . .]
Holistic scoring is a sorting or ranking procedure and is not designed to offer correction, feedback, or diagnosis. This is implicit and inherent in the nature of 'holism.' We are increasingly coming to view this as a severely limiting feature of holistic scoring, and to demand a richer definition of a 'valid' writing assessment.
[. . .]
In addition to the theoretical difficulties with holistic scoring, the nature of holistic judgments presents a practical weakness, since scores generated in this way cannot be explained either to the other readers who belong to the same assessment community and who are expected to score reliably together, or to the people affected by the decisions made through the holistic scoring process – the student writer, her parents and teachers, her academic counselors . . . To a greater or lesser degree depending on the individual reader, readers must give up their subjective holistic responses to the meaning and value of the text as text and adjust their responses to conform with those of other readers.
[. . .]

L. Hamp-Lyons

Primary trait scoring

Primary trait scoring is based on a view that one can only judge whether a writing sample is good or not by reference to its exact context, and that appropriate scoring criteria should be developed for each prompt. Thus, a primary trait scoring guide is designed separately for every writing task and consists of (a) the task, (b) the statement of the primary rhetorical trait to be elicited, (c) an interpretation of the task hypothesizing writing performance to be expected, (d) an explanation of how the task and primary trait are related, (e) a scoring guide, (f) sample papers, and (g) an explanation of scores on sample papers. Development of the scoring guide must be coupled with the careful development of prompts that test specified abilities such as the ability to write a certain mode of discourse or to write for a particular audience. The abilities specified must be those found to be salient for the context in which the writing assessment takes place: A primary trait scoring procedure is, then, very different from most holistic scoring procedures, which have often been transferred from the college or agency for which they were developed and used elsewhere. Not only must each school and college develop its own prompts and primary trait scoring guide, it must do so with almost the same expenditure of time and expertise for every new prompt.

★ Task B7.3

Consider the following two rating scales for speaking.

International Second Language Proficiency Ratings (ISLPR)

0	ZERO PROFICIENCY	Unable to communicate in the language.
0+	FORMULAIC PROFICIENCY	Able to perform in a very limited capacity within the most immediate, predictable areas of need, using essentially formulaic language.
1–	MINIMUM 'CREATIVE' PROFICIENCY	Able to satisfy immediate, predictable needs, using predominantly formulaic language.
1	BASIC TRANSACTIONAL PROFICIENCY	Able to satisfy basic everyday transactional needs.
1+	TRANSACTIONAL PROFICIENCY	Able to satisfy everyday transactional needs and limited social needs.
2	BASIC SOCIAL PROFICIENCY	Able to satisfy basic social needs, and routine needs pertinent to everyday commerce and to linguistically undemanding 'vocational' fields.
2+	SOCIAL PROFICIENCY	
3	BASIC 'VOCATIONAL' PROFICIENCY	Able to perform effectively in most informal and formal situations pertinent to social and community life and everyday commerce and recreation, and in situations which are not linguistically demanding in own 'vocational' fields.

3+	BASIC 'VOCATIONAL' PROFICIENCY PLUS	
4	'VOCATIONAL' PROFICIENCY	Able to perform very effectively in almost all situations pertinent to social and community life and everyday commerce and recreation, and generally in almost all situations pertinent to own 'vocational' fields.
4+	ADVANCED 'VOCATIONAL' PROFICIENCY	
5	NATIVE-LIKE PROFICIENCY	Proficiency equivalent to that of a native speaker of the same sociocultural variety.

Extract from the Fluency Rating Scale

Band 3

A candidate in band 3 will hardly ever misunderstand a question or be unable to respond to a question from the interviewer. On the odd occasion when it does happen a band 3 candidate will almost always ask for clarification from the interviewer.

Most pauses in the speech of a band 3 candidate will occur when they require 'thinking time' in order to provide a propositionally appropriate utterance. Time is sometimes needed to plan a sentence grammatically in advance, especially after making an error which the candidate then rephrases.

A band 3 candidate is very conscious of his/her use of lexis, and often pauses to think about the word which has been used, or to select another which they consider to be better in the context. The candidate may even question the interviewer overtly regarding the appropriacy of the word which has been chosen.

Often candidates in this band will give examples, counter examples or reasons to support their point of view.

(At band 3 and above there is an increasing tendency for candidates to use 'backchanneling' – the use of 'hm' or 'yeah' – when the interviewer is talking, giving the interview a greater sense of normal conversation, although many better candidates still do not use this device.)

Band 4

A band 4 candidate will only very rarely misunderstand a question of the interviewer, fail to respond, or dry up in the middle of an utterance.

A candidate in this band will exhibit a much greater tendency than candidates in any other band to express doubt about what they are saying. They will often use words such as 'maybe' and 'perhaps' when presenting their own point of view or opinion. More often than not, they will back up their opinion with examples or provide reasons for holding a certain belief. They will pause frequently to consider exactly how to express the content of what they wish to say and how they will present their views. (They will only rarely respond with a single word unless asked a polar question by the interviewer.)

There will be far fewer pauses to consider the grammatical structure of an utterance and pausing to consider the appropriacy of a lexical item chosen is rare. A candidate in this band will reformulate a sentence from time to time if it is considered to be inaccurate or the grammar does not allow the candidate to complete the proposition which he/she wishes to express.

The ISPLR, formerly known as the Australian Second Language Proficiency Ratings,[8] and the Fluency Rating Scale (Fulcher, 1996), have both been classified as 'detailed, holistic rating scales' (North, 1994).

➤ In the light of Hamp-Lyons's description of scale types, do you agree with this classification?

➤ Which rating scale would you find it easier to use, and why?

Multiple trait scoring

[. . .] The development of multiple trait scoring procedures has been motivated by the desire, first, to find ways of assessing writing which in addition to being highly reliable would also provide some degree of diagnostic information, to students and to their teachers and/or advisers; and second, to find ways of assessing writing with the level of validity that primary trait scoring has, but with enough simplicity for teachers and small testing programs in schools and colleges to apply in the development of their own writing tests.

'Multiple trait scoring' implies scoring any single essay on more than one facet or trait exhibited by the text. When proponents of holistic scoring object to methods that do this, they are usually reacting against the 'analytic' scoring used in the 1960s and 1970s, which focused on relatively trivial features of text (grammar, spelling, handwriting) and which did indeed reduce writing to an activity apparently composed of countable units strung together.

[. . .]

Multiple trait scoring procedures are grounded in the context for which they are used, and are therefore developed on-site for a specific purpose with a specific group of writers, and with the involvement of the readers who will make judgments in the context. Each is also developed as a response to actual writing on a single, carefully specified, topic type. Unlike primary trait instruments, however, multiple trait scoring instruments can be applied to a range of prompts, as long as those prompts fulfill the initial design criteria for prompts for which the multiple trait instrument was developed, and as long as the context remains essentially unchanged. This makes them more viable for small but committed groups of teachers to develop, pilot, and monitor in their own context, thereafter adding new prompts and paying close attention that new prompts pursue the same writing goals as the original prompts. Increasingly, the trend is to develop multiple trait scoring instruments to fit a particular view or construct of what writing is in this context, and to reflect what it is important that writers can do.

[. . .]

Advantages of multiple trait instruments

While multiple trait instruments are less costly than primary trait instruments because they can be used with multiple prompts that fit the design parameters for the instrument, they are considerably more costly than holistic scoring because of the extensive development efforts involved. What, then, are their advantages?

Salience. By 'salience' I mean that the writing qualities evaluated, and the kinds of writing samples collected are those that have been found appropriate in the context where the assessment takes place . . . Working in their own context, test developers and essay readers together can determine that 'control of register' (as an example) is or is not a salient trait for scale development. A more common example might concern the common college expectation of writing, and therefore exam prompts, for 'argument' or 'argumentative writing,' and the exploration of the local definition of 'argument.' In some contexts 'argument' implies an essay taking a position for or against some statement on an issue, as in a debate. In other contexts 'argument' requires more than that, expecting a consideration of *both* sides of the issue and a weighing of the evidence in the balance before arriving at a position. In two different local contexts, then, two multiple trait instruments would appear rather different because they would reflect the different types of argumentative writing called for and the different textual expectations of them. Because the multiple trait procedure, like primary trait scoring, involves prompt specification and development as well as scoring and reader training, a prerequisite of a multiple trait instrument is that there is a close match between the writing to be done and the skills and text facets to be evaluated.

Reality and community. One advantage of multiple trait scoring is that, once the initial process of data collection, prompt and rating guide development and validation is complete, and readers have been trained, readers' judgments are linked to something which is at once external and internal. More than this, a multiple trait instrument recognizes the readers' input, for it is built from that input, among the other data. Some of those who have to read assessment essays may dread the straightjacket that such a detailed instrument seems to imply, but a multiple trait rating guide, though closely specified, is not concrete. During training and refresher training discussions between readers about scores can be tied to the language of the criteria and standards, and discrepancies can be negotiated as each reader matches what she or he sees in a piece of writing with a personal interpretation of the language of the scale. This makes compromise easier to achieve than in the extremely concrete conditions of a placement system. Compromise is also easier to achieve than in the extremely abstract and personal conditions of holistic scoring, where each reader falls back on a personal reading and response without a shared language to talk about qualities in the writing, but is at the same time constrained by the holistic reading system to move to the same score as the majority of readers.

Increased information. The chief advantage of multiple trait scoring combined with profile reporting, and particularly important when working with ESL writers, is that the judgments made by assessment readers can be translated into information which can be shared with the writers, their academic advisors and other concerned parties. In contrast to holistic scoring, where the reader who notices an unevenness of quality in the writing has no way to report this observation, and must somehow reconcile it as a single score, multiple trait scoring permits performance on different components or facets of writing to be assessed and reported. Usually, the writing in any one sample looks rather similar from any perspective: I call a set of scores on multiple traits which arise from this kind of writing, with no visible peaks or troughs of skill, a 'flat profile.' But sometimes, and more often with ESL writers, the quality looks rather different from some perspectives than from others. I refer to this kind of uneven writing as 'marked', and to a set of scores which reflect the unevenness as a 'marked profile'.

[. . .]

If a writer's overall performance puts her into the category of those who will receive special courses or other special services, by looking *inside* the information provided by the multiple trait instrument, that is, by looking at the score profile, the writer, the class teacher, and the program administrator can make good decisions about which course offering or other kind of service would most help this individual writer make progress.

[. . .]

Conclusion

Scoring procedures are often decided only after a range of other test decisions have been made. I hope that this chapter has been able to show how decisions about scoring procedures are influenced by, and influence, all the other components of the process of developing a writing test. Designing and putting into operation a writing test is an iterative process – we must go back and forth between all the elements of our system, seeking to keep them in harmony. To wait until all the pieces are in place to think about how to score essay tests is to leave it far too late.

★ **Task B7.4**

Hamp-Lyons suggests that the following facets might be included in a multiple trait instrument:

- vocabulary
- grammatical competence
- textual competence
- accuracy
- fluency
- syntactic control
- rhetorical control

➤ Refer back to Unit 3A. Which of these would you retain to score an argumentative essay in a test of academic English? What other constructs might you wish to score?

➤ When judges are asked to rate using multiple traits, how many do you think they can use simultaneously when rating the same assignment?

➤ What dangers might be associated with asking a single rater to make too many independent judgments?

Summary

By their very nature, tests have to be relatively short. During the time available for the test enough information has to be collected on each individual for a reasonable inference to be made about the person's ability on the constructs of interest (see Unit A2). Tests of writing and speaking inevitably take up much more time than other tasks, and the number of samples that can be elicited is relatively small. It is therefore important that we maximize the information that is gained from each writing task or speaking task. One way to do this is to ensure that the rating scales focus attention on the constructs of interest, and that each of these constructs is carefully and empirically linked to the target domain of inference.

When it is possible to undertake multiple-trait rating, the information that we are extracting from each sample becomes much richer than is possible with other scoring methods. As Hamp-Lyons makes clear, this allows score-enhancement in the form of diagnostic feedback that can inform the learning process.

Perhaps the most important principle to emerge from this text is that designing the scoring system should be an integral part of a test design project; how we score tasks needs to be considered *as the tasks are being developed*, and not at some later stage. As we saw in Unit A6, scoring procedures should be part of the process of prototyping. Along with developing the rating scales upon data collected from task performance, this grounds rating scale design in the consideration of validity from the beginning of test design. Thus, it avoids the problem of having to train raters to use scales before there is any validity evidence at all for the use of the scale (see Fulcher, 2003a: 145–147).

Unit B8
Interlocutor training and behaviour

We now know that it is important to train the people who are going to be involved in test administration. At its most basic this involves the logistics of simply getting things done, such as providing the right-size chairs or making sure that the space for testing is properly organized (see Fulcher, 2003a: 152–153), through to ensuring that raters or interlocutors in a speaking test employ the behaviours that are needed to elicit a ratable speech sample. The importance of *standardization* lies in making sure that all test takers have the same experience, in so far as any variation in the administration may impact negatively upon their performance or scores.

The training of interlocutors is one of the most controversial areas of standardization. Although Shohamy (1994) has shown that simulated (tape-mediated) speaking tests do not contain the range of functions that are evidenced in tests where there is an interlocutor present, the absence of the interlocutor in the simulation leads to increased standardization. A preference for a tape-mediated test is expressed by those who see variation by the interlocutor as a potential threat to validity (Stansfield and Kenyon, 1992).

While removing the interlocutor from the speaking test completely increases standardization, introducing additional interlocutors in the form of other test takers may have the effect of increasing variation. But this may be the price we have to pay for claiming to measure a much more complex construct (see the discussion in Fulcher, 2003a: 186–190).

★ Task B8.1

Before reading the text selected for this Unit, consider these questions. Jot down your current views from your own experience of taking part in speaking tests.

➤ In a speaking test between candidate and interlocutor or rater:

(a) Should the interlocutor direct and change topic?
(b) How much should the interlocutor contribute to the interaction?
(c) Should the interlocutor help the test taker to 'perform at their best'?

➤ In a speaking test where two candidates talk to each other, do you think it would matter if they:

(d) did not speak the same first language?
(e) were at different proficiency levels?
(f) differed in age, gender, race, profession or personality?

➤ Do you think the scores from a tape-mediated test would be more 'interpretable' than the scores from a speaking test with human interlocutors?

The article in this Unit presents data taken from two tests of speaking. One candidate took two tests with two different interlocutors or interviewers. The two performances were then scored by eight raters. The two performances were qualitatively different, and the test taker would have received a different score. It is shown that the differences occur because of the contribution of the interlocutor and the interaction between interlocutor and test taker.

This text raises in its starkest form the dilemma of standardization. Should variation be eliminated through training or the use of ever more prescriptive interlocutor scripts? If this is the route we pursue, why should we not abandon the interlocutor and revert to tape-mediated tests? Or is the variation an essential part of the construct? And if it is, how can we claim that we are being 'fair' to test takers by providing them with a similar assessment experience?

In this text you will be looking at transcribed data from an oral proficiency interview. The transcription notation is described in Atkinson and Heritage (1984), and we provide the key elements here so that you can read the transcripts.

	(.)	Just noticeable pause
	(.3), (2.6)	Timed pauses
	↑word, ↓word	Onset of noticeable pitch rise or fall
A:	word [word	Square brackets aligned across adjacent lines
B:	[word	denote the start and end of overlapping talk.
	.hhh	Audible inhalation
	hhh	Audible exhalation
	wo(h)rd	(h) indicates that there is laughter within the word
	wor-	A sharp cut-off
	wo:rd	Colons show that the speaker has stretched the preceding sound.
	(words)	The speech is unintelligible and this is a guess at what might have been said
	( )	Speech which is unclear or in doubt.
A:	word=	The equals sign shows that there is no discernible
B:	=word	pause between two speakers' turns or, if put between two sounds within a single speaker's turn, shows that they run together

word, WORD	Underlined sounds are louder, capitals louder still
°word°	material between 'degree signs' is quiet
>word word<	Inwards arrows show faster speech,
<word word>	outward slower
→	Analyst's signal of a significant line
((text))	Non-verbal activity

Text B8
A. Brown

A. Brown (2003) 'Interviewer variation and the co-construction of speaking proficiency.' *Language Testing* 20, 1, 1–25

Introduction

Oral interviews, in which examiner and candidate take part in an unscripted discussion of general topics, have long been a popular method for assessing oral second language proficiency. Because they incorporate features of nontest or conversational interaction, they are claimed to allow second language learners to demonstrate their capacity to 'interact in an authentic communicative event utilising different components of communicative competence extemporaneously' (Ross, 1996: 3–4).

Conversational interviews are characterized by an unscripted and relatively unstructured format. Whilst interviewers are generally provided with guidelines that suggest topics and general questioning focus, specific questions are neither preformulated nor identical for each candidate; the interaction is intended to unfold in a conversational manner. However, whilst the unpredictability and dynamic nature of the interaction forms the basis of claims by proponents of the oral interview that it is a valid measure of conversational communicative competence, it has also long been argued that this unpredictability may compromise test reliability.

[. . .]

Interviewers have been found to vary in aspects of behaviour as diverse as:

■ the level of rapport that they establish with candidates (Lazaraton, 1996a; McNamara and Lumley, 1997; Morton *et al.*, 1997);
■ their functional and topical choices (Brown and Lumley, 1997; Reed and Halleck, 1997);
■ the ways in which they ask questions and construct prompts (Lazaraton, 1996b; Ross, 1996; Brown and Lumley, 1997);
■ the extent to which or the ways in which they accommodate their speech to that of the candidate (Ross, 1992; Ross and Berwick, 1992; Berwick and Ross, 1996; Lazaraton, 1996b; Brown and Lumley, 1997; Morton *et al.*, 1997); and
■ the ways in which they develop and extend topics (Berwick and Ross, 1996).

What is not clear, however, is which, if any, of these aspects of variation have an impact on ratings.

[. . .]

In the present study, two of the IELTS Speaking Module interviews which formed the basis of the study reported in Brown and Hill (1998) are analysed. These involved two interviewers who differed significantly in terms of their difficulty, and a single candidate. The analysis aims to show how the different strategies used by each of the interviewers resulted in qualitatively different performances in (and hence ratings for) the two interviews. In order to confirm the supposed link between interviewer behaviour and score outcomes (for this is all it can be at the level of the analysis of discourse), reference is made to comments produced by raters in retrospective verbal reports, where they discussed their reactions to the candidates' performance and the reasons for the scores they awarded.

A. Brown

Task B8.2

Consider the five ways in which researchers have discovered variation in interviewer behaviour, listed above.

➤ What do you think we mean by:

(a) establishing 'rapport' with a candidate?
(b) 'accommodating speech' to that of a candidate?

➤ Which of these five ways in which interviewers can vary is likely, in your experience, to have the greatest impact on the performance of the candidate?

The study

A. Brown

The two interviews were conducted on the same day and involved the same candidate, Esther, with each of two interviewers, Pam and Ian. [. . .] Table 1 shows that Esther received a mean score of 5.8 (over the 8 raters) for her interview with Pam, and a mean score of 5 for her interviews with Ian. In general, then, she appears to be perceived by the raters as being more proficient when being interviewed by Pam than when she is being interviewed by Ian.

Table 1 Interview ratings

Candidate	Interviewer	Scores								Mean	Median
Esther	Pam	5	5	5	6	6	6	6	7	5.8	6.0
Esther	Ian	4	5	5	5	5	5	5	6	5.0	5.0

The **IELTS** *interview*

. . . The emphasis of the test is on 'measuring candidates' communication skills in the language in everyday situations rather than formal knowledge of grammar, vocabulary or other elements of the language' (British Council *et al.*, 1996: 3). This orientation is captured within the IELTS band descriptors through the term 'communicative effectiveness', which refers to test-takers' ability to 'talk at length on a range of topics displaying a range of functional and discoursal skills (description, argument, narration and speculation, for example). This is in addition to the more traditional linguistic criteria of grammatical accuracy, syntactic complexity and vocabulary.

A. Brown

Methodology of the discourse analysis

Given the focus of the assessment on candidates' communicative effectiveness, the perspective taken within the analysis is also on communication, on the interplay between interviewer and candidate. As an analysis of interviewer moves alone would reveal little about their impact on candidate performance, the analysis consists not simply of a count of prespecified interviewer behaviours, but of a sequential analysis of the talk as a whole. This will allow us to ascertain not only the ways in which interviewer behaviour differs but also how these differences affect the quality of the candidate's talk and construct different pictures of her proficiency.

An approach to the analysis of spoken interaction which takes this perspective – the turn-by-turn construction of interaction – is conversation analysis (CA).

[. . .]

The analysis itself followed the convention of CA studies in that the transcription stage was an important part of the analysis, not a preliminary step. The analysis took topical sequences as the structural units within the interviews, and focused on the ways in which the two interviewers implemented their topical choices in order to elicit a performance from the candidate. Repeated close listening to the interviews allowed the researcher to build up a clear picture of each interviewer's style of topic development and conversational management, as well as its impact on the candidate's speech. It emerged that the interviewers differed along a number of dimensions, and that they did indeed – as Ross (1996) claims – exhibit stable styles. For the sake of brevity, the ways in which the two interviewers manage the interviews and elicit talk from the candidate are described here through a detailed analysis of a single sequence drawn from each interview. These sequences, it should be noted, were selected for detailed analysis here not because they stood out, but because they contained behaviours which were representative of the interviewers.

Analysis

Sequence 1   Tape 44   Interviewer: Pam   Candidate: Esther

    I   . . . do you live in a <u>fla:t</u>?
    C   er no hos<u>tel</u>
    I   in a <u>hos</u>tel.
    C   <u>Carl</u>ton College.
5   I   is it? [(.)] tell me about the hostel; (.) I haven't seen that one.
    C   [°mm°]
         (1.6)
    C   oh um: it's aum: international college, =
    I   = mm,
10   (0.8)
    C   er >I mean a hostel, < er: (1.0) and I knew- (.) I- (1.0) knew: that (.) hostel: by: (0.9) a counselling centre, (1.2) and: (1.9) and it's: (0.5) quite <u>good</u> for: (0.8) u:m: (.) >suitable for <u>me</u>;< [to live] there.
15   I   [is it?]
    I   what do you like about it Esther
    C   um: (3.0) er >the food_< (0.8) yeah is: >quite good< er: but it's (.) everyday f-western food.
    I   is it [(.) what] do they give you: to eat.
20   C   [yeah]

	C	er (.) potatoes.
	I	oh yes.
	C	yeah (.) everyday potatoes, er: and (0.6) sometimes got er(.) beef_ (0.8) lamb chops_(.) and: (.) others (.) like noodles, =
25	I	= mhm =
	C	= °°mm°°
	I	.hh (.) do you sometimes go and buy food (1.8)
	C	mm buy food for:_
30	I	d'you d'you go to: (.) maybe McDona:lds or K F C
	C	oh I seldom go:
	I	a:h y [es]
	C	[>be]cause<they: offer: tree meals (.) a day.
	I	so (.) yeah that's plenty for you [is it?] yes: yeah .hh =
35	C	[yeah]
	I	= ^what else do you like about (.) living in the hostel.
	C	mm:: (1.0) my friends are all there_
	I	ah good, [(.) yeah]
	C	[yeah all] came from (0.6) my: same school.
40	I	<u>did they</u> ye:s, yeah. .hh ......

The sequence begins with a closed question 'Do you live in a flat?', which introduces the topic 'living arrangements'. Esther responds, relevantly, with 'No', but elaborates then with the fact that she lives in a hostel and its name. Pam responds to this information with a newsmarker 'Is it?' (Heritage, 1995), which she immediately follows with a question that topicalizes the new information (the hostel) and explicitly elicits an extended response: 'Tell me about . . . '. The statement 'I haven't seen that one' also indicates a level of interest in Esther's response as it implies that she is familiar with other hostels and is therefore interested in learning how this one compares. After some hesitation (line 7) Esther begins an extended response to this prompt (lines 8–14).

[. . .]

Lazaraton . . . regards 'topic-priming' (as she terms it) as supportive, scaffolding behaviour, an attempt by the interviewer to make the upcoming 'interview' question understandable. However, as the strategy was found to be used by some interviewers more than others, Lazaraton argues that such variation will lead to unfairness in assessment as those candidates who are provided with this sort of scaffolding are likely to produce a better performance than those who are not given 'the benefit of assistance'.

Task B8.3

➤ Consider the following example of 'topic-priming'. Do you think that the interviewer is giving Esther an advantage through this kind of 'scaffolding' talk?

Extension

Extract 1:   Tape 44   Pam/Esther

I   . . . .hh so- (.) do you have a room, on your <u>own</u>?

C   <u>no</u> I'm sharing with my friend. =

I   = mhm can you describe your room to me!

C   er it's quite big [mm,] erm: (2.0) mm: (0.8) I'm sharing with my friend, (.) er
         Celia, (0.5) and: (1.3) we have (0.9) we have (.) two table for (0.5) >each of us,
         < [mm,] (0.7) an:d, (2.0) we have a double decker bed,

Returning to Sequence 1, once the topic has been introduced and Esther has completed her response to the first extended-response question ('Tell me about . . .'), Pam develops it further by (again) topicalizing information provided in Esther's previous response. This happens twice in Sequence 1. In line 16 Pam responds to Esther's response ('It's quite good for, suitable for me') with a newsmarker and a question that topicalizes the word 'suitable' ('Is it? What do you like about it Esther?'). This elicits a descriptive response. In line 19 again she incorporates the newly-introduced idea of 'food' ('The food is quite good but it's everyday western food') into her next question in the same way: 'Is it? What do they give you to eat?' Again, this approach to topic development is typical of Pam.

    [. . .]

After the three open-ended prompts in Sequence 1, Pam introduces a new line of questioning, 'eating out', a topic that is conceptually related to the previous one (i.e., 'food'). As before, she first produces a closed question, in which she seeks to ascertain whether Esther eats out at all (line 27). This potential new topic direction proves to be relatively fruitless, however: Esther responds that she rarely eats out. In response, Pam produces a formulation ('So yeah that's plenty for you is it?'), a typical topic-closing move that summarizes the gist of the previous talk (Heritage and Watson, 1979); in this case Esther's response is that she seldom eats out because the hostel provides three meals a day.

    [. . .]

Following the failed topic probe and its closure, Pam returns to the earlier topic of life in the hostel. She maintains topic continuity through a recycling of her earlier prompt, asking '*What else* do you like about living in the hostel?' and eliciting further detail in response to the earlier question. This technique for extending topics is again typical of Pam's interviewing technique. [. . .]

In addition to her consistent approach to topic introduction, development and maintenance, Pam also closes topics consistently and in a way that foreshadows topic shift for the candidate. Just as she produced a formulation to close off the failed topic direction described above, she tends to close all topics with formulations or assessments.

★ Task B8.4

➤ Pam's approach to interviewing is called 'supportive'. Do you think that her speech is more like that of a teacher? If you do, should we require all interviewers to adopt this kind of behaviour, or should we try to stop them from being 'supportive' in an attempt to recreate non-test and non-classroom-like interactions?

Turning now to Ian's interview we find that like Pam, he starts off with a closed question, in this case an or-question (Sequence 2 below). Esther provides a minimal response, selecting one of the alternatives provided: 'More Malay'. However, rather than following this with an extended-response question as Pam does, Ian produces an echo-and-tag question ('More Malay, is it?'). Esther appears to interpret this echo as a confirmation request, as she responds with agreement, 'mm'.

Sequence 2		Tape 50 Interviewer: Ian Candidate: Esther
	I	>in Ke<u>lan</u>g is it- is it many Ma<u>lay</u> or there a lot of <u>Chi</u>nese or (.) what is it (.) in Kelang(.) [the population.<]
	C	[yeah more] Malay.
	I	>mo<u>re</u> Malay is it. <
5	C	°°mm°°
	I	°right.° (1.2) erm (.) >what about the< <u>foo</u>ds there.
		(1.2)
	C	er: they are Indian food (.) Chinese food (.) a:nd Malay food
		[(.) th]ey are a:<u>ll</u> (0.8) <u>mix</u>
10	I	[mhm]
		(1.0)
	I	they're <u>mixed</u> are they.
	C	yea:h (0.4) all mix (0.6) <u>e</u>:verything ( ) hhnhhn lyeah? (.) >is it <u>good</u> that way is it.<
15	C	yeah hhh.
		(1.2)
	I	ah- which is the <u>spi</u>ciest food.
	C	um:: (0.7) <u>In</u>dian.
	I	°°Indian°°
20	C	°°mm°°
		(0.7)
	I	so- (.) <u>you</u>'re from the <u>Chi</u>nese community yourself is that [right?]
	C	[yes.]
	Y	>so do- <u>Chi</u>nese people eat a lot of <u>In</u>dian food< or is it mainly (.)Chinese food.
25	C	oh mainly Chinese food.
		(0.6)
	I	>but <u>some</u>times you eat Indian<
	C	e::r yeah sometimes
		(0.9)
30	I	sometimes Malay.
	C	mmm::
		(0.9)
	C	yeah [hnhnhn] .hh hh (.) not <u>very</u> often
35	I	[not <u>of</u>ten though]
	I	(°I see.°) (1.0) erm now tell me your plans are w-when . . .

Ian's 'acceptance' of this minimal response is followed by a long pause, which indicates that he is either waiting for Esther to add to her response or has not yet formulated a next question. Whatever the case, the pause is an indication that Esther's response was not as full as expected (Schegloff, 1982). When Esther also does not take up the turn – presumably having responded to her own satisfaction, if not Ian's – Ian eventually comes out with a next question.

A. Brown

With this question – 'What about the foods there?' – Ian shifts topic, introducing a new reference, 'food', to replace 'people'. Given the apparent inexplicitness of the question 'What about . . .?' Esther infers, appropriately, that she is being asked about ethnic styles of food, just as the previous question asked about the ethnic mix of people. She responds accordingly, naming the foods by ethnicity. Ian responds to this naming by producing a continuer ('*mhm*') followed by a 1-second pause, which indicates that he is expecting more than the minimal response Esther has provided. When no continuation is forthcoming Ian produces yet another echo-plus-tag ('They're mixed, are they?'), despite the earlier failure of this turn-type to elicit the expected response. Yet again the echo elicits only a confirmation from Esther, this time with an upgrading of force through the added repetition of her earlier response, 'Yeah, all mix, everything'. Ian follows this response with another closed question which again – given the long pause in line 16 following Esther's response – seems to be intended to elicit an elaborated response. A further closed question also elicits a minimal response and after a pause Ian shifts the focus of the talk to a related but new area, the eating habits of ethnic groups.

Here again, Ian produces a string of closed questions and, ultimately, statements, in lines 22, 24, 28 and 31, each of which appears to be intended to elicit extended responses, as can be inferred from the pauses following Esther's responses in lines 27, 30 and 33. Again, the topic tails off without Esther having produced anything more than a repetition of input or a series of agreement tokens. In fact, at Esther's level of pragmatic interpretation, her responses are fully appropriate: she responds to the first (or-)question with a selected response, and to the subsequent yes–no question (line 25) and statement (line 31) with confirmation tokens. It is noteworthy that after the final long pause (line 34) she appears to understand that more is expected. She produces an elaboration on her previous response ('not very often'). This overlaps with Ian's own elaboration, 'Not often though', which precedes a shift of topic.

In Sequence 2, although Ian is obviously attempting to elicit extended responses he is less explicit in his questioning than Pam. Whereas Pam's prompts consist either of open-ended questions or requests for the candidate to produce an extended piece of talk ('Tell me about . . .', etc.), Ian's tend to be framed as closed questions or statements, or consist of ambiguous moves such as echoes and tag questions . . . When Esther misinterprets the pragmatic force of Ian's moves, problems tend to arise in the smoothness of the interaction and the development of the topic. The interaction is studded by long pauses that follow minimal responses by the candidate. This failure to elicit extended speech from the candidate is compounded as Ian struggles to maintain the interaction and keep the topic alive, repeatedly producing closed questions (yes–no and or-questions) to elicit extended descriptive responses despite their failure to do so. Again, the examples of inexplicit or ambiguous prompts and closed questions seen here are not isolated incidents; Ian uses them regularly.

As we have seen, the problems that tend to develop in Ian's interviews occur because he is inexplicit about the type of response required. Esther often misinterprets the pragmatic force of the prompts, and her typically brief responses are often followed by a long pause while Ian waits for a response or formulates his next question, and these pauses give the discourse a sense of dis-fluency. Despite the obvious problems that Esther has with interpreting the pragmatic force of Ian's moves, Ian does not appear to have the strategies to reformulate when she misinterprets and produces an inadequate or insufficient response.

In Pam's interviews such misinterpretations are rare, not because Esther is more 'proficient' but simply because Pam's questions tend to be more explicit than Ian's.

In addition, on the rare occasion that Esther does misinterpret the pragmatics of a prompt (occurrences that indicate quite clearly that Esther herself is consistent across the two interviews), Pam has strategies that she uses to resolve the problem.

[. . .]

Ian also does not demonstrate the same skill as Pam in developing topics by integrating information provided in Esther's responses into the conversation. Because his questions tend to be closed, they do not elicit new content that can be topicalized, unlike Pam's open question. His attempts to elicit more on the topic tend to consist of tokens such as echo-plus-tag in (Sequence 1, lines 4 and 12: 'More Malay, is it?', 'They're mixed, are they?'), echo in line 19 ('Indian'), and other tokens such as 'yeah?' and 'mhm'. However, just as the use of closed questions failed to elicit extended responses, these also fail in the same way. Esther appears to interpret them as either providing feedback, which she acknowledges, or as seeking confirmation, which she also gives. In other words, she responds to them minimally rather than as a request to continue.

In fact, Esther is being consistent in her interpretation of such tokens across the two interviews; she does exactly the same in the interview with Pam, providing agreement or confirmation after the tokens 'do you?', 'yeah' and 'mm' (Sequence 1, lines 6, 20, 35). The difference is simply that Pam typically provides tokens such as these as feedback and not as turn-eliciting moves. In her interviews they are almost always immediately followed by further interviewer talk, which overlaps the candidate's minimal responses and which propels the interaction forward, whereas Ian uses them as prompts, which fail to elicit elaboration and are followed by a lapse in the talk, thus slowing down the rate of the interaction. So, in his interview, these tokens and their responses do not add substantial content to the previous talk, and the talk does not progress so fluidly. Esther, as candidate, is not able to capitalize on (or does not see) the opportunity to produce substantial content; she appears reactive rather than pro-active.

Ian is both less consistent and less explicit than Pam in providing markers of structural movement from one topic to another. Whereas Pam tends to close sequences with formulations or assessments that indicate both understanding and closure, in Ian's sequence there are few such explicit structural markers.

Task B8.5

Look at the following extract from Esther's interview with Ian:

I	so I'm <u>cu</u>rious_ is it <u>al</u>ways parents' (.) pressure or is it <u>per</u>sonal choice.
C	°°mm°°
	(1.0)
I	but for <u>you</u> it's personal choice,
C	yeah personal choice
I	°°right.°° >what do you< <u>li</u>ke about commerce.
I	°right.° (0.9) erm (1.2) oka:y, I ha- I have a list of things to °talk about here.° tell me in Port K— it's n- it's not a big (.) it's a small city.
C	°°mm°°
I	if you go to K L for example,
C	°°yeah°°
I	erm that's much bigger, (0.8)
C	nn yeah.
I	°°yeah?°° what o- what other differences are there between KL and K—.

➤ What questioning style does Ian use in this extract?

Brown argues that 'Ian's style of interviewing is in some ways more "casual" in that he uses conversational strategies to elicit talk rather than explicit questions. In this respect it reflects more closely nontest conversational interaction.'

➤ Return to your answer to Task B8.4. Do you now think it preferable to train interviewers to adopt a style like that of Ian?

Conclusions

[. . .] It appears from this study that standard approaches to the training and re-accreditation of examiners may be less than satisfactory. Interviewer training has generally tended to be somewhat overlooked in relation to rater training, with inter-viewer behaviour rarely being scrutinized once initial training is completed. With the emphasis in tests of second language proficiency being increasingly on relatively unstructured naturalistic interactions, however thorough the initial training, it is incumbent on test administrators to ensure that interviewers' styles do not over time become so diverse that they present different levels of challenge.

The final point concerns the test design, that is, the operationalization of the underlying construct. Communicative competence or effectiveness is an abstraction that is rarely defined with any precision in terms of actual test performance. What this means is that, as we saw here, differences in interviewer technique that might affect candidates' performance in relation to the construct are also not easily predictable. Differences in interviewer behaviour that might on the surface be taken as evidence of the natural variation that occurs amongst native speakers (and therefore evidence of test validity), may, as was the case here, turn out to be relevant to the construct. It is, it seems, simply not appropriate to assume that the variation that is allowed to occur is not relevant to the construct, especially where the construct can be interpreted as encompassing interpersonal communication skills.

★ Task B8.6

Review the section on interactional competence in Unit A3.

➤ Is it important to operationalize the construct of interactional competence in a speaking test?

➤ If variation in performance by interlocutor is central to the notion of inter-actional competence, how can this be considered 'fair' when a test taker might get a different score depending upon the selection of interlocutor?

➤ Depending on your answers to the previous two questions, what are the implications for interlocutor training?

Summary

Making decisions about test administration is not at all easy. Some of these decisions are routine, but important. Others are intimately connected with questions of validity and our understanding of the constructs we wish to measure. Administration therefore needs to be considered as part of the test design process. One such consideration might be whether to design and implement a so-called 'direct' speaking test with one or more interlocutors, or whether we might opt for an 'indirect' test in which the prompts are delivered by tape or computer.

The older term, test 'practicality', is only part of the question. Traditionally, this has referred to whether we have the resources to deliver the test we design (see Davies et al., 1999: 148), in a tripartite consideration of 'test reliability, validity and practicality'. What we have tried to show is that these 'practical' decisions are also linked to construct definition and to our concept of test fairness (see Unit A9).

There are no easy answers to the questions that we have raised through our consideration of Brown's study. Much research needs to be done, not only into interlocutor behaviour, but also into our theoretical understanding of interactional competence. As our knowledge and research base grows, it may be possible to devise a sounder theoretical basis for interlocutor training.

Unit B9
Ethics and professionalism

 Task B9.1

➤ In this excerpt, Alan Davies discusses ethical practice in language testing. His very first sentence concerns the role of ethics. Before reading this material, consider various settings in which you are active – school, clubs, business, to name but a few. What is the role of ethics in these various 'institutional settings'? Do the same standards of ethical behaviour apply in each? Are ethics universal? In each of your settings, does ethics serve a limiting role, as Davies suggests below?

Text B9
A. Davies

A. Davies (1997) 'Demands of being professional in language testing.' *Language Testing* 14, 3, 328–339

Definitions

Ethics has a clear role in institutional settings where there is concern to declare and to limit institutional duties and responsibilities. This applies particularly to business companies and to professions. House (1990: 91) offers this definition: 'Ethics are the rules or standards of right conduct or practice, especially the standards of a profession.' It is important to all stakeholders, both within the institution (e.g., medical doctors) and without (other medical colleagues, patients, the public in general) that professional standards of behaviour are stated explicitly (often in an authoritative code of practice) so that all stakeholders (including in this case medical doctors) know what is meant by right conduct and practice and therefore what can be expected and also what cannot.

Continuing his discussion of the ethics of educational evaluation, House (1990: 91) comments that in the most elaborate and widely disseminated set of standards, there are four areas of concern – utility, accuracy, feasibility and propriety. Under propriety, the standards are formal obligations, conflict of interest, full and frank disclosure, the public's right to know, rights of human subjects, human interactions, balanced reporting and fiscal responsibility. These standards relate mostly to privacy, protection of human subjects, and freedom of information.

Scriven (1991: 134) goes as far as to claim ethics as 'the emperor of the social sciences, imperial because it refers to considerations that supervene above all others, such as obligations to science, prudence, culture and nation'. Scriven (1991: 134) would have us accept that ethics has now been admitted into a central position in the social sciences. It is, he remarks, increasingly embarrassing to avoid this one great topic in policy analysis. These include work in game-theory (especially the treatment of the prisoner's dilemma), decision theory, latent function analysis, democratic theory in political science, moral stage theory, welfare economics, analytical and social jurisprudence, behavioural genetics, the codification and refinement of professional ethics.

The 'prisoner's dilemma' problem in game theory raises the issue of ethics both at a theoretical and an applied level. Two prisoners (A and B) are arrested for complicity in the commission of a crime. (They are in fact both guilty.) They are put in cells between which no communication is possible and then offered a deal. The deal is as follows:

1) If A confesses and B does not (or vice versa) then A is released and B gets ten years.
2) If both A and B confess they each get five years in prison.
3) If neither confesses they each get one year in prison.

The best (selfish) strategy for A is to confess. Then if B does not confess, B gets ten years and A is released. However, A does not know what B will do; it is possible that B will also confess, in which case they both get five years. The best strategy might therefore not work, indeed it could work to A's disadvantage. The best result would be obtained if neither A nor B confesses. However, this is still risky as a strategy for A since B may confess, in which case A would get ten years and B be released. What is necessary is for both A and B to think not of the best strategy for themselves alone (the selfish approach) but of the best outcome for them both (for 'the profession'). If they each take concern for the other then neither will confess, in which case they will both get one year.

Task B9.2

⭐

➤ The 'prisoner's dilemma' is a classical example of an ethical challenge thought exercise. Can you think up similar thought exercises about ethical practice in testing? Here's one that you and colleagues might enjoy.

Three students and close friends are finishing up with secondary school. They are all competing for limited college seats, and they have just completed a day-long national school-leaving exam. It is a frightful test that includes an obligatory foreign-language component – test takers can select from one of three foreign languages, but everybody who takes the test must go through at least one language exam. The overall result on the language test is factored into college entry decisions, and in addition (if an applicant does get into college), the result on that language test is used to place new college students into various levels of subsequent language courses.

Each of the three students prepared for and took the same foreign language test, although they have three different language teachers in school. As they leave the exam site on the testing day, they re-live the test and talk about its questions, in the manner that all students do right after an exam. It is clear to them that their three language teachers had conspired: their teachers must have had advance copies of the test, because all three students had seen the test questions – verbatim – in class during the weeks prior to the national test.

The country has long had rumours of rampant cheating on this particular test. The three friends feel some remorse, but more, they feel quite a bit of anger – why did the teachers put them into a potentially dangerous situation? What if the teachers are caught independent of the students' own realization? How could the teachers be so stupid? Many of their language classmates were at the test, and surely some of their mutual friends will also realize what has happened. The whole business seems incredibly volatile.

There seem to be three options:

1   If they immediately contact the government testing agency and explain what happened, the three of them would probably be allowed to re-take the test without penalty, but the teachers would probably be sacked. They feel this option is best for their careers – it would not impede their competitive college admission processes.
2   If they do nothing, the teachers still might be caught by independent means; one of the other classmates might say something. The three of them could then lie to authorities, friends and parents and say that they did not realize the advance exposure to test questions. They are uncertain what would happen in this case – would they be permitted to re-take the exam and compete for college admission, regardless?
3   If they do nothing and the teachers are not caught, then the three students have formed a permanent pact of silence, a secret bond they must keep up for ever. The three friends realize that their advance study of the test questions is a challenge to the test's validity, but all three feel they are fairly strong in the language in any case. The language test would help them get into college and they would be placed accurately into the highest-level classes for that language. Others who took the test and who are less fluent would be misplaced. The problem is that they must keep their mouths shut, for ever, while they see their classmates struggle in later college-level foreign language study.

➤   Re-read option 3 above, particularly: 'Others who took the test and who are less fluent would be misplaced.' Without calling it such, the students have stumbled on to the false positive/negative reasoning of truth tables, which we discuss in Task C9.3. A test taker will appear more fluent in the language than is the true case (a false positive), and if that test-taker does get into college, then subsequent foreign language placement will be inaccurate: the subsequent language class will be too difficult. As you write some of your own ethical thought exercises, try manipulating the false positive/negative dimension of test-based decisions. Many ethical dilemmas in testing involve truth tables.

➤ We also suggest that you write stories that touch on students and their lives, as we have done here. That is the best way to (actually) direct attention to the practices and administration of the test by others – by teachers, agencies, governments and others in power.

Scriven (1991: 276) concludes: 'The only solution is through prior irreversible commitment to treat the welfare of each other as comparable to their own, and this reflects the reason for ethical training of the young'. Being ethical comes at a cost to oneself (both A and B would have to go to prison for one year) but for the group/society/company/profession, etc., the cost is worth while since 'an ethical society has better survival value than a society of rational egoists' (Scriven, 1991: 276).

Following critical theorists in other social sciences, critical applied linguists have been asking questions about the ethics of applied linguistics and whether an ideologically neutral study of applied linguistics is possible. And where critical applied linguistics goes, there critical language testing follows. There is urgent reason therefore both to examine the state of ethics in academic language testing and language testing research and to encourage a move towards an explicit statement of good conduct or practice.

Three moralities

Institutional ethics or morality (and in particular professional morality) can be seen as standing between public morality on the one hand and individual morality on the other.

Public morality is concerned with large social issues in which there is a genuine public interest, e.g. genetic engineering, in vitro fertilization, female circumcision, capital punishment. Issues such as these may also be regarded by certain professions as coming within their sphere of concern. In vitro fertilization, for example, or euthanasia could be issues on which the medical profession and the legal profession would wish to establish a common professional position.

Task B9.3 ★

Large-scale tests have a moral history. Most notably, some have had a historical connection with human eugenics, which is the belief that our species could be made better by selective breeding. Some intelligence testing procedures were used in US sterilization cases in the early 1900s. Black (2003) and Kevles (1995) are excellent books about the disturbing interface between testing and eugenics. Another superb and readable volume is Gould (1996), which touches not only on eugenics but on other strangeness in testing's past. Finally, Hacking (1990) presents the nineteenth-century pre-history of modern testing and explains some of the set-up for the frightening social engineering phases that were to come.

Eugenics is by no means gone. Kevles and others warn of its possible rebirth through genetic engineering. To see eugenics in its modern incarnation, you

Extension

can visit the 'Future Generations' website at http://www.eugenics.net. Surfing this site is not for the faint of heart.

We do not endorse eugenics, but we feel that you should become familiar with it and with its historical connection to large-scale tests.

Professional morality is concerned with codes, contracts, professional training, professional ethical norms and standards, the systematic attempt to illuminate the ethos of a profession and to elaborate its norms (e.g., the medical profession, the American Psychological Association, the American Educational Research Association and language testing associations, such as the Association of Language Testers in Europe and the International Language Testing Association).

Individual morality is concerned with issues of conscience, which in some cases will be influenced by religion. Right conduct or practice for the individual will influence views as to such issues as divorce, abortion, military service. The public view in such cases may well be reflected in legal enactment, that is, divorce and abortion may be legalized; exemption from military service may be permitted in certain cases on the grounds of conscience. Individuals may, however, possibly for religious reasons, choose (or feel impelled) not to avail themselves of legal remedies because in their view what is legal is not acceptable morally. Except in the case of militant campaigners who wish to change the law in favour of a morality which they assert (e.g., pro-life campaigners against abortion) a conflict between a private and a public morality can be avoided. Where it cannot is when an individual is required to make a decision for him- or herself with regard to one of these disputed issues such as divorce and abortion. (Contraception and alcohol are other examples of issues where there is or has been a public–private moral dilemma.)

What this means is that the boundary between what is public (or indeed professional) and what is individual is not stable: what for me may well be a matter of individual ethics (or morality) may for others, for example, a church group, be a matter of public concern.

There is also the possibility of conflict between what is morally right within the code of conduct established by one's own profession and what is required by one's role as an individual member of society. Homan (1991: 2) points to the conflict for an academic researcher who is offered a post in a field which is entirely legal but which for him or her is unacceptable morally: 'the tension between individual morality and professional ethics is seen to be most problematic when legitimate scruples disqualify a student from taking up a research post or other opportunity'.

Research professions

Professions which involve research such as medicine, law, science, both inside and outside the academy, must be concerned about the ways their research, teaching, servicing and so on act both for and on society.

A research organization such as the Market Research Society offers a typical statement in its code of conduct as to the need to behave responsibly towards stakeholders: 'Research is founded upon the willing cooperation of the public and of business organisations. It [must be] conducted honestly, objectively, without unwelcome intrusion and without harm to informants' (Code of Conduct of the Market Research Society, 1986, cited in Homan, 1991: 3). Such a statement acts as a guarantee to the public of the profession's credibility as a profession (see the discussion below of the International Language Testing Association's draft 'Code of practice for foreign/ second language testing'). It resembles a degree certificate from a reputable university, a certificate of road worthiness for a vehicle that has been properly tested, or any examination certificate which states that the holder has reached a particular level in a skill or field of knowledge and is certified as having done so by the institution issuing the certificate.

The need for a professional morality

In part this explains the need for a professional morality in addition to individual morality, validation through the reputation of the promoting institution: clearly the American Medical Association or the British Medical Association is more likely to be paid attention to than the claim by an unknown neophyte medic that he or she has the necessary skills to be allowed to practice as a doctor. What a professional morality does therefore is to provide a contract for the profession and the individual with the public, thereby safeguarding all three. Professional research of a social nature is likely to state the profession's ethical position on issues having to do with informed consent, a taboo on the invasion of privacy, confidentiality, precautions against injury and distress, covert methods of conducting research (for example, recording conversations without gaining the permission of informants), and agreeing on conventions for writing and publishing.

There is a further reason, and that is that individual moralities differ, even of course among members of the profession. When therefore Hill and Parry (1994a) implicitly ask the question with regard to the teaching of international English 'what is the alternative to testing?' their very proper question may strike a chord with individual language testers. But the professional response of language testers as a collective has to be that testing is a valid activity.

We have maintained that both the public and the individual member of the profession need protection. But it is also relevant to point to the danger on the other side of overprotection. What is referred to here is the danger of an incestuous concern with the protection of members of the profession by avoiding and covering over complaints and offences to avoid legal actions being brought in a climate of an increasing likelihood of consequent (and expensive) litigation. Social science research does not in general have the life and death risks that medicine does but all public assessment provides for potential complaints and legal actions because of the use of assessment in selection and certification. Those excluded or rejected may well believe that the methods of assessment used were not valid and that they were therefore wrongly excluded or rejected. Safeguards for professional practitioners, in language testing as much as in medicine, are necessary but it is important that the safeguards are themselves also applicable to stakeholders other than the professionals themselves. Otherwise they become not safeguards but fortresses.

Querying the morality of language testing

For language testers the professional dilemma of ensuring a balance between the professional ethical code and the individual moral conscience is acute because of the intrusive nature of language testing and the normative role of tests. While a profession is primarily concerned with the relation between its purposes and its methods, it also needs from time to time to consider its right to exist, circular though such a question must be. Questioning its own activity and providing a rationale and a philosophy are necessary because otherwise the challenges from without will not be lacking. To a degree this is the current challenge from postmodernism that it questions the professionalism established by the children of the Enlightenment.

 Task B9.4

➤ Have you ever felt that dilemma? Have you ever been bothered by conflict between a professional ethic and your own moral consciousness?

➤ For example, have you ever proctored or invigilated a major high-stakes test and observed the tension in the room? Did you wish you could slice through the emotion with a knife of kindness, reach out to the test takers, help them, calm them, and make them feel better? Did you feel you could not do so because you were bound by professionalism: you and the other workers had to assure standard procedures and control for the sake of reliability?

We have already referred to the challenge made by Hill and Parry (1994a) with regard to the value of testing. In their view (a kind of 'critical testing' position) conventional tests of reading are inadequate (unethical) because they impose a particular meaning, or set of meanings on a text. The logic of their critique appears to be that every reader requires a separate test of reading, and possibly a different test for every reading occasion, even of the same text. Critical approaches of this kind are refreshing and salutary but somehow unsatisfying. They address the analysis, the programme, the evaluation the materials, the test, but offer no alternative solution to the practical problems these endeavours have grappled with.

They claim:

> In the final analysis, a test forces students to engage in arbitrary tasks under considerable time pressure. It is for this reason that many educators have replaced testing with . . . [alternative] assessment practices that provide students with not only greater freedom to select the work on which they will be assessed but more extended periods of time in which to execute it.
>
> (Hill and Parry, 1994b: 263)

Even though we may feel that Hill and Parry take a narrow and rather blinkered view of what constitutes testing, their claim needs to be addressed by carefully examining such statements as: 'arbitrary tasks', 'considerable time pressure', 'alternative assessment', 'freedom to select the work on which they will be assessed'. This is the proper role for the profession, that it states just what imposition is made on the public and why it is necessary to use the methods it does.

[. . .]

Task B9.5

➤ Select any test with which you are familiar – it could be one that you, yourself, went through in your schooling, or it could be one that you recently supervised. Imagine that a formal complaint has been lodged against the test, and that the complaint specifically mentions its 'arbitrary' questions and procedures. Defend the test in a written rebuttal: explain 'why it is necessary to use the methods it does'.

In Unit B9 we have selected an article on ethical practice as it relates to language testing. Davies touches on ethics both from a broad perspective and as it impinges on our everyday work in developing assessments. Our tasks seek to extend the constant debate (which is at the root of all ethical enquiry) and to challenge both the test and you – the reader – to explore the moral underpinning of our work.

Summary

Unit B10
Validity as argument

As with Canale and Swain's article (Unit B3), this paper has achieved seminal status. It is an early and much-cited statement of the need for argument in test validation.

⭐ **Task B10.1**

➤ What makes a paper seminal? Think about other reading you have done in your career. What seems to survive over long periods, and why?

Text B10
M. T. Kane

M. T. Kane (1992) 'An argument-based approach to validity.' *Psychological Bulletin* **112, 3, 527–535**

This article outlines a general, argument-based approach to validation, develops an interpretive argument for a placement test as an example, and examines some key properties of interpretive arguments. Validity is associated with the interpretation assigned to test scores rather than with the test scores or the test. The interpretation involves an argument leading from the scores to score-based statements or decisions, and the validity of the interpretation depends on the plausibility of this interpretive argument. The interpretive arguments associated with most test-score interpretations involve multiple inferences and assumptions. An explicit recognition of the inferences and assumptions in the interpretive argument makes it possible to identify the kinds of evidence needed to evaluate the argument. Evidence for the inferences and assumptions in the argument supports the interpretation, and evidence against any part of the argument casts doubt on the interpretation.

Validity is associated with the interpretations assigned to test scores rather than with the scores themselves or the test and involves an evaluation of the appropriateness of these interpretations (American Educational Research Association [AERA], American Psychological Association, & National Council on Measurement in Education, 1985; Cronbach, 1971; Messick, 1989). The kinds of evidence needed for the validation of a test-score interpretation can be identified systematically by focusing attention on the details of the interpretation.

⭐ **Task B10.2**

Validity as interpretation is now widely accepted. The typical way to illustrate it is to think of a test that is developed for one particular purpose but which is used to make quite a different decision (see discussion on retrofitting, p. 175). Suppose that a literary criticism test is developed for undergraduate students. The inference to be drawn is this: have the students learned from their first course in literary criticism? Suppose further that some test takers are non-native speakers of the language in which the literature is written. After the test is completed, the results are also used to send those students into additional language service courses.

➤ Is this an appropriate inference from the literary criticism test, or should those students also take a more general language proficiency test?

➤ Can you devise similar stories about tests that are designed for one purpose but (possibly) used by mistake for a different inference?

Task B10.3

Although validity as interpretation is widely accepted, common usage of the term 'validity' still ascribes it to a test: such-and-so test is (or is not) valid, claim its detractors.

➤ Review the above discussion by Kane and the various treatments of validity in this book. How would you explain to people that validity is supposed to relate to test inference, that it is not supposed to be an inherent characteristic of a test? Try out your explanation on people outside of education. Did it succeed?

➤ Has this validity-as-interpretation mantra perhaps become over-used? If a test is typically used for the same inferential decisions, over and over again, and if there is no evidence that it is being used for the wrong decisions, could we not simply speak to the validity of that particular test – as a characteristic of it? Or must we be on constant guard for misuse of all tests?

M. T. Kane

A test-score interpretation always involves an interpretive argument, with the test score as a premise and the statements and decisions involved in the interpretation as conclusions. The inferences in the interpretive argument depend on various assumptions, which may be more-or-less credible. For example, inferences from test scores to nontest behavior involve assumptions about the relationship between test behavior and nontest behavior; inferences from test scores to theoretical constructs depend on assumptions included in the construct. Because it is not possible to prove all of the assumptions in the interpretive argument, it is not possible to verify this interpretive argument in any absolute sense. The best that can be done is to show that the interpretive argument is highly plausible, given all available evidence.

To validate a test-score interpretation is to support the plausibility of the corresponding interpretive argument with appropriate evidence. The argument-based approach to validation adopts the interpretive argument as the framework for collecting and presenting validity evidence and seeks to provide convincing evidence for its inferences and assumptions, especially its most questionable assumptions. One (a) decides on the statements and decisions to be based on the test scores,

(b) specifies the inferences and assumptions leading from the test scores to these statements and decisions, (c) identifies potential competing interpretations, and (d) seeks evidence supporting the inferences and assumptions in the proposed interpretive argument and refuting potential counterarguments.

Practical arguments

The kind of reasoning involved in interpretive arguments has received increasing attention in the last 20 years, under various headings including 'practical reasoning,' 'informal logic,' and 'rhetoric' (Cronbach, 1982, 1988; House, 1980; Perelman & Olbrechts-Tyteca, 1969; Toulmin, Rieke, & Janik, 1979). Practical arguments address issues in various disciplines and in practical affairs. Because the assumptions in such arguments cannot be taken as given and because the available evidence is often incomplete and, perhaps, questionable, the argument is, at best, convincing or plausible. The conclusions are not proven.

This is a clear departure from traditional logic and mathematics, where the emphasis is on formal rules of inference. In logic and mathematics, the assumptions are taken as given, and the conclusions are proven (i.e., the proof is logically valid), if and only if the chain of inference from the premises to the conclusions follows certain explicit, formal rules. The rules of inference and the criteria for evaluating the application of these rules in formal arguments are sufficiently unambiguous that formal arguments can always be checked mechanically (e.g., by computer).

Practical arguments make use of traditional logic and mathematics in evaluating some inferences but also include inferences and assumptions that cannot be evaluated in this way. The evidence supporting practical arguments needs to address the appropriateness of various lines of argument in specific contexts, the plausibility of assumptions, and the impact of weak assumptions on the overall plausibility of the argument. There are three general criteria for evaluating practical arguments (see House, 1980; Toulmin et al., 1979, for discussions of practical argumentation).

Criterion 1: Clarity of the argument

Has the argument been stated clearly? The conclusions to be drawn and the inferences and assumptions used in getting to these conclusions should be specified in enough detail so that what is being claimed by the argument is known. The explicit statement of the details of the argument helps us to understand the conclusions and is also a necessary step in meeting the second and third criteria.

Criterion 2: Coherence of the argument

Is the argument coherent in the sense that the conclusions follow reasonably from the specified assumptions? The logical and mathematical inferences that occur in practical arguments can be judged against the rules of logic or mathematics (including probability theory and inferential statistics) and thereby judged to be either valid or invalid in the sense that these terms are used in logic and mathematics. Inferences that are based on a theory can be judged in terms of their consistency with the theory, and if the theory is stated mathematically, the theory-based inferences can also be judged unambiguously.

However, in practical arguments, there are always some inferences that are not based on logic, or mathematics, or on any formal theory. These inferences are often specific to the particular discipline or area of practice in which the argument is being developed and tend to become codified in textbooks and journals. For example, the Standards for Educational and Psychological Testing (AERA et al., 1985) provides a summary of many acceptable types of inferences for testing.

Criterion 3: Plausibility of assumptions

Are the assumptions used in the argument inherently plausible or supported by evidence? It is not possible to prove that the assumptions used in practical arguments are true, but it is usually possible to develop some empirical evidence for doubtful assumptions. If no single type of evidence is decisive in evaluating an assumption, several types of evidence may be developed. The plausibility of an assumption is judged in terms of all the evidence for and against it.

Some questionable assumptions may be checked directly (e.g., statistical inferences usually make distributional assumptions, and these can be checked empirically). Some assumptions may be supported by careful documentation and analysis of procedures (e.g., sampling assumptions). More general assumptions (e.g., that certain skills are being taught in a course) may be supported by several types of evidence (e.g., classroom observations, review of curriculum and teaching materials, and interviews with students).

An interpretive argument can be criticized for failing to meet any of these three criteria, but weak assumptions, especially weak 'hidden' assumptions, are typically the most serious problem. A vague argument can be developed more fully. Errors in logic and mathematics can be corrected, and loose inferences can be made more explicit. Weak assumptions, once recognized, can be supported by evidence. However, because hidden assumptions are not recognized as part of the argument, no effort is made to support them with evidence, and they may not be very plausible a priori. One of the main reasons for stating the argument clearly and for examining the inferences in some detail is to identify the assumptions being made.

Task B10.4

★

➤ Critically react to the three criteria of evaluation of a practical argument, which Kane lists above. Can you think of other characteristics of an argument that make it successful (or not)? What about tenacity, a method of knowing proposed by Peirce (see p. 65) – if the person building the argument seems emotionally wedded to it even in the face of reasonable refutation, is there some affective value to the argument that overrides Kane's practical considerations? Such personal defence of turf is actually rather common in testing, we find; people get defensive. Superficially, defensiveness may seem a weak component of an argument, but at a deeper level, it may indicate passion and commitment to a particular course of action – on which dialogue and change can be built. What do you think about the defensive side of human nature, as it applies to validation arguments?

M. T. Kane

Parallel lines of evidence and counterarguments

Parallel lines of evidence that support certain assumptions or parallel lines of argument that support certain conclusions play an important role in practical arguments. One may have high confidence in an assumption that is supported by several independent sources of evidence even though each source of evidence is questionable. Similarly a conclusion that can be reached in several ways is less vulnerable than a conclusion that depends on a single line of argument. The use of multiple independent sources of evidence to support a conclusion is often referred to as triangulation. In formal arguments, a second line of argument does not add anything to our confidence in a conclusion once the conclusion is proven. In practical arguments, redundancy can be a virtue.

The identification and refutation of plausible counterarguments can be a particularly effective way to reinforce practical arguments. If the potential counterarguments can be shown to be implausible, confidence in the initial argument is increased. By contrast, in formal systems, once a proposition has been proven, there is no need to disprove its negation.

To sum up, practical arguments may have some inferences and assumptions that can be evaluated unambiguously. Confidence in other inferences and assumptions depends on the accumulation of various kinds of evidence, none of which is completely decisive. The plausibility of the argument as a whole is limited by its weakest assumptions and inferences. Therefore, it is important to identify the assumptions being made and to provide supporting evidence for the most questionable of these assumptions.

Evaluating the interpretive argument

Interpretive arguments are practical arguments, and the criteria for evaluating an interpretive argument are the same as the criteria for evaluating any practical argument. The argument should be stated clearly so that what it claims and what it assumes are known. The argument should be coherent in the sense that the conclusions are reasonable, given the assumptions. The assumptions should be plausible a priori or supported by evidence. Parallel lines of evidence should be developed whenever this is possible, and plausible counterarguments should be considered.

The details of the interpretive argument depend on the specific interpretation being proposed, the population to which the interpretation is applied, the specific data collection procedures being used, and the context in which measurement occurs. The particular mix of evidence needed to support the interpretive argument will be different for each case. The remainder of this section describes several categories of interferences that appear regularly in interpretive arguments, the assumptions associated with these inferences, and the evidence that can support these inferences and assumptions.

Observation

Perhaps the most basic inference in interpreting a score is that the score results from an instance of the measurement procedure. The inference assumes that the methods used to assign the score were consistent with the definition of the measurement procedure. The evidence supporting this kind of inference is procedural. Some parts of the measurement procedure may be specified exactly. In attitude and personality inventories and in some tests, the questions and scoring keys are often standardized. The instructions given to examinees and the methods used to generate scores from the raw data are also specified in detail. It is assumed that these standardized procedures are followed exactly.

Other conditions of observation are specified by general guidelines rather than being uniquely determined. If responses are to be interpreted or evaluated by a scorer, the general qualifications of the scorer will be specified, usually in terms of training, experience, or knowledge. It is assumed that data collection follows these general guidelines.

Some conditions of observation are not explicitly limited and become relevant only if they are extreme. For example, the environment in which data are collected will typically be specified only in the most general terms, if at all, but can become an issue if these conditions are extreme (e.g., very hot, cold, or noisy). The existence of certain extreme conditions of observation may constitute a plausible competing interpretation for low scores.

Procedural evidence does not go very far in establishing the plausibility of an interpretive argument. However, it can be decisive in refuting an interpretive argument. If the procedures have not been followed correctly (e.g., the wrong scoring key was used, the sample of scores used to generate norms is inappropriate) or if the procedures themselves are clearly inadequate (e.g., no training for raters who are called on to make complex decisions), the interpretive argument would be effectively undermined.

Generalization

Most, if not all, test-score interpretations involve generalization from the specific observations being made to a broader universe of similar observations. In interpreting a test score, statements typically are not limited to a specific time, a specific place, a specific set of items, or a specific scorer. In reporting results with sentences such as, 'John got a 60 on the test' rather than the more cumbersome statement, 'John got a 60 on Form A of the test that he took on May 6, in Room 201, and that was scored by Professor Jones,' one is implicitly assuming that the particular time and place of testing, the choice of scorer, and the specific form of the test are not relevant to the interpretation. The observations are treated as if they have been sampled from some universe of observations, involving different occasions, locations, and observers that could have served equally well; in generalizing over conditions of observation, one draws conclusions about the universe of possible observations on the basis of a limited sample of actual observations. The assumptions supporting such inferences are invariance laws stating that the conditions of observation involved in the measurement can be allowed to vary along certain dimensions without changing the outcomes much (Kane, 1982); the results are largely invariant with respect to changes in the conditions of observation (within the limits imposed by the measurement procedure specifications).

The evidence needed to support assumptions about invariance is collected in reliability studies (Feldt & Brennan, 1989) or generalizability studies (Brennan, 1983; Cronbach, Gleser, Nanda, & Rajaratnam, 1972), which indicate how consistent scores are across different samples of observations (e.g., across samples of items, occasions). Reliability is a necessary condition for validity because generalization is a key inference in interpretive arguments, but it is not a sufficient condition because generalization is not the only inference in the argument.

Extrapolation

Most interpretive arguments also involve extrapolation; conclusions are drawn about behavior that is different in potentially important ways from that observed in the testing procedure. Scores on a reading test are interpreted as indicating the ability to comprehend a variety of written materials in a variety of contexts, even though the test may consist of discrete, multiple-choice items administered in one testing session. The use of test scores as an indication of nontest behavior assumes that the relationship between the scores and the target behavior is understood fairly well (Cronbach, 1982; Kane, 1982). The extrapolation may be based on fairly loose notions of similarity or on a detailed analysis of the specific processes used by examinees in responding in the two situations (Snow & Lohman, 1984, 1989).

In addition to qualitative analyses of the relationship between the behavior actually observed and the nontest behavior to which inferences are drawn, extrapolation can also be supported by empirical evidence showing a relationship between the test performance and nontest behavior. Criterion-related validity evidence seeks to establish a direct link between test behavior and nontest behavior.

Theory-based inferences

Essentially all interpretations also involve, at least implicitly, some theory-based inferences involving possible explanations or connections to other constructs (Cronbach & Meehl, 1955; Embretson, 1983; Messick, 1988, 1989). Some interpretations are primarily theory based, in that the observations in the measurement procedure are of interest mainly as indicators of unobservable constructs. However, even when the focus of the interpretation is more practical than theoretical, theory has a role in the interpretive argument.

Two kinds of formal theories have been widely discussed in relation to validity: nomological theories and process models (Embretson, 1983). If the construct being measured is interpreted in terms of its relationship to other constructs in a nomological theory, evidence comparing the observed pattern of relationships (based on the test scores and accepted measures of other constructs) with that predicted by the theory would be relevant to the plausibility of the interpretive argument. In addition, any other evidence supporting the theory would also support the theory-based interpretive argument. Nomological theories figure prominently in the original description of construct validity (Cronbach & Meehl, 1955) and are the basis for what Embretson (1983) called nomothetic span.

A second kind of theory involves the development of process models for test behavior (Pellegrino, 1988; Sternberg, 1985). If the process model provides an explanatory interpretation of test scores, the corresponding interpretive argument would incorporate the process model. To the extent that important aspects of test behavior (e.g., accuracy and speed) can be explained in terms of postulated component processes, the interpretive argument and therefore the interpretation of test scores in terms of these processes are supported. Embretson (1983) used the term construct representation to describe the role of process models.

In many cases, the theories that are used, implicitly or explicitly, as the basis for explaining test scores are neither normological nor process models but are, rather, loose collections of general assumptions. In such cases, validity evidence that is based on the theory is more effective in ruling out certain explanations than it is in establishing a particular theory-based interpretation. For example, analyses of multitrait–multimethod matrices can undermine proposed interpretations by showing that score differences are attributable largely to method variance (Campbell & Fiske, 1959). Similarly, evidence of racial or sex bias can cast doubt on a variety of interpretations (Cole & Moss, 1989).

Different possible assumptions about the processes involved in responding to test items are often the basis for competing interpretations. For example, Nedelsky (1965, p. 152) has suggested that items on science achievement tests must present novel situations–problems if they are to measure comprehension rather than simple recall. Of course, as Cronbach (1971) has pointed out:

> An item qua item cannot be matched with a single behavioural process. Finding the answer calls for dozens of processes, from hearing the directions to complex integration of ideas. The shorthand description in terms of a single process is justified when one is certain that every person can and will carry out all the required processes save one.
>
> (p. 453)

Collateral assumptions are clearly necessary if inferences about cognitive processes are to be drawn. However, analyses of content and procedures can effectively rule out some interpretations.

The evidence needed to support theory-based inferences depends on the theory. Because different kinds of theories can be used and because any given theory may be supported by different kinds of evidence, a wide range of different kinds of empirical evidence may be relevant to theory-based inferences (Messick, 1989).

Decisions

Most tests are also linked to some decision. If the test scores were not relevant to any decision, it is not clear why the test would be given. The legitimacy of test use rests on assumptions about the possible outcomes (intended and unintended) of the decision to be made and on the values associated with these different outcomes (Guion, 1974; Messick, 1975, 1980, 1981, 1988, 1989).

Task B10.5 ★

Nobody takes tests for fun, and nobody seems to write them as a hobby – so far as we know. Still, we find ourselves wondering about Kane's claim here. When the second author of this book taught in West Africa in the 1970s, his students would actually thank him for his tests. Whenever he gave an in-class quiz or major exam, the students would work hard, try their best, and in great number (often as they walked out the door) say: 'Thank you, Mr Davidson, for bringing us this test today.' Perhaps they felt the intrinsic value of schooling. Perhaps it caused Davidson to write a few more tests than he actually needed. The students seemed sincere; it did not feel like a scam, and it offered a way to motivate them to learn and to work harder.

➤ Can a test be given for no *decision* reason – can one be given purely to trigger positive affective response and instructional growth?

➤ Can a test be given for purposes of washback alone?

➤ Or is the problem more metaphysical in nature? If a test is given for purposes of washback alone, then by definition there must be a decision on whether the washback did or did not happen. Hence, the washback is the decision, and Kane's point is upheld.

➤ Or does he mean 'decision' to imply test-based inferences other than instructional growth? What is a 'decision' (in education), anyway?

Technical inferences

There are also a number of more technical inferences that frequently appear in interpretive arguments. For example, if scores on different forms of a test are equated, the inference from a score on the current form to the estimated score on the original form rests on statistical assumptions in the equating models and on assumptions about the appropriateness of these models (Holland & Rubin, 1982). If item-response models are used, assumptions about the fit of the model to the data are needed (Hambleton, 1989; Lord, 1980).

Summary

If the evidence for validity is to support the interpretive argument effectively, it must reflect the structure of the interpretive argument. Many different types of inferences appear in interpretive arguments, and each of these inferences rests on assumptions that provide justification for the inference. The acceptance of a number as a test score assumes that the number was assigned using certain procedures. Generalizations from a sample of behavior to some domain of behaviors rest on assumptions about the invariance of observed scores for different conditions of observation. Extrapolations are based on assumptions about the relationship between the behavior actually observed and the behavior to which the results are being extrapolated. Any theory-based inference assumes that the theory is credible. Decisions that are based on test scores make assumptions about the desirability of various kinds of outcomes, that is, about values.

Validity evidence is most effective when it addresses the weakest parts of the interpretive argument. Evidence that provides further support for a highly plausible assumption does not add much to the overall plausibility of the argument. The most questionable assumptions deserve the most attention. An assumption can be questioned because of existing evidence indicating that it may not be true, because of plausible alternative interpretations that deny the assumptions, because of specific objections raised by critics, or simply because of a lack of supporting evidence.

Characteristics of interpretive arguments

Interpretive arguments have four general characteristics that are especially relevant to validity: (a) Interpretive arguments are artefacts. They are made, not discovered. (b) Interpretive arguments are dynamic; they may expand or contract or simply shift their focus. (c) Interpretive arguments may need to be adjusted to reflect the needs of specific examinees or special circumstances. (d) Interpretive arguments are practical arguments, which are evaluated in terms of their degree of plausibility and not in terms of a simple valid or invalid decision.

Interpretive arguments are artefacts. The interpretation that is assigned to the test scores is not uniquely determined by the observations being made. The possible interpretations for any set of test scores vary along several dimensions, including their focus and their level of abstractions. For example, a test involving passages followed by questions about the passage could be interpreted simply as a measure of skill at answering passage-related questions, or as a measure of reading comprehension defined more broadly, or as one indicator of verbal aptitude, or as an indicator of some more general construct, such as intelligence. These different interpretations necessarily involve different interpretive arguments.

Because the procedures used to obtain a score do not uniquely determine the interpretations, the interpretation must be assigned to the test score. Someone or some group decides on the interpretation to be given to the reading comprehension scores.

Specifying the associated interpretive argument is of fundamental importance in evaluating the validity of the interpretation. One validates the interpretation by evaluating the plausibility of the interpretive argument, and some possible interpretive arguments are more plausible than others.

Therefore, an important first step in any effort to validate the interpretive argument is to state the argument clearly. The argument may be changed later, perhaps as a result of validation research, but if the effort to check on the assumptions and inferences in the interpretive argument is to make much progress, the effort needs to begin by specifying the details of the argument.

Interpretive arguments are dynamic. As new information becomes available, the interpretive argument may expand to include new types of inferences. Empirical results may support generalization to a wide domain or extrapolation to a new domain. Conversely, new results may refute assumptions that supported part of an interpretive argument, thus forcing a narrower interpretation. Society's priorities and values may change, leading to changes in how test scores are used.

The malleability of interpretations can make validation more difficult or easier. A changing interpretation presents the validator with a moving target. However, it may also be possible to make some adjustments in the intended interpretation, on the basis of validity data. That is, sometimes the case for the validity of the interpretive argument can be strengthened by changing some inferences and assumptions to fit the data.

The interpretive argument may need to be adjusted to reflect the needs of specific examinees or special circumstances that might have an impact on the test scores. The general version of the interpretive argument cannot take explicit account of all of the special circumstances that might affect an examinee's performance. In applying the argument in a specific case, it is assumed that the examinee is drawn from an appropriate population and that there are no circumstances that might alter the interpretation.

Adjustments in the interpretive argument may need to be made for subpopulations and for individuals. For example, within the subpopulation of examinees with a certain handicap, the interpretive argument may need to be adjusted to reflect the impact of the handicap (see Willingham, 1988). If testing procedures are adjusted to accommodate the needs of a handicapped student, it may be necessary to add evidence supporting the comparability of scores obtained under special testing procedures (Willingham, 1988). The general form of the interpretive argument may also need to be modified for individual examinees to reflect special circumstances (e.g., illness or lack of motivation).

Interpretive arguments make many assumptions that are plausible under ordinary circumstances (e.g., that examinees can hear instructions that are read to them) but that may be questionable for specific examinees (e.g., hearing-impaired examinees) or under special circumstances (a noisy environment). The assignment of an interpretation to a specific test score is an instantiation of the general form of the interpretive argument. The plausibility of the resulting specific interpretive argument depends on the reasonableness of the general form of the interpretive argument and on the extent to which the interpretive argument applies to the specific situation under consideration.

Interpretive arguments are practical arguments, which are evaluated in terms of their degree of plausibility. Initially, the intended interpretation is quite likely to be stated in very general terms, for example, in terms of reading comprehension or readiness for a particular course. The interpretive argument is then correspondingly loose. The interpretive argument may be made more explicit over time, but even the most highly developed interpretive arguments do not attain the precision of mathematical derivations. Interpretive arguments are practical arguments, and their evaluation does not involve a simple valid or invalid decision, as it might in logic or mathematics. The evaluation is necessarily judgmental, leading to conclusions about the plausibility of the interpretive argument rather than a simple yes or no decision.

In general, then, interpretive arguments are artefacts, they change with time, they may need to be modified for particular examinees or circumstances, and they are more-or-less plausible.

Advantages of an argument-based approach to validation

The argument-based approach to validity is basically quite simple. One chooses the interpretation, specifies the interpretive argument associated with the interpretation, identifies competing interpretations, and develops evidence to support the intended interpretation and to refute the competing interpretations. The amount of evidence and the types of evidence needed in a particular case depend on the inferences and assumptions in the interpretive argument.

The argument-based approach offers several advantages. First, it can be applied to any type of test interpretations or use: It is highly tolerant. It does not preclude the development of any kind of interpretation or the use of any data collection technique. It does not identify any kind of validity evidence as being generally preferable to any other kind of validity evidence. It does require that the interpretive argument be stated

M. T. Kane

as clearly as possible and that the validity evidence should address the plausibility of the specific interpretive argument being proposed.

Second, although the evaluation of an interpretive argument does not lead to any absolute decision about validity, it does provide a way to gauge progress. As the most questionable inferences and assumptions are checked and either are supported by the evidence or are adjusted so that they are more plausible, the plausibility of the interpretive argument as a whole can improve.

Third, the approach may increase the chances that research on validity will lead to improvements in measurement procedures. To the extent that the argument-based approach focuses attention on specific parts of the interpretive argument and on specific aspects of measurement procedures, evidence indicating the existence of a problem (e.g., inadequate coverage of content or the presence of some form of systematic error) may also suggest ways to solve the problem and thereby to improve the procedure.

The argument-based approach to validity is similar to what Cronbach (1989) called the strong program of construct validation: 'a construction made explicit, a hypothesis deduced from it, and pointedly relevant evidence brought in' (p. 162). The term argument-based approach to validity has been used here instead of construct validity or the strong program of construct validity to emphasize the generality of the argument-based approach, applying as it does to theoretical constructs as well as to attributes defined in terms of specific content or performance domains. The term construct validity has often been associated with theory-based interpretations (Cronbach & Meehl, 1955). Interpretive arguments may be, but do not have to be, associated with formal theories.

The expression argument-based approach offers some advantages. It is an approach to validity rather than a type of validity. The term argument emphasizes the existence of an audience to be persuaded, the need to develop a positive case for the proposed interpretation, and the need to consider and evaluate competing interpretations.

Task B10.6

Who makes test validity arguments? Usually, it is the producer of the test – a testing company or testing committee, for example. Who makes the refutations and challenges the arguments? Often, it is the same group of people. A well-made validity argument is one that anticipates its challenges and follows principles of good construction; this is the essential point of Kane's paper and of subsequent literature that amplifies this line of thinking (e.g. Chapelle 1994, 1999b). Kane is advocating two things in this paper: firstly, that our validation should be in the form of arguments, and secondly, that we should do all we can to make those arguments unassailable.

If we do things right, then, our validity arguments are a neatly sewn-up parcel, ready to go, before we ever present them to anybody on a website or (for commercial testing) in a sales promotion.

➤ Does this seem ethical?

What if the test developers – on purpose – allowed a test to go forward with an under-prepared validity argument? This would mean that the testers did not consider all aspects of support for the test score inferences, or perhaps that they had supportive evidence on hand but simply did not have time to write up the argument.

➤ Does that seem ethical?

Summary

The B10 excerpt seems a fitting paper to close this section of our book. Test validation as argument – by its very nature – engages a much wider range of concerns about testing practice. For example, the ethical questions we pose in the very last task (B10.6) echo concerns in Unit A9. And the inferential nature of validity is sounded throughout the entire book.

It is probably pedestrian to claim that all work on testing is a problem of validity, but there is some truth to that old chestnut. Certainly, if we keep the problem of validity arguments foremost in our consciousness as we build tests, then 'the best results will follow' (with a nod to Parkhurst, 1922: 225).

Validation arguments are yet another flavour of pragmatic effect-driven testing.

SECTION C
Exploration

Unit C1
Validity – an exploration

Task C1.1: The validity of love

Sarah and John have known each other for many years; in fact, they first met early in secondary school. Back then, they dated each other from time to time and almost never fought – their times together, as a couple, were characterized mostly by laughter and goofing off. As time passed, they stopped seeing each other. Each found and became involved with other people. Their lives grew and changed, and they matured – each in his or her own way, encountering both the nettles and the roses that accompany romantic life. Each married and divorced once, never having had children. Now in their mid-thirties, both Sarah and John came to an interesting realization. Over the past twenty years, when anguish or elation arose, each thought of the other and somehow communicated their emotional state. They have kept in touch over all these years: email, letters and occasional phone calls.

➤ Are Sarah and John in love?

➤ Write an argument. Choose either belief: yes, they are in love; no, they are not. Your argument should follow the style of test validation promoted by Chapelle (1994, 1999b). She advises that we lay forth two columns of reasoning: 'argues in favour', 'argues against'. The particular rows of the argument are up to you, but the rows should reflect the particulars of these two individual lives – think about the time that has elapsed, the need for each to communicate with the other, the fact that both married (but not to each other), the fact that both divorced, the fact that neither had children. Think about those dates in high school, 'characterized by laughter and goofing off'.

Task C1.2: The strength of the argument

Consult the reading by Kane in Unit B10. Review his discussion of three criteria to judge any validity argument: (1) the clarity of the argument, (2) the coherence of the argument and (3) the plausibility of the assumptions.

➤ Apply these three criteria to your argument about Sarah and John. What is your opinion of the argument as judged by Kane's criteria? Remember what we said in Unit A1:

> concepts become constructs when they are so defined that they can become 'operational' – we can measure them in a test of some kind by linking the term to something observable.

Task C1.3: Argument as targeting

➤ Find a test at your setting that nobody likes. Make a note of the test, because you can use it again for Task C4.4.

➤ In that test, find an item type that is famously disliked among your colleagues. Maybe it is some kind of multiple-choice test item or highly mechanical task – fill-in-the-blank, perhaps. Maybe it is an open-ended item that requires extensive work by a team of raters. Target it, remaining professional about the matter (of course), but target it.

➤ How could you re-operationalize the same concept? What other item types might test the same thing? Do you think such other item types yield more valid inferences? Build an argument in favour of these alternative item types.

Task C1.4: The wider nomological net

➤ Using the same test from the previous task, now interview teachers about classroom practice. How do they teach the construct(s) measured by the existing task? That is, given that they dislike the task, do they bring it into their teaching anyway? Or do they have alternative ways of seeing and of doing the thing in the classroom, and do those alternatives suggest an even broader array of potential reform?

We cannot avoid one problem here, one that vexes both test development and validity argumentation. Not everything that teachers do in classrooms can be transported into a formal test. There is an old saying: there are three things that drive test development – (1) money, (2) money and (3) money.

Task C1.5: A retroductive thought experiment

Select a test with which you are familiar, preferably one that is at present still in development. Imagine it is some two years hence. The test is fully operational. It yields results on which actual decisions are made.

Imagine two test takers walking out of your testing room in that future, engaged in a conversation:

A: Well, that was not as rough as I thought it would be.
B: Not too bad, I agree.
A: About what I expected.
B: Just about. I agree.
A: Then why do I feel I have not learned anything? Why do I feel that all I did was to take a test?
B: I don't know. I feel the same way.

Sherlock Holmes always seemed to get it right. You did not, in this case. Despite the Peircean dream-like assimilation, and despite all the creative energy you could muster, you now discover that the test did not foster learning.

The secret, we think, is to anticipate conversations like this now, before we write tests, and then adjust the test design to avoid such conversations later on.

➤ That said, what could you do to your test – now – to avoid such a conversation? This is where test development differs from Sherlock Holmes. He always worked with a crime already committed. Anticipate rightly, and you can avoid the crime entirely.

Task C1.6: And a return, to the wider net

Re-visit your answer to the previous task.

➤ Must all tests foster learning? Are there tests for which the sole purpose is to divide or filter people, allocating various resources or opportunities, preventing access in some cases and granting it in others? Are there social needs for tests that (to put the matter bluntly) don't care at all about washback?

Task C1.7: Suggestions for further research

C1.7.1 Proposed title: 'Validation in language testing: a comparison with the legal profession'

Background

Argument and reasoning are not limited to language testing. Rhetoric is really only recently acknowledged in educational test validation – arguably only since Messick's 1989 paradigm-shifting chapter and the Kane (1992) reading which we cite in Unit B10. We feel there is much to be learned from other human spheres of argument; surely, language testers are not the only scholars who use reasoning on a regular basis.

Possible procedure

You could interview scholars or practitioners in other areas of human activity which involve arguments. A good place to start would be the legal profession. Ask each lawyer how they establish their case in a courtroom or in a legal document – what is the form of reasoning involved? What kinds of evidence? When an argument fails (e.g. when a case is lost at trial), what weaknesses of reasoning might have been to blame?

Possible outcomes

You could critically analyse some arguments in a published validation study against the normal forms of reasoning employed in legal reasoning. This is a very practical form of research, intended to help build better validation arguments by borrowing from argument strategies outside of the testing profession.

C1.7.2 Proposed title: 'Validation of language tests via item tracking: Phase I'

Background

In many language tests the basic elements of the assessment are a series of items or tasks. Each item is a potential subject for validation: you can have a weak item in an otherwise (arguably) valid test. One way to catch this is to track the argument of validity for a particular item right from its genesis – from the point at which an item is actually created.

Possible procedure

Create a survey intended for experienced educators who write language test items regularly. This can be done retrospectively, introspectively or both. A retrospective survey would ask the educators to think back about some test questions they had written, whereas introspective enquiry would ask them to reflect as they are writing the test. Ask the educators to select items they feel ultimately worked well and those they feel did not. When an item did not work, what went wrong? How could such mis-steps have been anticipated in the item-writing process? Do the educators 'track' such bad items and fix them in subsequent tests?

Possible outcomes

This research will probably produce a set of recommended item-writing guidelines: a list of tips and tricks for future item writers. We think that such an outcome is immediately useful in any educational setting, for it will generate ideas that probably affect many different tests. This research can also be seen as the first phase of a two-phase project: the guidelines that emerge can become part of regular testing practice if they are written into test specifications. We will return to this idea in Unit C4, where we will propose 'Phase II' of this research project.

Unit C2
Assessment in school systems

 Task C2.1: Crafting an assessment statement

Exergue State University (ESU) is located in Obverse City, capital of Numismania. Term time is about to commence, and the Language Co-ordinator for the Department of French is meeting with instructors to review course plans for its introductory course sequence, known simply as French One to French Three. This is the first of five such meetings each term.

French One satisfies the notorious ESU 'second foreign language requirement', in which all ESU students must become fluent in a foreign language other than Numismanian, and then must study another (the 'second') foreign language for at least one academic term.

The Co-ordinator first reads off a memorandum from the Dean of their faculty, noting that all instructors must ensure that every ESU course prospectus is available to all students and to the general public, and that it must henceforward include a 'statement of assessment procedures and philosophy'. The French teachers nod knowingly, as there had been a high-profile complaint in the media during the previous year. Another department had been lax in distributing course information, and the information that was distributed said nothing about assessment. A student had failed a course and had complained of lack of advance warning about tests.

The French Language Co-ordinator says: 'We really don't have to worry. We have a prospectus for all of our courses, and we diligently distribute them to students on the first day of class. In addition, we are very careful to ensure that each is given at our department website. What concerns me is this assessment statement. I know that you say something about that to your students, but I am concerned about the comparability of our messages. I've been thinking a lot about it, and in fact it kept me awake much of last night. What I decided to do is this: please get into groups according to your French course. I'd like you to brainstorm a common assessment statement that fits the typical needs and strengths of ESU students at your instructional level. We have some large newsprint paper, markers and masking tape. Please write out your draft state-ment on to newsprint and put it on the wall. I want to see what you all come up with. I'll be circulating and helping. After we have the three statements, I want to see if it's feasible to come up with one common statement for the entire programme.'

After some two hours of work, following are the three draft assessment plans:

French One

Students in this class are measured against performance on two term tests and two face-to-face oral interviews. Term tests are written, and the test questions come from a bank of items that is routinely reviewed and renewed for item quality and reliability. We often have nearly two hundred students distributed across the various instructors, and so we make great use of item banks and of statistical analysis of item quality. As for the oral tests, those are conducted by a French teacher other than the student's contact instructor. Each oral test is clearly designed against a preparation plan, so that students know the topics of conversation before the interview begins; however, the interviewer or teacher has great latitude to select from a wide range of topics. Typically, the oral interviews are the most nerve-racking assessments, and so as those approach, there is a great deal of in-class practice prior to the testing.

French Two

Our students write essays in French and collect oral data of their French performance on audio tapes. They assemble these materials into a portfolio, which the contact teacher evaluates formally at least twice during the semester and once at the end to determine the final grade. We have a portfolio scoring scale that we have developed, which shows what a student must do in order to receive high marks during the class. We also ask the student to comment formally on the portfolio. Each student writes a 'PAM' or Portfolio Analysis Memo, which analyses the strengths and weaknesses of the work, and, most importantly, sets forth a formal contract-like statement of what improvement is needed. This year, we are applying for a research grant to move the entire portfolio process to digital media: the audio tapes will be replaced by digital recorders, and all written materials will be scanned (if handwritten) or typed directly into a word processor.

French Three

In the first week of class, our students design a 'Statement of Language Goals' or 'SLG', which is a written document about their perceptions of their current French ability, and which details at some length the goals they wish to accomplish during the course. We analyse all the SLGs and then we negotiate with the students if they have chosen some goals that are too easy, too difficult, or too time-consuming. The SLG is written entirely in French, and the nego-tiations about it are done in conference with the teacher, also conducted entirely in French. As the course term proceeds, periodic conferences are held with the teacher – again, conducted entirely in French. These help the teacher and student to monitor progress towards the goals. Our classrooms resemble workshops, with a lot of student-centred work and student-led small-group activities.

➤ What similarities and differences exist across the three levels?

➤ Clearly, the N-size of French Two and French Three is far less than that of French One. This 'second foreign language' requirement has boosted the class sizes at the first instructional level. Is a common statement even feasible for the entire programme? Why, or why not?

★ **Task C2.2: Shaping the message**

'These are good,' says the Co-ordinator, 'I was very involved with the discussion in all three groups, and it was quite active. In fact, I sense that a discussion like this would have been valuable even without the Dean's memo.

'As a veteran of teaching at all three levels, I think these three statements adequately capture what we need to say. Before we discuss whether a common statement is feasible or wise, I want us to break out again, and then to re-write each statement as if we are speaking to the student. Remember: the voice of each prospectus is aimed at our students. Each needs to be shaped.

'For example, I see that French Three says, "In the first week of class, our students design a Statement of Language Goals or SLG, which is a written document about their perceptions of their current French ability." They note that the statement should be written in French.

'What I need is something written to the student, for instance, "During Week One, you will write an SLG, or Statement of Language Goals. You will write this in French. Think about the learning you have done in French One and French Two. Consider any other study or exposure to French you may have had elsewhere. What do you want to learn in this class? What weaknesses do you have in French? How do you want to address those weaknesses?"'

One aspect of classroom assessment is communicating it to the students, to parents and to the public.

➤ Re-write the French Three statement for use by staff at this institution. Begin with the re-write indicated by the Co-ordinator, and then continue to revise the language of the rest of the statement.

➤ Repeat the activity with the French One and French Two statements.

➤ Does doing this help you to see any overall stylistic similarity in the three statements?

> 'Well,' says the Co-ordinator, 'it's nearly five o'clock, and for the past hour and a half we've been arguing whether or not a consolidated assessment statement is possible. I think that the energy of our discussion indicates that we need to talk more about it. Rather than decide it today, I'd like to implement the three statements as revised and shaped. Simply add the student-shaped statement to the prospectus in your class, and we are done. Be sure to get a copy to me in electronic form, and I'll pass it along to our webmaster.

> 'Here's what I plan to do this term. Let's set aside some ten or fifteen minutes at each co-ordination meeting to review and revisit the statements. Our meetings in-term are two hours each, and, as you are aware, there are often many topics to discuss. We can't give this too much time, but I am obligated to write to the Dean's office and illustrate how we have answered that memo, and all I'll do is send in the three statements. The memo does not require that we have one statement for the entire programme. I am, myself, not sure that is even feasible. But I am curious as to whether it is, and so we can study that problem in the coming months.'

Task C2.3: Rolling out with the system

➤ Do you think that this language instruction programme is moving towards similar assessment statements across all instructional levels? If so, is such a development wise? Why and/or why not?

Task C2.4: Suggestions for further research

C2.4.1 Proposed title: 'Alignment of assessment standards'

Background

> Many readers of this book work in systems where classroom teachers are obligated to produce tests that follow some co-ordinated assessment statements, often given as national guidelines. A Ministry of Education might issue descriptors about particular skills to be taught, and these descriptors might include guidance about how the skills are to be assessed. If you work in such a setting, we recommend a research study to investigate the comparability of test content across various teachers' classrooms, and in turn, the comparability of those teachers' tests to external guidelines and standards.

Possible procedure

Firstly, study the national guidelines and become very familiar with them; perhaps you, yourself, already teach in a class that is obligated to those guidelines. The purpose of this phase of the research is accurate and thorough description of the guidelines without actually including their content in your research report. What elements of style are common across such guidelines? What seems to be uniformly present and/or uniformly absent?

Secondly, survey a number of teachers about their familiarity with the guidelines. In our work, we find that teachers often work in guideline-driven systems without full knowledge of the guidelines. Design a survey or interview method that confirms or disconfirms this suspicion.

Thirdly, investigate the similarity of testing across a set of teachers, each of whom claims to be measuring the same elements of the guidelines. Analyse the content of the tests and compare it to the actual stated guidelines.

Fourthly, investigate the similarity of test results for the same set of teachers. You may need to consult with a statistician, because you may want to equate results across different teachers' practices.

Possible outcomes

Research such as this contributes to the validity argument for any test system. It allows the system to claim adherence to external standards, which helps with educational accountability. Interestingly, there is also a powerful opposing force that will – we are certain – arise in a vexing way. It is the age-old conflict between centralized educational control and local freedom, whether that be freedom of individual school buildings, of teachers or of students. We explore this age-old conflict in greater detail in the tasks in Unit C8, and, if you conduct research such as we suggest here, we suspect you will want to explore that philosophical tension as well.

C2.4.2 Research skills development

We would like to depart from our typical model of suggested research: title, background, procedure and outcome. Here and in Unit C7, we will include a 'research suggestion' that is not really about a particular project. Instead, we recommend the development of certain methodological expertise. In this case, we recommend that you develop skills of text analysis.

Our previous suggestion (C2.4.1) involves comparison of large amounts of text content: on the one hand, there would be the text of the teachers' assessments, and on the other, the text of various external guidelines and standards. The thought exercises in this unit for Exergue University also might involve comparison of texts. As the Dean's required 'statement of assessment procedures and philosophy' grows and evolves and changes in the French Department, texts will be produced that can be compared and analysed. There are other exercises in this book where evolution and change of text is central to the research enterprise – notably in Unit C4, in which we explore the evolution of test specifications, themselves a form of text.

Text content analysis is both a human and a machine activity. It involves reading and study of text in some formalized manner, and at the same time it involves management of the texts and the results of the content analyses (nowadays, on computers). There is a synergy between the two: a team of human analysts follow some protocol to study the texts, and in turn, they enter the results of that protocol into a database that yields summative results.

For example, what kind of text content analysis might apply to the previous research suggestion, C2.4.1? A starting point is the web page on alignment for the 'Council of Chief State School Officers' (CCSSO). This is an organization comprising the state education chiefs for the fifty states in the USA. Recent changes in US education law have necessitated greater coordination across the states and with the national government – this is the No Child Left Behind (NCLB) law, to which we shall return in Unit C8.

CCSSO is serving as a clearing house on alignment results and methodologies: of tests to standards, and of standards to standards; the latter complex problem arises when (for example) a local school government entity – like a state – has a set of assessment standards that fail to match national guidelines. You can access the web page at http://www.ccsso.org/Projects/surveys_of_enacted_curriculum/understanding_alignment_analysis/7847.cfm. Note particularly the discussion of content coding procedures: http://www.ccsso.org/content/pdfs/CodingProcedures.pdf. A natural byproduct of any text content analysis or comparison research is some kind of analytical formalism like those coding procedures. You may want to develop your own, adapt those of others or simply use existing coding schemes.

Unit C3
What do items really test?

Our activities here in Unit C3 will concern a particular test task, quoted from Davidson and Lynch (2002: 69–70) and known as 'the Barry item':

> Barry seemed _____; he had successfully predicted the outcome of seven major sporting events over the past month.
>
> a. surprised
> b. gifted
> *c. clairvoyant ['*' denotes the intended correct answer]
> d. upset

This is a strange little item, and Davidson and Lynch analyse it at some length. They argue that response data from test takers are critical to understanding what the item is measuring, because each choice is potentially correct. Choice (a) is possible if Barry has low self-esteem and a poor track record as a gambler. Choice (b) is possible if the assertion in the item is by an external observer – giftedness, we assume, is something that one does not assert about oneself. And finally, even choice (d) is feasible if Barry is a con artist who wishes to lose sometimes and thus dupe victims out of their money – conmen have trouble if they have a winning streak, because they cannot then control the perceived odds.

Let's see what happens if we try to view this item through each lens of some models discussed in Unit A3, and, along the way, we shall tweak the item from time to time, in an effort to make it agree with the various models discussed. As we do so, we will suggest various thought activities you can also perform, in an effort 'to articulate the theoretical rationale for our [item], and relate the meaning of specific [item] performance to language competence and ability for language use' (p. 51, Unit A3).

★ Task C3.1: The Barry item, variant 1: Measurement of vocabulary

Canale and Swain's original model included 'grammatical competence', which is (as one of our professors used to put it) 'grammar with a capital "G"', meaning all formal rule-governed or systematic taxonomies in a given language. Vocabulary control is part of 'G'rammar in this sense. Following is a variation on the Barry item in which we have attempted to pose a task that is still rather high-level, but for which the choice of the correct item is purely one of vocabulary. As is the case here, the usual way to produce a high-level vocabulary item is by selecting relatively low-frequency target words:

> Barry seemed _____; he had successfully predicted the outcome of seven major sporting events over the past month.
>
> a.   contrite
> b.   bankrupt
> *c. clairvoyant
> d.   myopic

In Units A4 and C4 we discuss test specifications, which are generative blueprints of test design. Specs involve guiding language, which is formulaic claims about how to construct given items or tasks. The key to writing good multiple-choice items is to specify the nature of the incorrect choices, known as the distracters. Here, (a) is plausible. Barry may be a contrite person, but we presume that somebody who has just predicted the future would feel some pride rather than contrition. Choice (b) does not make sense, assuming that Barry was (himself) gambling on the outcome of those events. And finally, (d) is a direct low-frequency antonym to the intended correct choice.

➤   We recommend that you do two things: first, try to write some other alterations to the Barry item, each of which keeps the item firmly in the 'grammar' competence of Canale and Swain: each of your items should measure features of vocabulary alone. Here is a hint – revise the correct choice from 'clairvoyant' to 'lucky', and see if you can write a parallel item that tests vocabulary, albeit at greater vocabulary frequency so as to make the item easier.

➤   Second, consider this question: do you think our revision of the Barry item really fits the Canale and Swain model? Is the distinction drawn among these lexical items largely a matter of control of lexis: contrite versus bankrupt versus clairvoyant versus myopic? Do other skills and abilities enter in as a test taker answers this item? Take the item to some high-level speakers of English as a foreign language and ask them to analyse the item with you – for best results, remove the asterisks and ask that the respondent answer the item.

Task C3.2: The Barry item, variant 2: Measurement of strategy

⭐

Suppose that the Barry item were revised and expanded like this:

> You have heard that Barry had successfully predicted the outcome of seven major sporting events over the past month. Imagine that you meet Barry one day on the street. You are aware of his successes at sports prediction, and you note that he is wearing a new broad-brimmed hat with

a sharp-looking hand-tooled leather strap. He seems to be in the money. You also know that Barry is rather a braggart, aware of his successes in sports gambling and willing to tell anybody about it. You are in a hurry, and the last thing you want this particularly busy day is to have to stand there and listen to Barry talking about his winnings. What will you say?

a.   Barry, my man, nice hat! I see that you've been doing well.
b.   Barry, my man, I see that you've been doing well.
*c. Barry, nice hat! Sorry, I can't talk – I gotta go; I'm late for a meeting.
d.   Barry, sorry I can't talk – I gotta go; I'm late for a meeting.

This item follows the 'magic formula' (Davidson and Lynch, 2002: 52). There are two elements in each choice – a greeting and a follow-up – and only when both are correct is the entire choice correct. Choice (a) has an overly friendly and engaging greeting ('my man') followed by a conversational opener that invites further dialogue – which you wish to avoid. Then choice (b) has the same dangerous invitation for conversation, but without the friendly opener. And finally, choice (d) seems wrong because there is no polite acknowledgment at all – simply an excuse not to talk. It seems that the item writer's choice for (c) shows a strategy to acknowledge Barry but immediately excuse further conversation – that is, the item tests the ability to acknowledge but excuse oneself from conversation.

As before, do you think this measures strategic competence? Consider in particular the difference between (c) and (d). Perhaps the acknowledgment is a matter not of strategy but of sociolinguistic politeness. What are the cultural assumptions when meeting an acquaintance on the street? Do you acknowledge the person before excusing yourself from further conversation? If so, that is a matter of sociolinguistic norms. Much as you wish that (d) might be a correct answer, (c) may be better, and if it is, that is because the line between strategies (what you plan to do) and sociolinguistics (what you must do according to norms) is indistinct.

Furthermore, the distinction between (a) and (b) is very interesting. Perhaps there is a norm in this language that compels speakers to compliment others who are wearing obviously new clothes. Do you think that Canale and Swain's conception of 'sociolinguistic' includes such interpersonal expectations? Or is that more a matter of personality variables: are some speakers more likely to acknowledge appearance of others and comment on it? If so, is that likelihood part of a construct of language knowledge, or, put another way, in order to be a competent speaker of this target language do you also have to figure out when to compliment others on their appearance – and when not?

➤ Does the Canale and Swain model really explain this variation of the Barry item? What about Canale's 1983b revisions of the model? Are they better at explaining this item?

Task C3.3: The Barry item, variant 3: Measurement of discourse

Suppose that the item – now more rightly called a 'task' – looks like this:

> Barry is an old and trusted friend. You and he go back years, to the early days of your schooling. As you grew up, you and he had many adventures – and chief among them was an episode of gambling in your teenage years. You and he used to seek out card games, bookies and even (as computers came in) online Internet wagering. Sometimes you did well, sometimes you both lost money.
>
> Once you both lost heavily. This soured you on gambling – forever, it seems, for you don't gamble.
>
> However, Barry rebounded. He scrounged some more money, wagered and placed bets, and gradually recouped his losses. You were envious, but you also started to worry about him. Your friendship had endured these events, but you noticed that he increasingly ignored the rest of his life responsibilities. He gained and lost girlfriends, held and lost jobs, and even bought a very nice semi-detatched house, and then sold it in a hurry to cover debts.
>
> Barry appears to have a gambling addiction.
>
>  Recently, Barry sent you an email with an attached image file. He said that he hit it big – he had won on seven major sporting events. He treated himself to an Australian 'Digger' or 'Slouch' hat and replica Vietnam-era uniform. He got the hat and uniform on the Internet and paid a lot of money. The attached image file showed Barry in his military splendour, and about the picture he wrote: 'I can't wait for our next costume party!'
>
> You are worried. Write a reply to Barry's email in which you discuss his gambling problem.

➤ Which of the models in Unit A3 seem to best explain this test task?

For instance, the Bachman model notes that language ability involves '[deciding] which abilities and knowledge we share with our interlocutor' (p. 45). Here, you have a large body of shared knowledge with Barry. You and he have been through much together, and the fact that you no longer gamble is probably known to Barry; we suspect he's tried to lure you back into that fold from time to time. Still, your friendship has endured. Have you expressed your worries to him before? Have you ever told him that he seems addicted to gambling? If so, those prior warnings are also part of the shared knowledge.

Perhaps you decide not to write a reply, but to speak to Barry. If you plan what you will say, then there are elements of strategic competence. We also suspect that interactional competence will play a role; 'responsibility for talk cannot be assigned to a single individual' (p. 49), and so the interaction will be co-constructed. If you talk to Barry, your personalities will emerge and the conversation may become a litany or repeat of past conversations, with repeated warnings (on your part) and repeated ignorance or side-stepping (on his).

The task above could lead to either a written or an oral response (a role-play, perhaps). And in either case, we suspect it will easily illustrate how the various models in Unit A3 are closely interrelated.

★ Task C3.4: The Barry item and the limits of language assessment contexts

Should foreign language tests include tests of interpersonal relationships (like the previous example) or refer to topics that may be culturally sensitive (like gambling)?

Clearly, difficult topics and complex interpersonal relationships are part of language use. We all have to talk about delicate matters from time to time, and we all have to seek and give counsel to loved ones and to friends. Let's list some more sensitive human interactions:

- a confessional with a priest
- a therapy session with a psychologist
- discussing with a close friend his or her recent diagnosis of cancer.

The models in A3 emphasize the importance of context in language use. These are language use contexts, but are they legitimate simulated contexts in a language test? Do we need to test such things?

Here is another list of possibly sensitive interactions:

- arguing a traffic ticket with a police officer
- negotiating a complex academic assignment (e.g. a research thesis) with a professor.

Imagine that the test taker is a second-language speaker of the TL, now living and studying in the TL country. Either of the above tasks is feasible, and either one may become sensitive and delicate, and (particularly for the second one) may involve past knowledge about interpersonal relationships.

➤ What is the nature of context, and, for each variant of the Barry item here, can you conceive of language test situations in which it would be appropriate to include it on a language test?

Task C3.5: Suggestions for further research

C3.5.1 Proposed title: 'Modelling language ability: a review of the debate'

Background

Several scholars have proposed models of foreign language ability, and we summarize some major models here. These models are evolutionary and often build on amplification or extension of a previous model, as when, for example, Canale expanded his model in 1983. What we do not do is cover discussion or criticism of the models by other scholars who themselves do not really build their own models in response. Our discussion here is about the evolution of these models, not about the reaction these models have triggered elsewhere in scholarship.

Possible procedure

Consult a bibliographic resource such as the Social Sciences Citation Index (SSCI).[9] Track and tabulate citations of these various models by other scholarly papers and authors. Summarize your findings, both numerically (which models get cited the most) and substantively (what is said).

Possible outcomes

First, there will be the rather pedestrian finding that the older models get more citations, but, beyond that, you should uncover some practical as well as theoretical criticism of the various views.

C3.5.2 Proposed title: 'Multiple-competency testing at lower ability levels'

Background

As we see with the Barry item here, it is possible to tweak and adjust test questions to tap various competences – or possibly to do so; debate on that point is the outcome we (very much) desire for the tasks in this unit. We also see that the tasks here are fairly high-level. Words like 'clairvoyant' and 'myopic' are antonyms, but both are low-frequency, so we surmise. A natural question arises: can we adapt some of these competences to lower-ability testing?

Possible procedure

Step 1: Assemble a discussion group of several language teachers. Try to find teachers whose experience involves beginner to intermediate students. Design a workshop based on the various language models in Unit A3, and show them how some of these competences may be testable at higher ability levels – use the Barry items or similar test tasks of your own construction. Ask the teachers to develop test questions that do the same thing but at lower ability levels.

Step 2: Now ask the teachers to compare the test tasks to activities and exercises typical of their classroom teaching. Are they actually training students in things like strategic competence, interactional competence, awareness of shared knowledge, and similar phenomena?

Possible outcomes

This study will help to enhance the validity of any tests it analyses or proposes, first and most easily, by comparing those tests to actual classroom instruction. Such a project is always valuable. The research goes further, however; it asks the teachers to push the edge of the envelope and try to come up with test tasks that do stretch out to new competences, even at lower ability levels. Davidson tried something like this in a workshop some years ago, and one group of teachers developed a test item for 'mooching', which is borrowing something minor with no intent to repay – a few sheets of paper, for example. Mooching is heavily culturally bound, full of formulaic interactions and very teachable even at a low level. And – so the teachers argued – it is fun.

C3.5.3 Proposed title: 'The cutting-room floor: an analysis of discarded language test items and tasks'

Background

Perhaps you have read this chapter and felt that you would not even try tasks like the Barry item or a question about mooching. We are curious whether items like this emerge and live, perhaps briefly, in the development of a test.

Possible procedure

We think this will work better for a larger test development situation, in which there are many items drawn from many test specifications (see Unit A4), and for which there is a reasonable chance of rejects. As in movie-making, where some scenes wind up on the cutting-room floor, there will be test item rejects which never make it into the operational test booklet. The research method is rather simple: to collect those rejects as comprehensively as possible. Doing so is rather tricky, because the testing agency may not wish its rejects to be known; we believe a collaborative approach is best. The rejects can be analysed: why were they denied a place in the test booklet? Clearly, some of them did not meet their specifications or had some other editing problems, but we think another reason may emerge.

Possible outcome

We believe that some items will get rejected because they do not test the intended target (they do not meet the spec) in a very particular way. They break into new competences. For example, an item on mooching might not make it into a vocabulary test. It might be too odd. Could its oddity actually represent a window into a wider, more creative array of test content, and might that window shine on to new competences that normally do not enter into test development? This was precisely the argument made by Davidson (1994, 2006), who discussed the richness of various English varieties and reasons why such richness might not make it into operational testing.

Unit C4
Evolution in action

In Unit A4 we reviewed test specifications, which are generative blueprints from which many equivalent test items or tasks can be created. We closed with some elements of spec-driven testing theory, repeated here:

- Specs exist.
- Specs evolve.
- The specs were not launched until ready.
- Discussion happens and that leads to transparency.
- And this is discussion to which all are welcome.

Our exploration of test specifications will focus on these key elements.

There is no dominant model of test specifications. Every testing textbook or test development project that uses specs eventually develops its own organizational style. As noted in Unit A4, all specs – regardless of style – share two common features: sample items or tasks that the spec generates, and guiding language about those items or tasks.

It is not important – really – to practise and train in a particular model of specs. Far more important is to practise the process of spec-driven test development. With that in mind, our exercises in this Unit focus not on a particular model of test specs but on some design considerations that arise as a spec evolves.

Task C4.1: A spec evolves

In the following we provide some guiding language and some sample test tasks from a larger test specification for a final examination in a language institute. This is for a fairly high-level listening or speaking class. The particular guiding language shown here concerns the scoring of the tasks.

[Version 1: Guiding language]

The general objective of this test specification is to produce a role-play task that involves the pragmatics of making a complaint. Students will be given a simple everyday situation in which something has gone wrong, and then asked to plan and then render the complaint in the target language, in a role-play with the teacher.

Scoring of the interaction will be as follows:

- [1] not competent – the student displayed little or no command of the pragmatics of the situation.
- [2] minimally competent – the student used language of complaint, but the interaction was hesitant and/or impolite.
- [3] competent – the student's interactions were smooth and generally fluent, and there was no evidence of impolite language use.
- [4] superb – the student's interactions were smooth and very fluent, and in addition, the student displayed subtle command of nuance.

[Version 1, sample one]

You have recently purchased a radio. When you got home, you discovered that a very important part was missing from the box. You want to return to the store and ask to speak to the manager about resolving the situation. Your task: (a) write out a rough plan of what you will say, then (b) role-play the conversation with your teacher.

[Version 1, sample two]

Yesterday, you went to the supermarket to buy groceries. After you got home and unpacked the bags, you discovered that a jar of peanut butter was open and that its seal had been punctured. You are worried that the peanut butter may be spoiled or unsafe to eat. You want to return to the store and speak to the manager about resolving the situation. Your task: (a) write out a rough plan of what you will say, then (b) role-play the conversation with your teacher.

Over time, teachers who use this test discover that they need further details in the scoring. The scoring scale changes in the next version of the spec:

[excerpt, Version 2, Scoring scale]

Scoring of the interaction will be as follows:

- [1] not competent – the student displayed little or no command of the pragmatics of the situation. If the student wrote a plan (at all), it was either inadequate or not implemented.
- [2] minimally competent – the student used language of complaint, but the interaction was hesitant and/or impolite. The student's plan may have been adequate, but the student was unable to implement it.

- ■ [3] competent – the student's interactions were smooth and generally fluent, and there was no evidence of impolite language use. The student wrote a viable plan and generally followed it during the interaction.
- ■ [4] superb – the student's interactions were smooth and very fluent, and in addition, the student displayed subtle command of nuance. The student wrote a viable plan and generally followed it during the interaction.

Still more time and try-outs ensue, and once again the spec goes through revisions. This time, a key change is made to the descriptor for level 4 in the scoring scale, while the rest of the scale remains the same:

[excerpt, Version 3, Scoring scale]

- ■ [4] superb – the student's interactions were smooth and very fluent, and in addition, the student displayed subtle command of nuance. The student wrote a viable plan and generally followed it during the interaction. Alternatively, the student wrote little (or no) plan, but seemed to be able to execute the interaction in a commanding and nuanced manner.

There are several interesting questions that arise:

➤ What has been learnt over time, about this spec and the task it generates?

➤ What (precisely) is the role of the written plan? Why do you suppose the teachers felt it necessary to have such a plan in the first version of their test? They have not jettisoned the plan (by Version 3), but have adapted the scoring scale to reflect alternative use of the plan. Why?

➤ Finally, do you suspect that any changes might be coming for level 3 on the scale? Do you suspect that the plan may prove to be an optional testing task, in general? Or do you think that the plan may prove unworkable?

Task C4.2: Planning causes debate and debate causes change

Over time, the number of teachers discussing this task has been relatively small. Perhaps it is only three or four colleagues, all of whom teach the same level in their language institute, and all of whom know each other very well.

A newcomer arrives at the faculty at a point in time between Version 2 and Version 3. This new teacher is energetic, even a bit abrasive, taking on the role of a productive debater in all instructional co-ordination meetings. Sooner or later, this complaint role-play task emerges for discussion, and the new teacher asks, 'Why have the students plan at all? Do we plan when we do this in real life? If we do plan, do we write it down?'

The newcomer causes the teachers to watch (carefully) the use of this task in the next test administration, and sure enough, there are high-level students for whom the plan is at best irrelevant and at worst a waste of time.

➤ Please consider the following questions: was the new teacher within his or her rights to point out this problem with the test? What obligations do teachers have to challenge each other and help make tests better?

➤ Read the discussion of 'Ownership' in the Davidson and Lynch excerpt (Unit B4). In your opinion, who 'owns' this spec? What ownership should be given to this new teacher or, for that matter, to any new teacher?

Task C4.3: And change stagnates

More time passes. The newcomer works at the institute for several academic seasons, and over time becomes a more and more trusted member of the faculty. There are many such debates – the complaint role-play is but one of many active dialogues this newcomer has sparked, and there is general agreement among the rest of the faculty (to put the matter bluntly) that this person was 'a very good hire.'

Gradually, an odd thing starts to happen with the role-play complaint task. Teachers stop teaching the written plan in their lessons, and gradually, most students do not produce one when doing that part of the test. Somehow the written plan is forgotten.

The spec stops evolving. It still gets used, primarily as a training tool for new teachers – and none of them have the engaging temerity of the previous newcomer to voice concerns, if, in fact, they have any concerns.

The faculty simply stop looking at the spec, they stop using a written plan, and the task evolves beyond reference to the spec.

➤ Is this a problem?

Suppose that one teacher does remember to teach written plans, that some of that teacher's students use the written plans in subsequent testing, and that they seem to benefit. Suppose, further, that the students tell their teacher that they feel they did better on the test, that the written plan helped, and that they were grateful for the reminder that it is acceptable to write out such a written plan.

➤ Should students be welcome to discussions of test evolution and change? Should teachers re-visit and re-affirm the wording of the spec, which (after all) does permit a plan? Or should they follow their own instinct and ignore this student feedback, encouraging (instead) role-plays without written plans?

➤ Should teachers, instead, continue to heed the advice of their 'good hire' and teach and prepare their students to do such tasks without written plans, because that is more authentic?

⭐ Task C4.4: Your turn

➤ Locate a test task or set of tasks from your teaching context or from your files. Conduct a reverse engineering day-long workshop with your colleagues, and argue strongly to them and to your superiors that financial investment is merited to make the workshop succeed. You will need breaks for coffee, tea and that most motivating of test development inducements, a decent lunch.

1 *Introduction and Welcome:* orient the participants to the tasks you have selected. The goal of this part of the workshop is not to revise the tasks but to make sure everybody knows what they are and whence they came. Orient them also to the basic design of all test specs: samples and guiding language. We'd suggest about twenty to thirty minutes for this. Do not show actual specs – the more of that you do, the more that the whole day slows down and, what's worse, people tend to think that the particular spec samples you show are how all specs should be written. In addition to the critical analysis that is the target of the day, you want an organic, bottom-up growth of specs. The style of the spec should reflect the tastes of the people in the room.

2 *Group Phase 1:* divide into groups or pairs. Each group is assigned the same set of tasks; we strongly suggest that you pick non-controversial tasks at this stage. Ask each group to do straight reverse engineering – write out what they think is the guiding language for the tasks without recommending any changes. This should be followed by a report back. It is good if each group writes its guiding language out on large newsprint tablets for all to see; the tasks you distributed are the sample items in this case. You can use non-harmful masking tape to mount group products on the room's walls, yielding a creative 'aura' of test development. An hour to an hour and a half is good for this.

3 *Vent Your Spleen:* The ancients believed that human anger and strong emotion locate in the spleen, a belief that gave us the modern adjective 'splenetic'. In the whole group, allow people to vent about test tasks they have never liked – tasks they did not analyse in Phase 1. We strongly recommend liberal use of the famous Quincy Jones quotation at this point: they should have 'left their egos in the hallway'. Based on the judgmental splenetic discussion that will certainly ensue, select a new set of tasks, and proceed to the next step. This may also need about an hour – perhaps less.

4 *Group Phase 2:* divide into groups or pairs again, and this time each group should do critical reverse engineering of some tasks about which somebody feels particularly splenetic. The goal is a set of specs that

improve testing at your situation. A similar report back should follow, again putting the results on newsprint on the wall. The aura will become healthily contentious. We suggest some two hours for this.

5 *'What's Next?'* (to quote a popular US television show – *West Wing*): The group now discusses which specs in the contentious aura stand a reasonable chance of implementation. Not everything that arises will be feasible. Some things will be too costly. But some should survive. This can be about an hour, and it should end the day with a hopeful sense of action.

Somebody needs to follow up, of course; and that will probably be you.

Task C4.5: A parting thought

One of our former students, Scott Walters, was fond of saying: 'Good tests are like art. They are never done. They just stop.'

➤ Do you agree? How do specs figure into this sentiment?

Task C4.6: Suggestions for further research

C4.6.1 Proposed title: 'Validation of language tests via item tracking: Phase II'

Background

This is a continuation of a task in Unit C1, in which we suggested communication with a group of educators who regularly write and revise language tests. The outcome of that study would be a set of general item-writing guidelines, learned from tracking the authorship of particular items. In Phase II we can formalize these guidelines, and in so doing we can learn some interesting details about spec writing.

Possible procedure

Conduct a spec-writing workshop with the items that seemed most discussed in Phase I. Ask the educators to reverse-engineer the items and produce full specs. During the workshop, have on hand the general guidelines from Phase I. Ask the educators to decide whether particular guidelines (from Phase I) apply across the entire test or whether they are restricted to given item types. For example, suppose that one bothersome Phase I item type was a close-reading item, such as the one we discussed in Unit A4. Some of the Phase I

317

guidelines might apply to that particular kind of close-reading multiple-choice item, and some of the guidelines might apply to all multiple-choice items.

Possible outcomes

The immediate practical outcome here is a better sense of guiding language that affects the entire test versus that which affects particular item types. This is of great value to any set of educators, to trainers in language testing, and to textbooks on how to write language tests. If you record and summarize the debate and consensus in this workshop, it will easily lead to audit trail research – a project we describe next.

C4.6.2 Proposed title: 'Audit narratives in spec-driven testing: what should be audited?'

Background

Li (2006) and Kim (2006) feature the notion of an 'audit trail' in their research, following a brief suggestion by Davidson and Lynch (2002: 9), who in turn advocated the use of 'validity narratives' in testing (Lynch and Davidson, 1997).

An audit trail is a metaphor borrowed from the business and accounting world. It is a formal tracking system of change, of response to feedback, and of accountability.

Li (2006) clarifies the distinction between a validity narrative and an audit trail. The narrative is the formal structure for the audit. Put another way, auditing is the function served by the narrative. Li proposes a four-step validity narrative model:

- 'how it was' – here, the test developer summarizes the current statements in the test spec(s) about one element or issue in the test development. In the above example, such an issue might be: 'the role of the written plan'.
- 'feedback' – this is a record of the feedback on that particular issue. In Li's work, the feedback is presented in excerpts from email dialogues about various problematic issues during her test's development, e.g. authenticity or checking for bias. Each issue emerged to form one complete narrative, but there can be many instances of feedback cited for a given narrative. Feedback can be critical discussion from other test development team members or stakeholders, or it can be interpretation from test try-outs, or both.
- 'how it changed' – this is a brief statement of how the test spec(s) changed as a result of the feedback.

■ 'reflection' – this is a brief paragraph or two on what this particular narrative reveals about the evolving validity of the test. It is a contribution to the validity argument of the test.

Possible procedure

For any test development project in which you are involved, or for any we suggest in this book (such as the two-phase tracking study above), you can implement Li's style of validity narratives. As Li found, we believe you will also find that not all elements of test development deserve audit narratives. For example, she discovered that things like bias checking and authenticity emerged as salient and frequent debates, and so she 'audited' them with one narrative each. These narratives became part of her validity argument.

Possible outcomes

Perhaps the most interesting outcome here would be the answers to two simple questions: What became a narrative? What did not? Furthermore, if audited narratives were employed across several test development projects, a cross-project comparison would help us better understand the unique vexations in test development – and these vexations may not be what the language testing textbooks tell us to expect.

Unit C5
To see a test in a grain of sand . . .

Over time, common concerns emerge in a testing system, and, while the 'minimalist' model of specs (discussed in Unit B4) may have attractive advantages, conversely, some test development systems want much more focused control. Evidence-centred design (ECD) can become such a technique – or more accurately, it was portrayed as such a fine-grained technique when first proposed in the literature.

ECD is basically an extremely elaborated specification model. It shares the classical goal of all test specifications – it is a generative engine to produce equivalent items and tasks. It is pragmatic and effect-driven, as all specs are. In addition, ECD attempts to unify and to standardize the creativity of test writing, for it asks test developers to clarify the guiding language behind a test according to pre-set taxonomic fine-grained schemes. A spec-driven testing system based on ECD compels all parties to justify the decisions they make as they engineer a test – it is a model that compels its users to forget nothing – and this obligation exists at a very precise level of analysis.

What would a spec-driven test development system look like if it were based on ECD? What strengths would it provide? We will explore that question in a series of tasks, using an ECD-style spec from Unit A5.

★ Task C5.1: Item coding

> Re-read Unit A5.3, *Describing items and tasks*. Focus your attention on subsections A5.3.1–4. If, as in Unit A5.3, we now take one item:
>
> impudent   insolent   audacious   pompous
>
> we may now code this as (2 b d e), and note that this coding could be used to select the correct number of items with this configuration for use in a test. This information would form part of the assembly model.

> ➤ What is involved in making this approach workable? Each item produced must be analysed and classified according to this scheme. Is that feasible in your setting? Why and/or why not?

Task C5.2: A coding thought experiment

Our sample ECD specification concerns textual competence with reference to lexical collocation and word sets.

Let us make some presumptions about the test:

- It has an item:spec ratio of 10:1 – ten items generated from each of ten specs will end up in the final operational test, which has 100 items.
- The specs test different skills, and, on average, each spec requires the item writer to code the item along four dimensions. For the sake of illustration, we shall simply fix the count at four codes per item.
- Each set of four codes requires close study of the item and of the spec. We shall refer to this as 'fine-grain' item development.
- Any item produced is coded both by its original author – the item writer – and by a colleague who reads the item and independently re-codes it – the item reviewer. This helps foster debate and refinement of the item, as well as feedback to and revision about the spec.
- The 100-item test is developed from a bank of twenty specifications; i.e., there are multiple versions of the test that support each test, such that, for any new form of the test, ten specs are not used.

This yields 160 item codes in the bank of specifications: four per item times ten specs (for any operational test) is forty. Each coding is done by the item writer and the item reviewer, yielding eighty codes. And finally, for any version of the test there are ten specs unused, waiting in the spec bank – 160 codes in total appear in this system. While for a given test version the teaching staff are concerned with only eighty codes, the general consciousness of the staff is doubled, depending on how frequently they produce new versions of the test.

➤ React to this thought experiment. In particular, ask yourself: what kind of test settings benefit most from a system of such complexity? Would a system like this work at your setting?

Task C5.3: One solution is suggested: test (far) less of each target domain

One way out is to vastly limit the domains to be tested. What if the sheer complexity of a 160-code bank of specs drives you and your testing team not to reduce the number of codes but rather to reduce the number of specs, perhaps to the extreme that the entire test comprises text items such as those presented here – the whole test becomes one of collocation and word sets?

➤ Please react to that possibility. What would you think of the validity of a textual competence exam if all of its items and questions tested only collocation and sets? What if you try a heavily coded system of many specs, and the coding becomes cumbersome such that entire specs are eliminated? What do you think of that possibility? Is it appropriate for the complexity of an evidentiary test development system to dissuade its users away from certain target test skills?

★ Task C5.4: Another solution is suggested: test the domains but sacrifice the analytical grain

Yet another way to manage such complexity is to reduce the number of codes. You could code these text items simply as 'collocation' or 'set', without concern about the actual features being tested. Suppose you can average about the same gain across the entire specbank: this would reduce the item-coding workload from 160 variables to eighty. There is a trade-off here: a larger range of skills is tested in the domain (we still have twenty specs) but only by sacrificing the fine-grained analysis of each skill (we now have something like two codes per spec rather than four).

➤ Please react to that possibility. What would you think of the validity of a test that loses some (but not all) of its analytical graininess?

★ Task C5.5: And one final solution is suggested: abandon codes

A final solution is simply to describe the item styles to be tested and eliminate the coding altogether; that is, this solution eliminates all of the analytical grain. This would change one element of our ECD spec:

Task features – alternative version

There must always be four words, and these are drawn from collocations or lexical sets. However, they may vary along a number of vectors that our theory predicts will influence the difficulty of the items. Hence, if a student can answer the more difficult items correctly we will draw the inference that he or she has *more textual competence* than someone who cannot answer those items correctly.

And this simpler 'task features' description could be coupled with a larger array of sample items. The samples would probably vary along the features we coded, if in fact that is a true representation of the construct in the real world, because we believe that our item writers – if given just enough guidance in the spec – would produce items and tasks that sample that construct domain. A spec without codes would rely on the creative force of sample items to help the generative function of the specs. If we extended this philosophy to the entire specbank and eliminated codes altogether, then we would retain our ability to specify a fairly wide domain of skills – there could still be twenty specs. At the same time, we could avoid worry about the complex coding job, both original and revised, because the specs do not compel their users to classify items according to the coding schemes. But it works only if the item writers instinctively sample across the rich complexity that we really want.

➤ What is the trade-off here? Can we still produce equivalent tests without such item coding? Do you trust the creative energy of the item writers to produce similar tasks in the absence of fine-grained coded guidance?

Task C5.6: What is evidence?

Consider all the permutations presented in our thought experiments here. We have roamed from highly articulated multi-coded specbanks to hyper-simple systems that shun codes.

We have two parting questions before we suggest some research.

➤ Consider once again the very controlled 160-code scenario. What impact would that have on maintaining test reliability and quality control? In large, standardized testing systems where much is at stake, do you think that such control is actually a very good idea?

➤ Consider even the simplest solutions above, for example the multiple-spec no-code solution. How, exactly, is that *not* evidentiary? Doesn't a simpler spec still serve as evidence as it later contributes to the test's validation?

Task C5.7: Suggestions for further research

C5.7.1 Proposed title: 'What is "evidence" in language test production? Phase I'

Background

We are curious whether any general guidelines (at all) can be crafted as to how specific or how general we need to be, in order to still claim that we are doing ECD.

Possible procedure

Assemble a group of colleagues who work on language testing. We strongly recommend that you get a range of experience, from new classroom teachers to seasoned veteran programme directors. Agree on some shared familiar test development problems. In this study it does not really matter what constructs(s) you set forth to test. Rather, the study is about the processes by which the testing happens. Ensure that the group has read articles about ECD; indeed, it would be good to include 'familiarity with ECD' as a criterion to select your participants. Conduct a test-specification workshop styled after Task C4.4, but with an important alteration: compel the group to write several versions of each spec, and to have each version exist at different levels of fine-grained analytical control. You might even stipulate that some fine-grained test specs should contain codes, as were proposed here for the textual competence item.

Possible outcome

There are two pure research questions to be addressed here, and we believe that this study would yield an important research paper. First, is there an optimal 'grain model'? For example, as the stakes of a test go up, should its items be subjected to finer and finer-grained evidentiary analysis? Second, what do the group think about the question in Unit C5.6 – 'What is evidence?' – and do they feel that all their specs are evidentiary, regardless of the complexity of the specs?

C5.7.2 Proposed title: 'What is "evidence" in language test production? Phase II'

Background

The general background of this proposed project is identical to the previous project. However, we want to expand the audience to which our evidence might speak. Evidence is something that should speak not only to the test developers, but also to test users: to test takers, to administrators who use the scores in decision making, perhaps to the general public (if you work in a setting where results are reported regularly in the media or on the Web), perhaps to parents (if you work in elementary or secondary education).

Possible procedure

Assemble a group of test users. As with Phase I, we recommend that you get a wide range of participants. Present the group with varying amounts and styles of evidence about test items and tasks. This is probably done best by giving the group previously used test tasks, and for each, a short summary of the evidence for each from its spec. In the example here, one extreme would be to (try to) explain to the group the four codes of the text item, whereas the opposite extreme would be to simply state that an item like this tries to measure 'what words seem to go together in natural language use'. The idea is to present a range of samples to the group of varying forms of evidence and then ask them the question: what seems to convince you that this test task is measuring what it claims to measure?

Possible outcome

The outcome of this project is also basic research: do test developers seem to think that 'evidence' is something different from what test users think it is? What if the test user wants diagnostic evidence? (The students in your Phase II group may well want such information.) How can you re-frame any ECD spec such that it provides evidence explained not only to the satisfaction of the test developers but also to the satisfaction of others?

Unit C6
Analysing items and tasks

⭐ Task C6.1: Distractor analysis

In Unit A6 we presented a table of results from five items. We reproduce it here without the item statistics, as the focus of our first task is on the data for each option for one of the items.

Table C6.1 Item statistics

	Option 1	Option 2	Option 3	Option 4	FV	DI
Item 1	2	9	0	3*	0.21	0.00
Item 2	9	3*	2	0	0.21	0.29
Item 3	0	10	3*	1	0.21	0.43
Item 4	10*	1	1	2	0.71	0.46
Item 5	1	2	7	4*	0.29	0.29

In multiple-choice testing the intended correct option is called the 'key' and each incorrect option is called a 'distractor'. Our example here will be Item 1. Option 4 is the key, and its distractors are options 1, 2 and 3.

A branch of item analysis is 'distractor analysis', in which the results of the distractors are examined. During test development, multiple-choice items can be improved depending on their results. Often, this improvement is seen not only in the key but also in the distractors.

Twenty-one per cent of the people answered item 1 correctly: three out of fourteen. Perhaps some difficult items are needed for the test; that is often the case if the test seeks to build out a bell-shaped curve for its total score distribution, a case when we must have a distribution of FVs. In that event, a problem may reside with the distribution of results across the distractors. Option 2 is overly distracting, relative to the other two options: nine people selected option 2, two chose option 1, and none selected the third option.

➤ In the next developmental stage for Item 1, what changes would you suggest? What would you do in revision of option 1 and option 3? For example, would you seek to make option 3 more attractive (more distracting)? Alternatively, do you think it is acceptable to have a difficult multiple-choice item for which one distractor is the most likely mistaken choice (put another way, if you use four-choice items, are you obligated to have three equally distracting wrong choices)?

Task C6.2: Mis-keying ⭐

Sometimes, a test question like Item 1 reveals a problem in test logistics and not in the item writing or in the spec from which the item is drawn. The item could be 'mis-keyed'.

Mis-keying happens like this. A test is built out carefully, and it is composed of many multiple-choice items. During the test development (and we strongly recommend this next step) each draft of the test booklet retains an asterisk to indicate the key. Here is an example which we discussed at great length in Unit C3, taken from Davidson and Lynch (2002) and known affectionately as the Barry item and for which the key is shown with an asterisk:

Barry seemed _____; he had successfully predicted the outcome of seven major sporting events over the past month.

a.   surprised
b.   gifted
*c.   clairvoyant
d.   upset

When the item actually appears in the test booklet, it must – of course – be presented without the asterisk.

After the test booklet is assembled, there comes a stage at which a scoring key is assembled. The scoring key is simply a list of item numbers and letters, showing the key for each item; there is a verb in test development – 'to key' a test means to assemble that list of item-to-key designations. A mis-keyed item happens when the scoring key has the wrong choice noted for a given item. Somebody makes a mistake, and, while the Barry item is faithfully reproduced in the test booklet, there is a mistake in the scoring – perhaps (d) is shown to be the right answer in the scoring key, when the intended correct choice is (c).

➤ What steps can be taken in test development to avoid mis-keying? Design a series of oversight procedures to avoid it. We suggest that these procedures involve careful human review. Think also about computer database technology. Shouldn't it be possible to generate a perfectly accurate scoring key through computer programming?

Mis-keying can also happen as more of a substantive problem, and it may even indicate a serious issue with the spec from which the item has been generated. The Barry item is controversial because each of the four choices could be correct, depending on the precise vocabulary inference intended by the test's designer. That is to say, the Barry item is an easy item to mis-key, not by oversight but rather by the design of the question itself. How can you avoid that in your oversight procedures, as well? Do you think that the spec for this item needs review?

★ Task C6.3: Double-keying

Once upon a time, there was a very large and reputable testing company. This company had been in business for nearly fifty years. It produced tests in a wide variety of school subjects – including languages – for use in many levels of education. Its tests pervaded every level of schooling in a major industrial country.

The company was hyper-precise in its procedures. It ran like an industrial factory, checking and re-checking everything. From prototyping through early trials and into final field testing, every step of the way, caution and precision were the rule.

Then one day, there was a multiple-choice test question in a test it had issued that had a strange problem. This test is a highly competitive secondary-school-leaving examination by which students can earn advance credit towards college-level courses. An extremely bright test taker with excellent memory actually remembered the question – verbatim – and noted its problem. The student reported the question to a newspaper, which contacted the company and offered it the chance to respond.

Through its procedures and policies, the company first checked internally and found out that the student had, indeed, recalled the item correctly. It then examined the item closely and found out that the student was right. The item had a problem. It was unintentionally double-keyed.

The intended correct choice – the key – was correct. Somehow, at some point in item development, a mistaken distractor had slipped through the system. This putative distractor was actually also acceptable. The item had two correct choices, and in psychometric parlance this is called 'double-keying', or, to be more accurate, 'unintentional double-keying', because only one correct choice was supposed to be possible.

The testing company verified that the student not only had remembered the item exactly but also had explained accurately why both choices were acceptable. The testing company verified all this to the newspaper, which, in turn, double-checked with some content-area experts to find out that indeed there were two correct answers.

Although based in one major city in the country, the newspaper actually serves as one of the most influential news sources all over the nation. It is printed (via satellite) at many other cities, and, while it bears the masthead of its source city, in effect it is a national paper. It is popular with a wide range of the nation's society; it is very popular among college professors.

The double-keyed item made the front page: the story about the mistake and the (rather complex) explanation of why both choices were correct appeared there, lower left, with a forceful headline.

The testing company did not conceal its mistake, but it did suffer the embarrassment of seeing the mistake, in print, all over the country. This was an operational high-stakes test – not a prototype, not a pilot, not a trial, not a field test. It offered free re-scoring of the exam (omitting the item at issue) to any test taker who wished it.

➤ What steps should the company take to prevent unintentional double-keying in the future? Why do you think this happened? Do you think that the company did the right thing by being open and responsive to the newspaper and by offering free re-scoring?

➤ For fun, what do you think was the headline of the newspaper story?

Task C6.4: Raters and test development

Our first three tasks here concerned multiple-choice items and problems that may emerge during test development:

- distractor analysis
- mis-keying
- (unintended) double-keying

Let us now consider rated assessment. Here are some problems that might emerge in rated testing, along with questions about how to handle each during the stages of test development:

➤ An oral interviewer suggests a topic to the test taker for discussion, something rather esoteric and uncommon. The test taker knows little about that topic, and so says little. The interviewer gives low marks for fluency, when (in actuality) had a different topic been suggested the student might have said more. Is the esoteric topic a problem? If so, what can be done to prevent such problems in later revision of the interview? What steps might you take in subsequent rater training to clarify the problem of topics during your oral interview?

➤ An essay exam is scored against a rubric. The rubric has five language components (e.g. organization, grammar, mechanics and punctuation, vocabulary usage, and register) and seven bands (e.g. low, low-intermediate, intermediate, high-intermediate, low-advanced, advanced and high-advanced). This is presented to raters in a descriptive table with thirty cells. Each cell has a brief descriptor. The table is presented online, and each cell is actually a hyper-link to web pages containing further information about the particular component or level score, along with excerpts of sample essays that illustrate that cell. Vast resources were invested to develop this system, and essay raters are required to use it. Over time, the raters start to rebel – the system is too complex, or, as one angry colleague puts it: 'This thing is like playing thirty-dimensional chess!' What steps could have been taken during the original test development to avoid the scoring complexity? How much rebellion would be needed in order to justify a re-building of the system to simplify the scoring?

⭐ Task C6.5: Project management and timelines

From prototyping through field tests and into operational testing, the production of any exam is a special instance of project management. Project management is a co-ordinated effort to assemble components, at the right time, from the best sources, with the proper oversight, such that a good product emerges at the end of a pre-set period of time. One way to do this is through PERT and Gantt charts. These are project management techniques that map out the steps in time order. Here are some examples from a media development project at Maricopa Community College:[10]

> The **PERT** (Project Evaluation and **R**eview **T**echnique) chart is a sort of flowchart of all the activities or tasks in the production phase of your project. The relationships between activities is clearly shown, completion times and names of persons assigned can be attached to each task. Except at the beginning and end of the chart, each task should be preceded and followed by another task. Tasks can also branch out and travel their own paths rejoining the main path at some later point. Any milestones such as points of review or completion can be indicated as well.
>
> The example is the original PERT chart for the whole 'Understanding Your Automobile' project. This gives you an idea what a PERT chart looks like. Your chart will look somewhat different because it will start at the Production phase of your project and contain a lot more detail than this one:

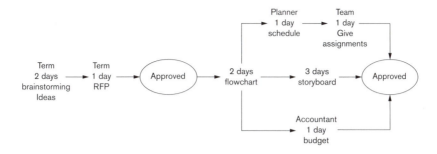

The **Gantt** chart is a timeline chart. It clearly shows when each task is to begin, the time it will take to complete each task, and which tasks will be going on simultaneously. You may want to use more than one level of Gantt chart. One chart may show the whole production phase from beginning to end. Another may show two or three weeks' activities. Another might show the current week's tasks. The example is a two week chart from the production phase of the 'Understanding Your Automobile' project:

	Feb									Mar				
Activity	21	22	23	24	25	26	27	28	29	1	2	3	4	5
Secure care dealership	████████													
Obtain dealership release						███								
Hire narrator	██													
Final draft of narration				███████████										
Hire graphic artist	████████													
Draw animation								███████████						
Hire programmer	██████													
Programming								███████████						
Photographer											███			

➤ Locate a testing project with which you are presently working, or, alternatively, imagine one of interest. You could select one of the rating problems in the previous task – for example, undoing the hyper-complexity of the essay scoring grid. Prepare both a PERT and a Gantt chart. Discuss them with colleagues and obtain feedback. In particular, seek feedback from colleagues who have themselves managed projects over time. Revise them as needed, and, if it is a real project, monitor the charts and adjust them as the project unfolds.

Task C6.6: Suggestions for further research

Our presentation of research ideas here is somewhat different, because test developmental stages actually resemble research very closely. When developing tests through such stages, you have goals and methodology, and you probably have reviewed literature relevant to your objectives; the entire enterprise is quite similar to a typical research project. Furthermore, during test development, new ideas and challenges emerge that point to additional interesting problems. Rather than suggest new research ideas here, we want to show how several of the tasks above can be elaborated into fuller enquiry that may yield an academic paper, a thesis or a conference talk.

■ *Mis-keying*: The problem identified here was that a test setting may inadvertently present the wrong choice as the item key. We believe that logistical reasons for this exist (somebody makes a mistake), and such logistical reasons do not really constitute territory for pure research. However, we also suggested that mis-keying could be due to a problem with the test spec. Have another look at the Barry item. What exactly does it measure? Sometimes, item analysis and discovery of an item-level problem (like mis-keying) lead to a deeper understanding of a fundamental issue in test design. In the Barry item there is a very subtle inference being assessed. The item may suggest an entire line of research about how to develop items that test such subtle areas of vocabulary inference and cultural knowledge.

■ *Double-keying*: Here, the testing company made a mistake and issued a faulty item in a high-stakes test. Clearly, we do not have the test item at hand here in this Unit, but this story could suggest research into double-keying. Note that we were very careful to call this 'unintended' double-keying. It is also possible to design tests that have intentionally been double (or triple) keyed. Doing so allows you to test several skills at once. This story suggests research on the intentionality of double-keying. Under what circumstances might several keys be desirable? What would constitute justifiable (intentional) double-keying?

■ *Score rubric complexity*: for the writing exam above, the problem was the hyper-complexity of the scoring rubric. A natural question emerges: just how much complexity can the raters tolerate? This suggests a qualitative research study, one in which score rubrics of varying detail are presented to raters. As with many suggested research projects in our book, the goal is both to benefit the local essay exam's setting and to derive general guidelines about scoring complexity for dissemination to the professional community.

Unit C7
Designing an alternative matrix

Task C7.1: A tale of two scoring universes

Ethelynn is a foreign language teacher. She has a class of eighteen students. At the end of the term, Ethelynn assembles score results into a master table, shown in Table C7.1. At the beginning of the term, Ethelynn announced to her students the following score weighting scheme. At term's end, what Ethelynn actually did was to compute each desired percentage weight as a decimal, representing 15 per cent as 0.15, 20 per cent as 0.20 and 30 per cent as 0.30. This is a more typical way to compute weights in scoring, as it avoids very large multiples.

Class attendance	15%
Class participation	15%
First test	20%
Second test	20%
Third and final (cumulative) test	30%

From left to right in her data (Table C7.1) the variables shown are structured as follows; this is a sample 'data structure' analysis as referenced later in Task C7.6.2:

Student	student identity number. (These are fictitious data.)
Absent	number of class days not present
Attend	number of class days attended; there were 45 days in the academic term, hence: 45 − absent = attend
Wattend	weighted attendance value: attend times 0.15
Partic	a holistic judgment of student participation (see Task C7.3, below) on a five-point scale, judged across the entire academic term, where 5 = excellent participation, and 1 = virtually no partipation.
Wpartic	weighted participation value: partic times 0.15
Test1	score on the first term test
Wtest1	test1 times 0.20
Test2	score on the second term test
Wtest2	test2 times 0.20
Final	score on the final test
Wfinal	final times 0.30

Table C7.1 Ethelynn's term-final results

student	absent	attend	wattend	partic	wpartic	test1	wtest1	test2	wtest2	final	wfinal	rawtot	rawrank	wgttot	wgtrank
s01	0	45	6.75	5	0.75	47	9.4	90	18.0	30	9.0	217	1	43.90	1
s02	3	42	6.30	2	0.30	40	8.0	80	16.0	26	7.8	190	4	38.40	4
s03	3	42	6.30	3	0.45	37	7.4	47	9.4	35	10.5	164	8	34.05	8
s04	2	43	6.45	4	0.60	40	8.0	37	7.4	25	7.5	149	14	29.95	14
s05	3	42	6.30	4	0.60	20	4.0	53	10.6	26	7.8	145	15	29.30	15
s06	1	44	6.60	4	0.60	23	4.6	77	15.4	25	7.5	173	7	34.70	7
s07	2	43	6.45	3	0.45	13	2.6	73	14.6	24	7.2	156	10	31.30	12
s08	7	38	5.70	1	0.15	17	3.4	63	12.6	35	10.5	154	12	32.35	10
s09	4	41	6.15	3	0.45	23	4.6	30	6.0	24	7.2	121	18	24.40	18
s10	1	44	6.60	4	0.60	40	8.0	90	18.0	33	9.9	211	2	43.10	3
s11	0	45	6.75	3	0.45	47	9.4	53	10.6	36	10.8	184	5	38.00	5
s12	0	45	6.75	5	0.75	37	7.4	57	11.4	34	10.2	178	6	36.50	6
s13	1	44	6.60	5	0.75	20	4.0	93	18.6	45	13.5	207	3	43.45	2
s14	2	43	6.45	4	0.60	30	6.0	47	9.4	34	10.2	158	9	32.65	9
s15	1	44	6.60	3	0.45	13	2.6	50	10.0	25	7.5	135	17	27.15	17
s16	4	41	6.15	3	0.45	23	4.6	53	10.6	22	6.6	142	16	28.40	16
s17	2	43	6.45	4	0.60	20	4.0	53	10.6	35	10.5	155	11	32.15	11
s18	1	44	6.60	4	0.60	21	4.2	52	10.4	30	9.0	151	13	30.80	13

Rawtot   sum of the raw (unweighted) components: attend + partic + test1 + test2 + final

Rawrank   student final ranking in class, based on rawtot, where 1 = highest and 18 = lowest

Wgttot   sum of the weighted components: wattend + wpartic + wtest1 + wtest2 + wfinal

Wgtrank   student final ranking, based on wgttot

Following are the descriptive statistics on the raw scores in Ethelynn's data table:

Variable	N	Mean	Std Dev	Minimum	Maximum
attend	18	42.94	1.76	38.00	45.00
partic	18	3.56	1.04	1.00	5.00
test1	18	28.39	11.39	13.00	47.00
test2	18	61.00	18.59	30.00	93.00
final	18	30.22	6.03	22.00	45.00

Note the situation with student 8 in the original data. This student's ranking on the raw total does not match that on the weighted total. The student moved up slightly, from rank 12 to rank 10. This is because the standard deviation on the final test, relative to its range of scores (maximum minus minimum), is slightly wider than that of previous components. The students are slightly more spread out on the final test.

Let us engage in a thought experiment. This time, we will conceive of an alternative universe, where this class is taught by Alternative Ethelynn. Her results for the eighteen students are given in Table C7.2, first the raw data, and then the descriptive statistics. She announced and employed the very same weighting scheme as Ethelynn. As far as score weighting was concerned, the two universes are identical. The difference – as we shall see – is in the distribution of the observed data.

In this case, the spread of scores is quite narrow for all components except the final, and the 'alternative student 8' benefited by a rank jump from a raw ranking of twelfth to fifth on the weighted total. Compare the means and standard deviations of Ethelynn's results with those obtained by Alternative Ethelynn.

Suppose that either Ethelynn and Alternative Ethelynn uses an Angoff-style cut score method to award final letter grades or overall marks for the class (see Unit A7). Suppose further that the final grade is based on the weighted totals, and not on the raw totals; after all, that is what students were told at the beginning of the term – that each component would be worth a particular amount in calculating the overall result of the course.

Table C7.2 Data from the alternative universe

student	absent	attend	wattend	partic	wpartic	test1	wtest1	test2	wtest2	final	wfinal	rawtot	rawrank	wgttot	wgtrank
s01	0	45	6.75	5	0.75	41	8.2	80	16.0	27	8.1	198	6.0	39.80	12.0
s02	3	42	6.30	2	0.30	42	8.4	80	16.0	26	7.8	192	15.0	38.80	17.0
s03	3	42	6.30	3	0.45	39	7.8	77	15.4	31	9.3	192	15.0	39.25	14.0
s04	2	43	6.45	4	0.60	40	8.0	77	15.4	28	8.4	192	15.0	38.85	16.0
s05	3	42	6.30	4	0.60	38	7.6	75	15.0	32	9.6	191	17.0	39.10	15.0
s06	1	44	6.60	4	0.60	39	7.8	77	15.4	33	9.9	197	7.5	40.30	10.0
s07	2	43	6.45	3	0.45	40	8.0	73	14.6	34	10.2	193	13.0	39.70	13.0
s08	7	38	5.70	1	0.15	41	8.2	69	13.8	45	13.5	194	12.0	41.35	5.0
s09	4	41	6.15	3	0.45	41	8.2	70	14.0	44	13.2	199	5.0	42.00	3.5
s10	1	44	6.60	4	0.60	40	8.0	80	16.0	36	10.8	204	2.5	42.00	3.5
s11	0	45	6.75	3	0.45	42	8.4	78	15.6	37	11.1	205	1.0	42.30	1.0
s12	0	45	6.75	5	0.75	39	7.8	77	15.4	38	11.4	204	2.5	42.10	2.0
s13	1	44	6.60	5	0.75	40	8.0	74	14.8	37	11.1	200	4.0	41.25	6.0
s14	2	43	6.45	4	0.60	39	7.8	75	15.0	34	10.2	195	10.5	40.05	11.0
s15	1	44	6.60	3	0.45	38	7.6	73	14.6	29	8.7	187	18.0	37.95	18.0
s16	4	41	6.15	3	0.45	40	8.0	72	14.4	40	12.0	196	9.0	41.00	8.0
s17	2	43	6.45	4	0.60	39	7.8	70	14.0	41	12.3	197	7.5	41.15	7.0
s18	1	44	6.60	4	0.60	38	7.6	71	14.2	38	11.4	195	10.5	40.40	9.0

Variable	N	Mean	Std Dev	Minimum	Maximum
attend	18	42.94	1.76	38.00	45.00
partic	18	3.56	1.04	1.00	5.00
test1	18	39.78	1.26	38.00	42.00
test2	18	74.89	3.60	69.00	80.00
final	18	35.00	5.58	26.00	45.00

In Ethelynn's universe, the impact on student 8 is not that severe. It triggers a change of only two ranks. In Alternative Ethelynn's universe, because of the narrow standard deviation on all scores except the final test, student 8 receives significant benefit, jumping from a rank of twelfth (rawrank) to fifth (wgtrank).

➤ Is this fair? Discuss the story with your colleagues. If the mood is right, enquire of colleagues whether any of them do this kind of percent-weighting approach to their teaching, or (and we caution that this may be even more sensitive) whether they supervise language teaching programmes in which such weights are mandated.

Task C7.2: Building a better universe

Clearly, you and your colleagues may feel that Alternative Ethelynn's situation is not fair, and that in the alternative universe, student 8 has benefited unreasonably. We suspect you are asking: what can be done?

There are several solutions to avoid a problem such as that encountered by Alternative Ethelynn:

1 Don't calculate course-final results on the basis of a cut score method, such as the Angoff approach.
2 Don't use rankings. This is a different solution, for you could do the Angoff approach on the raw totals.
3 Don't aggregate course results numerically at all. Instead, develop a performance scale with descriptors that cover your class objectives.

We prefer option (3), although it does have disadvantages. Firstly, it may be perceived as more subjective, simply because it is less numerical. Secondly, it is tricky to work out scale descriptors that discuss both the criterion-referenced expectation on given assignments and the overall aggregation across assignments. We believe such scales are feasible, but that they take time and patience and collaboration to develop. There is further discussion of performance scales and related matters (such as scoring rubrics) on pp. 93–100.

Alternatively, maybe you feel that student 8 deserves praise. In both universes, student 8 has figured out the system, and, despite poor performance all term, has worked hard on the final test, which (1) had the highest weight, and (2) by serendipity, had the widest standard deviation as well. Hence, the fourth and final solution is:

4   Nothing is wrong. Your teaching philosophy may be sympathetic with strategies such as those employed by student 8.

➤   Where do you stand on these four choices? How do all four solutions relate to the distinction between norm-referencing and criterion-referencing?

Task C7.3: Scaling the universes

Study the various performance rating scales given in Unit A7, such as the CEF (p. 99) or the five-level FSI scale (p. 94). As you do this task, bear in mind our critical analysis of the CEF, in particular.

➤   With colleagues, attempt to devise a set of five level descriptors that capture term-long participation in a foreign language course. Do you think that either Ethelynn or her Alternative has a viable method to measure participation? Is such a scale feasible?

Task C7.4: Parting thoughts and reflections on teaching

Maybe the entire issue lies not in the creation or nature of either Ethelynn's tests and measures, but rather in how she teaches the course. Perhaps she is too rigid in her application of this overall grading scheme. Perhaps she even feels trapped by it – what if these weights and an Angoff-style cut score aggregation are actually mandated by her school?

➤   What can Alternative Ethelynn – in particular – do to rectify the situation, in her teaching as opposed to her testing practices?

➤   Have you ever met somebody like student 8? Have you ever taught somebody like student 8? Discuss this with colleagues. Be careful. Discussion of score weighting can be seen as threatening. If a colleague comes to realize the principles we outline here, there may be an awkward silence. Learning the effect of score distributions and variability on weights can be an eye-opening (and interaction-closing) experience.

➤   Finally, did you, yourself, ever get through an academic course using strategies like those of student 8? Discuss this with yourself – in your diary, for example.

Task C7.5: Suggestions for further research

C7.5.1 Proposed title: 'Data mining in language teaching'

Background

Data mining is the process of working with data already at hand but not in the way for which the data were originally gathered. At your instructional setting, become familiar with the structuring of data for students. What kinds of information are routinely gathered? Write out the data structure, in a form like that given by Davidson (1996: 29) (Table C7.3).

The 'variable name' and 'description' tell us what information is contained in the database. 'Type' tells us how the information is stored in some computer file: as a 'char'acter or string variable, or as a 'num'eric variable; this is a useful distinction because the latter type permits subsequent mathematical operations, whereas string variables do not. The 'start–stop' columns show where the data are located in the computer file. This example is from a book published in the mid-1990s, when such column locations were still prevalent. Nowadays, we often speak of the particular column label – for example in a spreadsheet: Column A, Column B, Column C, and so on, and the width of the column is handled transparently by various analytical software routines. (This is one of the great advances in computer statistical software over the past decade or so.)

Table C7.3 Data mining structure

Variable name	Type	Description	Start–stop columns
NAME	Char	Student's name	01–05
COUNTRY	Char	Student's home country	08–12
L1	Char	Student's first language	14–20
SEX	Char	Student's sex	22
TIMEIN	Num	Student's time in institute	24
Student's grades:			
T1Q1	Num	Term 1, Quiz 1	26–27
T1Q2	Num	Term 1, Quiz 2	29–30
T1Q3	Num	Term 1, Quiz 3	32–33
T1FE	Num	Term1, Final Exam	35–37
T2Q1	Num	Term 2, Quiz 1	39–40
T2Q2	Num	Term 2, Quiz 2	42–43
T2Q3	Num	Term 2, Quiz 3	45–46
T2FE	Num	Term 2, Final Exam	48–50
T3Q1	Num	Term 3, Quiz 1	52–53
T3Q2	Num	Term 3, Quiz 2	55–56
T3Q3	Num	Term 3, Quiz 3	58–59
T3FE	Num	Term 3, Final Exam	61–63

Possible procedure

Once you have a structure for the data at your setting, then conduct a series of data mining interviews in which you find out the typical analyses conducted on such data, and the typical kinds of grade reports and summary documents generated from such data. As you interview each person, enquire what else they wish they could know from the database. For example, suppose that the main use of the Davidson (1996) data is to tell each student what score was given on each measure. Staff interviews may reveal a desire to compare results across the various measures: do students tend to do better on the first quizzes each term in comparison to the subsequent quizzes? That particular information is available in the database – it is possible to 'mine those data'. Staff may also be curious whether students with prior study at other language institutions do better (on any given measure) than students who originate at this particular school. That particular information is not in the database, because we have no variable for prior study – the answer to that question cannot be 'mined out' of the data.

Possible outcomes

The outcome of work like this is some sort of internal memorandum about alteration of the database so as to make it more responsive to staff needs. It can also serve as a pilot study for a wider research project, which we describe next.

C7.5.2 Proposed title: 'A data mining survey of language teaching programmes'

Background

This would be an extension of the previous project, in which you replicate the procedures and steps at other settings – in effect, the previous project would serve as a pilot study for this larger and broader work.

Possible procedure

Conduct a survey of data structures – a questionnaire could accompany a request for a formal data structure from each institution. The goal of the questionnaire would be to detect faculty satisfaction and dissatisfaction with the current data structures on hand at each institution. What similar variables are analysed? What similar variables are missing?

Possible outcomes

We see several interesting outcomes here. Firstly, the research could yield a beneficial meta-analysis of data management and analyses across a range of settings. Secondly, the analysis could provide feedback to professional organizations (like language teacher associations), which, in turn, could hold symposia and work with software publishers. Research like this could be the start of new analytical tools which receive widespread interest.

C7.5.3 Proposed title: 'Pushing the communicative envelope, or: picking up items from the cutting-room floor'

Background

Review Unit C3, and, in particular, note the discussion at C3.4. There, we asked whether certain language assessment tasks – while feasible under some models of language as a construct – were actually outside of the realm of possible school-based testing. Study also Task C3.5.3 and its metaphor of the cutting-room floor. We proposed that certain items simply will not make it into tests, because the items step outside some boundary of viable testing; our example there concerned a test item about the linguistic behaviour of mooching.

Possible procedure

Develop some test questions that you feel are outside of the testing envelope; we strongly recommend full use of group-based specification-driven testing, as outlined in Units A4 and C4. Seek test items like the mooching question or the Barry item and intentionally embed them into an existing test. Then track the item statistics. Do these items provide good discrimination values? Do they seem to fit the overall test's response models? Or do they 'bounce', a psychometric term for display of item statistics that seem wildly aberrant? You may run into some human-subjects regulations at your institution about disguised testing items in an otherwise normal test. Enquire of the authorities in your system whether or not you need some kind of phrase like this on the test booklet: 'Some of the items in this test are being developed and will be considered experimental. Those items will not count toward your overall score result.'

Possible outcomes

Testing a linguistic skill like mooching is, we admit, somewhat bizarre. What intrigues us is this: what might happen to some innocuous mooching questions if they are disguised in a test of otherwise standard and familiar language skills? Might they (simply) appear to be more difficult but otherwise display acceptable psychometric characteristics?

C7.5.4 Research skills development

As we did in Unit C2, we here depart from our usual research suggestion format. It is very important to acquire technical skills in analysis of test scores. To that end, here are a series of questions:

➤ What software do you already have on hand, and what is the capability of this software for data input, recoding and analysis? For example, you may have Microsoft Excel, which as of this writing has an add-on 'toolpak' with basic statistics.

➤ What software is readily available to you at no or little cost? For example, you may work at a school or institution that has a site-licence for some large statistical package such as SAS or SPSS.[11]

➤ Alternatively, there may be a computer lab nearby with such software installed. It is possible to obtain a licence yourself for these costly packages, but that will set you back a sizeable sum of money. Sometimes, site-licences are in hiding: you might be able to get one through an organization to which you belong, or perhaps by virtue of status in life (like being a senior citizen). Don't give up and pay the full cost without a rich battle! What training do you need to use such software, where can you get it and what does it cost? For example, a nearby computer lab may offer low-cost weekend tutorials or consulting, and websites are proliferating to help users of statistical software.

Throughout all of this learning, do not study only the sample data that come with various software but try to input and to analyse data of your own. The best learning and growth in this area come from work with data that you know very well. Furthermore, as you explore what you have and what is available, you may also discover a need for more actual study: a course on intermediate statistics, on data handling or on psychometrics may suggest itself. Likewise, survey what is available to you at little or no cost – although we find that these topics work best with some formal study, it is possible to teach yourself carefully and to check your learning with local consultants.

Unit C8
Administration and alignment

Often, language tests must document agreement with specific guidelines issued by some larger authority. Test specifications (as described in Units A4 and C4) are one way to do so, and governmental authorities often develop not only the guidelines themselves but intermediate generative specs from which actual test tasks can be produced. Sometimes, the guidelines or the specs are developed in a synthetic relationship between teachers and the government through a series of workshops; sometimes they are true pronouncements – rendered from a central star chamber about which everyday teachers know very little.

The governmental level involved can vary. A national government may issue statements of expected proficiency. A state or region may issue regulations that govern the amount of testing performed in a typical school year. And international organizations might publish codes of practice or guidelines about ethical test development (a topic which we discuss in Unit A9). 'Alignment' is the degree to which a test or its administration does in fact follow such stated mandates exerted by that larger authority. Usually, there are financial and political risks associated with failure to align with this larger authority. Many nations have systems of school inspectors that regularly examine school practice.

Recent testing practice in the USA has become quite cognizant of alignment. The long-standing tradition of state and local control over education is evolving; the USA is lurching towards a model of educational management that is actually very similar to that found in the rest of the world. These changes are documented in a series of national laws – the first of which was passed in the mid-1960s, and the latest of which was passed in January 2002: the 'No Child Left Behind' (NCLB) Act.[12]

We tell the story of demographic and political change at a fictional school building in western Columbia. As the story evolves, firstly, you can study and react to the particular case of this fictional school (a task which we call 'Columbia'); and secondly, you can apply the issues and topics they face to language testing alignment in your own setting (another task which we call 'Your setting'). Throughout, the tasks ask that you reflect on test administration, although we suspect that your reflection will carry over to issues of much greater reach.

Some background knowledge about Columbia – and all states in the USA – may help. The USA has a massively de-centralized educational system, and, as such, it is very different from many countries where something like a 'Ministry of Education' exists, and where curricula and testing are controlled by the national government. NCLB is challenging that de-centralized US educational civic tradition.

Each state has a state education agency (SEA), often bearing a name unique to the state. Illinois is the home state of the second author of this book, and his SEA is called the 'Illinois State Board of Education' (ISBE). In Columbia the corresponding body is called the 'Columbia Education Department' (CED). The SEA is generally the most powerful entity in school governance in US schools. Teachers and administrators are often highly sensitive to the pronouncements that come from their SEA. The SEA is usually located in the state capital – Buchanan, Columbia in the story below – although in large states there are often powerful SEA offices in other major urban areas as well. ISBE has a home office in Springfield (the capital of Illinois) but it also has an important office in downtown Chicago.

This state-based de-centralized system has a financial aspect. Schools receive funds from state revenue, which clearly shows how an SEA has political clout in its state. In addition, schools receive funds that are tied to the value of property in their location – this is revenue that comes from property taxes. Finally, schools do receive money directly from the national government, through a number of channels including things like competitive block grants to states. All funds to schools are administered through state government regardless of the source of the money, and so it is clear how the SEAs come to have strong regulatory influence.

The basic lever of NCLB is that it ties federal dollars that (eventually) reach schools to school performance indicators, and over recent years the relative proportion of federal money at US schools has increased. Federal dollars are associated with federal law, and so state and property tax dollars must also follow the statutes of the national government. This tension between national and state government is possibly a threat to the Constitution and to its principles of federalism, which concern the complex question of what activities a state may do and what activities are rendered to the national government. It is distinctly possible that challenges to NCLB may eventually reach the US Supreme Court.

Schools are organized within a state into units called 'districts'. Often, a district has many elementary schools of children aged 5 to about 10, some middle schools for ages 11 to 13, and then high schools that serve students to age 18. Some districts have only one high school. A district may or may not be the same as a 'county', which is a governmental entity that is a part of a state. In the story told below, we are assuming that the county and the district are the same entity.

Finally, a bit of background about the key players may help. In US education the leader of a school building is called a 'Principal' – this is equivalent to the 'Headmaster' or 'Head' in many other educational systems. There is at least one Vice-Principal per school, and often there are more than one. Each Vice-Principal is often also a classroom teacher, but with significant 'release time': a reduced teaching load to accommodate administrative work. A Vice-Principalship can lead to a Principalship, or even to a leadership position in a larger school management setting, such as a 'Superintendent' of an entire school district (or county) or a high-level post in an SEA. Typically, such administrative career paths carry greater salary increments than a career spent entirely in teaching.

We want to emphasize that this story below is a work of fiction – informed fiction, but fiction none the less.

Task C8.1: Getting things in line

Following is an email that went out to all staff at the fictional Chipp County High School, located in Livingston, Columbia.

> Date: Thu, 20 Mar 2003 09:52:18
> From: Arnold McCauley, Vice-Principal
> Subject: NCLB ELL Test Alignment Requirements
> To: CCHS Staff List
>
> Hello everybody
>
> This is the promised follow-up message to our faculty meeting of last Thursday, the 13th, in Pickens Auditorium. I have been on the telephone with people at CED in Buchanan off and on for several days.
>
> The situation boils down to this:
>
> (1) We have seen a growth of English Language Learners (ELLs) at our school over the last five years. These kids don't have sufficient command of English to succeed with grade-level peer students. The people in Buchanan tell me that we are not alone – this growth is impacting many counties in Columbia. While some ten years ago we had maybe thirty students for whom English is not the native language, this year we have over three hundred – and that represents about 15 percent of our student body.
>
> (2) For some years, we've used a commercial test to screen ELLs and determine if some kind of English language support is needed. We discussed this test at our meeting last Thursday, and as many of you point out, it has served us well. One or two of you 'veterans' recalled serving on a committee about twelve or thirteen years ago when the test was selected, and you still feel that the test is valid and reliable for our purposes: to decide if ELLs need English services and to track progress from year to year as the ELLs' English ability grows. On that note, I should tell you that Buchanan is very happy with our use of the test for program placement and tracking. Our database

– so says Buchanan – is a model for the entire state. That is not the problem.

(3) The problem is this: that particular test is not aligned with NCLB – or so Buchanan tells me. The tasks and items of the test do not appear to agree with the stated goals for training ELLs under NCLB guidelines – or so Buchanan tells me. And remember: CCHS receives 28 percent of our funding (across the board – all school programs) from federal sources. Buchanan believes strongly that the Feds are likely to withhold funding from local schools if they do not follow the strictures of NCLB. We are being told to toe the line, and carefully. In this case, that means one of three choices:

a. We must align the current test with NCLB; this is what the Buchanan folks call 'retrofitting'.

b. We must find a new test that is already aligned with NCLB; there are some out there, but they cost money and require us to 'buy in' to one of several consortiums of schools now forming, both in Columbia and in other states.

c. We must develop a new test and assure it is aligned with NCLB; this will drain our meager resources even more, I reckon, but we ought to look at it seriously.

(4) In cooperation with Principal Douglas, we are seeking volunteers to form a new testing committee. If you volunteer to serve on this committee, I will work to reduce your teaching load next year by one course, and we are guaranteeing staff support and long-distance telephone access in the main office. Please reply to this email within the next two weeks to indicate if you are willing to serve.

(5) I should note that Buchanan is very sensitive to our plight, and that we are not alone in not yet having a solution. They have negotiated with the Feds a grace period of one full academic year to have a workable aligned testing alternative announced, and an additional full academic year to have it implemented.

Thank you very much.

Arnie

P.S. I am aware that some of you know of all these NCLB developments through casual conversation among yourselves or with me. In addition to forming the new committee, I think we need another general faculty meeting to discuss larger issues and changes in federal governance here at CCHS. I am therefore calling another faculty meeting for Thurs Apr 10, again to be held in Pickens. And again, 7th period teachers: you may cancel class to attend, if you wish.

➤ *Columbia*: Imagine that you are the Vice-Principal, Arnie. You have got five very energetic teachers who are quite willing to serve on the new testing committee. What do you say to them at the first committee meeting? Consider the following questions which you may wish to pose; perhaps you can think of others:

1   *Identify guidelines*: What – precisely – are the NCLB guidelines that govern ELL education in CCHS? Perhaps the first activity of the committee should be thorough study of the NCLB website.
2   *Identify mis-alignment*: How – precisely – does current CCHS ELL testing violate NCLB guidelines? Perhaps the next activity should be a close point-by-point comparison of the existing test and its administration to the national law and regulations.

For example, the following guideline appears at the NCLB website:[13]

> Test scores will be broken out by economic background, race and ethnicity, English proficiency and disability. That way parents and teachers will know the academic achievement of each group of students and can work to ensure that no child will be left behind.

Perhaps also you discover that the current test does not allow breakdowns of student results by race and ethnicity, and that a new scoring sheet will be needed to accommodate that guideline. Are these two questions a sufficient starting point for your committee work: 'Identify guidelines' and 'Identify mis-alignment'?

➤ *Your setting*: For your teaching situation, consider the following generalized version of the two questions:

1   What language tests are given regularly, and to what extent are they governed by regional or national authority – such as a law (like NCLB) or a system of inspectors?
2   Do any practices at your setting violate external authority?

Task C8.2: 'Y'all need to leave Pickens alone'

Our story continues:

VP Arnie McCauley took it on himself to call another faculty meeting on 14 April, and that meeting was singularly acrimonious. Teachers were furious: too much testing, too much change, too little time, 'what about our contracts' (one furious teacher stood up and shouted: 'We don't have to DO this. We don't have to do so much testing! It isn't in the CONtract!').

Arnie sees resentment seething in the school. He reckons: if he can solve this problem it will be a feather in his cap, and maybe, just maybe, it will get him a leadership post in a year or two. Douglas won't help – he's an administrator who (Arnie is fond of saying to his wife) 'rarely sets foot out of his office except to go fishing at Columbia Lake'.

Additional faculty meetings are set – each Thursday for three weeks after 10 April. And each meeting is held in Pickens Auditorium. The auditorium is named for a major donor and now-deceased businessman in Livingston, who contributed over 80 per cent of its construction costs in 1989. Aside from the 'Town Hall' in the city centre, Pickens is the only true performance venue in the city. It was built to state-of-the-art standards, and it is eagerly sought by CCHS activities – like the Drama programme – as well as local civic and musical groups. Even today it remains one of the best high school performing arts facilities in the entire state.

And then, in early May, in the hallway Arnie runs into the Drama teacher, T. C. Rutter, who has some steam to vent: 'Now, Arnie, what's going on with all these faculty meetings? I gotta get the Spring play up and ready. Opening night is 24 May, and my kids just don't seem to have got it right yet. I need to rehearse every afternoon. Worse still, at your last meeting, somebody spilled a mocha or something all over two seats in the third row. It was a terrible mess, and I had to bring in some spray carpet cleaner to fix it. Arnie, y'all need to leave Pickens alone!'

Pickens is the only place in the school truly large enough to seat the entire faculty, whenever the entire faculty actually show up. In the school's culture, any meeting held in Pickens is seen as formal and important – the faculty like to meet there. What's more, the entire faculty is very upset about federal intrusion into testing at the school, not only of ELLS but in all content areas. The attraction of 'a meeting in Pickens' coupled with the faculty's irritation has generated an unusually high participation rate in this dialogue, which Arnie feels is a good thing. But now an old and trusted friend – T. C. – is causing Arnie to re-think matters.

Here are Arnie's management choices as he sees them:

- He could start talking to teachers one by one about their opinions on all this NCLB testing.
- He could attend department faculty meetings for each subject area, where he has heard that NCLB is a frequent topic of discussion, anyway.
- Or he could do nothing – NCLB is a federal mandate and the whole building basically has no choice, and everybody should let the Testing Committee just do its work so that the Buchanan deadlines can be met.

➤ *Columbia*: What should Arnie do?

➤ *Your setting*: Suppose that some true mis-alignment exists, and that some language tests at your school are mis-aligned with higher authority's dictates. Suppose further that you work out a method to resolve the matter, but that, in so doing, you step on the toes of others – perhaps even mildly offending an old friend of yours, like T. C. How do you handle such a problem?

Task C8.3: A new solution

Our final bit of the Columbia story unfolds to an interesting twist in the political fabric.

Most of a year has passed, and CCHS has a solution brewing, one that promotes a locally developed test to replace the commercial ELL measure. Arnie's teachers – particularly the committee of five – have worked very hard to write test specs that are aligned with NCLB. Those five colleagues have earned their release time, Arnie tells them – again and again.

The climate seems to be improving and the complaints seem to be lighter and less frequent. There are fewer all-faculty meetings, and, pleasantly, less pressure to use the valuable Pickens auditorium. Arnie has worked hard to balance all the competing pressures of this new NCLB-mandated ELL testing. He's built a network of compromises, and he has grown in his understanding and appreciation not only of the new national law – NCLB – but also of the complex pressures it has placed on all faculty at CCHS.

He tells his wife: 'Maybe we are gonna work this out. There seems to be a light at the end of the NCLB tunnel, and it *ain't* an oncoming train!'

One day, about a month before the required first report, Arnie is called into Principal Douglas's office. The Principal says, 'Well, Arnie, I just talked with Billy Mitchell – you know him, I believe – he's a principal over in Henderson County. He and I went to college together. He tells me that they have solved all their ELL testing problems. They've signed up with a consortium of Columbia schools that are using a new test developed up in Pennsylvania someplace. It's got some fancy name. I don't recall. I told Billy that we were working out our own local testing solution, and he warned me that was not a good idea. He said that Buchanan doesn't like that – they want a statewide solution, and this consortium test is a leading candidate for all of Columbia. So talk to your committee. I think y'all need to have a look at this consortium test. Your work is costing us a lot of money. That's quite a lot of release time I had to sign over for those five teachers. Let me know in a week or two. I don't want to send a report to Buchanan – much less the Feds – about a solution that we might not use.'

Arnie walks out of the Principal's office completely stunned. He'd talked with Buchanan regularly at the start of this entire process, but he'd forgotten to check with them in recent months. He thought he had unique authority to work out a solution to this mandate. Now, with very little time remaining before the first report is due, he suddenly has to re-tool his committee and his direction. Maybe all their work was in vain: the angry faculty meetings, the strained friendships, the networking, the political chips called in, the money spent. Maybe it was a waste. He feels torn: should he protest? Should he call Buchanan and see if Douglas is telling the truth? What if Douglas finds out that Arnie is checking up on matters?

Or should he just cave in – tell the committee of five that their work was wasted, and that he's been given a new directive? Take the heat, buck up, move on, live through it?

➤ *Columbi*a: What should Arnie do?

➤ *Your setting*: In language test development at your setting, is this scenario possible? Could there be a last-minute far-reaching change of plan? If you are in charge of testing at your setting, how do you react to such a change? How do you communicate such a change to those whom you supervise?

★ Task C8.4: Suggestion for further research

C8.4.1 Proposed title: 'Turmoil in language test administration: an ethnography'

Background

The story of Arnie and his school is a complex tale, and to understand it fully would take us well beyond the scope (and page limit) of this Unit. Properly rendered, a story like Arnie's would be an 'ethnography', which wikipedia.org defines as:

> **Ethnography** (from the Greek *ethnos* = nation and *graphein* = writing) refers to the qualitative description of human social phenomena, based on fieldwork. Ethnography is a holistic research method founded in the idea that a system's properties cannot necessarily be accurately understood independently of each other. The genre has both formal and historical connections to travel writing and colonial office reports. Several academic traditions, in particular the constructivist and relativist paradigms, claim ethnography as a valid research method.[14]

As background to this research suggestion, we suggest that you explore ethnographic research methods, perhaps by visiting Wikipedia's definition and some of the sources to which it links. Discuss ethnography with your research adviser(s) and colleagues, and see if they agree that study of change and protest in test administration necessitates an ethnographic approach.

Possible procedure

Our particular idea would be to find a setting like Arnie's. Perhaps it is your own school, or perhaps it is the regional governmental unit to which your school belongs – what is known as a 'district' in many US settings. Network and liaise with people in that setting, and find out the particular testing problems they face. Allow the research questions (if in fact they are stated as questions) to emerge from your networking – in ethnographic terms, the questions emerge from your own fieldwork. You may well discover a single test administration problem, like the use of the Pickens auditorium, which dominates the discussions.

Possible outcomes

Eventually, the result of research like this is a lengthy portrait or narrative of the setting. The distinction between 'procedure' and 'outcome' tends to fall apart, in that ethnographers often write the report as they go along.

Unit C9
In a time far, far away . . .

 Task C9.1: 'Do it, but do it with care'

Scree Valley Community College (SVCC) is a growing institution of higher education in a large industrialized country. The college has an extensive foreign language teaching programme. Many first-year students enrol in foreign language classes as part of degree requirements. Some students choose to continue a language studied in secondary school, and others decide to start a new language. For those who continue with a previously studied language, the college has used placement tests to determine the right course level.

Recent budget cutbacks have compelled the SVCC language faculty to co-ordinate all placement testing into a central office. Henceforward, the development and operation of placement tests will not be done by individual language departments but instead will be the responsibility of the Testing Office (TO).

➤ Following is a list of activities that SVCC TO could follow in the re-design and co-ordination of its language placement exam system. Consider Shohamy's advice about ethical testing: 'Do it, but do it with care.' One way to do testing with care is to ensure that no steps are overlooked in test development. Rate each activity below along the following scale, and discuss your ratings with colleagues:

■ [1] *Not necessary*: The activity would be useful for test development, but, given the budget crunch at SVCC, it is probably a luxury.
■ [2] *Optional*: The activity is a useful supplement to good test development, and, unless budgets are exhausted, it should be pursued.
■ [3] *Desirable*: The activity is a fundamental component of good test development, and, if not pursued, a strong argument is needed to justify its elimination.
■ [4] *Essential*: Without question, the activity must be pursued in good practice when developing new placement tests.

1	Literature review on placement testing	[1]	[2]	[3]	[4]
2	Literature review on testing in each of the particular foreign languages	[1]	[2]	[3]	[4]

3 Development of an overall blueprint of test   [1]   [2]   [3]   [4]
construction (e.g. specifying length of the
test, number of items per skill, and so on)

4 Development of full-text specifications for   [1]   [2]   [3]   [4]
each skill tested (in addition to an overall
blueprint, also write out rich text specs for
each particular skill and test method)

5 Investment in a rater training system, so that   [1]   [2]   [3]   [4]
constructed-response tasks are feasible and
the test need not be entirely multiple choice

6 Piloting of the test (i.e. informal try-out with   [1]   [2]   [3]   [4]
representative students on a very small scale)

7 Re-piloting of the test (i.e. repeat the pilot   [1]   [2]   [3]   [4]
after changes)

8 Formal trial of the test (i.e. a larger-scale trial   [1]   [2]   [3]   [4]
of the test that simulates – as much as possible
– the actual conditions of the operational
placement testing)

9 Installation of a new computer system: [1]   [2]   [3]   [4]
software, scanner (if optical mark sheets are
used), development of test reporting systems

10 Creation of a Test Advisory Committee   [1]   [2]   [3]   [4]
(TAC) who will oversee the operational
roll-out and quality control of the entire
placement testing system

11 Hiring a Manager of the TO, who will be   [1]   [2]   [3]   [4]
ex officio on the TAC

12 Development of a public information strategy   [1]   [2]   [3]   [4]
and outreach plan to explain the testing to
potential and new students, to the media, to
secondary schools which feed into the college,
and to students' families

13 [write your own: think of some test   [1]   [2]   [3]   [4]
development activity that could be pursued,
and then rate it on the scale on the right]

14 [write your own]   [1]   [2]   [3]   [4]

15 [write your own]   [1]   [2]   [3]   [4]

Task C9.2: Language testing in a bygone era ★

In 1917, Robert Yerkes and colleagues launched the US Army 'Alpha' testing
programme. Ultimately, 1.7 million recruits were tested for intelligence, as
part of the recruitment procedures into Army service in the First World War.
The idea of the project was simple: that placement into various military roles
and jobs would be a function of native intelligence, which could be measured

objectively – they reasoned – and so the best man would find the best job and the war would be prosecuted with greater efficiency and success.

As the project unfolded, it became apparent that some percentage of recruits were neither literate nor illiterate but rather that they were speakers of English as a second language and so the main intelligence testing was not valid. Yerkes and the team built a third test: in effect, this was the first English as a Second Language test developed on modern normative psychometric principles.

Yerkes and the team called this ESL measure 'the Linguality Test'. There was an individual and a group version of the Linguality Test. Its purpose was to screen recruits for whom there was a reasonable suspicion that English was not the native language, and, on the basis of the test's results, then to determine whether the recruit could proceed to the full intelligence screening measure.

➤ Following is the Group Linguality Test. Copy it out and administer it to colleagues. The instructions for the test are fairly simple: one person should read aloud the commands below, while the other works with the images shown on the pages that follow. In 1917, a 'cross' meant an 'X' in modern parlance. Bear in mind that the term 'swastika' did not have the pejorative implication that it has today. Item 28 shows the left-handed swastika, which is an ancient oriental religious symbol, not the right-handed swastika that was later associated with German National Socialism.

Yerkes notes that the Group Linguality Test was generally too difficult, and, in particular, that it reached too high a level of difficulty even for native speakers.

➤ What is your opinion of the ethics of this exam? Discuss the test with colleagues and reverse-engineer the intent of its designers: what features of language were they trying to control? Is this test ethical?

GROUP EXAMINATION.

The examiner then picks up a paper and pointing to the men says, 'Now, you take up your pencils; look here – number one on top here – see these pictures here – not the same as these (pointing to the blackboard); you do pictures here, Number 1, top.'

'Now, listen. You (pointing to men), make cross (drawing an X in the air) on the hat.'

'Now, look. On top again. These pictures. See the dog? Make a cross on the dog.'
During these two tests the orderlies move quickly and quietly among the men, making sure that they get started and saying, 'You know hat (or dog) – make a cross on the hat (dog).'

For these tests and the following ones the examiner must depend upon his judgment of the group as to how long each test should take, but in no instance should more than 10 seconds be allowed.

'Now, look here, Number 2. A boy – see – that's a boy.' (Make sure by repetition that the men have found the right place.) 'Make a cross on the boy's head.'

'Now, look, Number 3. A house.' (Repeat and point, if necessary.) 'Make a cross on the roof of the house.'

'Now, look, Number 4. A hand.' (Holds up hand.) 'Make a cross on the thumb.'

'Now, Number 5 – here. Make a cross on the envelope.

'Number 6 – here. Make a cross on the girl's eyelash.

'Number 7. What is it? Make a cross on the muzzle of the gun.

'Number 8. Make a cross above the pig's back.

'Number 9. Make a cross at the entrance to this house.

'Number 10. Make a cross on the rear wheel of the automobile.

'Number 11. Make a cross on the spout of the kettle.

'Number 12. Make a cross beneath the horizontal line.

'Number 13. Make a cross at the base of the tower.

'Now turn your papers over so – Number 14 – the letter – see.

'Number 14. Make a cross on the signature of the letter.

'Number 15. Make a cross on the pendulum of the clock.

'Number 16. The box. Make a cross on the partition.

'Number 17. Make a cross on the flange of the wheel.

'Number 18. Make a cross on the mosaic pattern.

'Number 19. See the two drawings? Make a cross at the point of conjunction.

'Number 20. Make a cross on the barb of the hook.

'Number 21. Make a cross on one of the tines.

'Number 22. Make a cross at the apex of the cone.

'Number 23. Make a cross on the filial descendant of the mare.

'Number 24. Make a cross on the caudal appendage of the squirrel.

'Number 25. Make a cross at the orifice of the jug.

'Number 26. Make a cross on the superior aspect of the pulpit.

'Number 27. Make a cross on the major protuberance of the bludgeon.

'Number 28. Make a cross on the sinister extension of the swastika.

'Number 29. Make a cross on the cephalic extremity of the homunculus.'

★ Task C9.3: Linguality, truth and warfare

The Linguality Test was designed as a pre-screening exam for the subsequent intelligence test, which (in turn) would be used to place recruits into various positions and duties in the Army. We ask the question: is the inference drawn from the Linguality Test correct? Philosophers approach this problem through something called a truth table:

	The state of the world, or: the world as God knows it, but as we do not	
The inference drawn from the test	YES	NO
YES	OK	False positive
NO	False negative	OK

A truth table is a heuristic device that helps us see the possible impact of a wrong decision. The rows of the table are known facts. What are the inferences we draw from the test? We say either 'yes, the recruit has sufficient command of English to proceed on to intelligence testing', or 'no, he does not'. The rows are simply a report of the inferential decision we have made on the test, and we know this inference as a fact: we can look at it on the score report.

The columns of the truth table are likewise labelled 'yes' and 'no'. However, these columns are a presumption. These columns represent the state of the world, something we admit to be fundamentally unknowable. We only surmise the world to be truly one or another thing: yes, the recruit has command of English, or no, he does not. Put another way, the state of the world is as only God would know it – we are ignorant of it, but we presume it for the sake of truth table analysis.

If our test matches the state of the world, then our decision is OK. In the table, there are two cells in which this is the case.

If our test does not match the state of the world, we have made a decision error. If we say 'yes, the recruit has sufficient command of English to proceed on to intelligence testing as part of the Army induction process' when – in fact – he does not have such command, this is known as a 'false positive'. Conversely, if we say that the recruit does not command English sufficiently well to sit the intelligence test, when in fact he does, that is known as a 'false negative.'

It seems to us that there is much more at stake with a false positive than with a false negative. In the false positive case, we'd say that the recruit's command of English is sufficient to do the induction intelligence test. The recruit would then sit the intelligence test and, we presume, do poorly on that test as a result not of innate intelligence but rather of his inability to process the English language of the test instructions and of the intelligence items. The recruit might be slated for some duty – perhaps a very dangerous duty, as this was wartime – for which he really does not display aptitude.

➤ Do you agree that a false positive is more ethically dangerous for the Linguality Test results than a false negative?

➤ Do you believe that subsequent intelligence testing – of any kind, delivered in any language – is a good predictor of success or failure of various tasks in armed service?

The Linguality Test never really saw the light of day. Yerkes and his team discovered the need for it very late in the testing project, and by the time that the Linguality Test was up and running, it was November 1918, and the war was over. If you draw the conclusion that the Linguality Test is ethically questionable, does the simple fact that it was never used make you feel better?

➤ Now consider some language test with which you are familiar – in the setting where you work, perhaps. What are the consequences of a false positive or a false negative in your situation?

★ Task C9.4: Suggestions for further research

C9.4.1 Proposed title: 'Review of language testing standards: Phase I'

Background

Davidson et al. (1995) conducted a survey of language test standards in many world settings. They operationalized the term 'standards' to mean codes of practice and ethical behaviour, and they found that the term actually encompassed a wider range of meanings; notably, the term meant, as it does now, a reference to expected levels of student performance. It would be interesting to see how the term is used now, and in so doing, to replicate their survey of 'standards' as implied by Unit A9, where we discuss ethics and fairness. The 1995 study provides a suggested methodology to do such work.

Possible procedure

Through networking with colleagues, a literature review and Web searches, locate a sample of documents which purport to state standards of ethical behaviour for language testers. Consult Davidson et al. (1995) and develop a similar common analytical scheme to compare the various documents. We recommend that you assemble a team of researchers who can look for documents in multiple languages.

Possible outcomes

Our reading and study of this matter suggests that there are far more statements of standards in language testing today than there were in 1995. We think that a simple descriptive report will be of great value to language testers worldwide. In fact, a survey like this is probably needed every ten years or so.

C9.4.2 Proposed title: 'Review of language testing standards: Phase II'

Background

This is a revision and extension of the above project. In this phase, you could expand the search (radically) to include a wide range of standards documents in other areas of educational, psychological and clinical measurement. The Davidson et al. (1995) project did this: it touched on documents that were targeted at language testers as well as those targeted at the wider general measurement field.

Possible procedure

This uses the same procedure as the previous project, but with a larger expansion of target documents. Such expansion necessitates more networking and a more extensive literature review. It is also very possible that your research in Phase I will uncover language testing standards documents that reference similar documents in general assessment and so help to shape the Phase II research.

Possible outcomes

The most interesting question here concerns the nature of language testing as a branch of ethics. To what extent are our activities and worries similar to those of people working in other measurement domains? What guidance can each offer to the other? What do language testers have to say to the rest of the measurement world, and vice versa?

C9.4.3 Proposed title: 'Tolerance of false positives and false negatives in [name the type of setting where you will conduct your research, e.g. "a college-level foreign language placement testing system"]'

Background

This project seeks to answer the question: how tolerant is a particular test setting of false positives versus false negatives? With some growth and extension, the project could be applied to several test settings, and thereby attain a broader survey flavour.

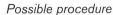
Possible procedure

First, gather some teachers or test developers at the setting of your choice. Conduct a workshop in which you develop some 'scenarios' about possible test takers for whom the decision (based on your test) is not correct. For each scenario the test taker is ultimately either a false positive or a false negative. Next, survey a wider range of teachers or administrators at your setting – these should be different participants from those who helped in the workshop. Ask them some questions about the level of tolerance of false positives and false negatives. This can be done with a short focused interview; we suspect that this research will work best through qualitative methodology.

Possible outcomes

The tolerance of false positives versus false negatives is very much linked with testing's ability to predict the future. In placement testing (for example), if a student is a false negative, then the student will waste time in subsequent service programmes. The student did not (truly) need the programmes, but we don't know that until we follow things out into the future. We suspect that the scenarios developed in your workshop will reflect this future orientation, and we suspect also that the tolerance levels will reflect issues of impact on the student and institution. We also suspect that this research will point towards possible improvement of the test, for the entire false positive/negative problem is, at its core, another form of validity evidence.

Unit C10
To boldly go

A correlation coefficient is an index of agreement between two sets of test results on the same set of people; we discuss this statistic in Unit A7. If the two tests rank the people exactly the same, then the correlation will be + 1.00. If the two tests rank inversely, then the correlation will be –1.00. If there is no relationship of ranking whatsoever, then the coefficient will be zero. In language testing, correlations are an important tool to measure agreement among raters, and, in turn, to help to train new raters.

For our logical exercise in this unit, we envision some relatively frequent cyclical testing – perhaps it is entry and placement testing before each of several academic terms per year, or perhaps it is some kind of periodic coordinated achievement testing at the end of instruction. Maybe it is both.

Our institution has committed to greater use of integrative language tasks in its tests, in the belief that such tasks are a better measure of communicative language ability. There is a logical price to pay for integrative complexity in language tests: the institution must hire more raters and must train them.

Task C10.1: The first pilot

Our testers develop a suite of integrative tasks. These tasks are piloted with four seasoned teachers in the system where the test is to operate. Raters are trained against the scoring rubric to be employed. The four teachers score a set of responses from students recruited to try out the test, and the following correlational results are obtained. This display of results is known as a correlation 'matrix'. There are ones on the diagonal; by definition, any correlation of a variable with itself is 1.00. This is a 'symmetric matrix', because the values above the diagonal are not given – they would be the same as those below:

	R1	R2	R3	R4
R1	1.00			
R2	0.61	1.00		
R3	0.70	0.80	1.00	
R4	0.58	0.84	0.81	1.00

Matrix 1: Inter-rater correlations, Pilot Test 1
(R1 is Rater 1, R2 is Rater 2, etc.)

➤ What is going on? Analyse the results for R1, in particular. What might the other raters say to that person before the raters proceed to further training?

★ Task C10.2: The second pilot

After discussion among the raters, and in particular, after the test developers and other three raters talk with R1, another set of student pilot results are elicited and are evaluated, and the following matrix is obtained among the same four raters:

	R1	R2	R3	R4
R1	1.00			
R2	0.79	1.00		
R3	0.83	0.89	1.00	
R4	0.84	0.83	0.82	1.00

Matrix 2: Inter-rater correlations, Pilot Test 2

Clearly, the raters are in greater agreement than in the first pilot test. The discussion with R1, in particular, seemed to effect this change.

➤ Why? What do you suppose R1 thought about while rating the second set of pilot data?

★ Task C10.3: The 'go/no-go' decision

After Pilot Test 2 is completed, the test developers meet and address the question: should they proceed to operational use of these integrative tasks? In testing parlance, this is one of many 'go/no-go' decisions we must make during test development. In effect, this decision is a form of validation reasoning, as follows:

1   The institution is committed to greater and greater use of integrative tasks.
2   Integrative tasks, by their nature, necessitate use of raters.
3   Raters must agree.
4   To achieve rater agreement, we must use rater training; the system did so, and
5   After two pilot tests, the inter-rater coefficients stabilized in the 0.79 to 0.89 range.

➤ The test developers face this decision: should they do another pilot test? What do you think? Suppose that a third pilot bought them only a very slight increase in the coefficients – maybe the strongest coefficient increases one point from 0.89 to 0.90. Would it be worth the time and the effort to continue to train these particular four raters?

Task C10.4: New raters arrive

Let us assume that our test developers did decide to go operational, and that the first operational use of this integrative test will be with the same four raters who participated in the pilot testing.

However, after some time the strain on the four raters is too great. They complain that the workload is too large, and they beg the developers (now functioning as test supervisors) to train up some new raters for the next testing cycle.

A new training session is called, and two more teachers are recruited as raters. They join the four seasoned veterans, and all six are asked to rate a sample of tests. The inter-rater correlations among the original four range much as they did in the second pilot: from the high 0.70s to the high 0.80s. However, both of the new raters correlate with the veterans at a lower level: from 0.55 to about 0.65. The supervisors conduct another cycle of rater training – in particular, they hold a dialogue among the original four veteran raters and the two new-comers. Another set of tasks are rated, and all six raters now display coefficients between the high 0.70s and the high 0.80s.

➤ Should the test supervisors be satisfied with the results obtained on the new raters? Can they (now) argue that the test is of better quality? Not only do they have a team of (now) six raters, but all six are achieving inter-rater coefficients of about the same level, and what is more, the rater training workshop has started to become very routine and easy to manage. Is this good?

Task C10.5: Two years out

Two years have passed since the operational go/no-go decision was made. There is now a cadre of twelve fully trained raters, cycling in and out of the operational testing. The workload problem has been solved, because all twelve people share fairly in the rating process.

From time to time, as new raters are inaugurated to the system, they participate in a training workshop – and the workshop routinely constitutes at least two full ratings. And with each workshop, inevitably the inter-rater coefficients stabilize in the standard coefficient range.

A student complains. The student feels the testing was unfair. The complaint alleges that peer students who performed similarly received higher marks. An enquiry is held following the institution's long-standing grievance procedures and regulations, and the test supervisors are called before an administrative panel. At this panel they defend the test by presenting the cyclical training and calibration that all raters follow. They present numerical analyses dating all the way back to the very first pilot, and they show how the training sessions routinely bring raters into agreement.

➤ In your opinion, what is the weight of this evidence in such a grievance? What value should the administrative panel place on the on-going numerical successes in the rater training?

⭐ Task C10.6: Six years out

That particular grievance is long since resolved, and very few others have arisen; the few complaints that have emerged are handled locally within the faculty's department. The rating system has hummed along for six years now, cycling regularly with the seasonal nature of all academic coursework. There is a sense of stasis, which is the warm confidence felt when a test system is stable and predictable (Davidson, 2004).

The operational raters have grown in number and have stabilized at fifteen – the exact number of faculty on staff. Everybody serves as a rater. There have been a few retirements from the teaching staff, and as new teachers are brought in they receive the rater training as part of their routine job orientations. Again and again, a two-cycle training workshop conducted with veterans and newcomers quickly brings the newcomers into agreement in the standard inter-rater coefficient range.

Then, one day, a particular new teacher arrives. This individual is something of a free spirit, an iconoclast hired from a progressive teacher-training institute. We shall call this person 'RX' for 'Rater X'.

A training session is called – it so happens that RX is the only newcomer on staff at that moment, so it is a simple workshop match-up: four veteran raters meet with RX for an afternoon's work.

Cycle 1 proceeds, and RX fails to correlate well with the other four: the RX coefficients are all in the 0.50 range.

Cycle 2 is then undertaken, and the same thing happens – weak coefficients are again observed with each pairing that involves RX, even though all other inter-rater correlations are in the now-standard range of acceptability. In fact, the second time around, RX correlates with one particular veteran at an even lower rate this time around: 0.45.

The veteran raters consult quickly, and for the first time that any of them can remember, they all agree to rate a third set of practice tests. The same thing happens. Despite all the discussion, despite the careful analysis of samples against the scoring rubric, despite deep theoretical and philosophical analysis of the test and its goals, RX continues to correlate poorly. The veterans note that the afternoon is drawing into the evening, and fatigue is starting to take its toll. Oddly, RX seems energized and excited by the procedures.

➤ What should be done?

Task C10.7: The X-factor

Ten years have passed since the operational roll-out of the integrative testing at this institution. RX is still on staff and has risen to the rank of Associate Director.

All parties like the test. Even the students have routinely praised its washback.

The rating system has been deconstructed frequently, and in fact (at RX's suggestion) the training workshop has become a far more flexible and – at times – contentious event. Everything is on the table during rater training: the tasks, the scoring rubric, the time limit of the testing, the number of tasks in the test, the variability or similarity among the tasks; in fact, the entire test specification is in a permanent state of creative flux.

RX has had an impact, but only in awakening an 'X-factor' among this faculty. These teachers are willing to talk and to dispel myths. They are democratic in their decision making, but they are unwavering in their commitment to con-sistent testing. None of them want to go through a serious grievance again, and hence their obligation to rater agreement remains firm. At the same time, they do not wish to become mere avatars for one another – mimicking the per-ceptions and tastes of one colleague upon another. The rater training sessions have long since abandoned any expectation of 'two cycles only'. Some last two cycles, some last three, or four, or sometimes even five. The rater training is as long as it needs to be, and if the training sparks changes elsewhere in the testing, such changes are entertained and explored, and, often, implemented.

RX was the catalyst. The faculty are the chemistry. And the whole reaction is proceeding well. Ten years out, not only has the system achieved stasis but it has also achieved something far more valuable: the willingness to upset the stasis when consensus dictates.

➤ Somebody did something right back at the very beginning. The impact is very positive, and the effects towards which the entire testing drove were laudatory. What do you think was done correctly, and when? Was it the design of the original test specs? Was it the original hiring in the institution, perhaps setting the stage for this moment ten years later? Was it some key decision made along the way, as the years and testing cycles rolled out?

➤ How did they get it right?

⭐ **Task C10.8: Suggestion for further research**

C10.8.1 Proposed title: 'Longitudinal tracking of test development: a feasibility study'

Background

Many of our exercises and examples in this book concern testing as a process. This reflects our pragmatic, effect-driven view of the world: that the ultimate determiner of a test's value lies not in the present moment but in time yet to come. We pose this research question: how feasible is long-term evolutionary data gathering?

Possible procedure

We suggest a survey and/or series of interviews with colleagues at your setting. The tracking of test evolution is going to involve strain on resources. There will be student databases to access (regularly) and keep clean (regularly). There will be tracking of test materials – like specs or rater training guidelines – and some kind of document management system is needed. Set these problems before your colleagues. Is your institution willing to pay for such work?

Possible outcome

As with many suggested research projects in this book, there is first and foremost an immediate payback to your local setting. Through dialogue with your colleagues, you will come to know what kind of evolutionary tracking is realistic. We also think that work like this will contribute to the field of language testing. Feasibility studies are not common in testing, but when they do happen they get quite a bit of attention – a good example is the research on which the computerization of the TOEFL was justified (Taylor et al., 1998).

C10.8.2 A testing diary

'It was . . . fun,' we are told, were the dying words of Captain Kirk of *Star Trek* fame – well, almost the dying words; he did go on to utter: 'Oh, my'.[15]

Reader and colleague, we have enjoyed this journey together. It has been fun. We feel no need also to say: 'Oh, my' – as if there were problems and challenges out there which we have overlooked or for which we have not adequately offered preparation.

Of course, we may have missed something – it is impossible to cover everything about testing even in a book with a unique structure such as this. If there is some testing vexation that haunts you and keeps you awake at night, and if a direct answer to that problem is not found in these pages, we acknowledge that oversight with respect. Let us know. Maybe we can persuade the publishers to think of a second edition.

Do we worry about our oversights? Not really. Something has kept the two of us battling away at testing all these donkey's years. Something has kept our spirit alive and our sense of humour active, for, without a spirit of enjoyment, work in testing would be at best plodding progress and at worst a traverse of ethical and moral quicksand. The two of us became ready to talk about testing some-where in our professional training, and we hope that we have conveyed to you a sense of preparation. If you read this book not only for its content but for its spirit, then all that still needs to be said is: 'feel ready'.

Feel ready to tell colleagues about reliability and validity. Feel ready to talk about effect-driven testing. Feel ready to explain the power and danger of tools readily available and yet possibly misunderstood. Feel ready to do so with diplomacy and tact, but with confidence.

➤ Keep a testing diary. Track your own awareness of testing and seek the pragmatic effect of this book. Continue to become a testing citizen, to participate in the dialectic that is testing, for it is a conversation to which all are welcome, and unless we all participate then it is not a dialogue at all but rather a monologue – and therein reside the same fears and powers which (we suspect) brought you to critical awareness of tests in the first place. Shohamy (2001) comes to the same conclusion in her masterful exploration of the power of language tests – that above all else, everything will be OK if we can just keep talking with each other.

Do all these things and feel ready to do them, but don't get stressed out.

Instead, have fun.

Glossary

BAND DESCRIPTOR

See also *rubric*. A term for a statement that describes what a student can do at a particular point on a rating scale. The descriptor is used by raters to match language samples from performance tests to a level on the scale. Also termed (simply) 'band'. Sometimes spelled 'descripter'.

COMPUTER-ADAPTIVE TEST

A computer-adaptive test selects items for each test taker on the basis of their history of responses. If a test taker gets items consistently correct, the algorithm that runs the test will select more difficult items for presentation. Similarly, if a test taker gets items consistently wrong, the algorithm selects easier items. The test therefore adapts to the ability level of the test taker and stops the test when it has made a reliable estimate of ability. Computer-adaptive tests are a special case of adaptive testing. Oral interviews are often adaptive by their very nature: adjusting the difficulty of tasks in real-time estimation (by the interviewer) of examinee ability.

CONCORDANCE

A table that shows how the scores on one test relate to the scores on one or more other tests. For example, it is said that a score of 550 on paper and pencil TOEFL is equivalent to a score of 213 on the computer-based test, and a score of 79–80 on TOEFL iBT.

CONGRUENCE, OR 'FIT-TO-SPEC'

Item writers are asked to produce new items that fit a task or item specification. The extent to which new items match, or 'fit' the *test specification*, is congruence.

CONSEQUENTIAL VALIDITY

The consideration of the *impact* test use has upon individuals, society, educational systems and other stakeholders. This includes the *impact* that the test may have because of its implicit values or theories, and its intended or unintended uses. It also includes test *washback* on teaching and learning.

CONSISTENCY

See *reliability*.

CONSTRUCT

Following Kerlinger and Lee (2000), a construct is a concept that is defined so that it can be scientifically investigated. This means that it can be *operationalized* so that it can be measured. Constructs are usually identified by abstract nouns, such as 'fluency', that cannot be directly observed in themselves but about which we need to make inferences from observations.

CONSTRUCT-IRRELEVANT VARIANCE

Changes in test scores that are caused by factors other than the construct of interest. For example, fluctuations that are caused by some aspect of the test administration would constitute construct-irrelevant variance. Note that a test may still (arguably) measure a construct without fluctuating, as when (for example) all the examinees get a particular test item correct. That is to say, mere fluctuation does not necessarily define a construct, but undesirable fluctation may indicate that the construct is not being measured.

CONSTRUCT UNDER-REPRESENTATION

Construct under-representation occurs when the content of the test does not adequately reflect the breadth or depth of the *construct* as defined for the purpose of the test.

CRITERION

There are two meanings to this term. Firstly, a criterion is a variable to which we may wish to make a prediction from a test score. If our test is designed to predict success in a future academic context, the criterion may be results on academic tests or the evaluation of communicative ability by subject specialists. Secondly, it is an area of content (sometimes called a domain) to which a test is referenced (see *criterion-referenced test*).

CRITERION-REFERENCED TEST (CRT)

A test that measures knowledge, skill or ability in a specific domain. Performance is usually measured against some existing criterion level of performance, above which the test taker is deemed to have achieved mastery. Also known as CRT, this approach is said to differ from *norm-referenced testing* (NRT) in that test takers are not compared with each other, only with a criterion of successful performance. CRTs typically do not seek to spread out student results. In contrast, NRTs are usually designed with spread in mind.

CRITERION STUDIES

A criterion study correlates scores from the test of interest to other tests. If we wish to know how a new test relates to its computer-based and paper-based versions, as in the case of the TOEFL iBT, the test scores are correlated and a *concordance* can be produced. This would be a concurrent criterion study. A *predictive* criterion study may correlate test scores to some future assessment of a test taker, such as assessment in a later course of study, or judgments made by subject teachers after entry to university.

CUT SCORE

A score on a test above which a test taker is considered to have achieved 'mastery' or met the requirements of some *criterion*. Cut scores are usually established by judgmental methods. One group of methods focuses on tests, or the probability of 'masters' correctly answering items. The second group of methods focuses on test takers, or the probability that individuals who have been independently judged to meet the *criterion* score above a certain level on the test.

DIRECT TEST

See also *indirect test*. It has often been claimed that a direct test is one in which we can 'directly' observe the constructs we wish to test. These have generally been performance tests that involve speaking and writing. A claim to 'directness' has usually implied a claim for test validity through other concepts such as 'authenticity'. Although this term remains in use, it is now accepted that all tests are 'indirect' in that performance must be interpreted through the lens of the constructs we wish to measure and the elements of performance we observe to make inferences about constructs.

DOMAIN

The domain is that part of the universe to which we wish to make a prediction from test scores. Domains are usually described in terms of language content, demands, functions, or other descriptions of actual language performance. For example, domains may be defined in relation to specific jobs, areas of language use, or discourse domain such as the language of academia. Domain analysis may be an important part of test content design in testing language for specific purposes.

EFFECT-DRIVEN TESTING

Effect-driven testing implies that as part of the design process we look into the future to picture the effect we would like the test to have. We then structure our test development to achieve this effect. A clear statement of intended effects enhances the clarity of test purpose and use, thus helping to avoid unintended consequences of test use.

FACET

See also *test method facets*. Some aspect of the test or the setting for the test that may have an impact upon test scores. One *construct-irrelevant* facet of a speaking test is the rater, and this facet is often studied to make sure that scores do not vary according to rater.

FALSIFICATION

See *verificationism*

FORM (OR TEST FORM)

In some usages, the term 'test' refers to the generic instrument, such as 'TOEFL' or 'IELTS'. When used in that sense, at any one time there may be many 'versions' of the test in use. Each version is referred to as a form. Forms should closely resemble each other in their content and the properties of the tasks and items. Only if forms are parallel can we claim that they are part of the same test. One way to assure such equivalence is through the use of test specifications.

FORMATIVE ASSESSMENT

Formative assessment is carried out during the learning process as an intervention that is designed to encourage further learning and change. It is frequently used in contrast to *summative assessment*.

FRAMEWORK

A selection of *constructs*, knowledge, skills or abilities, extracted from a *model* for their relevance to a particular domain of inference. Models of language competence are usually encyclopedic definitions of what it means to know and use a language. It is impossible to test everything that a model contains in any single test. If a test producer claims to be able to do this, it shows a fundamental misunderstanding of validity issues. Frameworks are mediating documents between a *model* and a *test specification* that provide rationales and empirical evidence to link the *constructs* tested to the explicit purpose for which the test is designed.

GENERALIZABILITY

There are two meanings to this term. Firstly, it can refer to the quality of being able to generalize the meaning of a test score beyond the specific items, tasks, other test method facets or test that generated the score. It is usual to investigate the generalizability of score meaning across tasks, raters and times. However, in many testing contexts users wish to generalize the meaning of the score to a range of communication tasks and situations that are not contained in the test. Secondly, in a meaning that is similar, it can refer to the extendability of research results to other research contexts. This latter definition is shared by many areas of research enquiry beyond language testing.

IMPACT

A term used to denote the effect of the use of a test on society, institutions, stakeholders and individual test takers. It may also include the effect of the test on the classroom, but this is more usually referred to by the more specific term *washback*.

INDIRECT TEST

See also *direct test*. An indirect test is one that does not require the test taker to demonstrate the skill being assessed in observable performance. For example, we may wish to make inferences to a test taker's ability to write from a test task that asks for the identification and correction of errors in written text. This would be an indirect test. However, there is a sense in which all tests are indirect because we can never directly observe the constructs to which we wish to make inferences.

INSTRUCTIONS

See also *rubric*. The directions given to test takers, either oral or written, on how to take the test or respond to item/task types.

INVIGILATOR

The person who monitors test takers during the test. Called a 'proctor' in US English.

LOGICAL POSITIVISM

See also *verificationism*. Logical positivists hold that only claims that are in principle verifiable or falsifiable using empirical methods are scientifically admissible. Other claims or beliefs are classed as meaningless. It is rare for researchers to hold strong positivist views today as the position makes it impossible to discuss most ethical, aesthetic or religious questions. Nevertheless, the principles of *verifiability* and *falsifiability* are closely associated with the concept of investigating alternative explanatory hypotheses for the meaning of test scores in the development of validity arguments.

MODEL

A description of what it means to know or use a language. Models may be abstract, such as the models of communicative competence or communicative language ability of Canale and Swain (1980; Canale, 1983b) or Bachman (1990), or they may be encyclopedic and taxonomic, like the Canadian Language Benchmarks or the Common European Framework of Reference. Models cannot be used directly for test design, or for comparing the purpose or content of specific tests. Rather, they are sources from which we select elements for inclusion in *frameworks*.

NOMOLOGICAL NET

A network of links between *constructs*, between *constructs* and observable variables, and between observable variables. A theory specifies the hypothesized nature of the relationships, which can be tested empirically.

NORM-REFERENCED TEST (NRT)

A test in which the score of any individual is interpreted in relation to the scores of other individuals in the population. It is common for a test to be given to a representative sample of the entire test-taking population in order to establish norms. Once the test is used in live testing, any score is interpreted in terms of where it falls on the curve of normal distribution established in the norm-setting study. See also *criterion-referenced test*.

OPERATIONALIZATION

The process of operationalizing a construct. Constructs by their very definition are abstract, and are usually named using abstract nominal groups, such as 'interactional competence' or 'fluency'. We cannot observe these constructs. Operationalizing a construct involves deciding what we can observe in order to make a decision how 'interactionally competent' or 'fluent' a test taker is. Operationalizing a construct therefore requires us to associate it with observable variables.

PRAGMATISM

A philosophy that insists on an intimate connection between theory and practice, and in which the meaning of a concept is best articulated as its conceivable practical consequences. For some this is a theory of meaning, and for others a theory of truth. Whichever line is taken, pragmatists are generally empiricists who believe that there is no division between the mind and the world, and that the meaning (or truth) of a claim lies in its utility in getting along with the world. Data from the world, and our perceptions of it in theory, are therefore interconnected and real, and essential to our understanding of any reality – including the validity of a test.

PROCTOR

See *invigilator*.

PROTOTYPE

A draft item or task type that we hypothesize will elicit behaviour that we can score, and from which we are able to make inferences to the intended constructs. Prototypes are used in alpha and beta testing to investigate whether the hypotheses are likely to be correct, before progressing to field testing. Prototypes are manipulated until they are accepted as part of the test, or rejected because they do not fulfil their intended role in the test as a whole.

PSYCHOMETRICS

The study of measurement in psychology and education. Psychometrics is primarily concerned with scoring models and the statistical aspects of test analysis.

RAPID PROTOTYPING

A term used in manufacturing for the process of testing pre-production components to ensure that they will fulfil the function they were designed for in the workings of a full-scale machine. In language testing, rapid prototyping refers to the testing of item or task types on small groups of students and giving them to expert judges for comment. Faults in the design can then be corrected, and the part quickly tested again. Only item or task types that pass rapid prototyping without serious faults being detected go on to field testing.

RASCH MODEL

Developed by the Danish mathematician Georg Rasch, the Rasch model is the most popular of a family of item response theory (IRT) models. It assumes that a response to a test item is a function of just two variables: the difficulty of the test item and the ability of the test taker. Item difficulty and test-taker ability can be calculated on a single scale of measurement, so that when a test taker's ability is the same as the difficulty of the item, the probability of getting the item correct will be 50 per cent. The Rasch model is equivalent to one-parameter IRT, in which both ability and difficulty are modelled. Two-parameter IRT also models item discrimination. Three-parameter IRT models the item threshold per-formance level, which is usually interpreted to mean an estimate of guessing on the item functioning.

RELIABILITY

Consistency of measurement, usually over time, rater or content. It is normally assumed that test takers should receive the same score (taking into account the error that is expected in all tests) if the test is taken twice within a reasonable period of time. Further, that they should receive the same score irrespective of whichever rater or scorer is used, and whichever *form* of the test is used.

RETROFITTING

Taking a test that was designed for one purpose and using it for another. When retrofitting takes place it is incumbent upon the test provider or the organi-zation that performs the retrofitting to create a new validity argument for the new purpose. In order to retrofit the test it may be necessary to make extensive modifications before it can be used. Failure to provide an explicit validity argument for a retrofitted test, especially when no modifications have taken place, should alert score users to the likelihood of invalidity and test misuse. The term was first used by Fulcher at the second EALTA conference in Voss, Norway (7 June 2005), to describe the use of existing language tests as part of an immigration decision without first creating a new validity argument.

REVERSE ENGINEERING

The process of taking a test, or item or task from a test, and trying to recreate the specification from which it was generated, to create a better specification, or to use the process of spec creation to understand the forces by which the test was created.

RUBRIC
See also *band descriptor*. *Rubric* is the term used in the United States to mean the same as *band descriptor* in the United Kingdom. However, in the United Kingdom the *test rubrics* usually refer to any instructions given in the test to help test takers understand how to respond to prompts.

SCORE CONSUMERS
Also *score users*. Whoever uses test scores, whether intended or unintended users of the scores. Intended score consumers may, for example, be parents or university admissions officers. One type of unintended user may be estate agents who push up house prices in successful school districts.

SEMANTIC DIFFERENTIAL
A rating process that requires the use of antonyms. These are placed at the opposite ends of a scale with blanks between, and the raters are asked to decide whether a language sample falls closer to one end or the other, as in this example:
Intelligible ___: __ : ___: __ : ___ Unintelligible

STAKEHOLDERS
All individuals or organizations with an interest in the use or *impact* of the test. Stakeholders include language testers, test takers and the families of test takers. However, those with an interest may also be Ministries of Education, school districts and individual educational establishments. In the use of Business English tests the stakeholders may also include companies that use the test for appointment and promotion purposes. In large-scale high-stakes tests the society of a country or region may have a stake in how a test is used. Test developers need to identify legitimate stakeholders for consultation in the test development process.

SUBSTANTIVE VALIDITY EVIDENCE
Substantive evidence is concerned with the processes used by test takers to answer items correctly, or successfully engage with language tasks. The means employed by successful test takers should be such that we are able to make predictions about the likely use of successful processes or strategies used in the target domain.

SUMMATIVE ASSESSMENT
Used in contrast to *formative assessment*, summative assessment is conducted at the end of a programme of study to assess whether and how far individuals or groups have been successful.

TEST METHOD FACETS
Aspects of the test method that may have an impact upon test scores, such as the *rubric*, input or expected response.

TEST SPECIFICATIONS	Generative blueprint or design documents for a test. Test specifications operate at the level of the item or task, and of the test as a whole (components or 'papers', mix of item or task types, response formats, length and so on); the latter whole-test level is often called a 'table of specifications'. Testers should be able to compile new equivalent forms from the test specifications, and item writers should be able to write new items or tasks that have *congruence* with the item specifications.
VALIDITY ARGUMENT	An argument is the defence of a claim, requiring grounds (data) to support the claim, and a warrant to justify the claim on the basis of the grounds. Validity arguments justify the claims that language testers make about the meaning of test scores.
VERIFICATIONISM	The view that a claim or belief is meaningful only if we can state the conditions under which it could be verified or falsified. That is, we need to state what empirical research would need to be done to show that the claim or belief was true, or false. Verifiability and falsifiability are associated with *logical positivism*.
WASHBACK	Sometimes referred to as 'backwash'. The effect of a test on learning and teaching. Washback studies focus on practices or behaviour that would not be present if it were not for the test. See also *impact*.

Notes

1 Test preparation, or 'cramming', has existed for as long as there have been tests. Galton (1874: 263) records that one of the demerits of the education provided for men of science is 'too much cramming for examinations'. In his life of Galton, Pearson (1914: 452) reports that by 1889 Galton was recommending increasing the number of standardized tests given by the army and the civil service as a measure to reduce the amount of 'cramming' for examinations. 'Probably marks will be given for a complete series of anthropometric tests, mental as well as physical. There can be no better remedy against cramming than examinations of this kind wherein it is quite easy to vary the tests, and to prevent anything but general intelligence and good physique scoring.'

2 There have been cases in which test discrimination has been argued to be 'unethical' because by definition tests do not treat individuals equally. See Wood (1991: 83) and Lynch (1997), and Unit A9 for further discussion of ethics in language testing.

3 Item variance is calculated as $s^2 = pq$, where s^2 is the variance of the item, p is the facility value (proportion correct) and q is the proportion incorrect. Notice that when $p = 0.5$ (and therefore $q = 0.5$), $s^2 = 0.25$. This is the maximum variance obtainable, and test designers try to include items with the largest variances, as these contribute to test reliability.

4 The standard deviation of the scores is 2.62, and test variance is the square of the standard deviation.

5 Spolsky (1995: 341) refers to the British approach to examination production as a 'cottage industry' as opposed to the US 'factory system'. This metaphor is attributed to Alan Maley.

6 Putnam (1990: 196) identifies this thinker as Kierkegaard.

7 This is a radically different position from the empiricism of Pragmatism. As James (1907: 99) says: 'Truths emerge from facts; but they dip forward into facts again and add to them; which facts again create or reveal new truth (the word is indifferent) and so on indefinitely. The "facts" themselves meanwhile are not *true*. They simply *are*. Truth is the function of the beliefs that start and terminate among them.' Italics in the original.

8 See Wylie, E. (no date) 'An overview of the international second language proficiency ratings.' Available on-line: http://www.gu.edu.au/centre/call/content4.html.

9 See http://scientific.thomson.com/products/ssci/.

10 See http://www.mcli.dist.maricopa.edu/authoring/studio/guidebook/prod_schedule.html.

11 See www.sas.com and www.spss.com.

12 http://www.ed.gov/nclb/landing.jhtml, downloaded 16 March 2006.

13 http://www.ed.gov/nclb/accountability/ayp/testing.html, downloaded 20 March 2006.

14 'Ethnography' at www.wikipedia.org, downloaded 13 May 2006.

15 'Memorable quotes from Star Trek: Generations'. Downloadable from imdb.com: http://www.imdb.com/title/tt0111280/quotes.

References

Aaron, B., Kromrey, J. D. and Ferron, J. M. (1998) 'Equating r-based and d-based effect size indices: problems with the common recommended formula.' Paper presented at the annual meeting of the Florida Educational Research Association, Orlando, FL (ERIC Document Reproduction Service. ED 433 353).

Abbs, B. et al. (1978) *Challenges: A Multimedia Project for Learners of English.* Harlow: Longman English Teaching Services.

Alderson, J. C. (1981) 'Reaction to the Morrow paper (3).' In Alderson, J. C. and Hughes, A. (eds) *Issues in Language Testing.* London: British Council, 45–54.

Alderson, J. C. (1983) 'The cloze procedure and proficiency in English as a foreign language.' In Oller, J. W. (ed.) *Issues in Language Testing Research.* Rowley, MA: Newbury House, 205–217.

Alderson, J. C. (1986) 'Innovations in language testing?' In Portal, M. (ed.) *Innovations in Language Testing.* London: NFER/Nelson, 93–105.

Alderson, J. C. (1990) 'Bands and scores.' In Alderson, J. C. and North, B. (eds) *Language Testing in the 1990s.* London: Modern English Publications and the British Council, 71–86.

Alderson, J. C. (2004) 'Foreword.' In Cheng, L., Watanabe, Y. and Curtis, A. (eds) *Washback in Language Testing: Research Contexts and Methods.* Mahwah, NJ: Erlbaum.

Alderson, J. C. and Buck, G. (1993) 'Standards in testing: a survey of the practice of UK examination boards in EFL testing.' *Language Testing* 10, 2, 1–26.

Alderson, J. C. and Hamp-Lyons, L. (1996) 'TOEFL preparation courses: a study of washback.' *Language Testing* 13, 3, 280–297.

Alderson, J. C. and Wall, D. (1993) 'Does washback exist?' *Applied Linguistics* 14, 2, 115–129.

Alderson, J. C., Clapham, C. and Wall, D. (1995) *Language Test Construction and Evaluation.* Cambridge: Cambridge University Press.

Allen, J. P. B. and Widdowson, H. G. (1974) 'Teaching the communicative use of English.' *International Review of Applied Linguistics* 12, 1, 1–21.

Almond, R. G., Steinberg, L. and Mislevy, R. J. (2001) *A Sample Assessment Using the Four Process Framework.* CSE Technical Report 543. Los Angeles: Center for the Study of Evaluation, CRESST.

American Council on the Teaching of Foreign Languages (1999) *Revised ACTFL Proficiency Guidelines – Speaking.* Yonkers, NY: American Council on the Teaching of Foreign Languages.

American Educational Research Association (AERA), American Psychological Association (APA) and National Council on Measurement in Education (NCME) (1985) *Standards for Educational and Psychological Testing.* Washington, DC: AERA.

American Educational Research Association (AERA), American Psychological Association (APA) and National Council on Measurement in Education (NCME) (1999) *Standards for Educational and Psychological Testing.* Washington, DC: AERA.

American Psychological Association (1954) 'Technical recommendations for psychological tests and diagnostic techniques.' *Psychological Bulletin* 51, 2, 2.

American Psychological Assocation (1955) *Technical Recommendations for Achievement Tests.* Washington, DC: National Educational Association.

American Psychological Association (1966) *Standards for Educational and Psychological Tests and Manuals.* Washington, DC: APA.

American Psychological Association (1974) *Standards for Educational and Psychological Tests.* Washington, DC: APA.

Angoff, W. H. (1984) *Scales, Norms and Equivalent Scores.* Princeton, NJ: Educational Testing Service.

Atkinson, M. and Heritage, J. (1984) *The Structure of Social Action.* Cambridge: Cambridge University Press.

Austin, J. L. (1962) *How to Do Things with Words.* Oxford: Clarendon Press.

Ayer, A. J. (1936) *Language, Truth and Logic.* London: Penguin Modern Classics.

Bachman, L. F. (1990) *Fundamental Considerations in Language Testing.* Oxford: Oxford University Press.

Bachman, L. F. (2000) 'What, if any, are the limits of our responsibility for fairness in language testing?' In Kunnan, A. J. (ed.) *Fairness and Validation in Language Assessment.* Studies in Language Testing 9. Cambridge: Cambridge University Press, 39–41.

Bachman, L. F. (2004) *Statistical Analyses for Language Assessment.* Cambridge: Cambridge University Press.

Bachman, L. F. (2005) 'Building and supporting a case for test use.' *Language Assessment Quarterly* 2, 1, 1–34.

Bachman, L. F. and Palmer, A. (1982) 'The construct validation of some components of communicative proficiency.' *TESOL Quarterly* 16, 4, 449–465.

Bachman, L. F. and Palmer, A. S. (1996) *Language Testing in Practice.* Oxford: Oxford University Press.

Bachman, L. F., Davidson, F., Ryan, K. and Choi, I. C. (1995) *An Investigation into the Comparability of Two Tests of English as a Foreign Language: The Cambridge–TOEFL Comparability Study.* Studies in Language Testing 1. Cambridge: Cambridge University Press.

Bailey, K. M. (1996) 'Working for washback: a review of the washback concept in language testing.' *Language Testing* 13, 3, 257–279.

Bailey, K.M. (1998) *Learnign About Language Assessment: Dilemmas, Decisions and Directions.* New York: Heinle & Heinle.

Bailey, K. M. (1999) *Washback in Language Testing.* Princeton, NJ: TOEFL Monograph No. MS-15.

Baker, R. (1997) *Classical Test Theory and Item Response Theory in Test Analysis.* Language Testing Update Special Report No. 2. Lancaster: University of Lancaster.

Beeston, S. (2000) 'The UCLES EFL Item Banking System.' *Research Notes* 2.

Bejar, I., Douglas, D., Jamieson, J., Nissan, S. and Turner, J. (2000). *TOEFL 2000 Listening Framework: A Working Paper.* TOEFL Monograph Series, Rep. No. 19. Princeton, NJ: ETS.

Benedict, R. (1934) *Patterns of Culture.* Boston: Houghton Mifflin.

Bernstein, R. J. (1985) *Beyond Objectivism and Relativism: Science, Hermeneutics, and Praxis.* Philadelphia: University of Pennsylvania Press.

Berwick, R. and Ross, S. (1996) 'Cross-cultural pragmatics in oral proficiency interview strategies.' In Milanovic, M. and Saville, N. (eds) *Performance Testing, Cognition and Assessment.* Selected papers from the 15th Language Testing Research Colloquium. Cambridge: Cambridge University Press, 34–54.

Bishop, S. (2004) 'Thinking about professional ethics.' *Language Assessment Quarterly* 1, 2&3, 109–122.

Black, E. (2003) *War against the Weak: Eugenics and America's Campaign to Create a Master Race.* New York: Four Walls Eight Windows.

Black, H. C. (1979) *Black's Law Dictionary*, 5th ed. St Paul, MN: West Publishing Co.

Brennan, R. L. (1983) *Elements of Generalizability Theory.* Iowa City, IA: American College Testing.

Bridgeman, B., Cline, F. and Powers, D. (2002). 'Evaluating new tasks for TOEFL: relationships to external criteria.' Paper presented at the annual meeting of Teachers of English to Speakers of Other Languages (TESOL), Salt Lake City, UT, April.

Brindley, G. (1998) 'Outcomes-based assessment and reporting in language learning programs: a review of the issues.' *Language Testing* 15, 1, 45–85.

Brindley, G. (ed.). (2000) *Studies in Immigrant English Assessment*, vol. 1. Sydney: Macquarie University, National Centre for English Language Teaching and Research.

British Council, University of Cambridge Local Examinations Syndicate and IDP Education Australia (1996) *Assessment Guide for the Speaking Module*, 2nd ed. Cambridge: University of Cambridge Local Examinations Syndicate.

Brookhart, S. (2003) 'Developing measurement theory for classroom assessment purposes and uses.' *Educational Measurement: Issues and Practice* 22, 4, 5–12.

Brown, A. (2003) 'Interviewer variation and the co-construction of speaking proficiency.' *Language Testing* 20, 1, 1–25.

Brown, A. and Hill, K. (1998) 'Interviewer style and candidate performance in the IELTS oral interview.' In Woods, S. (ed.) *Research Reports 1997*, vol. 1. Sydney: ELICOS, 173–191.

Brown, A. and Lumley, T. (1997) 'Interviewer variability in specific-purpose language performance tests.' In Huhta, A., Kohonen, V., Kurki-Suonio, L. and Luoma, S. (eds) *Current Developments and Alternatives in Language Assessment Proceedings of LTRC 96.* Jyväskylä: University of Jyväskylä and University of Tampere, 137–50.

Brown, J. D. and Hudson, T. (2002) *Criterion-referenced Language Testing.* Cambridge: Cambridge University Press.

Brumfit, C. (1984) *Communicative Methodology in Language Teaching: The Roles of Fluency and Accuracy.* Cambridge: Cambridge University Press.

Butler, F., Eignor, D., Jones, S., McNamara, T. and Suomi, B. (2000). *TOEFL 2000 Speaking Framework: A Working Paper.* TOEFL Monograph Series, Rep. No. 20. Princeton, NJ: ETS.

Campbell, D. T. and Fiske, D. W. (1959) 'Convergent and discriminant validation by the multitrait–multimethod matrix.' *Psychological Bulletin* 56, 81–105.

Canale, M. (1983a) 'From communicative competence to communicative language pedagogy.' In Richards, C. and Schmidt, R. W. (eds) *Language and Communication.* London: Longman, 2–27.

Canale, M. (1983b) 'On some dimensions of language proficiency.' In Oller, J. W. (ed.) *Issues in Language Testing Research.* Rowley, MA: Newbury House, 333–342.

Canale, M. and Swain, M. (1980) 'Theoretical bases of communicative approaches to second language teaching and testing.' *Applied Linguistics* 1, 1, 1–47.

Candlin, C. N. (1977) Preface to M. Coulthard, *An Introduction to Discourse Analysis.* London: Longman.

Carroll, B. J. (1980) 'Specifications for an English language testing service.' In Alderson, J. C. and Hughes, A. (eds) *Issues in Language Testing.* ELT Documents 111. London: British Council, 66–110.

Carroll, J. B. (1961) 'Fundamental considerations in testing for English language proficiency of foreign students.' In *Testing the English Proficiency of Foreign Students*. Washington, DC: Center for Applied Linguistics. Reprinted in Allen, H. B. and Campbell, R. N. (eds) (1972) *Teaching English as a Second Language: A Book of Readings*. New York: McGraw-Hill.

Celce-Murcia, M., Dörnyei, Z. and Thurrell, S. (1995) 'Communicative competence: a pedagogically motivated model with content specifications.' *Issues in Applied Linguistics* 2, 5–35.

Chalhoub-Deville, M. (1995) 'Deriving oral assessment scales across different tests and rater groups.' *Language Testing* 12, 1, 16–33.

Chalhoub-Deville, M. (1997) 'Theoretical models, assessment frameworks and test construction.' *Language Testing* 14, 1, 3–22.

Chalhoub-Deville, M. (2003) 'Second language interaction: current perspectives and future trends.' *Language Testing* 20, 4, 369–383.

Chalhoub-Deville, M. and Fulcher, G. (2003) 'The oral proficiency interview: a research agenda.' *Foreign Language Annals* 36, 4, 498–506.

Chapelle, C. (1994) 'Are c-tests valid measures for L2 vocabulary research?' *Second Language Research* 10, 2, 157–187.

Chapelle, C. (1998) 'Construct definition and validity inquiry in SLA research.' In Bachman, L. F. and Cohen, A. D. (eds) *Interfaces between Second Language Acquisition and Language Testing Research*. Cambridge: Cambridge University Press, 32–70.

Chapelle, C. (1999a) 'From reading theory to testing practice.' In Chalhoub-Deville, M. (ed.) *Issues in Computer-adaptive Testing of Reading*. Cambridge: Cambridge University Press, 150–166.

Chapelle, C. (1999b) 'Validity in language assessment.' *Annual Review of Applied Linguistics* 19, 254–272.

Chapelle, C. and Brindley, G. (2002) 'Assessment'. In Schmitt, N. (ed.) *An Introduction to Applied Linguistics*. London: Arnold, 267–288.

Chapelle, C., Grabe, W. and Berns, M. (1997) *Communicative Language Proficiency: Definition and Implications for TOEFL 2000*. TOEFL Monograph Series, Rep. No. 10. Princeton, NJ: ETS.

Cheng, L. and Watanabe, Y. (eds) (2004) *Washback in Language Testing*. Mahwah, NJ: Erlbaum.

Chomsky, N. (1973) 'Linguistic theory.' In Oller, J. W. and Richards, J. C. (eds) *Focus on the Learner: Pragmatic Perspectives for the Language Teacher*. Rowley, MA: Newbury House.

Clapham, C. (1996) *The Development of the IELTS: A Study of the Effect of Background Knowledge on Reading Comprehension*. Cambridge: Cambridge University Press.

Clark, J. L. D. (1972) *Foreign Language Testing: Theory and Practice*. Philadelphia: Center for Curriculum Development.

Code of Fair Testing Practices in Education (1988). Washington, DC: Joint Committee on Testing Practices (Mailing Address: Joint Committee on Testing Practices, American Psychological Association, 750 First Avenue, NE, Washington, DC, 20002-4242). Available on-line: http://www.apa.org/science/FinalCode.pdf.

Cole, N. S. and Moss, P. A. (1989) 'Bias in test use.' In R. L. Linn (ed.) *Educational Measurement*. New York: American Council on Education/Macmillan, 201–219.

Coniam, D. (2005) 'The impact of wearing a face mask in a high-stakes oral examination: an exploratory post-SARS study in Hong Kong.' *Language Assessment Quarterly* 2, 4, 235–261.

Cook, V. J. (1978) 'Some ways of organising language.' *Audio Visual Language Journal* 16, 2, 89–94.

Cortázar, J. (1968) *Hopscotch*. London: Harvill.

Council of Europe (2001) *Common European Framework of Reference for Languages: Learning, Teaching and Assessment.* Cambridge: Cambridge University Press. Available on-line: http://www.coe.int/t/dg4/linguistic/Source/Framework_EN.pdf.

Criper, C. and Davies, A. (1988) *ELTS Validation Project Report: Research Report 1(i).* Cambridge: British Council and the University of Cambridge Local Examinations Syndicate.

Crocker, L. and Algina, J. (1986) *Introduction to Classical and Modern Test Theory.* Orlando, FL: Holt, Rinehart and Winston.

Cronbach, L. J. (1971) 'Test validation.' In Thorndike, R. L. (ed.) *Educational Measurement.* Washington, DC: American Council on Education, 443–507.

Cronbach, L. J. (1982) *Designing Evaluations of Educational and Social Programs.* San Francisco: Jossey-Bass.

Cronbach, L. J. (1984) *Essentials of Psychological Testing,* 4th ed. New York: Harper and Row.

Cronbach, L. J. (1988) 'Five perspectives on validity argument.' In Wainter, H. (ed.) *Test Validity.* Hillsdale, NJ: Erlbaum, 3–17.

Cronbach, L. J. (1989) 'Construct validation after thirty years.' In R.E. Linn (ed.) *Intelligence: measurement, theory, and public policy.* Urbana, IL: Univesity of Illinois Press, 147–171.

Cronbach, L. J. and Meehl, P. E. (1955) 'Construct validity in psychological tests.' *Psychological Bulletin* 52, 281–302.

Cronbach, L. J., Gleser, G. C., Nanda, H. and Rajaratnam, N. (1972) *The Dependability of Behavioral Measurements: Theory of Generalizability for Scores and Profiles.* New York: Wiley.

Cumming, A. (1996). 'The concept of validation in language testing.' In Cumming, A. and Berwick, R. (eds) *Validation in Language Testing.* Clevedon: Multilingual Matters, 1–44.

Cumming, A., Kantor, R., Powers, D., Santos, T. and Taylor, C. (2000) *TOEFL 2000 Writing Framework: A Working Paper.* TOEFL Monograph Series MS-18. Princeton, NJ: Educational Testing Service.

Cumming, A., Grant, L., Mulcahy-Ernt, P. and Powers, D. E. (2005) *A Teacher-Verification Study of Speaking and Writing Prototype Tasks for a New TOEFL.* TOEFL Monograph Series MS-26. Princeton, NJ: Educational Testing Service.

Cummins, J. (1984) *Bilingualism and Special Education: Issues in Assessment and Pedagogy.* Clevedon: Multilingual Matters.

Darling-Hammond, L. (1994) 'Performance-based assessment and educational equity.' *Harvard Educational Review* 64, 1, 5–30.

Davidson, F. (1994) 'The interlanguage metaphor and language assessment.' *World Englishes* 13, 3, 377–386.

Davidson, F. (1996) *Principles of Statistical Data Handling.* Thousand Oaks, CA: Sage.

Davidson, F. (2004) 'The identity of language testing.' *Language Assessment Quarterly* 1, 1, 85–88.

Davidson, F. (2006) 'World Englishes and test construction.' In Kachru, B., Kachru, Y. and Nelson, C. (eds) *The Handbook of World Englishes.* Malden, MA: Blackwell, 709–717.

Davidson, F. and Bachman, L. F. (1990) 'The Cambridge–TOEFL Comparability Study: an example of the cross-national comparison of language tests.' *AILA Review* 7, 24–45.

Davidson, F. and Lynch, B. K. (2002) *Testcraft: A Teacher's Guide to Writing and Using Language Test Specifications.* New Haven, CT: Yale University Press.

Davidson, F., Alderson, J. C., Douglas, D., Huhta, A., Turner, C. and Wylie, E. (1995) *Report of the Task Force on Testing Standards to the International Language Testing Association.* International Language Testing Association. Available on-line: http://www.iltaonline.com/tfts_report.pdf.

Davidson, F., Turner, C. E. and Huhta, A. (1997) 'Language testing standards.' In Clapham,

C. and Corson, D. (eds) *Encyclopedia of Language and Education*, vol. 7: *Language Testing and Assessment*. Amsterdam: Kluwer Academic Publishers, 303–312.

Davies, A. (1975) 'Two tests of speeded reading.' In Jones, R. L. and Spolsky, B. (eds) *Testing Language Proficiency*. Arlington, VA: Center for Applied Linguistics.

Davies, A. (1990) *Principles of Language Testing*. Oxford: Blackwell.

Davies, A. (1991) *The Native Speaker in Applied Linguistics*. Edinburgh: Edinburgh University Press.

Davies, A. (1997a) 'Introduction: the limits of ethics in language testing.' *Language Testing* 14, 3, 235–241.

Davies, A. (1997b) 'Demands of being professional in language testing.' *Language Testing* 14, 3, 328–339.

Davies, A. (1997c) 'Australian immigrant gatekeeping through English language tests: how important is proficiency?' In Huhta, A., Kohonen, V., Kurki-Suonio, L. and Luoma, S. (eds) *Current Developments and Alternatives in Language Assessment*. Jyväskylä: University of Jyväskylä, 71–84.

Davies, A. (2004) 'Introduction: language testing and the golden rule.' *Language Assessment Quarterly* 1, 2&3, 97–108.

Davies, A., Brown, A., Edler, C., Hill, K., Lumley, T. and McNamara, T. (1999) *Dictionary of Language Testing*. Studies in Language Testing 7. Cambridge: Cambridge University Press.

De Waal, C. (2005) *On Pragmatism*. Belmont, CA: Thomson Wadsworth.

Dewey, J. (1888) 'The ethics of democracy.' In Menand, L. (Ed.) *Pragmatism: A Reader*. New York: Vintage Books, 182–204.

Dewey, J. (1938) *Logic: The Theory of Inquiry*. New York: Henry Holt.

Dewey, J. (1981–91) *The Later Works*, 17 vols. Carbondale: Southern Illinois University Press.

Douglas, D. (2000) *Assessing Languages for Specific Purposes*. Cambridge: Cambridge University Press.

Edgeworth, F. Y. (1888) 'The statistics of examinations.' *Journal of the Royal Statistical Society* 51, 599–635.

Edgeworth, F. Y. (1890) 'The element of chance in competitive examinations.' *Journal of the Royal Statistical Society* 53, 644–663.

Educational Testing Service (2002) *ETS Standards for Quality and Fairness*. Princeton, NJ: Educational Testing Service.

Educational Testing Service (2005) *TOEFL iBT Tips: How to Prepare for the Next Generation TOEFL Test*. Princeton, NJ: Educational Testing Service.

Elatia, S. (2003) 'History of the baccalaureat: a study of the interaction between educational legislation, government policy, and language theory in the national language examination.' Unpublished PhD thesis, University of Illinois at Urbana-Champaign.

Elder, C. (1993) 'How do subject specialists construe classroom language proficiency?' *Language Testing* 10, 233–254.

Elman, B. A. (2000) *A Cultural History of Civil Examinations in Late Imperial China*. Los Angeles: California University Press.

Ely, C. (1986) 'An analysis of discomfort, risk taking, sociability, and motivation in the L2 classroom.' *Language Learning* 36, 1–25.

Embretson, S. (1983) 'Construct validity: construct representation versus nomothetic span.' *Psychological Bulletin* 93, 179–197.

Ennis, R. H. (1999) 'Test reliability: a practical exemplification of ordinary language philosophy.' *Philosophy of Education Yearbook*. Urbana-Champaign, IL: Philosophy of Education Society. Available on-line: http://www.ed.uiuc.edu/EPS/PES-yearbook/1999/ennis_body.asp). Retrieved 14 February 2006.

Enright, M. and Cline, F. (2002) 'Evaluating new task types for TOEFL: relationship between skills.' Paper presented at the annual meeting of Teachers of English to Speakers of Other Languages, Salt Lake City, UT.

Enright, M., Grabe, W., Koda, K., Mosenthal, P., Mulcahy-Ernt, P. and Schedl, M. (2000) *TOEFL 2000 Reading Framework: A Working Paper.* TOEFL Monograph Series MS-17. Princeton, NJ: Educational Testing Service.

Epp, L. and Stawychny, M. (2001) 'Using the Canadian Language Benchmarks (CLB) to benchmark college programs/courses and language proficiency tests.' *TESL Canada Journal* 18, 2, 32–47.

Feldt, L. S. and Brennan, R. L. (1989) 'Reliability.' In R. L. Linn (ed.) *Educational Measurement.* New York: American Council on Education/Macmillan, 105–146.

Fish, S. (1995) 'What makes an interpretation acceptable?' In Goodman, R. B. (ed.) *Pragmatism.* New York and London: Routledge.

Foucault, M. (1975) *Discipline and Punish: The Birth of the Prison.* New York: Vintage.

Fradd, S. H. and McGee, P. L. (1994) *Instructional Assessment: An Integrative Approach to Evaluating Student Performance.* New York: Addison-Wesley.

Fransson, A. (1984) 'Cramming or understanding? Effects of intrinsic and extrinsic motivation on approach to learning and test performance.' In Alderson, J. C. and Urquhart, A. H. (eds) *Reading in a Foreign Language.* London: Longman.

Frederiksen, J. R. and Collins, A. (1989) 'A systems approach to educational testing.' *Educational Researcher* 18, 9, 27–32.

Freedman, S. (1991) *Evaluating Writing: Linking Large-Scale Testing and Classroom Assessment.* Occasional Paper 27. University of California, Berkeley: Center for the Study of Writing.

Fulcher, G. (1991) 'The role of assessment by teachers in schools.' In Caudery, T. (ed.) *New Thinking in TEFL.* The Dolphin Series No. 21. Aarhus: Aarhus University Press, 138–158.

Fulcher, G. (1995) 'Variable competence in second language acquisition: a problem for research methodology?' *System* 23, 1, 25–33.

Fulcher, G. (1996) 'Does thick description lead to smart tests? A data-based approach to rating scale construction.' *Language Testing* 13, 2, 208–238.

Fulcher, G. (1997) 'The testing of speaking.' In Clapham, C. and Corson, D. (eds) *Language Testing and Assessment.* Encyclopedia of Language and Education, vol. 7. Dordrecht: Kluwer Academic Publishers, 75–86.

Fulcher, G. (1998) 'Widdowson's model of communicative competence and the testing of reading: an exploratory study.' *System* 26, 281–302.

Fulcher, G. (1999a) 'Assessment in English for academic purposes: putting content validity in its place.' *Applied Linguistics* 20, 2, 221–236.

Fulcher, G. (1999b) 'Ethics in language testing.' *TAE SIG Newsletter* 1, 1, 1–4.

Fulcher, G. (2000a) 'The "communicative" legacy in language testing.' *System* 28, 4, 483–497.

Fulcher, G. (2000b) 'Computers in language testing.' In Brett, P. and Motteram, G. (eds) *A Special Interest in Computers: Learning and Teaching with Information and Communications Technologies.* Manchester: IATEFL Publications, 93–107.

Fulcher, G. (2003a) *Testing Second Language Speaking.* London: Longman/Pearson Education.

Fulcher, G. (2003b) 'Interface design in computer based language testing.' *Language Testing* 20, 4, 384–408.

Fulcher, G. (2003c) 'Few ills cured by setting scores.' *Education Guardian,* 17 April. Retrieved 5 March 2006: http://education.guardian.co.uk/tefl/story/0,5500,937988,00.html.

Fulcher, G. (2004) 'Deluded by artifices? The Common European Framework and harmonization.' *Language Assessment Quarterly* 1, 4, 253–266.

Fulcher, G. (2005) 'Better communications test will silence critics.' *Guardian Weekly,*

18 November. Available on-line: http://education.guardian.co.uk/tefl/story/0,5500, 1645011,00.html.

Fulcher, G. (2007) 'Criteria for evaluating language quality.' In Shohamy, E. (ed.) *Language Testing and Assessment*. Encyclopedia of Language and Education, vol. 7. Amsterdam: Springer.

Fulcher, G. and Bamford, R (1996) 'I didn't get the grade I need. Where's my solicitor?' *System* 24, 4, 437–448.

Fulcher, G. and Márquez Reiter, R. (2003) 'Task difficulty in speaking tests.' *Language Testing*, 20, 3, 321–344.

Galton, F. (1874) *English Men of Science: Their Nature and Nurture*. London: Macmillan.

Gass, S. M. and Mackey, A. (2000) *Simulated Recall Methodology in Second Language Research*. Mahwah, NJ: Erlbaum.

Gee, S. (1997) 'Teaching writing: a genre-based approach.' In Fulcher, G. (ed.) *Writing in the English Language Classroom*. London: Prentice Hall and The British Council, 24–40.

Genesee, F. and Upshur, J. A. (1996) *Classroom-Based Evaluation in Second Language Education*. Cambridge: Cambridge University Press.

Ginther, A. (2001) *Effects of the Presence and Absence of Visuals on Performance on TOEFLCBT Listening-comprehensive Stimuli*. TOEFL Research Rep. No. 66. Princeton, NJ: ETS.

Gipps, C. (1994) *Beyond Testing: Towards a Theory of Educational Assessment*. London: Falmer Press.

Goddard, H. H. (1914) *Feeble-mindedness: Its Causes and Consequences*. New York: Macmillan.

Goddard, H. H. (1919) *Psychology of the Normal and the Subnormal*. London: Routledge. Reprinted 1999, London: Routledge.

Gould, S. J. (1996) *The Mismeasure of Man: Revised and Expanded*. London: Penguin.

Grabe, W. (1999) 'Developments in reading research and their implications for computer-adaptive reading assessment.' In Chalhoub-Deville, M. (ed.) *Issues in Computer-adaptive Testing of Reading Proficiency*. Studies in Language Testing 10. Cambridge: Cambridge University Press, 11–47.

Grant, L. (1997) 'Testing the language proficiency of bilingual teachers: Arizona's Spanish proficiency test.' *Language Testing* 14, 1, 23–46.

Green, A. (1998) *Verbal Protocol Analysis in Language Testing Research*. Cambridge: Cambridge University Press.

Guion, R. M. (1974) 'Open a window: validities and values in psychological measurement.' *American Psychologist* 29, 287–296.

Gullikwen, H. (1950) 'Intrinsic validity.' *American Psychologist* 5, 511–517.

Hacking, I. (1990) *The Taming of Chance*. Cambridge: Cambridge University Press.

Haertel, E. H. (1999) 'Validity arguments for high-stakes testing: in search of the evidence.' *Educational Measurement: Issues and Practice* 18, 4, 5–9.

Halliday, M. A. K. (1973) 'Relevant models of language.' In Halliday, M. A. K. *Explorations in the Functions of Language*. New York: Elsevier North-Holland.

Halliday, M. A. K. and Hasan, R. (1976) *Cohesion in English*. London: Longman.

Hambleton, R. K. (1989) 'Principles and selected applications of item response theory.' In Linn, R. L. (ed.) *Educational Measurement*. New York: American Council on Education/Macmillan, 147–200.

Hamp-Lyons, L. (1991) 'Scoring procedures for ESL contexts.' In Hamp-Lyons, L. (ed.) *Assessing Second Language Writing in Academic Contexts*. Norwood, NJ: Ablex, 241–276.

Hamp-Lyons, L. (1997a) 'Ethics in language testing.' In Clapham, C. and Corson, D. (eds)

Encyclopedia of Language and Education, vol. 7: *Language Testing and Assessment.* Dordrecht: Kluwer Academic Publishers, 323–333.

Hamp-Lyons, L. (1997b) 'Washback, impact and validity: ethical concerns.' *Language Testing* 14, 3, 295–303.

Hamp-Lyons, L. (2000a) 'Social, professional and individual responsibility in language testing.' *System* 28, 4, 579–591.

Hamp-Lyons, L. (2000b) 'Fairnesses in language testing.' In Kunnan, A. J. (ed.) *Fairness and Validation in Language Assessment.* Studies in Language Testing 9. Cambridge: Cambridge University Press, 30–34.

Hamp-Lyons, L. (2001) 'Ethics, fairness(es) and developments in language testing.' In Elder, C., Brown, A., Grove, E., Hill, K., Iwashita, N., Lumley, T., McNamara, T. and O'Loughlin, K. (eds) *Experimenting with Uncertainty: Essays in Honour of Alan Davies.* Studies in Language Testing 11. Cambridge: Cambridge University Press, 222–227.

Hamp-Lyons, L. and Kroll, B. (1997). *TOEFL 2000–Writing: Composition, Community, and Assessment.* TOEFL Monograph Series, Rep. No. 5. Princeton, NJ: ETS.

Hansen, E. G., Mislevy, R. J., Steinberg, L. S., Lee, M. J. and Forer, D. C. (2005) 'Accessibility of tests for individuals with disabilities within a validity framework.' *System* 33, 107–133.

Harris, D. and Bell, C. (1986) *Evaluating and Assessing for Learning.* London: Kogan Page.

Hawthorne, L. (1997) 'The political dimension of English language testing in Australia.' *Language Testing* 14, 3, 248–260.

He, A. W. and Young, R. (1998) 'Language proficiency interviews: a discourse approach.' In Young, R. and He, A. W. (eds) *Talking and Testing: Discourse Approaches to the Assessment of Oral Proficiency.* Amsterdam: John Benjamins, 1–24.

Henning, G. (1987) *A Guide to Language Testing: Development, Evaluation, Research.* Cambridge, MA: Newbury House.

Heritage, J. (1995) 'Conversation analysis: methodological aspects.' In Quasthoff, U. M. (ed.) *Aspects of Oral Communication.* Berlin: Walter de Gruyter, 391–417.

Heritage, J. C. and Watson, D. R. (1979) 'Formulations as conversational objects.' In Psathas, G. (ed.) *Everyday Language: Studies in Ethnomethodology.* New York: Irvington, 123–62.

Hill, C. and Parry, K. (1994a) 'Models of literacy: the nature of reading tests.' In Hill, C. and Parry, K. (eds) *From Testing to Assessment: English as an International Language.* London: Longman, 7–34.

Hill, C. and Parry, K. (1994b) 'Assessing English language and literacy around the world.' In Hill, C. and Parry, K. (eds) *From Testing to Assessment: English as an International Language.* London: Longman, 253–271.

Holland, P. W. and Rubin, D. B. (1982) *Test Equating.* San Diego, CA: Academic Press.

Holmes, O. W. (1919) 'Abrams v. United States.' In Menand, L. (ed.) (1997) *Pragmatism: A Reader.* New York: Vintage Books.

Homan, R. (1991) *The Ethics of Social Research.* London: Longman.

Hood, S. and Parker, L. (1991) 'Minorities, teacher testing, and recent U.S. Supreme Court holdings: a regressive step.' *Teachers College Record* 92, 4, 603–618.

House, E. R. (1980) *Evaluating with Validity.* Beverly Hills, CA: Sage.

House, E. R. (1990) 'Ethics of evaluation studies.' In Walberg, H. J. and Haertel, G. C. (eds) *The International Encyclopedia of Educational Evaluation.* Oxford: Pergamon Press, 91–94.

Hughes, A. (1989) *Testing for Language Teachers*, 1st ed. Cambridge: Cambridge University Press.

Hughes, A. (2003) *Testing for Language Teachers*, 2nd ed. Cambridge: Cambridge University Press.

Hughes, A., Porter, D. and Weir, C. (eds) (1988) *ELTS Validation Project: Proceedings of a Conference Held to Consider the ELTS Validation Project Report: Research Report 1(ii).*

Cambridge: British Council and the University of Cambridge Local Examinations Syndicate.

Hymes, D. (1967) 'Models of the interaction of language and social setting.' In Macnamara, J. (ed.) 'Problems of bilingualism.' *Journal of Social Issues* 23, 8–28.

Hymes, D. (1968) 'The ethnography of speaking.' In Fishman, J. (ed.) *Readings in the Sociology of Language*. The Hague: Mouton.

Hymes, D. (1972) 'On communicative competence.' In Pride, J. B. and Holmes, J. (eds) *Sociolinguistics: Selected Readings*. Harmondsworth: Penguin, 269–293.

ILTA (2000) *Code of Ethics*. International Language Testing Association. Available on-line: http://www.iltaonline.com/code.pdf.

Jacoby, S. and McNamara, T. (1999) 'Locating competence.' *English for Specific Purposes*, 18, 3, 213–241.

Jacoby, S. and Ochs, E. (1995) 'Co-construction: an introduction.' *Research on Language and Social Interaction* 28, 3, 171–183.

James, W. (1907) *Pragmatism*. In Gunn, G. (ed.) (2000) *Pragmatism and Other Writings by William James*. London: Penguin.

Jamieson, J., Jones, S., Kirsch, I., Mosenthal, P. and Taylor, C. (2000) *TOEFL 2000 Framework: A Working Paper*. TOEFL Monograph Series, Rep. No. 16. Princeton, NJ: ETS.

Johnson, D. M. (1993) *Approaches to Research in Second Language Learning*. London: Longman.

Johnson, K. and Morrow, K. (1978) *Communicate: The English of Social Interaction*. Reading: Centre for Applied Language Studies, University of Reading.

Jones, R. L. (1977) 'Testing: a vital connection.' In Philips, J. K. (ed.) *The Language Connection: From the Classroom to the World*. Skokie, IL: National Textbook Company.

Jonsen, A. R. and Toulmin, S. (1988) *The Abuse of Casuistry: A History of Moral Reasoning*. Berkeley: University of California Press.

Kane, M. T. (1982) 'A sampling model for validity.' *Applied Psychological Measurement* 6, 125–160.

Kane, M. T. (1992) 'An argument-based approach to validity.' *Psychological Bulletin* 112, 3, 527–535.

Kane, M. T. (2001) 'Current concerns in validity theory.' *Journal of Educational Measurement* 38, 4, 319–342.

Kane, M. T. (2002) 'Validating high stakes testing programs.' *Educational Measurement: Issues and Practice* 21, 1, 31–41.

Kane, M. T., Crooks, T. and Cohen, A. (1999) 'Validating measures of performance.' *Educational Measurement: Issues and Practice* 18, 2, 5–17.

Kant, I. (1785) *Groundwork of the Metaphysic of Morals*. Trans. Patron, J. (1972) *The Moral Law*. London: Hutchinson.

Kasper, G. and Kellerman, E. (1997) *Communication Strategies: Psycholinguistic and Sociolinguistic Perspectives*. London: Longman.

Kaulfers, W. V. (1944) 'War-time developments in modern language achievement tests.' *Modern Language Journal* 70, 4, 136–150.

Kehoe, J. (1995). 'Writing multiple-choice test items.' *Practical Assessment, Research & Evaluation*, 4, 9. Retrieved 4 January 2006 from http://PAREonline.net/getvn.asp?v=4&n=9.

Kerlinger, F. N. and Lee, H. B. (2000) *Foundations of Behavioral Research*, 4th ed. Orlando, FL: Harcourt Brace.

Kevles, D. J. (1995) *In the Name of Eugenics: Genetics and the Uses of Human Heredity*. Cambridge, MA: Harvard University Press.

Kim, J. T. (2006) 'The effectiveness of test-takers' participation in development of an innovative web-based speaking test for international teaching assistants at American colleges.' Unpublished PhD thesis: University of Illinois at Urbana-Champaign.

Kramsch, C. J. (1986) 'From language proficiency to interactional competence.' *Modern Language Journal* 70, 4, 366–372.

Kramsch, C. (1998) *Language and Culture.* Oxford: Oxford University Press.

Kuhn, T. S. (1970) *The Structure of Scientific Revolutions.* Chicago: University of Chicago Press.

Kunnan, A. (1998) 'Approaches to validation in language assessment.' In A. Kunnan (ed.) *Validation in Language Assessment.* Mahwah, NJ: Erlbaum, 1–18.

Kunnan, A. J. (2000) 'Fairness and justice for all.' In Kunnan, A. J. (ed.) *Fairness and Validation in Language Assessment.* Studies in Language Testing 9. Cambridge: Cambridge University Press, 1–14.

Lado, R. (1961) *Language Testing.* London: Longman.

Lantolf, J. P. and Frawley, W. (1985) 'Oral proficiency testing: a critical analysis.' *Modern Language Journal* 69, 4, 337–345.

Lantolf, J. P. and Frawley, W. (1988) 'Proficiency: understanding the construct.' *Studies in Second Language Acquisition* 10, 2, 181–195.

Lazaraton, A. (1996a) 'Interlocutor support in oral proficiency interviews: the case of CASE.' *Language Testing* 13, 151–172.

Lazaraton, A. (1996b) 'A qualitative approach to monitoring examiner conduct in the Cambridge Assessment of Spoken English (CASE).' In Milanovic, M. and Saville, N. (eds) *Performance testing, cognition and assessment: selected papers from the 15th Language Testing Research Colloquium.* Cambridge: Cambridge University Press, 18–33.

Lazaraton, A. (2002) *A Qualitative Approach to the Validation of Oral Language Tests.* Studies in Language Testing 14. Cambridge: Cambridge University Press.

Lewkowicz, J. A. (2000) 'Authenticity in language testing: some outstanding questions.' *Language Testing* 17, 1, 43–64.

Li, J. (2006) 'Introducing audit trails to the world of language testing.' Unpublished MA thesis: University of Illinois.

Linn, R., Baker, E. and Dunbar, S. (1991) 'Complex, performance-based assessment: expectations and validation criteria.' *Educational Researcher* 20, 8, 15–21.

Lord, F. M. (1980) *Applications of Item Response Theory to Practical Testing Problems.* Hillsdale, NJ: Erlbaum.

Lowe, P. (1986) 'Proficiency: panacea, framework, process? A reply to Kramsch, Schulz, and particularly Bachman and Savignon.' *Modern Language Journal* 70, 4, 391–397.

Lowe, P. (1987) 'Interagency language roundtable proficiency interview.' In Alderson, J. C., Krahnke, K. J. and Stansfield, C. W. (eds) *Reviews of English Language Proficiency Tests.* Washington, DC: TESOL, 43–47.

Lynch, B. (1997) 'In search of the ethical test.' *Language Testing* 14, 3, 315–327.

Lynch, B. (2001) 'The ethical potential of alternative language assessment.' In Elder, C., Brown, A., Grove, E., Hill, K., Iwashita, N., Lumley, T., McNamara, T. and O'Loughlin, K. (eds) *Experimenting with Uncertainty: Essays in Honour of Alan Davies.* Studies in Language Testing 11. Cambridge: Cambridge University Press, 228–239.

Lynch, B. and Davidson, F. (1997) 'Is my test valid?' Presentation at the 31st Annual TESOL Convention, Orlando, FL, March.

McDonough, S. (1981) *Psychology in Foreign Language Teaching.* Hemel Hempstead: Allen and Unwin.

McGroarty, M. (1984) 'Some meanings of communicative competence for second language students.' *TESOL Quarterly* 18, 257–272.

McNamara, T. F. (1996) *Measuring Second Language Performance.* London: Longman.

McNamara, T. F. (1997) '"Interaction" in second language performance assessment: whose performance?' *Applied Linguistics* 18, 4, 446–465.

McNamara, T. (2006) 'Validity in language testing: the challenge of Sam Messick's legacy.' *Language Assessment Quarterly* 3, 1, 31–51.

McNamara, T. F. and Lumley, T. (1997) 'The effect of interlocutor and assessment mode variables in overseas assessments of speaking skills in occupational setting.' *Language Testing* 14, 140–56.

Markee, N. (2000) *Conversational Analysis.* Mahwah, NJ: Erlbaum.

Menand, L. (2001) *The Metaphysical Club: A Story of Ideas in America.* New York: Farrar, Straus and Giroux.

Messick, S. (1975) 'The standard problem: meaning and values in measurement and evaluation.' *American Psychologist* 30, 955–966.

Messick, S. (1980) 'Test validity and the ethics of assessment.' *American Psychologist* 35, 1012–1027.

Messick, S. (1981) 'Evidence and ethics in the evaluation of tests.' *Educational Researcher* 10, 9–20.

Messick, S. (1988) 'The once and future issues of validity: assessing the meaning and consequences of measurement.' In Wainer, H. and Braun, H. (eds) *Test Validity.* Hillsdale, NJ: Erlbaum, 33–45.

Messick, S. (1989) 'Validity.' In Linn, R. L. (ed.) *Educational Measurement.* New York: Macmillan/American Council on Education, 13–103.

Messick, S. (1994) 'The interplay of evidence and consequences in the validation of performance assessments.' *Educational Researcher* 23, 2, 13–23.

Messick, S. (1996) 'Validity and washback in language testing.' *Language Testing* 13, 241–256.

Miles, M. and Huberman, A. (1994) *Qualitative Data Analysis: An Expanded Sourcebook,* 2nd ed. Thousand Oaks, CA: Sage Publications.

Mill, J. S. (1859) *On Liberty.* In Gray, J. (ed.) (1998) *John Stuart Mill's On Liberty and Other Essays.* Oxford: Oxford University Press.

Mislevy, R. J. (2003a) *On the Structure of Educational Assessments.* CSE Technical Report 597. Los Angeles: Center for the Study of Evaluation, CRESST.

Mislevy, R. J. (2003b) *Argument Substance and Argument Structure in Educational Assessment.* CSE Technical Report 605. Los Angeles: Center for the Study of Evaluation, CRESST.

Mislevy, R. J., Almond, R. G. and Lukas, J. F. (2003) *A Brief Introduction to Evidence-centered Design.* Research Report RR-03–16. Princeton, NJ: Educational Testing Service.

Mislevy, R. J., Steinberg, L. S. and Almond, R. G. (1999) *On the Roles of Task Model Variables in Assessment Design.* CSE Technical Report 500. Los Angeles: Center for the Study of Evaluation, CRESST.

Morris, B. (1972) *Objectives and Perspectives in Education: Studies in Educational Theories.* London: Routledge and Kegan Paul.

Morrow, K. E. (1977) *Techniques of Evaluation for a Notional Syllabus.* Reading: Centre for Applied Language Studies, University of Reading (study commissioned by the Royal Society of Arts).

Morrow, K. (1979) 'Communicative language testing: revolution or evolution?' In Brumfit, C. K. and Johnson, K. (eds) *The Communicative Approach to Language Teaching.* Oxford: Oxford University Press, 143–159.

Morrow, K. (1986) 'The evaluation of tests of communicative performance?' In Portal, M. (ed.) *Innovations in Language Testing.* London: NFER/Nelson.

Morton, J., Wigglesworth, G. and Williams, D. (1997) 'Approaches to the evaluation of interviewer performance in oral interaction tests.' In Brindley, G. and Wigglesworth, G.

(eds) *Access: Issues in English Language Test Design and Delivery.* Sydney: National Centre for English Language Teaching and Research, 175–196.

Moss, P. (1992) 'Shifting conceptions of validity in educational measurement: implications for performance assessment.' *Review of Educational Research*, 62, 3, 229–258.

Moss, P. (1994) 'Can there be validity without reliability?' *Educational Researcher* 23, 2, 5–12.

Moss, P. (1995) 'Themes and variations in validity theory.' *Educational Measurement: Issues and Practice* 14, 2, 5–13.

Moss, P. (2003) 'Reconceptualizing validity for classroom assessment.' *Educational Measurement: Issues and Practice* 22, 4, 13–25.

Munby, J. (1978) *Communicative Syllabus Design.* Cambridge: Cambridge University Press.

Nedelsky, L. (1965) *Science Teaching and Testing.* New York: Harcourt, Brace and World.

Nietzsche, F. (1887) *On the Genealogy of Morals.* Trans. Kaufmann, W. and Hollingdale, R. J. (1969). New York: Random House.

Nietzsche, F. (1906) *The Will to Power.* Trans. Kaufmann, W. and Hollingdale, R. J. (1968). New York: Random House.

North, B. (1994) *Scales of Language Proficiency: A Survey of Some Existing Systems.* Strasbourg: Council of Europe, Council for Cultural Cooperation, CC-LANG(94)24.

North, B. (1995) 'The development of a common framework scale of descriptors of language proficiency based on a theory of measurement.' *System* 23, 4, 445–465.

North, B. (2000) *The Development of a Common Framework Scale of Language Proficiency.* Oxford: Peter Lang.

North, B., Figueras, N., Takala, S., Van Avermaet, P. and Verhelst, N. (2003) *Relating Language Examinations to the Common European Framework of Reference for Languages: Learning, Teaching, Assessment (CEF).* Strasbourg: Council of Europe. Document: DGIV/EDU/LANG 5 rev.1. Available on-line: http://www.coe.int/T/DG4/Portfolio/?L=E&M=/documents_intro/Manual.html.

Norton, B. (1997) 'Accountability in language assessment.' In Clapham, C. and Corson, D. (eds) *Encyclopedia of Language and Education*, vol. 7: *Language Testing and Assessment.* Dordrecht: Kluwer Academic Publishers, 313–322.

Ockenden, M. (1972) *Situational Dialogues.* London: Longman.

O'Laughlin, K. (2001) *The Equivalence of Direct and Semi-direct Speaking Tests.* Studies in Language Testing 13. Cambridge: Cambridge University Press.

Oller, J. W. (1976) 'Language testing.' In Wardhaugh, R. and Brown, H. D. (eds) *A Survey of Applied Linguistics.* Ann Arbor: University of Michigan Press.

Oller, J. W. (1979) *Language Tests at School.* London: Longman.

Oller, J. W. (1983a) 'A consensus for the 80s.' In Oller, J. W. (ed.) *Issues in Language Testing Research.* Rowley, MA: Newbury House, 351–356.

Oller, J. W. (1983b) 'Response to Vollmer: "g", what is it?' In Hughes, A. and Porter, D. (eds) *Current Developments in Language Testing.* London: Academic Press, 35–37.

Oller, J. W. and Hinofotis, F. (1980) 'Two mutually exclusive hypotheses about second language ability: indivisible or partially divisible competence.' In Oller, J. W. and Perkins, K. (eds) *Research in Language Testing.* Rowley, MA: Newbury House, 13–23.

O'Sullivan, B., Weir, C. and Saville, N. (2002) 'Using observation checklists to validate speaking test tasks.' *Language Testing* 19, 1, 33–56.

Oxford Dictionary of Business (1996). Oxford: Oxford University Press.

Palmer, A. S. (1978) 'Measures of achievement, communication, incorporation, and integration of two classes of formal EFL learners.' Paper read at the 5th AILA Congress, Montreal, August. Mimeo.

Parkhurst, H. (1922) *Education on the Dalton Plan.* New York: E. P. Dutton.

Pearson, K. (1914) *The Life, Letters and Labours of Francis Galton*, vol. 2. Cambridge: Cambridge University Press.

Pearson, I. (1988) 'Tests as levers for change.' In Chamberlain, D. and Baumgardner, R. (eds) *ESP in the Classroom: Practice and Evaluation*. ELT Document 128. London: Modern English Publications.

Peirce, C. S. (undated) *Lecture I of a Planned Course*, MS 857: 4–5. Available on-line: http://www.helsinki.fi/science/commens/terms/abduction.html.

Peirce, C. S. (1877) 'The fixation of belief.' In Moore, E. C. (ed.) (1998) *The Essential Writings of Charles S. Peirce*. New York: Prometheus Books.

Peirce, C. S. (1878) 'How to make our ideas clear.' In Moore, E. C. (ed.) (1988) *The Essential Writings of Charles S. Peirce*. New York: Prometheus Books.

Pellegrino, J. W. (1988) 'Mental models and mental tests.' In Wainer, H. and Braun, H. (eds) *Test Validity*. Hillsdale, NJ: Erlbaum, 49–59.

Pennycook, A. (1994) *The Cultural Politics of English as an International Language*. Harlow: Longman/Pearson Education.

Perelman, C. and Olbrechts-Tyteca, L. (1969) *The New Rhetoric: A Treasure on Argumentation*. Notre Dame, IN: University of Notre Dame.

Philips, S. E. (1991) 'Diploma sanction tests revisited: new problems from old solutions.' *Journal of Law and Education* 20, 2, 175–199.

Pica, T., Kanagy, R. and Falodun, J. (1993) 'Choosing and using communication tasks for second language instruction and research.' In Crookes, G. and Gass, S. M. (eds) *Tasks and Language Learning: Integrating Theory and Practice*. Cleveland: Multilingual Matters, 9–34.

Plato. *Theaetetus*. Trans. Cornford, F. M. in Hamilton, E. and Cairns, H. (eds) (1975) *The Collected Dialogues of Plato*. New York: Pantheon Books, 845–919.

Popham, W. J. (1978) *Criterion Referenced Measurement*. Englewood Cliffs, NJ: Prentice Hall.

Popper, K. (1959) *The Logic of Scientific Discovery*. London: Hutchinson.

Powers, D. E. and Fowles, M. E. (1997) *Effects of Disclosing Essay Topics for a New GRE Writing Test*. GRE Board Research Report No. 93-26aR. ETS Research Report 96-26. Princeton, NJ: Educational Testing Service.

Powers, D. E., Albertson, W., Florek, T., Johnson, K., Malak, J., Nemceff, B., Porzuc, M., Silvester, D., Wang, M., Weston, R., Winner, E. and Zelazny, A. (2002) *Influence of Irrelevant Speech on Standardized Test Performance*. TOEFL Research Report 68. Princeton, NJ: Educational Testing Service.

Putnam, H. (1990) 'A reconsideration of Deweyan democracy.' *Southern Californian Law Review* 63, 1671–1697. Reprinted in Goodman, R. B. (ed.) (1995) *Pragmatism: A Contemporary Reader*. London: Routledge, 183–204.

Raimes, A. (1990). 'The TOEFL test of written English: causes for concern.' *TESOL Quarterly* 24, 3, 427–442.

Reed, D. J. and Halleck, G. B. (1997) 'Probing above the ceiling in oral interviews: what's up there?' In Kohonen, V., Huhta, A., Kurki-Suonio, L. and Luoma, S. (eds) *Current Developments and Alternatives in Language Assessment: Proceedings of LTRC 96*. Jyväskylä: University of Jyväskylä and University of Tampere, 225–238.

Roach, J. O. (1945) *Some Problems of Oral Examinations in Modern Languages. An Experimental Approach Based on the Cambridge Examinations in English for Foreign Students*. University of Cambridge Examinations Syndicate: Internal report circulated to oral examiners and local representatives for these examinations.

Roden, C. (ed.) (2000) *The Memoirs of Sherlock Holmes by Arthur Conan Doyle*. Oxford: Oxford University Press.

Rorty, R. (1999) *Philosophy and Social Hope*. London: Penguin.

Rosenfeld, M., Leung, S. and Oltman, P. (2001) *The Reading, Writing, Speaking, and Listening Tasks Important for Academic Success at the Undergraduate and Graduate Levels.* TOEFL Monograph Rep. No. 21. Princeton, NJ: ETS.

Ross, S. (1992) 'Accommodative questions in oral proficiency interviews.' *Language Testing* 9, 2, 173–86.

Ross, S. (1996) 'Formulae and inter-interviewer variation in oral proficiency interview discourse.' *Prospect* 11, 3–16.

Ross, S. and Berwick, R. (1992) 'The discourse of accommodation in oral proficiency interviews.' *Studies in Second Language Acquisition* 14, 159–176.

Ruch, G. M. (1924) *The Improvement of the Written Examination.* Chicago: Scott, Foresman and Company.

Savignon, S. J. (1972) *Communicative Competence: An Experiment in Foreign-language Teaching.* Philadelphia: Center for Curriculum Development.

Schegloff, E. A. (1982) 'Discourse as an interactional achievement: some uses of "uh huh" and other things that come between sentences.' In Tannen, D. (ed.) *Analyzing Discourse: Text and Talk.* Washington, DC: Georgetown University Press, 71–93.

Scollon, S. (1999) 'Confucian and Socratic discourse in the tertiary classroom.' In Hinkel, E. (ed.) *Culture in Second Language Teaching and Learning.* Cambridge: Cambridge University Press.

Scriven, M. (1991) *Evaluation Thesaurus,* 4th ed. Newbury Park, CA: Sage.

Shavelson, R. J., Eisner, E. W. and Olkin, I. (2002) 'In memory of Lee J. Cronbach (1916–2001).' *Educational Measurement: Issues and Practice* 21, 2, 5–7.

Shepard, L. A. (2003) 'Commentary: intermediate steps to knowing what students know.' *Measurement: Interdisciplinary Research and Perspectives* 1, 2, 171–177.

Shohamy, E. (1994) 'The validity of direct versus semi-direct oral tests.' *Language Testing* 11, 2, 99–123.

Shohamy, E. (2000) 'Fairness in language testing.' In Kunnan, A. J. (ed.) *Fairness and Validation in Language Assessment.* Studies in Language Testing 9. Cambridge: Cambridge University Press, 15–19.

Shohamy, E. (2001) *The Power of Tests: A Critical Perspective on the Uses of Language Tests.* London: Longman.

Smith, J. K. (2003) 'Reconsidering reliability in classroom assessment and grading.' *Educational Measurement: Issues and Practice* 22, 4, 26–33.

Snow, R. E. and Lohman, D. E. (1984) 'Toward a theory of cognitive aptitude for learning from instruction.' *Journal of Educational Psychology* 76, 347–376.

Snow, R. E. and Lohman, D. E. (1989) 'Implications of cognitive psychology for educational measurement.' In Linn, R. L. (ed.) *Educational Measurement.* New York: American Council on Education/Macmillan, 263–331.

Sowden, C. (2005) 'Plagiarism and the culture of multilingual students in higher education abroad.' *ELT Journal* 59, 3, 226–233.

Spence-Brown, R. (2001) 'The eye of the beholder: authenticity in an embedded assessment task.' *Language Testing* 18, 463–481.

Spolsky, B. (1985) 'The limits of authenticity in language testing.' *Language Testing* 2, 31–40.

Spolsky, B. (1995) *Measured Words.* Oxford: Oxford University Press.

Spolsky, B. (1997) 'The ethics of gatekeeping tests: what have we learned in a hundred years?' *Language Testing* 14, 3, 242–247.

Stansfield, C. W. (1993) 'Ethics, standards and professionalism in language testing.' *Issues in Applied Linguistics* 4, 2, 189–206.

Stansfield, C. W. and Kenyon, D. (1992) 'Research on the comparability of the oral proficiency interview and the simulated oral proficiency interview.' *System* 20, 347–364.

Stansfield, C. W. and Kenyon, D. (1996) 'Comparing the scaling of speaking tasks by language teachers and by the ACTFL guidelines.' In Cumming, A. and Berwick, R. (eds) *Validation in Language Testing*. Clevedon: Multilingual Matters, 124–153.

Stendhal (1975) *Love*. London: Penguin Classics.

Stern, H. H. (1978) 'The formal–functional distinction in language pedagogy: a conceptual clarification'. Paper read at the 5th AILA Congress, Montreal, August. Mimeo.

Sternberg, R. J. (1985) *Human Abilities: An Information Processing Approach*. New York: W. H. Freeman.

Swain, M. (1985) 'Large-scale communicative testing.' In Lee, Y. P., Fok, C. Y. Y., Lord, R. and Low, G. (eds) *New Directions in Language Testing*. Hong Kong: Pergamon Press.

Swender, E. (1999) *ACTFL Oral Proficiency Interview Tester Training Manual*. Yonkers, NY: ACTFL.

Swender, E. (2003) 'Oral proficiency testing in the real world: answers to frequently asked questions.' *Foreign Language Annals* 36, 4, 520–526.

Tarone, E. (1998) 'Research on interlanguage variation: implications for language testing.' In Bachman, L. F. and Cohen, A. D. (eds) *Interfaces between Second Language Acquisition and Language Testing Research*. Cambridge: Cambridge University Press, 71–89.

Taylor, C. S. and Nolen, S. B. (1996) 'What does the psychometrician's classroom look like? Reframing assessment concepts in the context of learning.' *Educational Policy Analysis Archives* 4, 17.

Taylor, C., Jamieson, J., Eignor, D. and Kirsch, I. (1998) *The Relationship between Computer Familiarity and Performance on Computer-Based TOEFL Test Tasks*. Princeton, NJ: Educational Testing Service.

Thompson, B. (2000) 'A suggested revision to the forthcoming 5th edition of the APA Publication Manual.' Retrieved September 5, 2002, from http://www.coe.tamu.edu/~bthompson/apaeffec.htm

Thrasher, R. (2004) 'The role of a language testing code of ethics in the establishment of a code of practice.' *Language Assessment Quarterly* 1, 2&3, 151–160.

Toulmin, S. (1972) *Human Understanding*, vol. 1: *The Collective Use and Evolution of Concepts*. Princeton, NJ: Princeton University Press.

Toulmin, S. (2003) *The Uses of Argument*, 2nd ed. Cambridge: Cambridge University Press.

Toulmin, S., Rieke, R. and Janik, A. (1979) *An Introduction to Reasoning*. New York: Macmillan.

Underhill, N. (1982) 'The great reliability validity trade-off: problems in assessing the productive skills.' In Heaton, J. B. (ed.) *Language Testing*. London: Modern English Publications, 17–23.

Underhill, N. (1987) *Testing Spoken Language*. Cambridge: Cambridge University Press.

Upshur, J. and Turner, C. (1995) 'Constructing rating scales for second language tests.' *English Language Teaching Journal* 49, 1, 3–12.

Van Avermaet, P., Kuijper, H. and Saville, N. (2004) 'A code of practice and quality management system for international language examinations.' *Language Assessment Quarterly* 1, 2&3, 137–150.

Van Ek, J. A. (1976) *Significance of the Threshold Level in the Early Teaching of Modern Languages*. Strasbourg: Council of Europe.

Vernon, P. E. (1956) *The Measurement of Abilities*, 2nd ed. London: University of London Press.

Vollmer, H. J. and Sang, F. (1983) 'Competing hypotheses about a second language ability:

a plea for caution.' In Oller, J. W. (ed.) *Issues in Language Testing Research.* Rowley, MA: Newbury House, 29–79.

Vygotsky, L. (1978) *Mind in Society.* Cambridge, MA: Harvard University Press.

Wall, D. (1996) 'Introducing new tests into traditional systems: insights from general education and from innovation theory.' *Language Testing* 13, 3, 334–354.

Wall, D. (1997) 'Impact and washback in language testing.' In Clapham, C. and Corson, D. (eds) *Encyclopedia of Language and Education,* vol. 7: *Language Testing and Assessment.* Dordrecht: Kluwer Academic Publishers, 291–302.

Wall, D. (2000) 'The impact of high-stakes testing on teaching and learning: can this be predicted or controlled?' *System* 28, 4, 499–509.

Weigle, S. C. (2002) *Assessing Writing.* Cambridge: Cambridge University Press.

Weir, C. (2004) *Language Testing and Validation: An Evidence Based Approach.* Basingstoke: Palgrave.

Wenger, E. (1998) *Communities of Practice: Learning, Meaning, and Identity.* Cambridge: Cambridge University Press.

Widdowson, H. G. (1978) *Teaching Language as Communication.* London: Oxford University Press.

Widdowson, H. (1983) *Learning Purpose and Language Use.* Oxford: Oxford University Press.

Wilds, C. (1975) 'The oral interview test.' In Jones, R. L. and Spolsky, B. (eds) *Testing Language Proficiency.* Arlington, VA: Center for Applied Linguistics, 29–44.

Wilkins, D. A. (1976) *Notional Syllabuses.* London: Oxford University Press.

Wilkins, D. A. (1978) 'Approaches to syllabus design: communicative, functional or notional'. In Johnson, K. and Morrow, K. (eds) *Functional Materials and the Classroom Teacher: Some Background Issues.* Reading: Centre for Applied Language Studies, University of Reading.

Willingham, W. (1988) 'Testing handicapped people – the validity issue.' In Wainer, H. and Braun, H. (eds) *Test Validity.* Hillsdale, NJ: Erlbaum, 89–103.

Wilson, N. (1998) 'Educational standards and the problem of error.' *Educational Policy Analysis Archives* 6, 10.

Wood, R. (1991) *Assessment and Testing: A Survey of Research.* Cambridge: Cambridge University Press.

Young, R. F. (2000) 'Interactional competence: challenges for validity.' Paper presented at a joint symposium 'Interdisciplinary Interfaces with Language Testing' held at the annual meeting of the American Association for Applied Linguistics and the Language Testing Research Colloquium, 11 March 2000, Vancouver, British Columbia, Canada. Available on-line: http://www.wisc.edu/english/rfyoung/IC_C4V.Paper.PDF. Retrieved 20 November 2005.

Zieky, M. J. and Livingston, S. A. (1977) *Manual for Setting Standards on the Basic Skills Assessment Tests.* Princeton, NJ: Educational Testing Service.

Index